WILDEST LIVES
OF THE FRONTIER

Through the Eyes of Jesse James,
George Armstrong Custer,
and Other Famous Westerners

EDITED BY JOHN RICHARD STEPHENS

TWODOT®

GUILFORD, CONNECTICUT
HELENA, MONTANA

This book is dedicated to Elaine Molina

A · TWODOT® · BOOK

An imprint and registered trademark of Rowman & Littlefield

Distributed by NATIONAL BOOK NETWORK

British Library Cataloguing-in-Publication Information available

Library of Congress Cataloging-in-Publication Data

Names: Stephens, John Richard, editor.
Title: Wildest lives of the frontier : America through the words of Jesse James, George Armstrong Custer, and other famous Westerners / edited by John Richard Stephens.
Description: Guilford, Connecticut : TwoDot, [2017] | Includes bibliographical references and index.
Identifiers: LCCN 2016025143 (print) | LCCN 2016040656 (ebook) | ISBN 9781493024414 (paperback : alkaline paper) | ISBN 9781493024421 (e-book)
Subjects: LCSH: Frontier and pioneer life—West (U.S.)—Sources. | West (U.S.)—Biography. | West (U.S.)—History—Sources.
Classification: LCC F596 .W57985 2017 (print) | LCC F596 (ebook) | DDC 978—dc23
LC record available at https://lccn.loc.gov/2016025143

Contents

ACKNOWLEDGMENTS

John Richard Stephens would like to thank Elaine Molina; Martha and Jim Goodwin; Scott Stephens; Marty Goeller and Dorian Rivas; Terity, Natasha, and Debbie Burbach; Brandon, Alisha, and Kathy Hill; Jeff and Carol Whiteaker; Christopher and Doug Whiteaker; Gabriel, Aurelia, Elijah, Nina, and Justin Weinberger; Rachel, Roxanne, Lotus, and Sage Nunez; Jayla, Anthony, Sin, and Bobby Gamboa; Pat Egner; Baba and Mimi Marlene Bruner; Anne and Jerry Buzzard; Krystyne Göhnert; Eric, Tim, and Debbie Cissna; Norene Hilden; Doug and Shirley Strong; Barbara Main; Joanne and Monte Goeller; Irma and Joe Rodriguez; Danny and Mary Schutt; Les Benedict; Dr. Rich Sutton; Jeanne Sisson; Michael and Roz McKevitt; Carmen Shaffer; Dr. Rick Roth; Steve and Shelly Alexander; and his agent, Charlotte Cecil Raymond.

A Note About the Text

I've placed these selections roughly in chronological order, but there is some overlap in time between the selections. I understand there will be the temptation to jump around and read the selections out of order, but I guarantee they will make a lot more sense if you read them in the order presented. And I suspect you'll find that the selections you think will be the least interesting will end up being among the most interesting.

While putting this book together, I thought long and hard about how to deal with typos, misspellings, and old-style punctuation. If this was a scholarly book intended primarily for historians, I would have left the texts in their original state with all their flaws, adding corrections in brackets. But since this book is primarily for the general reader, I decided that too many brackets would be a distraction. Therefore I have corrected typos that appeared in the originals and have fixed misspelled words and names. I have also corrected capitalization and have modernized punctuation.

While it is sometimes interesting to read a person's letters with all its flaws and idiosyncrasies, that also makes reading them much more difficult and can obscure their meaning. Also, some of the texts were already corrected for their initial publication, while others were still in raw form. I felt that by putting raw text next to someone else's polished text could falsely give the impression that the former person was less intelligent than the latter. One person's unedited writings might make them seem ignorant by today's standards, while giving the opposite impression of someone whose writings had already been corrected. Even the best-educated scholars sometimes make mistakes in their hastily written notes and personal correspondence. In addition, when the selections in this book were written, spelling wasn't as formalized as it is now. Lewis and Clark's uncorrected journals are excellent examples of this. Spelling didn't really become standardized until about the beginning of the twentieth century.

As Mark Twain once humorously put it, "I don't give a damn for a man that can only spell a word one way." Actually he fought hard for standardization, saying of the English alphabet, "It can hardly spell any word in the language with any degree of certainty." At that time people even spelled their own names several different ways. I once saw a legal document where someone's last name was spelled three different ways. So while alternate spellings were acceptable and common in the nineteenth century, these are now seen as errors and signs of ignorance; therefore I decided to update spellings to today's accepted standards.

In some instances I have also inserted missing words, but only where there was no doubt as to what the author intended that word to be. And I have corrected the tense of a few words, so they matched the rest of the paragraph. I have not rewritten any sentences to correct the grammar. Neither have I made any changes that might alter the author's meaning. If the meaning was ambiguous, I left apparent errors uncorrected.

Ultimately I decided it was more important to make the texts easier to read and understand. By removing errors that would prove distracting, I hope I have enabled the reader to better focus on the fascinating stories these remarkable people have to tell.

Going West

John Richard Stephens

Out of the frontier West the American character was formed ...
—DEE BROWN, HISTORIAN

Frontier is a relative term. During the Colonial period, it was everything outside the thirteen colonies. Essentially, the Appalachians and beyond were all called "the wilderness" back then. Generally it was unexplored, except by Native Americans, trappers, and mountain men. Later on it was everything west of the Mississippi River. The expansion west kept pushing the frontier in front of it up until gold was discovered in California. Then suddenly a huge number of people jumped over to the West Coast and the frontier began to be pushed back toward the east.

With the end of the Civil War, veterans from both sides flooded west to start new lives and the Wild West period began. (For more on this you should check out my book *Wildest Lives of the Wild West*.) As the frontier was squeezed from east and west, the Indian Wars of the Plains took place. These ended a few years after the deaths of George Custer and many of his men. By then the Native Americans were confined to reservations.

The people who headed into the frontier were searching for a better life. They were willing to brave its dangers and hardships. Some hoped to strike it rich quick, especially during the Gold Rush, where prospectors literally pulled fortunes right out of the ground. (For more on this I recommend *Gold*, my book on the California Gold Rush.) Many others just wanted to become successful farmers and ranchers, shop owners, and businessmen. This brought a clash of cultures between the new arrivals and the long-established residents—the Native Americans. Prejudices, fear, and misunderstandings led to conflicts and death.

All across the frontier, new towns sprang up, bringing laws and government with them. And the wilderness was tamed and corralled behind barbed-wire fences.

All of this—both good and bad—formed the birth of the western United States. It was a period of history that, for the most part, spanned just over a century—from the end of the 1700s through the beginning of the 1900s. It was the creation of a new way of life. Unfortunately many were killed along the way.

The frontier was a dangerous place and it attracted brave and interesting personalities, some of whom became the celebrities of that era. People throughout the East were fascinated by life in the West and in the people who lived it. Explorers and mountain men, soldiers and Indians, prospectors and robbers could become famous for their exploits. Many of them are still famous today. In selecting the best-known of these frontier celebrities, I've gathered their own firsthand accounts of the most interesting incidents in their lives. Here they describe their personal experiences of life on the frontier in their own words—what they did, what they saw, and how they felt.

Claiming the Kentucky Wilderness

Daniel Boone

Daniel Boone

"Daniel Boone will always occupy a unique place in our history as the archetype of the hunter and wilderness wanderer," wrote Teddy Roosevelt. "He was a true pioneer, and stood at the head of that class of Indian-fighters, game-hunters, forest-fellers, and backwoods farmers who, generation after generation, pushed westward the border of civilization from the Alleghenies to the Pacific. As he himself said, he was 'an instrument ordained of God to settle the wilderness.'"

Buffalo Bill Cody divided the history of the West into three periods, distinguished by three men and three types of firearms. The men were Daniel Boone, Davy Crockett, and Kit Carson. He wrote,

In the life of Boone we have a history of that period corresponding with the age, so to speak, of the flint-lock rifle, from 1770-1820; Crockett lived in the secondary period, or when the percussion-cap rifle had superseded the unreliable pan-flashing weapon of the very early settlers, his active career beginning at the close of that of Boone's and ending, as we have seen, in a blaze of heroism, in 1836. Carson belonged to the tertiary epoch of Western settlement, when the frontier had been pushed across the plains to the shores of the beating sea, and during whose eventful career the repeating rifle was invented and first brought into use. . . . We have, therefore, in the history of these three men a description of the reclamation and development of a belt of our country west of the Alleghenies, and south of the Mason and Dixon Line, and incidentally, sketches of many of the brave men who helped make the first trail across the continent.

The exploration of the West began in what is now considered the East. Back when the thirteen British colonies dotted the East Coast and most of the continent was largely unexplored and unknown, traveling west into the wilderness was considered to be very dangerous. It was something left to mountain men, hunters, trappers, and Indian traders.

Daniel Boone's interest in the Western wilds was piqued when he met John Finley while serving in the French and Indian War. Years later he made several excursions into the wilderness of Kentucky. In 1769 he, John Finley, and four others set out on a long hunting expedition that ended up lasting two years. They passed through the Cumberland Gap into Kentucky. Six months later Boone and another hunter were captured by a party of Shawnee, who considered the two hunters to be poaching on their hunting grounds. After confiscating their pelts, the Natives told them to leave and never return. They didn't, and continued hunting and exploring, reaching as far west as where Louisville is now located, before returning to Boone's home in North Carolina.

In 1773, at the age of thirty-eight, Boone and his family—along with about fifty others—set out to be the first to establish a settlement in Kentucky. He described this in *The Adventures of Col. Daniel Boon, Formerly a Hunter; Containing a Narrative of the Wars in Kentucky,* which was published in John Filson's book, *The Discovery and Settlement of Kentucke* (1884). This—the first of two autobiographies by Boone—was ghostwritten by Filson from interviews with Boone and, though somewhat embellished, is considered to be pretty accurate.

Boone's second autobiography—*Biographical Memoir of Daniel Boone, the First Settler of Kentucky* (1833)—was actually written by Timothy Flint, who loosely based his book on interviews with Boone. This book is so exaggerated that it's largely considered to be fiction. Still, it became one of the bestselling biographies of the nineteenth century. While the first book made Boone internationally famous, the second one turned him into a folk legend.

This selection is from Daniel Boone's first autobiography. With the movement west and the clash of two very different cultures, it was inevitable that conflicts would arise between the pioneers and the land's Native inhabitants.

I returned safe to my old habitation and found my family in happy circumstances. I sold my farm on the Yadkin, and what goods we could not carry with us; and on the twenty-fifth day of September, 1773, bade a farewell to our friends and proceeded on our journey to Kentucke in company with

A portrait of Daniel Boone by John James Audubon. Audubon met Boone in about 1810 and painted this portrait sometime later.

five families more, and forty men that joined us in Powell's Valley, which is one hundred and fifty miles from the now settled parts of Kentucke. This promising beginning was soon overcast with a cloud of adversity; for upon the tenth day of October, the rear of our company was attacked by a number of Indians, who killed six and wounded one man. Of these my eldest son was one that fell in the action. Though we defended ourselves and repulsed the enemy, yet this unhappy affair scattered our cattle, brought us into extreme difficulty, and so discouraged the whole company that we retreated forty miles to the settlement on Clench River.

We had passed over two mountains, viz. Powell's and Walden's, and were approaching Cumberland Mountain when this adverse fortune overtook us. These mountains are in the wilderness, as we pass from the old settlements in Virginia to Kentucke, are ranged in a S. West and N. East direction, are of a great length and breadth, and not far distant from each other. Over these, nature hath formed passes that are less difficult than might be expected from a view of such huge piles. The aspect of these cliffs is so wild and horrid that it is impossible to behold them without terror. The spectator is apt to imagine that nature had formerly suffered some violent convulsion; and that these are the dismembered remains of the dreadful shock; the ruins, not of Persepolis or Palmyra, but of the world!

I remained with my family on Clench until the sixth of June, 1774, when I and one Michael Stoner were solicited by Governor Dunmore of Virginia to go to the Falls of the Ohio [near what is now Louisville], to conduct into the settlement a number of surveyors that had been sent thither by him some months before; this country having about this time drawn the attention of many adventurers. We immediately complied with the Governor's request, and conducted in the surveyors, completing a tour of eight hundred miles, through many difficulties, in sixty-two days.

Soon after I returned home, I was ordered to take the command of three garrisons during the campaign, which Governor Dunmore carried on against the Shawnee Indians: After the conclusion of which, the Militia was discharged from each garrison, and I being relieved from my post, was solicited by a number of North Carolina gentlemen that were about purchasing the lands lying on the S. side of Kentucke River from the Cherokee Indians to attend their treaty at Wataga in March 1775 to negotiate with them and mention the boundaries of the purchase. This I accepted, and at the request of the same gentlemen, undertook to mark out a road in the best passage from the settlement through the wilderness to Kentucke, with such assistance as I thought necessary to employ for such an important undertaking.

I soon began this work, having collected a number of enterprising men, well armed. We proceeded with all possible expedition until we came within fifteen miles of where Boonsborough now stands, and where we were fired upon by a party of Indians that killed two and wounded two of our number; yet, although surprised and taken at a disadvantage, we stood our ground. This was on the twentieth of March 1775. Three days after, we were fired upon again and had two men killed and three wounded. Afterwards we proceeded on to Kentucke River without opposition; and on the first day of April began to erect the fort of Boonsborough at a salt lick, about sixty yards from the river on the S. side.

The Revolutionary War was just beginning at this point. Many of the Native Americans in the area were upset by the new settlements, so they sided with the British. Most of the battles in this part of the country were between settlers and Natives.

On the fourth day, the Indians killed one of our men. We were busily employed in building this fort until the fourteenth day of June following, without any farther opposition from the Indians; and having finished the works, I returned to my family on Clench.

In a short time I proceeded to remove my family from Clench to this garrison, where we arrived safe without any other difficulties than such as are common to this passage, my wife and daughter being the first white women that ever stood on the banks of Kentucke River.

On the twenty-fourth day of December following we had one man killed and one wounded by the Indians, who seemed determined to persecute us for erecting this fortification.

On the fourteenth day of July 1776, two of Col. Calaway's daughters and one of mine were taken prisoners near the fort. I immediately pursued the Indians with only eight men and on the sixteenth overtook them, killed two of the party and recovered the girls. The same day on which this attempt was made, the Indians divided themselves into different parties and attacked several forts—which were shortly before this time erected—doing a great deal of mischief. This was extremely distressing to the new settlers. The innocent husbandman was shot down while busy cultivating the soil for his family's supply. Most of the cattle around the stations were destroyed. They continued their hostilities in this manner until the fifteenth of April 1777, when they attacked Boonsborough with a party of above one hundred in number, killed one man and wounded four. Their loss in this attack was not certainly known to us.

On the fourth day of July following, a party of about two hundred Indians attacked Boonsborough, killed one man and wounded two. They besieged us forty-eight hours; during which time seven of them were killed, and at last, finding themselves not likely to prevail, they raised the siege and departed.

The Indians had disposed their warriors in different parties at this time and attacked the different garrisons to prevent their assisting each other, and did much injury to the distressed inhabitants.

On the nineteenth day of this month, Col. Logan's fort was besieged by a party of about two hundred Indians. During this dreadful siege they did a great deal of mischief, distressed the garrison, in which were only fifteen men, killed two and wounded one. The enemies loss was uncertain, from the common practice which the Indians have of carrying off their dead in time of battle. Col. Harrod's fort was then defended by only sixty-five men and Boonsborough by twenty-two, there being no more forts or white men in the country, except at the Falls, a considerable distance from these, and all taken collectively, were but a handful to the numerous warriors that were everywhere dispersed through the country, intent upon doing all the mischief that savage barbarity could invent. Thus we passed through a scene of sufferings that exceeds description.

On the twenty-fifth of this month [July 1777] a reinforcement of forty-five men arrived from North Carolina, and about the twentieth of August following, Col. Bowman arrived with one hundred men from Virginia. Now we began to strengthen, and from hence, for the space of six weeks, we had skirmishes with Indians in one quarter or other almost every day.

The savages now learned the superiority of the Long Knife, as they call the Virginians, by experience; being out-generaled in almost every battle. Our affairs began to wear a new aspect, and the enemy, not daring to venture on open war, practiced secret mischief at times.

On the first day of January 1778, I went with a party of thirty men to the Blue Licks, on Licking River, to make salt for the different garrisons in the country.

On the seventh day of February, as I was hunting to procure meat for the company, I met with a party of one hundred and two Indians, and two Frenchmen, on their march against Boonsborough, that place being particularly the object of the enemy.

They pursued and took me, and brought me on the eighth day to the Licks, where twenty-seven of my party were, three of them having previously returned home with the salt. I, knowing it was impossible for them to escape, capitulated with the enemy and, at a distance in their view, gave notice to my men of their situation with orders not to resist, but surrender themselves captives.

The generous usage the Indians had promised before, in my capitulation, was afterwards fully complied with, and we proceeded with them as prisoners to Old Chillicothe, the principal Indian town on Little Miami, where we arrived, after an uncomfortable journey in very severe weather, on the eighteenth day of February, and received as good treatment as prisoners could expect from savages.

On the tenth day of March following [1778], I and ten of my men were conducted by forty Indians to Detroit, where we arrived the thirtieth day and were treated by Governor Hamilton, the British commander at that post, with great humanity.

During our travels, the Indians entertained me well; and their affection for me was so great that they utterly refused to leave me there with the others, although the Governor offered them one hundred pounds Sterling for me, on purpose to give me a parole to go home. Several English gentlemen there, being sensible of my adverse fortune and touched with human sympathy, generously offered a friendly supply for my wants, which I refused with many thanks for their kindness, adding that I never expected it would be in my power to recompense such unmerited generosity.

The Indians left my men in captivity with the British at Detroit and on the tenth day of April brought me towards Old Chillicothe, where we arrived on the twenty-fifth day of the same month. This was a long and fatiguing march through an exceeding fertile country, remarkable for fine springs and streams of water. At Chillicothe I spent my time as comfortably as I could expect; was adopted, according to their custom, into a family where I became a son, and had a great share in the affection of my new parents, brothers, sisters, and friends. I was exceedingly familiar and friendly with them, always appearing as cheerful and satisfied as possible, and they put great confidence in me. I often went a hunting with them, and frequently gained their applause for my activity at our shooting-matches.

I was careful not to exceed many of them in shooting, for no people are more envious than they in this sport. I could observe in their countenances and gestures, the greatest expressions of joy when they exceeded me, and when the reverse happened, of envy. The Shawnee king took great notice of me and treated me with profound respect, and entire friendship, often entrusting me to hunt at my liberty. I frequently returned with the spoils of the woods, and as often presented some of what I had taken to him, expressive of duty to my sovereign. My food and lodging was in common with them, not so good indeed as I could desire, but necessity made everything acceptable.

I now began to meditate an escape and carefully avoided their suspicions, continuing with them at Old Chillicothe until the first day of June following [1778], and then was taken by them to the salt springs on Sciotha [Sciota River in what is now Ohio], and kept there making salt ten days. During this time I hunted some for them and found the land, for a great extent about this river, to exceed the soil of Kentucke, if possible, and remarkably well watered. When I returned to Chillicothe, alarmed to see four hundred and fifty Indians of their choicest warriors, painted and armed in a fearful manner, ready to march against Boonsborough, I determined to escape the first opportunity.

On the sixteenth before sunrise, I departed in the most secret manner and arrived at Boonsborough on the twentieth, after a journey of one hundred and sixty miles, during which I had but one meal.

I found our fortress in a bad state of defense, but we proceeded immediately to repair our flanks, strengthen our gates and posterns, and form double bastions, which we completed in ten days. In this time we daily expected the arrival of the Indian army; and at length, one of my fellow prisoners, escaping from them, arrived, informing us that the enemy had an account of my departure and postponed their expedition three weeks.

The Indians had spies out viewing our movements and were greatly alarmed with our increase in number and fortifications. The Grand Councils of the nations were held frequently, and with more deliberation than usual. They evidently saw the approaching hour when the Long Knife would dispossess them of their desirable habitations, and anxiously concerned for futurity, determined utterly to extirpate the whites out of Kentucke. We were not intimidated by their movements, but frequently gave them proofs of our courage.

About the first of August [1778], I made an incursion into the Indian country with a party of nineteen men in order to surprise a small town up Sciotha, called Paint-Creek-Town. We advanced within four miles thereof, where we met a party of thirty Indians on their march against Boonsborough intending to join the others from Chillicothe. A smart fight ensued betwixt us for some time. At length the savages gave way and fled. We had no loss on our side. The enemy had one killed and two wounded. We took from them three horses and all their baggage, and being informed by two of our number that went to their town that the Indians had entirely evacuated it, we proceeded no further and returned with all possible expedition to assist our garrison against the other party. We passed by them on the sixth day, and on the seventh we arrived safe at Boonsborough.

On the eighth, the Indian army arrived—being four hundred and forty-four in number, commanded by Capt. Duquesne, eleven other Frenchmen, and some of their own chiefs—and marched up within view of our fort with British and French colors flying; and having sent a summons to me in his Britannick Majesty's name to surrender the fort, I requested two days consideration, which was granted.

It was now a critical period with us. We were a small number in the garrison. A powerful army before our walls, whose appearance proclaimed inevitable death, fearfully painted, and marking their footsteps with desolation. Death was preferable to captivity, and if taken by storm, we must inevitably be devoted to destruction. In this situation we concluded to maintain our garrison, if possible. We immediately proceeded to collect what we could of our horses and other cattle, and bring them through the posterns into the fort. And in the evening of the ninth, I returned answer that we were determined to defend our fort while a man was living.

"Now," said I to their commander who stood attentively hearing my sentiments, "We laugh at all your formidable preparations. But thank you for giving us notice and time to provide for our defense. Your efforts will not prevail, for our gates shall forever deny you admittance."

Whether this answer affected their courage or not, I cannot tell, but contrary to our expectations, they formed a scheme to deceive us, declaring it was their orders from Governor Hamilton to take us captives and not to destroy us, but if nine of us would come out and treat with them, they would immediately withdraw their forces from our walls and return home peaceably. This sounded grateful in our ears and we agreed to the proposal.

We held the treaty within sixty yards of the garrison on purpose to divert them from a breach of honor, as we could not avoid suspicions of the savages. In this situation the articles were formally agreed to and signed, and the Indians told us it was customary with them on such occasions for two Indians to shake hands with every white-man in the treaty, as an evidence of entire friendship. We agreed to this also, but were soon convinced their policy was to take us prisoners.

They immediately grappled us, but although surrounded by hundreds of savages, we extricated ourselves from them and escaped all safe into the garrison, except one that was wounded through a heavy fire from their army. They immediately attacked us on every side, and a constant heavy fire ensued between us day and night for the space of nine days.

In this time the enemy began to undermine our fort, which was situated sixty yards from Kentucke River. They began at the water-mark and proceeded in the bank some distance, which we understood by their making the water muddy with the clay, and we immediately proceeded to disappoint their design by cutting a trench across their subterranean passage. The enemy discovering our counter-mine by the clay we threw out of the fort, desisted from that stratagem. And experience now fully convincing them that neither their power nor policy could effect their purpose, on the twentieth day of August they raised the siege and departed.

During this dreadful siege, which threatened death in every form, we had two men killed and four wounded, besides a number of cattle. We killed of the enemy thirty-seven and wounded a great number. After they were gone, we picked up one hundred and twenty-five pounds weight of bullets, besides what stuck in the logs of our fort, which certainly is a great proof of their industry.

Soon after this, I went into the settlement and nothing worthy of a place in this account passed in my affairs for some time.

Every day we experienced recent mischiefs. The barbarous savage nations of Shawnee, Cherokee, Wyandot, Tawas, Delawares, and several others near Detroit, united in a war against us and assembled their choicest warriors at Old Chillicothe to go on the expedition in order to destroy us and entirely depopulate the country. Their savage minds were inflamed to mischief by two abandoned men, Captains McKee and Girty. These led them to execute every diabolical scheme, and on the fifteenth day of August, commanded a party of Indians and Canadians of about five hundred in number, against Briant's Station, five miles from Lexington. Without demanding a surrender, they furiously assaulted the garrison, which was happily prepared to oppose them, and after they had expended much ammunition in vain and killed the cattle round the fort, not being likely to make themselves masters of this place, they raised the siege and departed in the morning of the third day after they came, with the loss of about thirty killed and the number of wounded uncertain. Of the garrison four were killed and three wounded.

What follows is Boone's account of the Battle of Blue Licks, which was one of the final battles of the Revolutionary War. In this battle 182 Kentucky militiamen were ambushed and routed by about 50 British rangers and 300 Native Americans.

On the eighteenth day [of August 1782] Col. Todd, Col. Trigg, Major Harland, and myself, speedily collected one hundred and seventy-six men, well-armed, and pursued the savages. They had marched beyond the Blue Licks to a remarkable bend of the main fork of Licking River, about forty-three miles from Lexington, as it is particularly represented in the map, where we overtook them on the nineteenth day. The savages observing us, gave way; and we, being ignorant of their numbers, passed the river. When the enemy saw our proceedings, having greatly the advantage of us in situation, they formed the line of battle, represented in the map from one bend of Licking to the other, about a mile from the Blue Licks. An exceeding fierce battle immediately began for about fifteen minutes, when we, being over-powered by numbers, were obliged to retreat with the loss of sixty-seven men, seven of whom were taken prisoners. The brave and much lamented Colonels Todd and Trigg, Major Harland and my second son, were among the dead. We were informed that the Indians, numbering their dead, found they had four killed more than we; and therefore, four of the prisoners they had taken, were, by general consent, ordered to be killed in a most barbarous manner by the young warriors in order to train them up to cruelty; and then they proceeded to their towns.

On our retreat we were met by Col. Logan, hastening to join us with a number of well-armed men. This powerful assistance we unfortunately wanted in the battle, for—notwithstanding the enemy's superiority of numbers—they acknowledged that if they had received one more fire from us, they should undoubtedly have given way. So valiantly did our small party fight, that, to the memory of those who unfortunately fell in the battle, enough of honor cannot be paid. Had Col. Logan and his party been with us, it is highly probable we should have given the savages a total defeat.

I cannot reflect upon this dreadful scene, but sorrow fills my heart. A zeal for the defense of their country led these heroes to the scene of action, though with a few men to attack a powerful army of experienced warriors. When we gave way, they pursued us with the utmost eagerness, and in every quarter spread destruction. The river was difficult to cross and many were killed in the flight—some just entering the river, some in the water, others after crossing in ascending the cliffs. Some escaped on horse-back, a few on foot; and, being dispersed everywhere in a few hours, brought the melancholy news of this unfortunate battle to Lexington.

Many widows were now made. The reader may guess what sorrow filled the hearts of the inhabitants, exceeding anything that I am able to describe. Being reinforced, we returned to bury the dead and found their bodies strewed everywhere, cut and mangled in a dreadful manner. This mournful scene exhibited a horror almost unparalleled. Some torn and eaten by wild beasts; those in the river eaten by fishes; all in such a putrefied condition, that no one could be distinguished from another.

As soon as General Clark, then at the Falls of the Ohio—who was ever our ready friend, and merits the love and gratitude of all his countrymen—understood the circumstances of this unfortunate action, he ordered an expedition with all possible haste to pursue the savages, which was so expeditiously effected that we overtook them within two miles of their towns, and probably might have obtained a great victory had not two of their number met us about two hundred poles before we come up. These returned quick as lightning to their camp with the alarming news of a mighty army in view. The savages fled in the utmost disorder, evacuated their towns, and reluctantly left their territory to our mercy. We immediately took possession of Old Chillicothe without opposition, being deserted by its inhabitants. We continued our pursuit through five towns on the Miami Rivers—Old Chillicothe, Pecaway, New Chillicothe, Will's Towns, and Chillicothe—burnt them all to ashes, entirely destroyed their corn, and other fruits, and everywhere spread a scene of desolation in the country. In this expedition we took seven prisoners and five scalps, with the loss of only four men, two of whom were accidentally killed by our own army.

This campaign in some measure damped the spirits of the Indians and made them sensible of our superiority. Their connections were dissolved, their armies scattered, and a future invasion put entirely out of their power, yet they continued to practice mischief secretly upon the inhabitants in the exposed parts of the country.

In October following [1782], a party made an excursion into that district called the Crab Orchard and one of them, being advanced some distance before the others, boldly entered the house of a poor defenseless family in which was only a Negro man, a woman and her children, terrified with the apprehensions of immediate death. The savage, perceiving their defenseless situation, without offering violence to the family attempted to captivate the Negro, who happily proved an over-match for him, threw him on the ground, and in the struggle, the mother of the children drew an ax from a corner of the cottage and cut his head off while her little daughter shut the door. The savages instantly appeared, and applied their tomahawks to the door. An old rusty gun-barrel without a lock lay in a corner, which the mother put through a small crevice, and the savages, perceiving it, fled. In the meantime, the alarm spread through the neighborhood. The armed men collected immediately and pursued the ravagers into the wilderness. Thus Providence, by the means of this Negro, saved the whole of the poor family from destruction.

From that time, until the happy return of peace between the United States and Great Britain, the Indians did us no mischief. Finding the great king beyond the water disappointed in his expectations and conscious of the importance of the Long Knife, and their own wretchedness, some of the nations immediately desired peace; to which, at present [1784], they seem universally disposed, and are sending ambassadors to General Clark at the Falls of the Ohio with the minutes of their Councils, a specimen of which, in the minutes of the Piankashaw Council, is subjoined.

To conclude, I can now say that I have verified the saying of an old Indian who signed Col. Henderson's deed. Taking me by the hand, at the delivery thereof, "Brother," says he, "we have given you a fine land, but I believe you will have much trouble in settling it."

My footsteps have often been marked with blood and therefore I can truly subscribe to its original name. Two darling sons, and a brother, have I lost by savage hands, which have also taken from me forty valuable horses and abundance of cattle. Many dark and sleepless nights have I been a companion for owls, separated from the cheerful society of men, scorched by the Summer's sun, and pinched by the Winter's cold, an instrument ordained to settle the wilderness. But now the scene is changed: Peace crowns the sylvan shade.

What thanks, what ardent and ceaseless thanks are due to that all-superintending Providence which has turned a cruel war into peace, brought order out of confusion, made the fierce savages placid, and turned away their hostile weapons from our country!

The war ended in September 1783 and Boone's account was published the following year. After the war Boone worked as a surveyor, horse trader, and land speculator. He operated a tavern and a trading post. He also served three terms in the Virginia General Assembly—the first was during the war. Overall, he ended up failing as a businessman and was swept up in a wave of lawsuits involving his land deals. Apparently he wasn't ruthless enough and was reluctant to profit at the expense of others. In 1789 he ignored a summons to testify in court and a warrant was issued for his arrest. He fled the country to Missouri, which was then part of Louisiana and controlled by Spain.

He was appointed by the Spanish governor as a magistrate and military leader of the Femme Osage district. He was given some large land grants, but after Louisiana was bought by the United States in 1804, he ended up selling off most of it to pay off his debts back in Kentucky. He continued hunting and trapping almost up until he died in 1820 at the age of eighty-five.

As his legend grew, he became one of the first frontier heroes and the tall tales of his adventures greatly influenced the legends of later heroes of the West. He inspired some parts of James Fenimore Cooper's *The Last of the Mohicans* (1826) and was mentioned by Lord Byron in several stanzas of his famous poem *Don Juan*. Here is the first of those stanzas:

> Of all men, saving Sylla the man-slayer,
>   Who passes for in life and death most lucky,
> Of the great names which in our faces stare,
>   The General Boon, back-woodsman of Kentucky,
> Was happiest amongst mortals anywhere;
>   For killing nothing but a bear or buck, he
> Enjoy'd the lonely, vigorous, harmless days
> Of his old age in wilds of deepest maze.

Sacagawea

Lewis and Clark

Meriwether Lewis

Wm Clark

At the beginning of the nineteenth century, the United States was still a young country. The Revolutionary War had ended just seventeen years earlier, and in that time the population of the United States had almost doubled to just over five million. But even though almost two centuries had passed since the Europeans began building settlements in America, two thirds of the US population clung to the edge of the continent within fifty miles of the Atlantic Ocean. To the west were scattered settlements, separated from the original colonies by the Appalachian Mountain Range—about one hundred miles of mountains, crossed by only four roads.

Then, in 1803, President Thomas Jefferson purchased the Louisiana territory from Napoleon for fifteen million dollars. While France claimed the territory, Napoleon had no way to enforce the claim and he knew the Americans were about to overrun it. The primary reason Jefferson wanted the territory was to ensure the right to ship goods down the Mississippi River to New Orleans, since at that time the Mississippi marked the western edge of the United States. From New Orleans, goods could be shipped to the East Coast. Another reason was that US citizens were already moving into the area, and he wanted to make sure they didn't secede from the Union. The westward expansion of the United States was already under way, but with the purchase, the size of the country doubled overnight.

On acquiring the new territory, President Jefferson wanted to find out more about what he had bought, so he commissioned Lewis and Clark to explore the uncharted land to the west of the Mississippi. He hoped they would find a water route to transport goods from the Columbia and Missouri Rivers to the Pacific—they didn't. He had books that said they would find woolly mammoths, erupting volcanoes,

William Clark and Meriwether Lewis posed for these portraits in 1807.

mountains made entirely of salt, and seven-foot-tall beavers. This goes to show just how little was known of the West at that time. But while this land was a large blank space on maps, that doesn't mean it was unoccupied. It's difficult to estimate the Native American population in 1800, but, keeping that in mind, rough estimates put the number for the area now occupied by the forty-eight contiguous states at between half a million and one million. The Expedition would have to cross the territories of a number of Native American nations.

Jefferson chose his personal secretary-aide, the twenty-nine-year-old Captain Meriwether Lewis, to lead the Expedition, but Lewis thought it better if he had a co-commander with him, so he talked Jefferson into allowing Lewis's friend William Clark to join the Expedition. Clark was thirty-three. Ten years earlier when Lewis was an ensign, he had served under Lieutenant Clark fighting the British and Native Americans. Clark was still a lieutenant when they set off, but Captain Lewis hid this from his men by referring to him as "Captain" Clark. The two were opposites in some respects—Lewis was quiet, introspective, and scientific, while Clark was friendly, outgoing, and practical—but they complemented each other well and made an excellent team.

The Expedition of the Corps of Discovery was made up of thirty-three permanent members plus Lewis's dog and about twenty others who joined them for portions of the journey, not including the various Natives they hired as guides along the way. They were to document the languages, customs, and medical knowledge of the Natives, along with details of plants and animals, minerals, mountains, and rivers. The journey covered more than eight thousand miles and took two years and four months.

Setting out from Camp Dubois in the Illinois Territory, just outside of St. Louis, in May 1804,they proceeded up the Missouri River to near present-day Washburn, North Dakota, where there was a large group of five Mandan-Hidatsa Indian villages and they decided to spend the winter of 1804–1805 there, building Fort Mandan. This was the largest "city" on the Missouri River. At that time St. Louis, at the southern end of the river, had a population of less than one thousand—most of whom primarily spoke French—and only around two hundred buildings. At the Mandan-Hidatsa villages, on the other hand, there lived about forty-five hundred Native Americans, making it more populous than Albany or Schenectady, New York; Savannah, Georgia; New Haven, Connecticut; Portland, Maine; or even Washington, D.C. In fact, only fourteen US cities were larger. This is in spite of the fact that the Mandan-Hidatsa population had shrunk drastically in the previous century, largely because of smallpox and other epidemics. Still, it remained one of the most important Native American trading centers of the Midwestern plains.

(Note: By the 1770s, epidemics had reduced the Mandan–Hidatsa population to about 12,000—about the same size as Baltimore at the time—then the 1780–1781 smallpox epidemic hit them, killing another 60 percent to 70 percent of the people. The survivors moved to the five-village area, where they remained until the 1837 epidemic decimated them again, reducing the Hidatsa to about 500 and the Mandan to about 125 people.)

The five villages covered a ten-mile stretch along the Missouri River. The Mandan had lived in the area at the least since around 1000 A.D. and the Hidatsa since the 1600s. They lived in large earth lodges. These, with their community centers, were enclosed into a circular village by earthen walls. The Mandan-Hidatsa were primarily farmers, growing most of their food—corn, pumpkin, squash, beans, and sunflowers—in well-tended fields, though they did hunt buffalo when the herds migrated

The Mandan Village painted by George Catlin, 1837–1839

into the area. These Natives were familiar with the Europeans and had been trading with the French for more than one hundred years and with the British for several decades.

The Expedition arrived here on October 25, 1804. This was where Lewis and Clark met someone who would become one of the most famous members of their Expedition—an approximately sixteen-year-old pregnant girl named Sacagawea. They met her through her husband, a part-French, part-Indian fur trapper named Toussaint Charbonneau, who they hired as a translator for the journey. At about the age of forty-seven, he was the oldest member of the Expedition, and Sacagawea was one of his wives. Her story is one of the most interesting elements of the Expedition.

The selections here are from three sources. The first is Lewis and Clark's *History of the Expedition under the Command of Captains Lewis and Clark* (1814), which was edited by lawyer Nicholas Biddle with some assistance from law student George Shannon. Clark pulled together a variety of material and Biddle reworked it into a coherent narrative, which was presumably approved by Clark. The second source is The *Journals of Lewis and Clark* (1893), which was edited by Elliott Coues. The third is *Original Journals of the Lewis and Clark Expedition, 1804–1806* (1905), edited by historian and author Reuben Thwaites.

Contrary to the popular myth, Sacagawea was not one of Lewis and Clark's guides. They brought her as a translator and to serve as a "white flag." Since Native Americans never took women on war parties, the presence of a woman—especially one with a baby—indicated their peaceful intensions. In this capacity she probably saved their lives several times. She also ended up being valuable to the Expedition in many other ways.

CAPTAIN WILLIAM CLARK'S JOURNAL.

Sunday, November 4, 1804; Mandan and Hidatsa Indian villages on the Upper Missouri near what is now Stanton, North Dakota: A Frenchman by name Charbonneau, who speaks the Big Belly language, visited us. [The name Big Belly is from "Gros Ventre," an early French name for the Hidatsa.] He wished to hire and informed us his two squaws were Snake Indians [Shoshone]. We engaged him to go on with us and take one of his wives [Sacagawea] to interpret the Snake language. The Indian's horses and dogs live in the same lodge with themselves.

Charbonneau primarily spoke French and, by his own admission, even after living for decades with the Hidatsa, he spoke their language poorly. Since he couldn't speak English, other members of the Expedition had to translate Charbonneau's French into English.

LEWIS AND CLARK'S *HISTORY OF THE EXPEDITION*.

Thursday, November 22, 1804; Mandan and Hidatsa Indian villages on the Upper Missouri near what is now Washburn, North Dakota at a fort they built for the winter called Fort Mandan: The morning was fine, and the day warm. We purchased from the Mandan [tribe] a quantity of corn of a mixed color, which they dug up in ears from holes made near the front of their lodges, in which it is buried during the winter. This morning the sentinel informed us that an Indian was about to kill his wife near the fort. We went down to the house of our interpreter where we found the parties, and after forbidding any violence, inquired into the cause of his intending to commit such as atrocity. It appeared that some days ago a quarrel had taken place between him and his wife, in consequence of which she had taken refuge in the house where the two squaws of our interpreter lived. By running away she forfeited her life, which might have been lawfully taken by the husband. About two days ago she had returned to the village, but the same evening came back to the fort much beaten and stabbed in three places, and the husband now came for the purpose of completing his revenge. He observed that he had lent her to one of our sergeants for a night, and that if he wanted her he would give her to him altogether. We gave him a few presents and tried to persuade him to take his wife home. The grand chief too happened to arrive at the same moment, and reproached him with his violence, till at length they went off together, but by no means in a state of much apparent love.

CAPTAIN MERIWETHER LEWIS'S JOURNAL.

Monday, February 11, 1805; Fort Mandan: The party that were ordered last evening set out early this morning. The weather was fair and cold. Wind N.W. About five o'clock this evening, one of the wives of Charbonneau was delivered of a fine boy. It is worthy of remark that this was the first child which this woman [Sacagawea] had born, and as is common in such cases her labor was tedious and the pain violent. Mr. La Jeunnesse [another French interpreter for the expedition] informed me that he had frequently administered a small portion of the rattle of the rattlesnake, which he assured me had never failed to produce the desired effect—that of hastening the birth of the child. Having the rattle of a snake by me, I gave it to him, and he administered two rings of it to the woman, broken in small pieces with the fingers, and added to a small quantity of water. Whether this medicine was truly the cause or not, I shall not undertake to determine, but I was informed that she had not taken it more than ten minutes, before she brought forth. Perhaps this remedy may be worthy of future experiments, but I must confess that I want faith as to its efficacy.

LEWIS AND CLARK'S *HISTORY OF THE EXPEDITION*.

Friday, April 5, 1805; Fort Mandan: Fair and pleasant, but the wind high from the northwest. We were visited by a number of Mandan, and are occupied in loading our boats in order to proceed on our journey.

LEWIS AND CLARK'S *HISTORY OF THE EXPEDITION*.

Sunday, April 7, 1805; Fort Mandan: Having made all our arrangements, we left the fort about five o'clock in the afternoon. The party now consisted of thirty-two persons. . . . The wife of Charbonneau also accompanied us with her young child, and we hope may be useful as an interpreter among the Snake Indians. She was herself one of that tribe, but having been taken in war by the Minitaree [aka the Hidatsa], by whom she was sold as a slave to Charbonneau, who brought her up and afterwards married her.

Native Americans did not have slaves like the African Americans in the South. They captured people from other tribes and usually adopted them as family members, though they were often treated like Cinderella and made to do much of the work. Some were treated as servants and some as property.

While women did most of the work, the Hidatsa had a matrilineal society. In the United States, married women were not allowed to own property—it belonged to the husband. Hidatsa women, on the other hand, owned the earth lodges and gardens. On getting married, the husband moved into his mother-in-law's lodge, unless his wife happened to own one.

According to Hugh Monroe (aka Rising Wolf), Sacagawea told him that the Hidatsa man who captured her and her best friend Otter Woman, lost them to Charbonneau in a game of hide-the-bone after gambling all night.

One of the Mandan likewise embarked with us, in order to go to the Snake Indians and obtain a peace with them for his countrymen. All this party with the baggage was stowed in six small canoes and two large pirogues [canoes hacked out of logs]. We left the fort with fair pleasant weather though the northwest wind was high, and after making about four miles encamped on the north side of the Missouri, nearly opposite the first Mandan village. At the same time that we took our departure, our barge manned with seven soldiers, two Frenchmen, and

Mr. Gravelines as pilot, sailed for the United States loaded with our presents and dispatches.

Though the United States had just made the Louisiana Purchase, it was not commonly thought of as part of the United States yet.

Captain Meriwether Lewis's Journal.
Monday, June 10, 1805; Missouri and Marias Rivers near what is now Fort Benton, Montana: We drew up the red pirogue into the middle of a small island at the entrance of Marias River, and secured and made her fast to the trees to prevent the high floods from carrying her off. Put my brand on several trees standing near her, and covered her with brush to shelter her from the effects of the sun. At 3 p.m. we had a hard wind from the S.W., which continued about an hour, attended with thunder and rain. As soon as the shower had passed over we drew out our canoes, corked, repaired, and loaded them.

I still feel myself somewhat unwell with the dysentery, but determined to set out in the morning up the south fork or Missouri, leaving Captain Clark to complete the deposit and follow me by water with the party. Accordingly, gave orders to Drouilliard, Joseph Fields, Gibson, and Goodrich to hold themselves in readiness to accompany me in the morning. Sacagawea, our Indian woman, is very sick this evening. Captain Clark bled her. The night was cloudy with some rain.

Lewis and Clark's *History of the Expedition.*
Sunday, June 16, 1805; Great Falls of the Missouri near what is now Great Falls, Montana: Some rain fell last night, and this morning the weather was cloudy and the wind high from the southwest. We passed the rapid by doubly manning the pirogue and canoes, and halted at the distance of a mile and a quarter to examine the rapids above, which we found to be a continued succession of cascades as far as the view extended, which was about two miles. About a mile above where we halted was a large creek falling in on the south, opposite to which is a large sulfur spring falling over the rocks on the north....

Since leaving Marias River the wife of Charbonneau, our interpreter, has been dangerously ill, but she now found great relief from the mineral water of the sulfur spring. It is situated about two hundred yards from the Missouri, into which it empties over a precipice of rock about twenty-five feet high. The water is perfectly transparent, strongly impregnated with sulfur, and we suspect iron also, as the color of the hills and bluffs in the neighborhood indicates the presence of that metal. In short the water to all appearance is precisely similar to that of Bowyer's sulfur spring in Virginia.

CAPTAIN MERIWETHER LEWIS'S JOURNAL.

Wednesday, June 19, 1805; Great Falls of the Missouri: The Indian woman was much better this morning. She walked out and gathered a considerable quantity of the white apples, of which she ate so heartily in their raw state, together with a considerable quantity of dried fish without my knowledge, that she complained very much and her fever returned. I rebuked Charbonneau severely for suffering her to indulge herself with such food, he being privy to it and having been previously told what she must only eat. I now gave her broken doses of diluted niter until it produced perspiration, and at 10 p.m., 30 drops of laudanum [a tincture of opium], which gave her a tolerable night's rest.

CAPTAIN WILLIAM CLARK'S JOURNAL.

Saturday, June 29, 1805; Great Falls of the Missouri: Finding that the prairie was so wet as to render it impossible to pass on to the end of the portage, determined to send back to the top of the hill at the creek for the remaining part of the baggage left at that place yesterday—leaving one man to take care of the baggage at this place—I determined to proceed on to the falls and take the river. Accordingly, we all set out. I took my servant and one man. Charbonneau, our interpreter, and his squaw accompanied. Soon after I arrived at the falls, I perceived a cloud which appeared black and threatened immediate rain. I looked out for a shelter, but could see no place without being in great danger of being blown into the river if the wind should prove as turbulent as it is at some times.

About a quarter of a mile above the falls, I observed a deep ravine in which were shelving rocks under which we took shelter near the river, and placed our guns, the compass, etc., under a shelving rock on the upper side of the creek, in a place which was very secure from rain. The first shower was moderate, accompanied with a violent wind, the effects of which we did not feel. Soon after, a torrent of rain and hail fell, more violent than ever I saw before. The rain fell like one volley of water falling from the heavens and gave us time only to get out of the way of a torrent of water which was pouring down the hill into the river with immense force, tearing everything before it, taking with it large rocks and mud.

I took my gun and shot pouch in my left hand and with the right scrambled up the hill, pushing the interpreter's wife—who had her child in her arms—before me, the interpreter himself making attempts to pull up his wife by the hand, much scared and nearly without motion. We at length reached the top of the hill safely, where I found my servant in search of us, greatly agitated for our welfare. Before I got out of the bottom of the ravine, which was a flat dry rock when I entered it, the water was up to my waist and wet my watch. I scarcely got out before it rose ten feet deep with a torrent which was terrible to behold, and by the time I reached the top of the hill, at least fifteen feet water.

I directed the party to return to the camp, at the run, as fast as possible to get to our load, where clothes could be got to cover the child, whose clothes were all lost; and the woman, who was but just recovering from a severe indisposition and was wet and cold, I was fearful of a relapse. I caused her, as also the others of the party, to take a little spirits, which my servant had in a canteen, which revived them very much.

On arrival at the camp on the Willow Run, met the party, who had returned in great confusion to the run, leaving their loads in the plain, the hail and wind being so large and violent in the plains, and them [nearly] naked [which was how they dressed on account of the heat]; they were much bruised, and some nearly killed—one knocked down three times— and others without hats or anything on their heads, bloody and complained very much. I refreshed them with a little grog.

Soon after, the run began to rise and rose six feet in a few minutes. I lost at the river in the torrent the large compass, an elegant fusee, tomahawk, umbrella, shot pouch and horn with powder and ball, moccasins, and the woman lost her child's bier [papoose] and clothes, bedding, etc.

The compass is a serious loss, as we have no other large one. The plains are so wet that we can do nothing this evening, particularly as two deep ravines are between ourselves and the load [their baggage].

CAPTAIN MERIWETHER LEWIS'S JOURNAL.

Same day: Soon after a most violent torrent of rain descended accompanied with hail. The rain appeared to descend in a body and instantly collected in the ravine and came down in a rolling torrent with irresistible force, driving rocks, mud and everything before it which opposed its passage. Captain Clark fortunately discovered it a moment before it reached them and seizing his gun and shot pouch with his left hand with the right he assisted himself up the steep bluff, shoving occasionally the Indian woman before him, who had her child in her arms. Charbonneau had the woman by the hand endeavoring to pull her up the hill, but was so much frightened that he remained frequently motionless and, but for Captain Clark, both himself and his woman and child must have perished. So sudden was the rise of the water that before Captain Clark could reach his gun and begin to ascend the bank, it was up to his waist and wet his watch, and he could scarcely ascend faster than it arose till it had obtained the depth of fifteen feet with a current tremendous to behold. One moment longer and it would have swept them into the river just above the great cataract [i.e., waterfall] of 87 feet where they must have inevitably perished.

Charbonneau lost his gun, shot pouch, horn, tomahawk, and my wiping rod. Captain Clark his umbrella and compass or circumferenter. They fortunately arrived on the plain safe, where they found the black man, York, in search of them. York had separated from them a little while before the storm, in pursuit of some buffalo and had not seen them enter the ravine. When this gust came on, he returned in search of them and not being able to find them for some time was much alarmed.

The bier in which the woman carries her child and all its clothes were swept away as they lay at her feet, she having time only to grasp her child. The infant was therefore very cold and the woman also who had just recovered from a severe indisposition was also wet and cold. Captain Clark therefore relinquished his intended route and returned to the camp at Willow Run—in order also to obtain dry clothes for himself—and directed them to follow him.

CAPTAIN MERIWETHER LEWIS'S JOURNAL.

Sunday, July 28, 1805; Three Forks of the Missouri, about ninety miles north of Yellowstone in what is now Southwestern Montana: Our present camp is precisely on the spot that the Snake Indians were encamped at the time the Minitaree of the Knife River first came in sight of them five years since. From hence they retreated about three miles up Jefferson's River and concealed themselves in the woods. The Minitaree pursued, attacked them, killed four men, four women, a number of boys, and made prisoners of all the females and four boys. Sacagawea, our Indian woman, was one of the female prisoners taken at that time [at about the age of twelve], though I cannot discover that she shows any emotion of sorrow in recollecting this event, or of joy in being again restored to her native country. If she has enough to eat and a few trinkets to wear, I believe she would be perfectly content anywhere.

LEWIS AND CLARK'S *HISTORY OF THE EXPEDITION.*

Tuesday, July 30, 1805; Three Forks of the Missouri: Captain Clark was this morning much restored; and, therefore, having made all the observations necessary to fix the longitude, we reloaded our canoes and began to ascend Jefferson River. The river now becomes very crooked and forms bends on each side. The current, too, is rapid and cut into a great number of channels, and sometimes shoals, the beds of which consist of coarse gravel. The islands are unusually numerous: on the right are high plains occasionally forming cliffs of rocks and hills; while the left was an extensive low ground and prairie intersected by a number of bayous or channels falling into the river.

Captain Lewis, who had walked through it with Charbonneau, his wife, and two invalids, joined us at dinner a few miles above our camp. Here the Indian woman said was the place where she had been made prisoner. The men, being too few to contend with the Minitaree, mounted their horses and fled as soon as the attack began. The women and children dispersed and Sacagawea, as she was crossing at a shoal place, was overtaken in the middle of the river by her pursuers.

CAPTAIN MERIWETHER LEWIS'S JOURNAL.

Wednesday, August 14, 1805; near what is now Dillon, Montana: This evening Charbonneau struck his Indian woman, for which Captain Clark gave him a severe reprimand.

Leaving the Corp behind, Captain Lewis and three men went to the Shoshone village to establish contact with the tribe. One of the men was half Native American and could communicate using sign language.

LEWIS AND CLARK'S *HISTORY OF THE EXPEDITION*.

Thursday, August 15, 1805; what is now the Clark Canyon Reservoir in Southwestern Montana: Captain Lewis rose early, and having eaten nothing yesterday, except his scanty meal of flour and berries, felt the inconveniences of extreme hunger. On inquiry he found that his whole stock of provisions consisted of two pounds of flour. This he ordered to be divided into two equal parts, and one half of it boiled with the berries into a sort of pudding and, after presenting a large share to the [Shoshone] chief, he and his three men breakfasted on the remainder. Cameahwait [the chief] was delighted at this new dish. He took a little of the flour in his hand tasted and examined it very narrowly, asking if it was made of roots. Captain Lewis explained the process of preparing it, and he said it was the best thing he had eaten for a long time.

This being finished, Captain Lewis now endeavored to hasten the departure of the Indians [to accompany Lewis], who still hesitated and seemed reluctant to move, although the chief addressed them twice for the purpose of urging them. On inquiring the reason, Cameahwait told him that some foolish person had suggested that he was in league with their enemies the Pahkee [Piegan Blackfeet], and had come only to draw them into ambuscade, but that he himself did not believe it. Captain Lewis felt uneasy at this insinuation. He knew the suspicious temper of the Indians—accustomed from their infancy to regard every stranger as an enemy—and saw that if this suggestion were not instantly checked, it might hazard the total failure of the enterprise.

The Shoshone—Sacagawea's tribe—had about seven hundred horses and the expedition desperately needed some in order to survive crossing the mountains. Though they were rich in horses, the tribe was otherwise very poor. Their neighbors, the Blackfeet, had obtained modern rifles by trading with the whites and had chased the Shoshone off the plains. In the mountains, the Shoshone were forced to survive on berries, roots, and what buffalo they could kill on their annual hunts. They were practically starving, as were Lewis and his men, though at least Lewis's men could use their rifles to hunt game in these bare mountains.

Cameahwait knew he needed to trade with the whites in order to regain an equal footing with their enemies, but he was very wary, knowing the whites were friends of his enemies. This put Lewis and the expedition in a very tight spot. Not only would their expedition probably fail if they didn't obtain the horses they needed, the Shoshone might have attacked them on the spot at the first sign of treachery.

Lewis lured Cameahwait with the promise that the government would begin trading guns with his tribe, even though Lewis knew it was Thomas Jefferson's policy not to trade guns with Indians. Lewis also told them Captain Clark had a woman from their tribe with him and one of his men told them about York, Clark's black servant, which really aroused their curiosity.

Assuming therefore a serious air, he told the chief that he was sorry to find they placed so little confidence in him, but that he pardoned their suspicions because they were ignorant of the character of white men, among whom it was disgraceful to lie or entrap even an enemy by falsehood; that if they continued to think thus meanly of us they might be assured no white men would ever come to supply them with arms and merchandise; that there was at this moment a party of white men waiting to trade with them at the forks of the river; and that if the greater part of the tribe entertained any suspicion, he hoped there were still among them some who were men, who would go and see with their own eyes the truth of what he said, and who, even if there was any danger, were not afraid to die.

To doubt the courage of an Indian is to touch the tenderest string of his mind and the surest way to rouse him to any dangerous achievement. Cameahwait instantly replied, that he was not afraid to die, and mounting his horse, for the third time harangued the warriors. He told them that he was resolved to go if he went alone; or if he were sure of perishing, that he hoped there were among those who heard him some who were not afraid to die, and who would prove it by mounting their horses and following him. This harangue produced an effect on six or eight only of the warriors, who now joined their chief.

With these Captain Lewis smoked a pipe, and then fearful of some change in their capricious temper, set out immediately. It was about twelve o'clock when his small party left the camp, attended by Cameahwait and the eight warriors. Their departure seemed to spread a gloom over the village. Those who would not venture to go were sullen and melancholy, and the women were crying and imploring the Great Spirit to protect their warriors as if they were going to certain destruction. Yet such is the wavering inconstancy of these savages, that Captain Lewis's party had not gone far when they were joined by ten or twelve more warriors, and before reaching the creek which they had passed on the morning of the 13th, all the men of the nation and a number of women had overtaken them, and had changed from the surly ill temper in which they were two hours ago, to the greatest cheerfulness and gayety.

Unfortunately the view of the Natives as "savages" and other cultural misunderstandings resulted in many years of unnecessary violence.

We continued on for two miles, till we reached in the evening a small bottom covered with clover and a few cottonwood trees: here we passed the night near the remains of some old Indian lodges of brush. The river is as it has been for some days shallow and rapid; and our men, who are for hours together in the river, suffer not only from fatigue, but from the extreme coldness of the water, the temperature of which is as low as that of the freshest springs in our country. In walking along the side of the river, Captain Clark was very near being bitten twice by rattlesnakes, and the Indian woman narrowly escaped the same misfortune.

LEWIS AND CLARK'S *HISTORY OF THE EXPEDITION.*
Friday, August 16, 1805; what is now the Clark Canyon Reservoir: As neither our party nor the Indians had anything to eat, Captain Lewis sent two of his hunters ahead this morning to procure some provision. At the same time he requested Cameahwait to prevent his young men from going out, lest by their noise they might alarm the game, but this measure immediately

revived their suspicions. It now began to be believed that these men were sent forward in order to apprise the enemy of their coming, and as Captain Lewis was fearful of exciting any further uneasiness, he made no objection on seeing a small party of Indians go on each side of the valley under pretense of hunting, but in reality to watch the movements of our two men. Even this precaution however did not quiet the alarms of the Indians, a considerable part of whom returned home, leaving only twenty-eight men and three women.

After the hunters had been gone about an hour, Captain Lewis again mounted with one of the Indians behind him, and the whole party set out. But just as they passed through the narrows, they saw one of the spies coming back at full speed across the plain. The chief stopped and seemed uneasy. The whole band were moved with fresh suspicions and Captain Lewis himself was much disconcerted, lest by some unfortunate accident some of their enemies might have perhaps straggled that way.

The young Indian had scarcely breath to say a few words as he came up, when the whole troop dashed forward as fast as their horses could carry them; and Captain Lewis, astonished at this movement, was borne along for nearly a mile before he learnt with great satisfaction that it was all caused by the spy's having come to announce that one of the white men had killed a deer. Relieved from his anxiety he now found the jolting very uncomfortable, for the Indian behind him being afraid of not getting his share of the feast had lashed the horse at every step since they set off. He therefore reined him in and ordered the Indian to stop beating him. The fellow had no idea of losing time in disputing the point and, jumping off the horse, ran for a mile at full speed. Captain Lewis slackened his pace and followed at a sufficient distance to observe them.

When they reached the place where Drouillard had thrown out the intestines, they all dismounted in confusion and ran tumbling over each other like famished dogs. Each tore away whatever part he could and instantly began to eat it. Some had the liver, some the kidneys, in short no part on which we are accustomed to look with disgust escaped them. One of them who had seized about nine feet of the entrails was chewing at one end, while with his hand he was diligently clearing his way by discharging the contents at the other.

It was indeed impossible to see these wretches ravenously feeding on the filth of animals, and the blood streaming from their mouths, without deploring how nearly the condition of savages approaches that of the brute creation. Yet though suffering with hunger, they did not attempt, as they might have done, to take by force the whole deer, but contented themselves with what had been thrown away by the hunter.

Captain Lewis now had the deer skinned, and after reserving a quarter of it gave the rest of the animal to the chief to be divided among the Indians, who immediately devoured nearly the whole of it without cooking.

They now went forward towards the creek where there was some brushwood to make a fire, and found Drouillard who had killed a second deer. The same struggle for the entrails was renewed here, and on giving nearly the whole deer to the Indians, they devoured it even to the soft part of the hoofs. A fire being made, Captain Lewis had his breakfast, during which Drouillard brought in a third deer. This too, after reserving one quarter, was given to the Indians, who now seemed completely satisfied and in good humor. At this place they remained about two hours to let the horses graze and then continued their journey, and towards evening reached the lower part of the cove; having on the way shot an antelope, the greater part of which was given to the Indians.

As they were now approaching the place where they had been told by Captain Lewis they would see the white men, the chief insisted on halting. They therefore all dismounted and Cameahwait, with great ceremony and as if for ornament, put tippets or skins round the necks of our party, similar to those worn by themselves. As this was obviously intended to disguise the white men, Captain Lewis—in order to inspire them with more confidence—put his cocked hat and feather on the head of the chief, and as his own over-shirt was in the Indian form, and his skin browned by the sun, he could not have been distinguished from an Indian. The men followed his example and the change seemed to be very agreeable to the Indians.

In order to guard however against any disappointment, Captain Lewis again explained the possibility of our not having reached the forks in consequence of the difficulty of the navigation, so that if they should not find us at that spot, they might be assured of our not being far below.

They again all mounted their horses and rode on rapidly, making one of the Indians carry their flag so that we might recognize them as they approached us. But to the mortification and disappointment of both parties, on coming within two miles of the forks, no canoes were to be seen. Uneasy, lest at this moment he should be abandoned and all his hopes of obtaining aid from the Indians be destroyed, Captain Lewis gave the chief his gun, telling him that if the enemies of his nation were in the bushes he might defend himself with it; that for his own part he was not afraid to die, and that the chief might shoot him as soon as they discovered themselves betrayed. The other three men at the same time gave their guns to the Indians, who now seemed more easy, but still wavered in their resolutions.

As they went on towards the point, Captain Lewis, perceiving how critical his situation had become, resolved to attempt a stratagem which his present difficulty seemed completely to justify. Recollecting the notes he had left at the point for us, he sent Drouillard for them with an Indian, who witnessed his taking them from the pole. When they were brought, Captain Lewis told Cameahwait that on leaving his brother chief at the place where the river issues from the mountains, it was agreed that the boats should not be brought higher than the next forks we should meet, but that if the rapid water prevented the boats from coming on as fast as they expected, his brother chief was to send a note to the first forks above him to let him know where the boats were; that this note had been left this morning at the forks, and mentioned that the canoes were just below the mountains and coming slowly up in consequence of the current.

Captain Lewis added that he would stay at the forks for his brother chief, but would send a man down the river, and that if Cameahwait doubted what he said, one of their young men would go with him whilst he and the other two remained at the forks. This story satisfied the chief and the greater part of the Indians, but a few did not conceal their suspicion, observing that we told different stories, and complaining that the chief exposed them to danger by a mistaken confidence. . . .

On ascending an eminence Captain Clark saw the forks of the river and sent the hunters up. They must have left it only a short time before Captain Lewis's arrival, but fortunately had not seen the note which enabled him to induce the Indians to stay with him. From the top of this eminence he could discover only three trees through the whole country, nor was there along the sides of the cliffs they had passed in the course of the day, any timber except a few small pines. The low grounds were supplied with willow, currant bushes, and serviceberries. After advancing half a mile further we came to the lower point of an island near the middle of the river, and about the center of the valley. Here we halted for the night, only four miles by land, though ten by water, below the point where Captain Lewis lay. Although we had made only fourteen miles, the labors of the men had fatigued and exhausted them very much. We therefore collected some small willow brush for a fire and lay down to sleep.

LEWIS AND CLARK'S *HISTORY OF THE EXPEDITION.*

Saturday, August 17, 1805; what is now the Clark Canyon Reservoir: On setting out at seven o'clock, Captain Clark with Charbonneau and his wife walked on shore, but they had not gone more than a mile before Captain Clark saw Sacagawea—who was with her husband one hundred yards ahead—begin to dance and show every mark of the most extravagant joy, turning round him and pointing to several Indians, whom he now saw advancing on horseback, sucking her fingers at the same time to indicate that they were of her native tribe.

As they advanced Captain Clark discovered among them Drouillard dressed like an Indian, from whom he learnt the situation of the party. While the boats were performing the circuit, he went towards the forks with the Indians, who as they went along, sang aloud with the greatest appearance of delight.

We soon drew near to the camp and just as we approached it, a woman made her way through the crowd towards Sacagawea, and recognizing each other, they embraced with the most tender affection. The meeting of these two young women had in it something peculiarly touching, not only in the ardent manner in which their feelings were expressed, but from the real interest of their situation. They had been companions in childhood. In the war with the Minitaree, they had both been taken prisoners in the same battle, they had shared and softened the rigors of their captivity, till one of them had escaped from the Minitaree with scarce a hope of ever seeing her friend relieved from the hands of her enemies.

While Sacagawea was renewing among the women the friendships of former days, Captain Clark went on and was received by Captain Lewis and the chief, who after the first embraces and salutations were over, conducted him to a sort of circular tent or shade of willows. Here he was seated on a white robe and the chief immediately tied in his hair six small shells resembling pearls—an ornament highly valued by these people, who procured them in the course of trade from the seacoast. The moccasins of the whole party were then taken off, and after much ceremony the smoking began.

After this the conference was to be opened, and glad of an opportunity of being able to converse more intelligibly, Sacagawea was sent for. She came into the tent, sat down, and was beginning to interpret, when in the person of Cameahwait she recognized her brother. She instantly jumped up and ran and embraced him, throwing over him her blanket and weeping profusely. The chief was himself moved, though not in the same degree.

After some conversation between them, she resumed her seat and attempted to interpret for us, but her new situation seemed to overpower her and she was frequently interrupted by her tears. After the council was finished, the unfortunate woman learnt that all her family were dead except two brothers—one of whom was absent—and a son of her eldest sister, a small boy, who was immediately adopted by her.

The canoes arriving soon after, we formed a camp in a meadow on the left side a little below the forks, took out our baggage, and by means of our sails and willow poles, formed a canopy for our Indian visitors. About four o'clock the chiefs and warriors were collected, and after the customary ceremony of taking off the moccasins and smoking a pipe, we explained to them in a long harangue the purposes of our visit, making themselves one conspicuous object of the good wishes of our government, on whose strength as well as its friendly disposition we expatiated. We told them of their dependence on the will of our government for all future supplies of whatever was necessary, either for their comfort or defense. That as we were sent to discover the best route by which merchandise could be conveyed to them, and no trade would be begun before our return, it was mutually advantageous that we should proceed with as little delay as possible. That we were under the necessity of requesting them to furnish us with horses to transport our baggage across the mountains and a guide to show us the route, but that they should be amply remunerated for their horses, as well as for every other service they should render us. In the meantime our first wish was that they should immediately collect as many horses as were necessary to transport our baggage to their village, where, at our leisure we would trade with them for as many horses as they could spare.

The speech made a favorable impression. The chief in reply thanked us for our expressions of friendship towards himself and his nation and declared their willingness to render us every service. He lamented that it would be so long before they should be supplied with firearms, but that till then they could subsist as they had heretofore done.

LEWIS AND CLARK'S *HISTORY OF THE EXPEDITION.*

Saturday, August 24, 1805; what is now the Clark Canyon Reservoir: As the Indians who arrived yesterday had a number of spare horses, we thought it probable they might be willing to dispose of them, and desired the chief to speak to them for that purpose. . . . They now said that they had no more horses for sale, and as we had now nine of our own, two hired horses, and a mule, we began loading them as heavily as was prudent, and placing the rest on the shoulders of the Indian women, left our camp at twelve o'clock. We were all on foot, except Sacagawea, for whom her husband had purchased a horse with some articles which we gave him for that purpose. An Indian however had the politeness to offer Captain Lewis one of his horses to ride, which he accepted in order better to direct the march of the party.

LEWIS AND CLARK'S *HISTORY OF THE EXPEDITION.*

Monday, August 26, 1805; Lewis camped about four miles north of what is now Tendoy, Idaho, while Clark camped about five miles southeast of what is now Salmon, Idaho: The morning was excessively cold, and the ice in our vessels was nearly a quarter of an inch in thickness: we set out at sunrise, and soon reached the fountain of the Missouri. . . . One of the women who had been leading two of our pack horses halted at a rivulet about a mile behind and sent on the two horses by a female friend. On inquiring of Cameahwait the cause of her detention, he answered with great appearance of unconcern that she had just stopped to lie in, but would soon overtake us. In fact we were astonished to see her in about an hour's time come on with her newborn infant and pass us on her way to the camp, apparently in perfect health....

The Shoshone are a small tribe of the nation called Snake Indians, a vague denomination, which embraces at once the inhabitants of the southern parts of the Rocky Mountains and of the plains on each side. The Shoshone with whom we now are, amount to about one hundred warriors, and three times that number of women and children. Within their own recollection they formerly lived in the plains, but they have been driven into the mountains by the Pawkees [Piegan Blackfeet]—or the roving Indians of the Saskatchewan—and are now obliged to visit occasionally, and by stealth, the country of their ancestors.

Their lives are indeed migratory. From the middle of May to the beginning of September, they reside on the waters of the Columbia, where they consider themselves perfectly secure from the Pawkees who have never yet found their way to that retreat. During this time they subsist chiefly on salmon, and as that fish disappears on the approach of autumn, they are obliged to seek subsistence elsewhere. They then cross the ridge to the waters of the Missouri, down which they proceed slowly and cautiously, till they are joined near the three forks by other bands, either of their own nation or of the Flatheads, with whom they associate against the common enemy.

Being now strong in numbers, they venture to hunt buffalo in the plains eastward of the mountains, near which they spend the winter, till the return of the salmon invites them to the Columbia. But such is their terror of the Pawkees, that as long as they can obtain the scantiest subsistence, they do not leave the interior of the mountains. And as soon as they collect a large stock of dried meat, they again retreat, and thus alternately obtaining their food at the hazard of their lives, and hiding themselves to consume it.

In this loose and wandering existence they suffer the extremes of want. For two thirds of the year they are forced to live in the mountains, passing whole weeks without meat and with nothing to eat but a few fish and roots.

Nor can anything be imagined more wretched than their condition at the present time, when the salmon is fast retiring, when roots are becoming scarce, and they have not yet acquired strength to hazard an encounter with their enemies. So insensible are they however to these calamities, that the Shoshone are not only cheerful but even gay. And their character, which is more interesting than that of any Indians we have seen, has in it much of the dignity of misfortune. In their intercourse with strangers they are frank and communicative, in their dealings perfectly fair, nor have we had during our stay with them, any reason to suspect that the display of all our new and valuable wealth, has tempted them into a single act of dishonesty. While they have generally shared with us the little they possess, they have always abstained from begging anything from us.

With their liveliness of temper, they are fond of gaudy dresses and of all sorts of amusements—particularly to games of hazard—and, like most Indians, fond of boasting of their own warlike exploits, whether real or fictitious. In their conduct towards ourselves, they were kind and obliging, and though on one occasion they seemed willing to neglect us, yet we scarcely knew how to blame the treatment by which we suffered, when we recollected how few civilized chiefs would have hazarded the comforts or the subsistence of their people for the sake of a few strangers.

This manliness of character may cause or it may be formed by the nature of their government, which is perfectly free from any restraint. Each individual is his own master and the only control to which his conduct is subjected, is the advice of a chief supported by his influence over the opinions of the rest of the tribe. The chief himself is in fact no more than the most confidential person among the warriors, a rank neither distinguished by any external honor, nor invested by any ceremony, but gradually acquired from the good wishes of his companions and by superior merit. Such an officer has therefore strictly no power; he may recommend or advise or influence, but his commands have no effect on those who incline to disobey, and who may at any time withdraw from their voluntary allegiance. His shadowy authority, which cannot survive the confidence which supports it, often decays with the personal vigor of the chief or is transferred to some more fortunate or favorite hero.

In their domestic economy, the man is equally sovereign. The man is the sole proprietor of his wives and daughters and can barter them away or dispose of them in any manner he may think proper. The children are seldom corrected. The boys, particularly, soon become their own masters. They are never whipped, for they say that it breaks their spirit and that after being flogged they never recover their independence of mind, even when they grow to manhood.

A plurality of wives is very common, but these are not generally sisters, as among the Minitaree and Mandan, but are purchased of different fathers. The infant daughters are often betrothed by the father to men who are grown, either for themselves or for their sons, for whom they are desirous of providing wives. The compensation to the father is usually made in horses or mules, and the girl remains with her parents till the age of puberty—which is thirteen or fourteen—when she is surrendered to her husband. At the same time the father often makes a present to the husband equal to what he had formerly received as the price of his daughter, though this return is optional with her parent.

Sacagawea had been contracted in this way before she was taken prisoner, and when we brought her back, her betrothed was still living. Although he was double the age of Sacagawea and had two other wives, he claimed her, but on finding that she had a child by her new husband, Charbonneau, he relinquished his pretensions and said he did not want her.

The chastity of the women does not appear to be held in much estimation. The husband will, for a trifling present, lend his wife for a night to a stranger, and the loan may be protracted by increasing the value of the present. Yet strange as it may seem, notwithstanding this facility, any connection of this kind not authorized by the husband, is considered highly offensive and quite as disgraceful to his character as the same licentiousness in civilized societies.

The Shoshone are not so importunate in volunteering the services of their wives as we found the Sioux were, and indeed we observed among them some women who appeared to be held in more respect than those of any nation we had seen. But the mass of the females are condemned, as among all savage nations, to the lowest and most laborious drudgery. When the tribe is stationary, they collect the roots and cook; they build the huts, dress the skins and make clothing; collect the wood, and assist in taking care of the horses on the route; they load the horses and have the charge of all the baggage.

The only business of the man is to fight. He therefore takes on himself the care of his horse—the companion of his warfare—but he will descend to no other labor than to hunt and to fish. He would consider himself degraded by being compelled to walk any distance; and were he so poor as to possess only two horses, he would ride the best of them and leave the other for his wives and children and their baggage. And if he has too many wives or too much baggage for the horse, the wives have no alternative but to follow him on foot. They are not however often reduced to those extremities, for their stock of horses is very ample. Notwithstanding their losses this Spring, they still have at least seven hundred, among which are about forty colts and half that number of mules.

There are no horses here which can be considered as wild. We have seen two only on this side of the Muscleshell River which were without owners; and even those, although shy, showed every mark of having been once in the possession of man. The original stock was procured from the Spaniards, but they now raise their own. The horses are generally very fine, of a good size, vigorous and patient of fatigue as well as hunger. Each warrior has one or two tied to a stake near his hut both day and night, so as to be always prepared for action. The mules are obtained in the course of trade from the Spaniards—with whose brands several of them are marked—or stolen from them by the frontier Indians. They are the finest animals of that kind we have ever seen and at this distance from the Spanish colonies are very highly valued. The worst are considered as worth the price of two horses, and a good mule cannot be obtained for less than three and sometimes four horses.

LEWIS AND CLARK'S *HISTORY OF THE EXPEDITION.*

Sunday, January 5, 1806; on the Lewis and Clark River, just a few miles south of the Oregon side of the Columbia River near what is now Astoria, Oregon at a fort they built for the winter called Fort Clatsop: Two of the five men who had been dispatched to make salt returned. . . . The appearance of the whale seemed to be a matter of importance to all the neighboring Indians, and as we might be able to procure some of it for ourselves, or at least purchase blubber from the Indians, a small parcel of merchandise was prepared and a party of the men held in readiness to set out in the morning. As soon as this resolution was known, Charbonneau and his wife requested that they might be permitted to accompany us. The poor woman stated very earnestly that she had traveled a great way with us to see the great water, yet she had never been down to the coast, and now that this monstrous fish was also to be seen, it seemed hard that she should not be permitted to see neither the ocean nor the whale. So reasonable a request could not be denied. They were therefore suffered to accompany Captain Clark, who, after an early breakfast set out with twelve men in two canoes.

CAPTAIN WILLIAM CLARK'S JOURNAL.
Monday, August 4, 1806; Missouri River in what is now McKenzie County in Western North Dakota: On this point the mosquitoes were so abundant that we were tormented much worse than at the point. The child of Charbonneau has been so much bitten by the mosquitoes that his face is much puffed up and swollen.

CAPTAIN WILLIAM CLARK'S JOURNAL.
Saturday, August 17, 1806; Chief Big White's Mandan village on the Upper Missouri River near Fort Mandan and what is now Washburn, North Dakota: We were visited by all the principal chiefs of the Minitaree to take their leave of us. At 2 o'clock we left our encampment after taking leave of Colter, who also set out up the river in company with Messrs. Dickson and Handcock. We also took our leave of T. Charbonneau, his Snake Indian wife and their son child who had accompanied us on our route to the Pacific Ocean in the capacity of interpreter and interpretess.

T. Charbonneau wished much to accompany us in the said capacity if we could have prevailed the Minitaree chiefs to descend the river with us to the U. States, but as none of those chiefs of whose language he was conversant would accompany us. His Services were no longer of use to the U. States and he was therefore discharged and paid up. We offered to convey him down to the Illinois if he chose to go, he declined proceeding on at present, observing that he had no acquaintance or prospects of making a living below and must continue to live in the way that he had done.

I offered to take his little son—a beautiful, promising child who is 19 months old—to which they both himself and wife were willing, provided the child had been weaned. They observed that in one year the boy would be sufficiently old to leave his mother and he would then take him to me, if I would be so friendly as to raise the child for him in such a manner as I thought proper; to which I agreed, etc.

LEWIS AND CLARK'S *HISTORY OF THE EXPEDITION*.

Same day: This man [Charbonneau] has been very serviceable to us, and his wife particularly useful among the Shoshone. Indeed, she has borne with a patience truly admirable, the fatigues of so long a route, encumbered with the charge of an infant, who is even now only nineteen months old. We therefore paid him his wages, amounting to five hundred dollars and thirty-three cents [roughly $132,000 in today's money], including the price of a horse and a lodge purchased of him.

Red Hair and Long Knife

Sacagawea

Not surprisingly, Sacagawea herself had a very different way of looking at things than did Lewis and Clark. Most of this was due to cultural differences. Her background was obviously very different, and her unique perspective is what makes her account so interesting.

Obviously she wasn't able to write down her experiences herself. They were passed down orally through one of her friends. Storytelling was a very important part of Native American culture. In a society without movies, television, computers, or books, one of the main sources of entertainment was telling accounts of important events. Also, because these tribes didn't have a written language, a strong emphasis was placed on remembering oral histories. Accounts were repeated over and over so that people would be able to remember them, because this was how tribal history was preserved.

Personal experiences were viewed as being possessions of the narrators, who needed to be compensated in advance for their accounts, therefore narrators were invited for dinner and given gifts before being asked to talk. It was a form of showing respect for the knowledge and wisdom the person had gained from their experiences. Among the Hidatsa, storytelling was only permitted between the summer and winter solstices, starting on the summer solstice and stopping just before the winter solstice. Otherwise it was believed a long, difficult winter would ensue.

Contact narratives were particularly important because they portrayed cultural differences and, of course, exploration narratives would have been significant for revealing new worlds. Sacagawea's accounts were both. Because her experiences were so unique, she no doubt recounted her experiences many times. One of those who listened to her was Sakwaihki, "Earth Woman."

Sakwaihki was born in one of the five villages in 1804. She was the daughter of one of the Mandan chiefs who welcomed Lewis and Clark. She listened to Sacagawea relate her experiences before she left the area in the 1820s. (About that time she married Captain James Kipp of the American Fur Company, becoming Mrs. James Kipp.) Sakwaihki then relayed them to James Willard Schultz in the 1880s.

At the age of seventeen, Schultz traveled west to experience life on the frontier in 1877 and ended up becoming part of a Blackfeet tribe. His Piegan Blackfeet name was Apikuni. He became fluent in the Blackfeet language and married a Blackfeet woman. He published thirty-seven books about his life with them, their culture, their tales, and their experiences. His most popular book is *My Life as an Indian* (1907). He translated Sacagawea's narrative that he had copied down from Sakwaihki—along with those of Hugh Monroe, who was also known as Rising Wolf—and published them as *Bird Woman* (1918).

How accurately her words were passed on and translated is uncertain. Readers will have to decide that for themselves. They do give some insight into how Native Americans viewed things and offer another perspective on the Lewis and Clark expedition.

Just as Lewis and Clark had difficulty pronouncing Sacagawea's name, prompting Clark to call her "Janey," Sacagawea had other names for them. Using the Indian custom of giving names related to something distinctive about a person, Sacagawea called Clark "Red Hair," obviously because of his red hair, and Lewis was called "Long Knife" because of the sword he carried. Both of them were called "the Long Knife chiefs."

I did not, of course, attend the great council of our chiefs with the Long Knife chiefs [at the Mandan-Hidatsa villages]; women were not allowed in it. But my man was there, and as soon as it was over he came to me and said, "The Long Knife chiefs will winter here with us, and when they go on westward they want a guide to show them the way, and someone to take them to the Snakes, in order to purchase horses from them. They will need many horses for riding and for carrying their goods when they arrive at the head of the river and leave their boats—"

"They cannot take their boats to the head of the river. They will not be able to get them up over the big falls, a long way this side of the mountains," I told him.

"Oh, well, wherever they abandon the boats, there they must have horses with which to go on. I shall tell them that I will be their guide and interpreter."

"But you do not know the way, you cannot even understand my Snake language!" I told him.

"Fool!" he cried. "You shall show me the way—and I will lead them to your people!"

Can you imagine how my heart beat when he said that? Here, after all the years, was a chance to see my own people again! At the thought of it I was so happy that I cried. And Otter Woman was happy, too. She sprang up and danced around and around, crying, "We are going to the mountains! We are going to the mountains! We shall see our Snake people, our dear relations!"

"Come! Let us go to the Long Knives at once, and tell them that we will guide them, and interpret for them," I said.

"No! We shall let them find out that we are the only ones that can do this for them. Then they will come to us about it, and so we shall get bigger pay than if we ran to them to offer our services," our man answered.

As our man said, so it had to be. Oh, how anxious Otter Woman and I became as the days passed and we had no word from the white men! Our man became anxious, too, and one day went down and visited the white men, where they were building a fort, some distance below the lower Mandan village. They said nothing to him about engaging us at that time. More and more long days passed. We became more and more uneasy, and finally our man took us down to visit the whites and to see their fort. It was not completed, but we were filled with wonder at it, the first white men's building that we had ever seen. It was wonderful how they had put heavy logs one on top of another, up and up to make the walls. As a great rock is in the middle of a river's swift current, so was that fort there in the timbered bottom. Storms could not even shake it. Nor could all the warriors of our three tribes take it by attack, for there were cunningly cut holes in the walls through which the whites could shoot their many guns and kill off the attackers as they came!

The great white chiefs, Long Knife [Captain Clark] and Red Hair [Meriwether Lewis], greeted us very pleasantly, and made us feel that we were really welcome in their camp. They showed their many strange things, things beautiful and useful, and made us presents of some of them. They had us to eat with them, too, and at that evening meal Otter Woman and I first tasted bread; we thought it the best-flavored food that we had ever eaten. Just as soon as I looked at those two white chiefs, and put my hand in theirs, my heart went out to them, for I knew that, although very brave, truly fearless of all things, yet were they of gentle heart. I could not keep my eyes off them. I felt that I wanted to work for them; to do all that I could for them. Think, then, how happy I was when, that very evening, it was arranged that we should all come and live with them as soon as their fort was completed, our man to be their Minitaree interpreter, and hunter at times. Nothing was then said about our going west with them in the spring, but I felt sure that that would be asked of us later on.

A few days later the fort was completed, and we moved down with our belongings and were given a room in it. Oh, what a pleasant place that room was, with its fireplace, its windows of oiled skin, and its comfortable couches! The white men visited us in it, and we often visited in their rooms, especially the room of the two chiefs. They were always having visitors from the villages above, and were always getting them to describe what they knew of the country and the people who inhabited it, especially those to the west of us. Night after night they got me to tell them about my Snake people and their country, and I told them all, even to telling them how my people were persecuted by the Blackfeet, the Minitaree, the Assiniboine, and how I, myself, had been taken into captivity. I told them, too, that my people starved more than half the time, because, without guns, they were driven from the plains by their powerful enemies every time that they came out after buffalo. And at that Long Knife and Red Hair both told me that one of their objects in coming to the country was to make peace between all the tribes in it, and, anyhow, if they would not agree to that, the traders who would follow the trail that they were to make would furnish my Snake people plenty of guns, and they would then be able to hold their own against all enemies.

Those were happy days for us, there in the fort of the white men. I was happier than I had ever been, until the time came for me to have my child, and then I suffered terribly. There was another Frenchman and his family with us in the fort, and I could see by the way he talked with the white chiefs that he thought I was about to die. I thought so myself, and, oh, I didn't want to die! I wanted to live! I prayed the gods to help me! At last, when I thought that I could bear the pain no longer, the white chiefs and the Frenchman got together and decided to give me a powerful medicine. I took it. It was powerful; soon after I drank it I gave birth to my child, and then, when I found that it was a boy, I was happier than ever. And what do you think was the medicine that they gave me? You could never guess. It was the rattles of a poison snake, crushed fine in water! It may be that I would not have drank it had I known what it was, and when all was over I was glad that they had not told me.

Upon my man's return to the fort the boats were all loaded. We had two large ones and six small ones, and we abandoned the fort and headed up the river. At the same time that we started, Long Knife and Red Hair sent their very large boat down the river in charge of some of their men. It was loaded with many skins, bones, and other things, presents for the great chief of the whites. Counting in my son, we were thirty-three people in our eight boats. I was given a place in one of the two large ones.

As we went on and on up the river, sometimes making a long distance between the rising and the setting of the sun, I was, at times, I believe, happier than I had ever been in my life, for each day's travel brought me so much nearer my people whom I so much longed to see. Then at other times, whenever I thought of what was before us, I would become very unhappy. I would say to myself that we could not possibly survive the dangers we should be sure to encounter along the way. I may as well say it: my good, kind white chiefs were not cautious; they were too brave, too sure of themselves. From the very start they and their men would foolishly risk their lives by attacking all the man-killing bears that came in sight of us. At night they would build great fires that would be sure to attract to us any wandering war party that might be in the country. After we passed the mouth of the Yellowstone and entered the country of the Blackfeet, I begged my chiefs to be more cautious. I asked them to stop always a short time before dark and build little cooking-fires, and then, after our meal, to put out the fires, and then go on until dark and make camp in the darkness. But they only laughed at me, and answered, "We have good guns and know how to use them. Big fires are a great comfort to us, so we must have them."

I often said to myself, "Strange are these white men! Strange their ways! They have a certain thing to do, to make a trail to the west to the Everywhere-Salt-Water. Why, then, are we not on horseback and traveling fast and far each day? Here we are in boats, heavily loaded with all kinds of useless things, and when the wind is bad or the water swift, we make but little distance between sun and sun! We could have got all the horses that we needed from the Earth House tribes, and had we done that, we should long since have arrived at the mountains. Yes, right now I should probably be talking with my own people!"

And those medicine packages of theirs, packages big and little piled all around me in the boat in which I rode, how my chiefs valued them! One day a sudden hard wind struck our sail and the boat began to tip and fill with water. More and more it filled, and the men in it and those on the shore went almost crazy with fear. But I was not afraid. Why should I be when I knew that I could cast off my robe and swim ashore with my little son? More and more water poured into the boat and the medicine packages began to float out of it. I seized them one by one as they were going, and kept seizing them and holding them, and when, at last, we reached the shore, my good white chiefs acted as though I had done a wonderful thing in saving their packages; it seemed as though they could not thank me enough for what I had done. Thinking about it, after it was all over, and when the things had been spread out to dry, I said to myself, "Although I cannot understand them, these little instruments of shining steel and these writings on thin white paper [Clark's journals] must be powerful medicine. Hereafter, whenever we run into danger, I shall, after my son, have my first thought for their safety, and so please my kind white chiefs."

After leaving the mouth of Little River [in what is now Montana], or, as my white chiefs named it, Milk River, we went up through a part of the Big River Valley that I had not seen, for, when I was captured by the Minitaree, we had, after leaving the valley at the mouth of Bear River aka Marias River], struck across to Little River and then followed it down. We were many, many days in getting the boats up this long, winding, and ever swifter part of the river. The farther up it we went the more I looked for signs of the enemy, the Blackfeet, and their war brothers, the Big Bellies, but, look as I would, I could never find even a single footprint that they had made nor any tracks of their horses. I thought that very strange. When we arrived at the mouth of the stream my white chiefs named the Musselshell, some of the men went up it during the afternoon, and, returning, told of a stream coming into it from the plain on the right. My chiefs then told me that it should have my name, as they called it, Sah-ka-ja´-we-ah.

I asked my man to tell them that I wished they would give it my right name, Bo-i´-naiv, Grass Woman.

But he laughed at me, and answered, "Never mind! It doesn't matter what they call it!"

I thought that it did matter, but I could not at that time speak French more than a few words, and so I was bashful about asking them to make the change.

"It seemed to matter when they named a creek after you," I said. "You were pleased enough!"

"Yes, but I am a man! Important! Women—their names to things do not matter," he answered. And I said nothing more. What could I say? Nothing.

It was some days after passing the mouth of the Other-Side-Bear-River, the Musselshell, that we arrived at the mouth of a small river coming in from the south, and there came upon a not long deserted campground of the enemy, either Blackfeet or their war brothers, the Big Bellies. There had been a great camp of them at the mouth of the small river, and another opposite it on the north side of Big River [the Missouri River]. Just below the little river they had decoyed a herd of buffalo to death over a cliff, and wolves were still eating the meat of old and poor animals that the hunters had not thought worth taking.

As I looked at the abandoned fireplaces of the camp, I said to myself, "It will not be long before we are discovered by the enemies who were recently here, and when that happens our end will come! Brave though my white chiefs and their men are, they are too few to win a fight with the hundreds of warriors who will come against them!"

My heart was very low as we went on up the river. I felt that, after all, I was not to see my country and my people again. I made up my mind that I would not be captured again; before the enemy could lay hands upon me, I would kill my little son, and then myself! I now kept constant watch of the river bottoms ahead, and the tops of the cliffs on each side of the narrow valley, expecting at every turn we made to see the enemy approaching us.

At last we came, one morning, to the mouth of Bear River and made camp. I was now in country that I knew. Here I had left Big River with my Minitaree captors, and struck off across the plain to Little River. On horseback it was but a day from here up to the falls of Big River. Look as I would, I could find no fresh signs of the enemy, not a fireplace, not a track of man or horse, and I began to think that we might, after all, reach the mountains without being discovered by the Blackfeet. I prayed for that! Oh, how I prayed the gods to keep the eyes of the enemy from us while we went on and on to the head of the river and over the mountains to my people!

To my surprise, after my white chiefs had made medicine with their strange instruments, we did not go on. One of the chiefs went up Big River and the other up Bear River, each with a few men, leaving us to be easily killed by the enemy should they discover us. Red Hair, who went up Big River, was gone from us three days, and Long Knife, who went up Bear River, did not return until the evening of the fifth day. After his return we remained there still another day, drying our things after the heavy rain that had fallen, hiding some of them in a hole the men dug in the ground, and leaving one of our boats on an island. And why, do you think, they were gone so long up the two rivers? They were all that time learning which of them was Big River, the one that they wanted to follow! And there I was; I could have told them which one it was, and they had not asked me! When my man told me what they had been doing I scolded him, and asked him to tell Long Knife and Red Hair that I was very sorry they had not told me what was their trouble, for I could have saved them these five days of wandering. He would not do it. "I can't. They would then blame me for not having asked you about it," he answered. Ah, well, that is one great fault in men: they think that women are so foolish that it is a waste of time to question them about anything!

On our last night at the mouth of Bear River, I fell sick. While I slept, some Blackfeet or other enemy ghost, wandering there, had found me and put its badness into my body. As we went on up the river I became more and more sick day by day, and began to think that I was about to die. If I did, then my little son, lacking the milk of my breast, would die, too. I said to myself that for his sake I must not die. I prayed and prayed the gods for help. I made sacrifice to them. I begged them to sustain life in me until I could reach their stinking-water spring at the falls and drink its healing water. They did help me. I fought and fought the ghost's evil that was inside me, and at last, when we neared the place, I told my man where the spring was, and sent him to bring me some of the water. I drank and drank it, and by the time we went into camp near the spring I began to feel better. Two days later I was worse again, but I continued to pray to the gods, and drink the medicine water, and finally the evil work of the enemy ghost went from me.

I had thought that when we arrived at the long stretch of falls and swift water in the river, we should abandon the boats and go on to my country on foot. But no! As soon as we arrived at the first of the bad water, the men began at once to cut down a big tree from which to saw round pieces upon which to draw the boats—all but the largest one—the long, rough, and steep way to the almost-still water above the upper falls, and this caused a long delay, many days of hard toil. And while their men worked, dragging the boats upon the log slices up the trail, and carrying the many packages of goods upon their backs, Long Knife and Red Hair made medicine with their queer, little instruments at each of the falls, not once but many times. I could not understand why they did that; it seemed to me useless work. They were making a trail to the west. Well, no boats nor men could go up over the falls, so why not plainly mark the beginning of the trail around them and its end up at the still water and be done with it? That was the one fault with my good white chiefs: they were—I hate to say it—time-wasters.

At last a camp was made above the falls, and one day we in the lower camp started out to move the last of the boats and the goods packages up to it. I went ahead of the party with Red Hair, the black white man [York, Captain Clark's slave], and my man. It was a bad day; low, black clouds everywhere shutting out the blue, and rain falling. We had not gone very far on the trail when there came a terrible wind and the hardest rain that

I ever saw. The black white man was on ahead. Red Hair, my man, and I ran down into a coulee and stood under a rock wall that formed its right bank. The rain came harder and harder until it made the day so dark that we could no more than see the other bank of the coulee, not ten steps across from us. I knew that so heavy a rain would soon make a river where we stood, and was about to tell my man that we had best get out of the coulee, when, suddenly, we saw a great flood of it coming down upon us. I had set my little son down at my feet, spreading his wraps upon his carrying-case for him to lie upon, and as I snatched him up, Red Hair and my man seized hold of me and we made a run for the steep bank across the way. Before we could reach it the water began to rise and foam about us, and roll stones that bruised our legs and nearly took us off our feet. And who do you think it was that saved me and my little son? My man? No. By his hard pulling and pushing, Red Hair saved the three of us from being taken by the awful rise of roaring water and stones down the coulee into Big River, and down it to our death in the falls! Can you wonder that I loved Red Hair more than ever? When I was sick he tried to doctor me; he was always doing something for me and my little son; and now he had, at the risk of his own life, saved us from death in the terrible flood. He was a real father to me. From that time on to the end of our long trail I did all the poor little things that I could for him. He was the best man that I ever knew! My man, Charbonneau—I have said some hard things about him. I shall say some more. But do not think that I hated him. He was the father of my child. He was a child himself—for all his bigness and strength, nothing but a child. And so I pitied him, and did all that I could for his comfort, yes, to the very end, although at times it was hard to do.

<hr>

We remained in this camp several days, and then, after resuming our way, soon came to the place where the Minitaree had pursued me into the river and snatched me up before him on his horse. A hundred times I had dreamed about it, awaking with shrieks of terror! A hundred times I had seen the place with my dream eyes, and now I saw it with my awake eyes, and could see no change in it since that terrible day of my capture. No, there had been no change in it. The crumbling bank sloping down to the ford was still there; the wide, swift water on the ford was no deeper; and the timber on the far shore remained as it had been, untouched by fire, unswept by the floods of spring. But I had changed. I was no longer the little girl that had been snatched up out there in the river, and had tried to scratch and bite her captor as she was borne away. Right there I asked myself if I was sorry that I had been captured, and I had to answer that I was not sorry. True, I had suffered much at first, but my captor—all the Minitaree—had been good to me. True, I had lost my Mandan sweetheart, and I had not wanted to become the white man's woman, but those sorrows were over. During all the winters and summers since I had been carried away from this place I had lived in warm lodges, safe from all enemies, had been given plenty of good food and good clothing, and, best of all, I had become a mother—I had my little son, snuggling warm at my breast. What I had suffered from being taken from my people was nothing to the happiness I had gained through having him. And had I not been captured, I should never have met these great white chiefs with whom I was traveling, and for whom I felt that I would die if that were necessary for their happiness. They were so great, so wise, brave, and good, that at times I felt that they must be more than just men, that they must be gods!

After passing the place of my capture Long Knife took my man and several others with him, and set out ahead to try to find my people. I asked Long Knife to allow me to go, too, but that was not to be. He answered that he would gladly take me along with my man were it not for my little son. With him to carry and care for, he believed that I could not stand the hardships that they were sure to encounter. And so they went on and were absent from us a number of days, coming to our camp again as we were passing the Beaver's Head. They had found no fresh signs of my people. My man was worn out, his feet very sore. I gave him some marrow grease to rub into them.

On the following day Long Knife again went on ahead with three men, taking for one of them the half-Indian, Drouillard, in place of my man, for he, too, was a good sign-talker. Again I begged to be taken along with the lead party, begged harder than ever, for we were now right up in the edge of the country of my people, and I feared that, without me with them to explain that they were friends, my people would attack and kill them. I had known ever since I had seen that smoke signal, some days back, that my people were aware that we were moving up the valley, and that, of course, they believed we were a war party of their enemies. As I entreated Long Knife now to take me with him and his men, I could see that he had a mind to do it. I felt hopeful that he would. And then my man told him that he did not want me to go; that, with my little child, my place was in the boat! That ended it. Long Knife laughed a little, said something to Red Hair, told me that he was sorry he could not take me along, and then departed with his men. I was so disappointed that I cried!

WITH HER OWN PEOPLE AGAIN

Days passed. We made slow progress up the swift, and now often shallow, river, so shallow that, for the most of the time, I walked ahead on the shore while the men dragged the boats over the bars. One morning, as soon as the start for the day was made, Red Hair and my man and I went on ahead of the boats. We had not traveled far up along the shore when I discovered some riders hurrying toward us. They were rounding a bend, were close upon us. I could see their faces. I did not recognize them. How could I after all these winters? But by their dress, by the very shape of their bodies, I knew that these riders were my own people, some of them, perhaps, my very own relatives.

I raised my hands to them in greeting. I cried out to them, "My people! My people! I am your long-lost Grass Woman!" And then I whirled around and signed to Red Hair, who was behind me, "These are my people! These are my people!" And then I turned again and ran to meet them, crying, laughing, and so happy, so filled up with happiness that I went almost crazy with it. And now I saw that our half-Indian man was with them, that he had on Snake clothing, and by that I knew that Long Knife was safe, that my people had not killed him, and I felt that the gods had been more than good to us, that more happiness than I had right then would kill me!

And now we met, these riders and I, and again I called out to them my name, and they cried "Yes! Yes! We know you, Grass Woman! This is a great day! This is a medicine day, this day of your return to us!" And then they raised our Snake song of greeting and happiness, and turned and

A Shoshone village in Wyoming's Wind River Mountains in 1870

went on up the bottom with us, up around the bend toward the camp that they had made, and where, one of them told me, a number of my people, with the white chief and his men, awaited our coming.

As we neared the place some women advanced to meet us, and when they had come quite near, the lead one stopped suddenly and stared at me and I stared at her, and then, crying, laughing, crying, we ran together and hugged and kissed and kissed one another, "It is you! It is you, Grass Woman!" she cried.

I could not answer! I could not speak for the happiness that was in me, for this was Leaping Fish Woman, she who had so long since fled from the Minitaree village. I had often thought of her, mourned for her. I had not believed that she could possibly escape the dangers of the long trail that she had to follow, and here she was! But, oh, how thin she was! Hunger stared at me out of her big, sunken eyes. I could see it in the eyes of the other women who came running to embrace me. It was with my people as it had ever been. And out there on the plain were countless herds of buffalo! Oh, how I wanted to help them, my persecuted, defenseless, helpless people!

We could not let go of each other, Leaping Fish Woman and I. We stood there in close embrace, she asking me question after question, the other women standing close around and listening to us, and then, suddenly, my man came to me and hurried me to where the Snake warriors were gathered with Red Hair and Long Knife in a small, poor lodge of willow brush. I was wanted to interpret for them. As I took my seat near the entrance and laid my little son down in his wrappings, the chief asked one of his warriors to pass him a small pipeloading stick. His voice sounded much like one that I had known, but somewhat deeper. I looked up at him. I knew him. He was my elder brother!

I sprang across to him, crying, "Oh, brother! Oh, Black Bow! Elder brother, don't you know me? I am your little sister, Grass Woman!" And with that I put my blanket around his shoulders and embraced and kissed him. I could feel him tremble.

"So you are!" he answered. "I recognize you! I am glad! But take courage! There must be no tears on my face, here, before these white chiefs. Take courage, little sister, and interpret for us!"

"I will try to do so," I answered. "But just think, brother! After all these winters I am here with you, here where I thought that I was never again to come!"

"Yes, truly, the gods have been kind," he answered. "But now dry your tears. Interpret to me the words of these white chiefs. After the council is ended, you and I will talk."

At that I tried my best to stop crying. Long Knife said a few words to my man, who interpreted them to me, and then I began to tell my brother what had been said. My thoughts were too much for me. I could not stop crying. I could not even remember what I was to interpret. My man got angry at me; called me bad names. But Red Hair and Long Knife took pity upon me; they saw how I felt, and at once halted the council, saying that they would put it off until I was myself again. They arose and went out, and I was left with my brother.

"Tell me all. Tell me about our family," I said to him.

"Our father was killed on the day that the enemy took you from us," he said.

"Yes, I know. I saw him dead and scalped beside the trail," I told him.

"Our mother is dead, and our two sisters. Our sister, Red Willow Woman, left a little boy [named Bazil]. Our brother is not here. I sent him to one of our tribes with a message."

"Where is the little boy?" I asked, after I had cried some more.

"In our camp on the other side of the pass."

"Brother, give him to me. Let me be his mother. I will be a good mother to him," I said.

"Take him. I know that you will be good to him," he answered. And thoughts of what I should do for the little one helped me dry my tears.

And now my brother began asking me many questions. He wanted to know all about my life with the Minitaree; how many they were; how many guns they had and where they obtained them. And at last, after I had answered them all, and had told him much that he did not ask about, he said to me, "Truly, the gods are good to us. Here you are, returned to your own people. And here are these white men with many guns and much food for them. No longer shall we starve. I have sent messengers to all the tribes of our people and to the Flatheads, asking them to come and help us kill these white men. When we have done that and have taken their guns, we shall go out upon the plains and live there all the time, for we shall then be able to kill off the plains enemies when they come to attack us!"

When my brother said that, I thought that he was joking. I looked at him, saw that he really meant what he had said, and my body went cold. What, kill my good, kind chiefs, and their men? Here was a terrible situation! And it was my own brother who was planning to do this! What could I say to him to make him change his mind? I prayed the gods to help me and began:

"Brother," I said, "these two white chiefs and their men have been good to me; if you kill them, I must die too!"

"What are their lives compared to the lives of our people?" he cried. "Nothing! Only by killing these white men and taking their guns can we go out and hold our own against our enemies on the buffalo plains!"

"For how long?" I asked. "After just one fight with your enemies you would have used up all the food for the guns. Then what would you do? Could you make more of the black sand, and more of the heavy, round balls? No, you could not! And after you had killed many of the enemy, those who survived would go home and gather together all the warriors of the three tribes of the Earth House people, and the number of those who would come to attack you would be as many as the grass. Not one of you would live to see these mountains again!"

"But you can help us! You must!" he cried. "You have been with the white men a long time and have seen them make gun food; you shall teach us how to make it!"

"Not even Red Hair and Long Knife, great chiefs though they are, know how to make the black sand," I told him. "I have inquired about that, and have learned that the making of it is a great secret, known only to some wonderful white medicine men who live far in the east."

My brother groaned. He humped over in his seat.

I saw that I had hit him, and went on, "I know these white men. Their talk is as straight as the straightest pine tree that you ever saw. They do not know how to lie. They say that they have come to make a trail from the far east to the shore of the Everywhere-Salt-Water, to make peace with the different tribes along the way, and to get the tribes to make peace with one another. They promise that white traders shall follow this trail, and bring to you plenty of guns and gun food, and plenty of all the different useful and beautiful things of white men's make. Brother, be wise! Do that which is best for us all. Send messengers at once to tell the warriors of the different tribes to remain where they are, for the white men are not to be attacked!"

"You will not tell your white chiefs anything about this?" he asked.

"I should be ashamed to let them know that my brother had so foolishly made plans against them," I answered.

"I was foolish," he agreed, "but I meant well for my people. I just thought of the many guns we should get. Why—oh, why didn't I see at once that they would become as useless to us as the few that we have, as soon as the black sand that we should take with them should be used up! Yes. I will send a man at once to our camp on the other side of the pass, and he shall send messengers from there to the tribes to tell them that we are not to fight the white men!"

And at that he called a young man to us, and we both explained to him what he was to do, and away he went to camp to send out the messengers. So were my white chiefs and their men saved from sudden end there in the mountains.

———

All the horses were bought that my people could spare, but still we had not all that we wanted. The Blackfeet and the Minitaree had stolen the most of their horses. The last two that we got were bought at a very high price, a gun, a pistol, and much food for them, and even at that the owners did not like to let them go.

Although he had said nothing to me about it, my brother had counted upon my man and me parting from Red Hair and Long Knife and turning back with him to the buffalo plains.

I was surprised when he now said to me, "Tomorrow your white men go upon their way; I have by my waiting upon them too long delayed taking my hungry people out to meat. You had better get your things out from the white men's camp this evening, so that we can make an early start in the morning."

"What do you mean?" I asked him. "I have had no thought of turning back with you. What made you think that I should?"

"I talked with your man about it. He doesn't understand signs very well, but I understood him to say that you and he would leave the white men and join us," he answered.

My man was right there with us, and I asked him about it, what he had said to my brother. "I told him that I didn't want to go any farther west," he replied. "Nor do I. I have gone far enough with these white men. I have slaved enough for them. It is best that we leave them right here!"

"We cannot do it. You promised them that we should go with them to the Everywhere-Salt-Water and back to the Minitaree village. You put your name to that promise, and what was written cannot be rubbed out!" I said.

"There is a way out of it, a good way," he told me. "You can become sick, very sick, too sick to go on with them, and then, of course, I shall have to leave the party and take care of you!"

"I shall not be sick! I am strong to go on!" I said.

"Well, if you don't care for yourself and for me, you ought to care for our little son," he pleaded. "We are almost starving now, and from all that I can learn, to the west there is no food at all after the fish turn about and go down the rivers. If we go on, we go to die from starvation!"

"Then we die with Red Hair and Long Knife, with good company!" I answered. "But we shall not do that. To the west are many tribes of people, and where they find food we can find it."

"Some of those tribes are very powerful. If we escape starvation, we shall be killed for the goods that we take with us," he said.

"You know as well as I do that Red Hair and Long Knife are great chiefs; that they have powerful medicine; that their men are also very brave. Enemy tribes cannot stop them from doing what they have set out to do!" I answered.

And at that my man sprang up, and, without another word to me, went off to the other camp.

I then explained to my brother why we could not leave the white men, and asked him to take good care of my adopted son until I could return and care for him myself. He promised to do that; said that he had taken the best of care for him since his mother's death. And so we parted. I felt very sad as I walked back to our camp. I thought of the terrible risk my people were about to take in going out after buffalo. And, although I had talked bravely enough about it, I, too, feared the long trail that we were about to follow into the west.

To the Everywhere-Salt-Water

We broke camp early the next morning, my people striking out to the east, we to the west and north. Old Diving Eagle, his sons, and a young man going with a message to the Flatheads, accompanied us. Owing to our lack of horses, the most of our men were still on foot. Almost at once our troubles began. For five days we traveled up and down and up and down in very steep, high mountains, in rain and snow, and then, on the fifth day, we had some good luck. On that afternoon we came upon a large camp of Flatheads, on their way to go out upon the plains with my people, and bought some horses from them. They were at first so afraid of us, never having seen any white men, that the women all ran off and the men stood trembling, not knowing what to do until they saw that we meant them no harm. They then became very friendly, and held a long council with Red Hair and Long Knife, and told all that they knew about the country and the tribes along the trail which we sought. I made their hearts glad when I told them that, in the vicinity of the falls of the Big-River-of-the-Plains, the country was black with buffalo, and that we had seen no enemies anywhere along that river.

After leaving the Flatheads—the old man, Diving Eagle, and one of his sons going on with us—we soon got into the roughest, most barren-of-game country that any of us had ever seen. After some days of it, so great was our hunger that we began killing our horses for food. Then we lost the trail in the new-falling snow, and Red Hair took some of the men and went on ahead to try to find a way on through the great mountains that broke sharp up into the blue in all directions as far as we could see. We suffered from cold, from wet, from hunger, for we killed our horses very sparingly. We began to despair: we thought that there would be no end to the mountains, that we should soon have to kill the last of our horses, and then, of course, we should die.

At last, after many days of hard travel and suffering, we rode down into warmer country [in what is now northwest Idaho] and met some of Red Hair's men bringing food to us and good news. We had no more mountains to cross; a large camp of Nez Percés was nearby, and we could obtain food from them. We made the camp that night, and there found Red Hair and his men. The Nez Percés, we found, were in many bands scattered over a great plains country and along its rivers. They had many horses and boats as well, and in every lodge were great quantities of dried salmon and dried camas and other roots. We bought all that we wanted of this food, ate plenty of it, and soon after eating nearly all of our party became sick. However, sick as the men were and my white chiefs, too, we moved camp down the river to where it was joined by another river and began building boats. Four very large logs and one not so large were cut, and fires were built upon them to burn out their insides. While this was going on, day after day, Red Hair and Long Knife kept me busy interpreting for them, and that was not easy, for only two or three of the Nez Percé understood a little of my language, and they were all very poor sign-talkers. The most important news that we got from them was, that, although there were some rapids ahead, we could boat down this river into the truly Big-River-of-the-West-Side, and down that to its great falls. White men had been seen at the falls, which were not a very great distance from the Everywhere-Salt-Water.

When the boats were finished, we loaded our goods into them, left our horses with the Nez Percés, and went on. On our second night down the river, Diving Eagle had a terrible dream. He told me about it while we were eating our morning meal, and asked me if I did not think it was a warning to him to turn back to our people. I answered that the snow in the mountains would prevent him going to them, and he said no more. But soon after we had set out, he and his son got out of the boat in which they were traveling, and started up the shore as fast as they could run, and we saw no more of them. I cried a little over his going. He had been good company to me, with his evening tales about my people. And now all the interpreting and questioning of the different tribes that we should meet, fell upon me. I prayed the gods to give me the wisdom to do it all. We had with us two Nez Percé chiefs, both of whom understood a little of my language, and through them I hoped to be able to do all that my white chiefs asked of me.

This was not a gentle river; we had much trouble in its rapids. After some days we arrived at the place where it entered the real Big River, and then, for a time, had better water. Then we came to the beginning of terrible rapids and falls along it, and twice had to drag the boats around bad places. All this time on the lesser river we were meeting different tribes of the Nez Percés. At the falls of the Big River we came upon the first of other tribes, people who lived in houses and went about in boats. As we of the mountains fearlessly traveled along great cliffs and across steep slides upon our horses, so did they travel in their boats, [the] water [being] so bad that it did not seem possible that they could survive its terrible waves and swirlings. Time was when I should have thought that the people of these different tribes were very rich. They had great quantities of dried salmon, salmon pemmican, and dried roots. I once had loved this food. I now despised it. And I saw how very poor these people were. The only rich people are those of the plains: the Earth House people, the Blackfeet, the Crows. With their great bands of horses they wander here and there over their endless plains, and wherever they go there is their food, real food upon all sides of them—buffalo, antelope, elk, deer—all easily to be killed as wanted.

After passing the last swift water of this Big River we found it to become ever wider the farther we went. Truly, as a mountain stream is to the Big-River-of-the-Plains, so is that river to this Big-River-of-the-West, just a little creek and nothing more. Why, at last this river became so wide that, looking across it on a clear day, one could not possibly see a man on the farther shore! And now strange things began to happen. Twice, between sunrise and sunrise, the current of this great river turned and ran back, and the rising, backing water tasted of salt. Red Hair told me that this was because the Everywhere-Salt-Water was close at hand, and was pushing back the river water, but I could not understand that. Why should the Great Salt Water want to fight the river water, I should like to know? We had no sooner set out one morning, I sitting in the bow of my boat, then a terribly fierce appearing water animal thrust its head and part of its body out of the water, so close that I could have put my hand upon it, opened wide its mouth and roared at me, made a splash that threw water all over me, and then disappeared as suddenly as it came. It was a water-dog! A fishdog! Yes, it had the head and body of a dog, but much larger, and it had fishlike fins where its front legs should have been, and its body ended in a fishlike tail. Yes, and the noise that it made was much like the barking of a dog. Red Hair told me not to be afraid of it; that it and its kind did not harm people; but I could not help being afraid of it. I thought what would happen to my little son and me if we were to be upset: without doubt these animals would at once seize us and drag us down into the deep water and eat us!

We had now come into a different country [what is now Oregon]; a country of much rain and fog, and that, too, Red Hair told me, was caused by the Everywhere-Salt-Water. We were boating on one morning, when, suddenly, Red Hair and Long Knife and all the men began to cry out with joy and point ahead, and, as I wondered what it was all about, Red Hair signed to me, "There it is, the Everywhere-Salt-Water!"

I looked and looked for it, but could see nothing, nothing but the wide river running on and on ahead of us to where it was hidden in dark fog, from which came a roaring noise. I was soon to know what that roaring was. We made camp, and such waves as I had never thought there could be, came roaring and pouring upon us, wetting us and all our goods, and tossing drift trees and wood all around us. That was the beginning of some terrible days of rain, strong wind, high waves, and of hunger. We were on the north side of the river. Some of the men went on ahead, in boats, on foot, looking for a good place for us to camp, but could find none that would do. We then, on a still day, crossed the river, and more parties went out, and at last a good place was found. It was on a little river, some distance back from the salty Big River. There, on a little hill, in good pine woods, the men built a fort and we wintered in it. There Indians from different tribes came to visit us and sell us their bad food, fish, and roots. Also they brought women to lend to our men. Red Hair and Long Knife would have nothing to do with these women, and that often made them angry.

There were quite a number of elk and deer around our fort, and the men often brought in some of them. They were poor in flesh, but better than no meat. The best food that we had was the meat of the dogs that we bought off the Indians. We soon used the last of our salt, and several men were sent to the shore of the Everywhere-Salt-Water to boil this water and make salt. Not long after they had gone, one of them returned with some salt, and told about a great fish that the Indians had found on the shore of the Everywhere-Salt-Water. I could hardly believe that there was ever so large a fish as this one they described, but, whatever its size, I wanted to see it, and see, too, the Great Water that the men were always talking about. Red Hair and several of the men were to go after some of the fat of the big fish, and I told him that I wanted to go, too, as my man was to be one of the party, and he said that I could go. I was glad. I was tired of sitting day after day in the fort.

We traveled for three days in bad, low country, and over a high mountain on our way to the big fish. We struck the Everywhere-Salt-Water on the second day, and, great though I had expected to find it, still was I astonished at the size of it. In whatever direction I looked out upon it, I saw that it had no farther shore; that it went on and on to the edge of the world. There was no wind, but still was that great water angry, breaking in roaring waves higher than a fort upon the sand and rocks of the shore! From the top of the high mountain at its edge we could see still farther out upon it, but still could see no farther shore. But we did see the Big-River-of-the-West running into it, and several villages of the Indians that were built along its shores. That night I could not sleep because of the roaring of the waves, which, day and night, are ever rushing upon the shore.

At last, on the third day, we came to the big fish, or what was left of it, just its skeleton; the Indians had taken all its meat and most of its intestines. At first I could not believe that those bones were bones and the bones of a fish. Why, the backbone was larger around than my body, and the rib bones curving up around from it were so high that a man could not touch the tips of them with the muzzle of his upheld gun! In between those ribs, where' the stomach had been, we could have piled all the boats in which we had come down Big River from the Nez Percés' country, and even then there might have been space for one or two more! As the sun looks down upon me, I tell you in his sight that, truly, that was the size of the skeleton of the big fish! I did not go very close to it. I was afraid of it. Its ghost was thereabouts, of course, and I prayed hard that it would do me and mine no harm. Red Hair explained to me how the great fish came to be there. He said that it had, no doubt, been chasing smaller fish, to eat, and that it had got into shallow shore water and the waves had pushed it out upon the shore where, lacking water, it soon died. After he told me that I feared the waves more than ever.

There were two villages where the big fish had been wave-pushed ashore to die, and the Indians living in them, and Indians from other villages, had taken all its meat and fat. I saw much of it. I saw with my own eyes pieces of its fat that were as thick as the body of a buffalo! Red Hair bought some of it, and some of the oil that the Indians had made from it, and he and his men said that it was good food. Myself, I did not even touch it. I believed it to be bad medicine; all I asked was that the ghost of the big fish would do me and mine no harm. It hurt me, though, to refuse to eat it when Red Hair asked me to join in the feast. I thought so much of him that I wanted always to do what he asked of me. But this was too much. I was glad when I saw that he was not angry because I refused to eat the fat. I thought over things he had done for me and I for him. He had saved my son and me from the flood at the falls of the Big-River-of-the-Plains. He had bought a horse from my people for me to ride. He had brought me here to see the Everywhere-Salt-Water and this big fish's bones. I had given him my bead belt, with which to buy an otter-skin robe that he wanted, and, when he fell sick, I had given him a piece of bread that I had long been saving for my little son. Best of all, I had saved him—and all the party—from terrible trouble with my Snake people. But I had not done enough for him. I prayed the gods that night to show me how to do more for him, great chief that he was.

We had no real winter, no deep snow, where we were, near the Everywhere-Salt-Water. Instead of snow we had rain; almost continuous rain. It was in the middle of our stay there that we went to see the big fish. After that game became more and more scarce, and we often went hungry to bed. The men, too, became weak and often sick. We longed more and more for Red Hair and Big Knife to give the word for us to abandon the fort and take our back trail, but they kept saying that we must wait a little longer, so as not to strike the great mountains until the summer sun had melted the tribe of Flatheads, who were as mean to us as the tribe at the falls had been. We made camp near their village, and they tried to steal things from us. On the next day, as we were passing through the village, the pack on the horse which my man was leading came off, and an Indian ran off with a robe which he stole from it. That made Long Knife very angry. "We have got to stop this thieving right now, else we shall never get through the country," he said. "Yes, we shall make a stand and kill some of these people unless they give up the robe!" And then he ordered my man to tell me to ride on as fast as I could and tell Red Hair and his men to come back and help him fight the camp.

I was on a fat and very eager little horse and I started him off up the trail at a swift lope. As I left the village there was great outcry in it, women running with their children to hide, and men calling to one another as they rushed about after their weapons and prepared to make a stand against Long Knife. Off to my left I saw a man mount his horse and take after me, and well I knew that, if he succeeded in catching me, in killing me, Long Knife and his men would be killed there in the village, and then, later on, Red Hair and his men would be wiped out. I had the lead of the Flathead, but I saw at once that his horse was more powerful, more swift than mine; from the very start he gained upon me. My little son, upon my back, prevented me from whipping my horse to faster speed, for with one hand I had to clutch hard the edges of the robe by which I held him to me, and with the other hold the bridle rope; all that I could do was to thump and keep thumping my heels against the sides of the animal!

I did not know how far ahead of me Red Hair and his men were. The trail was through groves of timber and across hilly small prairies. I rode through two groves, across two prairies, and as I entered the third grove, the Flathead was so close behind me that I could hear him whipping his horse. "I am gone," I said to myself, "but I will keep on going to the very end!"

That grove of pines was not wide. I tore on through it, out upon a prairie and up a rise in it, and, topping it, there I saw Red Hair and his men not far ahead! I cried out to them. They heard me and saw me and came hurrying to meet me. I looked back, and looked just in time to see the Flathead come to the top of the little rise and turn and at once ride back out of sight! Then, as I met Red Hair, I signed to him, "Come! Long Knife calls you! We are to fight!"

"Yes!" he signed back to me. And away we went toward the village. We topped the little rise and I looked for my pursuer, but could see nothing of him. On we went. I expected at every jump of my horse to hear the guns of Long Knife and his men as they fought for their lives, and feared that we should not be in time to save them. And then, oh, how glad I was when we at last rode into sight of the village and saw them gathered at the edge of the lodges. One of the men had found the robe where the thief had hidden it, and, after all, the Indians had not dared fight for it. As soon as we came up to them, Long Knife gave the warriors a terrible scolding, told them that we should do some killing if they ever again attempted to steal from us, and then we went our way.

The next people we came to were the Wallawalla, who had been friendly to us the summer before, and were friendly to us now. We got from them a few more horses, and had many talks with them through a captive they had, a young man belonging to a far western tribe of my nation. I had never met one of that tribe before. His language was somewhat different from mine, but not so much that we could not well understand one another. My chiefs, through me, had many talks with him, and got from him much that we had not known about the country and the different tribes that lived in it. I told him that he could now be free; that my chiefs would take him with us to my tribe of our nation. But he answered that he no longer wished to return to his people. He was in love with a Wallawalla girl and hoped soon to have her. He spoke the Wallawalla language very well, and so, through the both of us, my chiefs had also many talks with the Wallawalla chiefs, and became greater friends than ever with them.

We got more horses from the Wallawalla, and went on to our best friends of the west side, the Nez Percés. They had taken good care of our horses that we had left with them the summer before, and soon collected them and turned them over to us. Red Hair and Long Knife were for packing up and going on at once, but the Nez Percés told them that we should not be able to cross the mountains for a long time to come, nearly two moons. So we remained there in the low country, visiting one and another of the villages of the Indians, and hunting, and starving mostly, for food was very scarce. We had a lot of sickness in our camp. My own little son fell sick, too, and for a time I thought that he would die. Many of the Indians were also sick; one, especially, a chief who had not been able to move for a summer and a winter. Red Hair and Long Knife doctored him and made him well, as they did all the others who came to them, and that made the people like us better than ever. Some of the young women were very beautiful, so it is no wonder that our men liked them. They would go to the village to be with them as often as they could be spared from our camp. There was one young woman, tall, slender, long-haired, who fell in love with Red Hair, and followed him wherever he went and loved him more and more every day. When we at last started on, she begged him to take her with us, and when Red Hair told her that he could not possibly do that, she went off into the woods and hung herself from a limb of a tree. Her people discovered her just in time to save her life, and said that they would keep close watch upon her until she recovered from her grief.

And now, a little way below the mouth of the Yellowstone [on what is now the border between Montana and North Dakota], Long Knife and his men also overtook us, and, again a united party, we went on down Big River [the Missouri River], and a few days later, after passing two white men, free trappers, we sighted the Minitaree villages. Hunters from them had seen us and spread the news of our coming, and there was a great crowd to meet and greet us when we landed at the little village of the Black Moccasins, at the mouth of Knife River.

With the crowd was Otter Woman, thin, gray-faced, so old-appearing that I hardly knew her. She threw herself upon me and wept, crying out to me, "Oh, Grass Woman! Pity me! Comfort me! I have lost my little son! He fell sick one night and died before the rising of the sun!"

I did comfort her all that I could by telling her about meeting our people in the previous summer. But when she learned that I had seen not even signs of them on our way back, she became very sad again. She soon died of the coughing disease; of that, and mourning for her little son.

Now, after my chiefs had met the chiefs of the Earth House people in a great council, they asked my man and me to go downriver with them and visit the great chief of the Long Knives. My man answered that we should go with them, and that made me very happy. Wherever Red Hair went, I was more than glad to go. I began at once to beg pretty and useful things from my friends, so that I should have many presents to give the great white chief when we arrived in his village. But that very evening my man had a talk with some Nor'westers, who had come from the Assiniboine River Fort to trade, and the next morning he told me, and then Red Hair and Long Knife, that we should not go downriver. Here, in the buffalo country, where he had lived so long, was the place for him, he said.

"But you can go as interpreter for the chiefs that we are taking with us," they told him. "You shall be paid for going, and some of our men shall bring you all back to this place."

"No, I feel that I can't go, that this is the one place for me," my man answered again.

And that ended it. Oh, but I was angry at him! But what could I do? Nothing! Women can never do anything that they want to do, because of their men! The truth was, the Nor'westers had talked him out of going with Red Hair and Long Knife! And so, with but little delay, my good chiefs and their men got into their boats and set out for their faraway country. I watched them until they went out of sight around the bend of the river, and then I went off by myself and cried.

So ends my story.

After the expedition, Lewis and Clark were national celebrities. By appointment of President Jefferson, Lewis became governor of the Louisiana Territory in 1808, but he was a poor administrator and in 1809 he was called to Washington, DC, to answer complaints. On the way there he died violently while spending the night at a tavern in Tennessee, about seventy miles southwest of Nashville. It's still debated today whether he committed suicide or was murdered. He was thirty-five.

Jefferson appointed Clark as the Superintendent of Indian Affairs for the Louisiana Territory in 1807 and promoted him to brigadier general of the territory's militia. His headquarters was in St. Louis. He held these posts until 1813, when he was appointed governor of the newly formed Missouri Territory. Missouri became a state in 1820 and Clark lost his campaign to be elected governor. Two years later President Monroe again appointed him Superintendent of Indian Affairs, where he eventually had to supervise the relocation of the "Five Civilized Tribes"—under President Jackson's Indian Removal Act, which began in 1831—to Indian Territory in what is now Oklahoma and Arkansas. Jackson's main goal was to clear the Native Americans from the South, but also to end a crisis between the Cherokee and the state of Georgia, which wanted to gain access to Cherokee lands after gold was discovered there. The result was that in 1838 Georgia got the land and the Cherokee were forced to march the Trail of Tears. Of the seventeen thousand Cherokee moved, about four thousand perished in prison camps and along the road. In exchange, Georgia gave up claims on what would become the states of Alabama and Mississippi. In spite of this, Clark retained a reputation for honesty and fairness up until his death in 1838 at the age of sixty-eight.

While dealing with the difficulties and the stress of leading the expedition, one of the high points for Clark was watching the antics of Sacagawea's son, Jean Baptiste. He became very attached to the child and must have felt like something of an uncle. Just four days after parting company with the Charbonneaus, on the way back to St. Louis—knowing that Sacagawea played a significant role in the success of the Expedition—Clark wrote to Charbonneau that he felt Sacagawea deserved much more than he had officially been able to give her and offered to provide for their son's schooling.

While Captain Lewis didn't think much of Charbonneau, describing him as "a man of no peculiar merit" and "useful as an interpreter only," Clark had a higher opinion of him, writing:

You have been a long time with me and have conducted yourself in such a manner as to gain my friendship, your woman who accompanied you that long dangerous and fatiguing route to the Pacific Ocean and back deserved a greater reward for her attention and services on that route than we had in our power to give her at the Mandans. As to your little son (my boy Pomp) you well know my fondness for him and my anxiety to take and raise him as my own child. I once more tell you if you will bring your son [Jean] Baptiste to me, I will educate him and treat him as my own child. I do not forget the promise which I made to you and shall now repeat them that you may be certain. Charbonneau, if you wish to live with the white people and you will come to me, I will give you a piece of land and furnish you with horses, cows and hogs. If you wish to visit your friends in Montreal, I will let you have a horse and your family shall be taken care of until your return. If you wish to return as an interpreter for the Menetarras [i.e., the people of the Menetarra, the largest of the Hidatsa villages] when the troops come up to form the establishment, you will be with me ready and I will procure you the place—or if you wish to return to trade with the Indians and will leave your little son Pomp with me, I will assist you with merchandise for that purpose from time [to time] and become myself concerned with you in trade on a small scale; that is to say, not exceeding a pirogue load at one time. If you are disposed to accept either of my offers to you and will bring down your son, your famn [wife] Janey had best come along with you to take care of the boy until I get him.

The parents decided it was a generous offer, but thought it best to wait until the infant was weaned before he was parted from his mother. It was not until 1809 that Charbonneau and Sacagawea brought Jean Baptiste—who was just shy of six years old—and her sister's son she had adopted, Bazil, to St. Louis to be educated. Charbonneau bought some farmland from Clark and his wife, but Charbonneau soon decided he didn't like that lifestyle and sold the land back. By 1811 he was tired of "civilized" life and one of his wives wasn't well, so they returned to the five villages where Charbonneau went back to trapping. This could have been Sacagawea, Otter Woman, or a third wife that he was vaguely mentioned as having in 1804.

It's said Charbonneau had at least five wives throughout his life—all of them Native American teenagers. In 1837 at Fort Clark, F. A. Chardon wrote in his journal, "Old Charbonneau, an old man of 80, took to himself and others a young wife, a young Assiniboine of 14, a prisoner that was taken in the fight of this summer . . . The Old gentleman gave a feast to the men, and a glass of grog—and went to bed with his young wife, with the intention of doing his best." It's thought he died six years later, at about the age of eighty-six.

Baptiste's education came in handy. He became fluent in English, French, and several Native American languages. He could also read Classical Greek and Latin. When he was nineteen he met Duke Paul Wilhelm, who was known as Prince Paul and was the nephew of Fredrick I, the king of Württemberg. Baptiste was hired as a translator and guide for the duke on a natural history expedition in the West. They became friends and the duke took him back to Europe, where he lived at the palace for almost six years. Here he toured Europe, visited Northern Africa, and played the violin for Beethoven. He also learned to speak German, Spanish, and Italian.

By 1829 he was ready to head back to the West, so he and the duke launched another expedition. After that he became a mountain man for fifteen years, but when beavers became scarce, he gave up trapping to be a guide for expeditions throughout the West. On one of these in 1842, he crossed paths with explorers John Frémont and Kit Carson. Frémont wrote, "There was a quaint humor and shrewdness of his conversation, so garbed with intelligence and perspicuity, that he at once insinuated himself into the good graces of listeners, and commanded their admiration and respect."

In 1848 Baptiste joined the gold rush to California, living there for seventeen years. Most historians believe he then headed for what is now Montana to search for gold, but caught pneumonia while passing through Oregon and died there in 1866. A few say he returned to live with the Shoshone and his mother on the Wind River Indian Reservation in the Wyoming Territory until his death in 1885.

Not much is known of Sacagawea's later life, and there is considerable debate about where and when she died. According to one vague account, she died in 1812. John C. Luttig, a clerk at the Fort Manuel Lisa Trading Post, wrote in his journal, "This evening the wife of Charbonneau, a Snake squaw, died of a putrid fever [i.e., typhus]. She was a good and best woman in the fort. Aged about 25 years, she left a fine infant girl." Sacagawea had been ill, but this could easily have been his other Shoshone wife, Otter Woman, so this is inconclusive.

There is an adoption document dated August 11, 1813, making Luttig the guardian of "Toussaint Charbonneau, a boy about ten years, and Lizette Charbonneau, a girl about one year old." Sometime later Luttig's name was crossed out and replaced with Clark's. Baptismal records indicate Toussaint is actually Baptiste, but oral testimony says Toussaint was Otter Woman's child. Little is known of Lizette, except that she died in 1832 at age twenty-one.

The only thing that makes it likely Sacagawea died in 1812 is that sometime between 1825 and 1828 Clark noted that she had died. Still, it is possible he had faulty information. Clark did list someone else as dead who was actually still alive. There is a Shoshone oral tradition that she died young, but there is also one that she didn't.

Sakwaihki—the woman who relayed Sacagawea's account to Schultz—and her childhood friend, Crow Woman, told Schultz that after returning from St. Louis to the five villages in about 1811, Sacagawea and Charbonneau were interpreters on several trading expeditions to the Shoshone. One of these expeditions was with William or Milton Sublette, which would have been in the 1820s, and they took one of their sons with them. Eventually they left on one of these trips and never returned to the five villages.

According to the daughter of Hidatsa tribal historian Poor Wolf, who was born about nine years after Sacagawea, in about 1820 Charbonneau married a young Hidatsa girl named Eagle. She repeated Eagle's story:

When Charbonneau took me down the river among the white people we came to a great town called St. Louis. We stayed there a year or so when Charbonneau found one of his Shoshone wives, the "Bird Woman" Sacagawea, in a little town about St. Louis, called Portage [Portage des Sioux]. This woman had two sons with her, one was about 18 and the other 16. The older one was called Bazile, the other Baptiste. They were bright young men and talked French quite well. The Shoshone woman, herself, talked French too.

After a while Charbonneau wanted to take his wife back and I consented, then we lived together for a little while at St. Louis, when Charbonneau was employed by the [Missouri] Fur Company and we were sent southwest on a big river, almost as big as the Missouri River. On this trip we came to a great many trading posts and we stayed at one place for a year, and we stopped another place two years. We came among many Indian tribes that I never heard of, some were called Wichita, some were called Comanche, and Ute, and other tribes who came to trade at these posts where we were. After [a] while Charbonneau, my husband, took another wife, a pretty Ute woman. I did not complain but Bird Woman made serious complaint and made it unpleasant for the Ute Woman. Finally Charbonneau punished her severely and in a day or so afterwards she disappeared. At this time her two boys were away on a trip. . . . When the boys came back, they made it very serious for Charbonneau and they were not friends after that.

Hugh Monroe (Rising Wolf) said that he met Baptiste at mountain man Jim Bridger's trading post and he said his father had died and his mother was living with the Shoshone. This would have been in the 1840s.

A second version of Sacagawea's death comes from people living on the Wind River Indian Reservation in Wyoming and from the Comanche in Oklahoma. They came from Shoshone and Comanche relatives, missionaries, teachers, and Indian agents who said they knew her from the early 1860s until her death in 1884.

They mainly knew her by her Comanche name Porivo, meaning "Chief," and as "Bazil's mother," but a few also called her by the Comanche name Pohenive—"Grass Woman." They say that sometime after leaving St. Louis, Porivo married a Comanche named Jerk-Meat and lived with him in Oklahoma for twenty-six or twenty-seven years. They had five children, three of whom died as infants. The second born was a boy named Ticannaf, according to his daughter. This was supported back in Wyoming by James McAdams, Bazil's grandson, who said Porivo told him she left a son named Ticannaf with the Comanche. Eventually Jerk-Meat died in battle, and friction with the rest of the tribe caused Porivo to leave, taking one of her daughters with her.

Porivo then lived for about thirty years with her son Bazil near Fort Bridger, which would later be called Fort Washakie on what would eventually be the Wind River Indian Reservation in Wyoming. Baptiste visited her in 1874 and eventually moved there. They say she was kind, gentle, well loved, and highly respected. She moved equally well among the various tribes, as among white society. She was treated extremely well by the whites and was allowed to travel on stagecoaches for free. The Natives used her as a translator and intermediary with reservation and government officials, since she could speak French, Shoshone, Hidatsa, Comanche, and Assiniboine.

They described her as about five feet five inches tall with long, slightly gray hair. She usually wore buckskin and a blanket. Both she and Bazil had light complexions, while Baptiste was dark. Finn Burnett said she looked as young or younger than her son Bazil, adding, "She was pleasing in appearance, a woman full of brightness and smartness." Charles Bocker said she was "quite lovely looking for an old woman, and she could ride horses as well as any of them." Engha Peahrora said that "she always had kind feelings toward white people, and they had a great liking and respect for her."

So far nothing besides these accounts connects Porivo with Sacagawea. If it was her, she would have been in her nineties when she died in 1884. It's said her two sons, Baptiste, who died in 1885, and Bazil, who died in 1886, were buried next to her.

Brushes with Death

Davy Crockett

David Crockett [signature]

Moving back east to Tennessee, here was the second of the men Buffalo Bill believed typified the three periods of the western expansion. David "Davy" Crockett—as with many other famous Western figures—is now more of a folk legend, holding the title of "the King of the Wild Frontier," largely because of the Walt Disney TV shows and movies.

The real Davy Crockett was a pioneer, hunter, scout, Indian fighter, adventurer, and very colorful politician. He had almost no education and had run away from home at age thirteen, but with a reputation for honesty, he was elected to three terms in the US House of Representatives in 1826, 1828, and 1833, and was nominated as a presidential candidate. According to one version of his comments after failing to get re-elected to Congress in 1835, he said, "Since you have chosen to elect a man with a timber toe to succeed me, you may all go to hell, and I will go to Texas." That's what he did. He took a break from politics by joining the Texas Revolution and was killed at the Alamo when he was forty-nine years old—either in the final minutes of the thirteen-day siege, or he may have been executed after the battle.

Buffalo Bill Cody wrote, "If I were asked to name the most singular—and in many respects the most remarkable—man in the history of pioneer settlement in the great West, I should without a moment's consideration of others say, 'Davy Crockett.' . . . He possessed those bolder traits and faculties of pride and ambition, a heart that was absolutely fearless as it was honest, open, generous and sympathetic."

By the early 1830s, he was famous and many myths about his life began forming. A satirical play about him called *The Lion of the West* (1831) contributed to this. Its main character was Colonel Nimrod Wildfire, who wore buckskins and a wildcat skin cap and was a very thinly veiled parody of Crockett. Though the play made fun of him, it greatly expanded his fame. A series of at least forty-four comic almanacs from 1835 to 1856 gave him the name "Davy" and made him a superhero, riding lightning bolts and such.

After his death a supposed autobiography with entries from his diary at the Alamo were published as *Col. Crockett's Exploits and Adventures in Texas...Written by Himself* (1836), but this book is considered to be fiction, probably written by Richard Penn Smith.

More authentic is Crockett's autobiography, *A Narrative of the Life of David Crockett of the State of Tennessee* (1834). Though Crockett was uneducated, he was able to write, as his last known letter—written January 9, 1836—shows.

Davy Crockett, 1830s

I must say as to what I have seen of Texas it is the garden spot of the world. The best land and the best prospects for health I ever saw, and I do believe it is a fortune to any man to come here. There is a world of country here to settle. . . . I have taken the oath of government and have enrolled my name as a volunteer and will set out for the Rio Grand[e] in a few days with the volunteers from the United States. But all volunteers is entitled to vote for a member of the convention or to be voted for, and I have but little doubt of being elected a member to form a constitution for this province. I am rejoiced at my fate. I had rather be in my present situation than to be elected to a seat in Congress for life. I am in hopes of making a fortune yet for myself and family, bad as my prospect has been.

Still, Crockett did receive help writing this book from his friend and roommate, Thomas Chilton, who was a congressman from Kentucky. Chilton used Crockett's notes and worked closely with him to get this book the way Crockett wanted it. As

Crockett wrote to his son in a letter dated January 10, 1834, "I am engaged in writing a history of my life and I have completed one hundred and ten pages and I have Mr. Chilton to correct as I write it." On February 23 he wrote to his publishers, "The manuscript of the book is in his (Chilton's) handwriting though the entire substance of it is truly my own. The aid which I needed was to classify the matter, but the style was not altered." On its release, it was an immediate bestseller and it's now considered a masterpiece of frontier literature.

Here are some of his more interesting—and dangerous—adventures from it. But one should be aware that he did use exaggeration and sarcasm as a form of humor—a style of writing that was later improved and perfected by Mark Twain. He also put a bit of a spin on things to present himself as your average backwoods frontiersman in order to gain popularity among the voters.

I continued at home now, working my farm for two years, as the war [the War of 1812] finally closed soon after I quit the service. The battle at New Orleans had already been fought, and treaties were made with the Indians which put a stop to their hostilities.

But in this time, I met with the hardest trial which ever falls to the lot of man. Death, that cruel leveler of all distinctions—to whom the prayers and tears of husbands, and of even helpless infancy, are addressed in vain—entered my humble cottage, and tore from my children an affectionate good mother, and from me a tender and loving wife.

It is a scene long gone by, and one which it would be supposed I had almost forgotten; yet when I turn my memory back on it, it seems as but the work of yesterday. It was the doing of the Almighty, whose ways are always right, though we sometimes think they fall heavily on us; and as painful as is even yet the remembrance of her sufferings, and the loss sustained by my little children and myself, yet I have no wish to lift up the voice of complaint. I was left with three children; the two oldest were sons, the youngest a daughter, and, at that time, a mere infant. It appeared to me, at that moment, that my situation was the worst in the world. I couldn't bear the thought of scattering my children, and so I got my youngest brother, who was also married, and his family to live with me. They took as good care of my children as they well could, but yet it wasn't all like the care of a mother. And though their company was to me in every respect like that of a brother and sister, yet it fell far short of being like that of a wife. So I came to the conclusion it wouldn't do, but that I must have another wife.

There lived in the neighborhood, a widow lady whose husband had been killed in the war. She had two children, a son and daughter, and both quite small, like my own. I began to think, that as we were both in the same situation, it might be that we could do something for each other; and I therefore began to hint a little around the matter, as we were once and a while together. She was a good industrious woman, and owned a snug little farm, and lived quite comfortable. I soon began to pay my respects to her in real good earnest; but I was as sly about it as a fox when he is going to rob a hen-roost. I found that my company wasn't at all disagreeable to her; and I thought I could treat her children with so much friendship as to make her a good stepmother to mine, and in this I wasn't mistaken, as we soon bargained, and got married, and then went ahead. In a great deal of peace we raised our first crop of children, and they are all married and doing well. But we had a second crop together . . .

The next fall after this marriage, three of my neighbors and myself determined to explore a new country. Their names were Robinson, Frazier, and Rich. We set out for the Creek country, crossing the Tennessee River; and after having made a day's travel, we stop'd at the house of one of my old acquaintances, who had settled there after the war. Resting here a day, Frazier turned out to hunt, being a great hunter; but he got badly bit by a very poisonous snake, and so we left him and went on.

We passed through a large rich valley, called Jones's Valley, where several other families had settled, and continued our course till we came near to the place where Tuscaloosa now stands. Here we camped, as there were no inhabitants, and hobbled out our horses for the night. About two hours before day, we heard the bells on our horses going back the way we had come, as they had started to leave us. As soon as it was daylight, I started in pursuit of them on foot, and carrying my rifle, which was a very heavy one. I went ahead the whole day, wading creeks and swamps, and climbing mountains; but I couldn't overtake our horses, though I could hear of them at every house they passed. I at last found I couldn't catch up with them, and so I gave up the hunt, and turned back to the last house

I had passed, and stayed there till morning. From the best calculation we could make, I had walked over fifty miles that day; and the next morning I was so sore, and fatigued, that I felt like I couldn't walk anymore. But I was anxious to get back to where I had left my company, and so I started and went on, but mighty slowly, till after the middle of the day. I now began to feel mighty sick [from malaria], and had a dreadful headache. My rifle was so heavy, and I felt so weak, that I lay down by the side of the trace, in a perfect wilderness too, to see if I wouldn't get better.

In a short time some Indians came along. They had some ripe melons, and wanted me to eat some, but I was so sick I couldn't. They then signed to me, that I would die, and be buried; a thing I was confoundedly afraid of myself. But I asked them how near it was to any house. By their signs, again, they made me understand it was a mile and a half. I got up to go; but when I rose, I reeled about like a cow with the blind staggers, or a fellow who had taken too many [drinking] "horns." One of the Indians proposed to go with me, and carry my gun. I gave him half a dollar, and accepted his offer.

We got to the house, by which time I was pretty far gone, but was kindly received, and got on to a bed. The woman did all she could for me with her warm teas, but I still continued bad enough, with a high fever, and generally out of my senses. The next day two of my neighbors were passing the road, and heard of my situation, and came to where I was. They were going nearly the route I had intended to go, to look at the country; and so they took me first on one of their horses, and then on the other, till they got me back to where I had left my company. I expected I would get better, and be able to go on with them, but, instead of this, I got worse and worse; and when we got there, I wasn't able to sit up at all. I thought now the jig was mighty nigh up with me, but I determined to keep a stiff upper lip.

They carried me to a house, and each of my comrades bought him a horse, and they all set out together, leaving me behind. I knew but little that was going on for about two weeks; but the family treated me with every possible kindness in their power, and I shall always feel thankful to them. The man's name was Jesse Jones. At the end of two weeks I began to mend without the help of a doctor, or of any doctor's means. In this time, however, as they told me, I was speechless for five days, and they had no thought that I would ever speak again—in Congress or any where else. And so the woman, who had a bottle of Bateman's Drops [a tincture of opium], thought if they killed me, I would only die anyhow, and so she would try it with me. She gave me the whole bottle, which throwed me into a sweat that continued on me all night; when at last I seemed to wake up, and spoke, and asked her for a drink of water. This almost alarmed her, for she was looking every minute for me to die. She gave me the water, and, from that time, I began slowly to mend, and so kept on till I was able at last to walk about a little. . . .

But when I got so I could travel a little, I got a waggoner who was passing along to hawl me to where he lived, which was about twenty miles from my house. I still mended as we went along, and when we got to his stopping place, I hired one of his horses, and went on home. I was so pale, and so much reduced, that my face looked like it had been half soled with brown paper.

When I got there, it was to the utter astonishment of my wife; for she supposed I was dead. My neighbors who had started with me had returned and took my horse home, which they had found with their's; and they reported that they had seen men who had helped to bury me; and who saw me draw my last breath. I know'd this was a whapper of a lie, as soon as I heard it. . . .

The place on which I lived was sickly, and I was determined to leave it. I therefore set out the next fall to look at the country which had been purchased of the Chickasaw tribe of Indians. I went on to a place called Shoal Creek [near what is now Lawrenceburg, Tennessee], about eighty miles from where I lived. . . . We remained here some two or three years, without any law at all; and so many bad characters began to flock in upon us, that we found it necessary to set up a sort of temporary government of our own. . . . But we met, and appointed magistrates and constables to keep order. We didn't fix any laws for them, tho'; for we supposed they would know law enough, whoever they might be; and so we left it to themselves to fix the laws.

I was appointed one of the magistrates; and when a man owed a debt, and wouldn't pay it, I and my constable ordered our warrant, and then he would take the man, and bring him before me for trial. I would give judgment against him, and then an order of an execution would easily scare the debt out of him. If anyone was charged with marking his neighbor's hogs, or with stealing anything, which happened pretty often in those days,—I would have him taken, and if there was tolerable grounds for the charge, I would have him well whip'd and cleared. . . . whenever I told my constable, says I—"Catch that fellow, and bring him up for trial"—away he went, and the fellow must come, dead or alive; for we considered this a good warrant, though it was only in verbal writings. But after I was appointed by the assembly, they told me, my warrants must be in real writing, and signed; and that I must keep a book, and write my proceedings in it. This was a hard business on me, for I could just barely write my own name; but to do this, and write the warrants too, was at least a huckleberry over my persimmon. I had a pretty well-informed constable, however; and he aided me very much in this business. Indeed I had so much confidence in him, that I told him, when we should happen to be out anywhere, and see that a warrant was necessary, and would have a good effect, he needn't take the trouble to come all the way to me to get one, but he could just fill out one; and then on the trial I could correct the whole business if he had committed any error. In this way I got on pretty well, till by care and attention I improved my handwriting in such manner as to be able to prepare my warrants and keep my record book without much difficulty. My judgments were never appealed from, and if they had been they would have stuck like wax, as I gave my decisions on the principles of common justice and honesty between man and man, and relied on natural born sense, and not on law, learning to guide me; for I had never read a page in a law book in all my life. . . .

About this time I met with a very severe misfortune, which I may be pardoned for naming, as it made a great change in my circumstances, and kept me back very much in the world. I had built an extensive grist mill, and [black] powder mill, all connected together, and also a large distillery. They had cost me upwards of three thousand dollars, more than I was worth in the world. The first news that I heard after I got to the Legislature, was, that my mills were—not blown up sky high, as you would guess, by my powder establishment,—but swept away all to smash by a large fresh [*sic*], that came soon after I left home. I had, of course, to stop my distillery, as my grinding was broken up; and, indeed, I may say, that the misfortune just made a complete mash of me. I had some likely negroes, and a good stock of almost everything about me, and, best of all, I had an honest wife. She didn't advise me, as is too fashionable, to smuggle up this, and that, and t'other, to go on at home; but she told me, says she, "Just pay up, as long as you have a bit's worth in the world; and then everybody will be satisfied, and we will scuffle for more." This was just such talk as I wanted to hear, for a man's wife can hold him devilish uneasy, if she begins to scold, and fret, and perplex him, at a time when he has a full load for a railroad car on his mind already.

And so, you see, I determined not to break full handed, but thought it better to keep a good conscience with an empty purse, than to get a bad opinion of myself, with a full one. I therefore gave up all I had, and took a bran-fire new start.

Having returned from the Legislature, I determined to make another move, and so I took my eldest son with me, and a young man by the name of Abram Henry, and cut out for the Obion [River in western Tennessee]. I selected a spot when I got there, where I determined to settle; and the nearest house to it was seven miles, the next nearest was fifteen, and so on to twenty. It was a complete wilderness, and full of Indians who were hunting. Game was plenty of almost every kind, which suited me exactly, as I was always fond of hunting.

In the fall of 1825, I concluded I would build two large boats, and load them with pipe staves for market. So I went down to the lake, which was about twenty-five miles from where I lived, and hired some hands to assist me, and went to work; some at boat building, and others to getting staves. I worked on with my hands till the bears got fat, and then I turned out to hunting, to lay in a supply of meat. I soon killed and salted down as many as were necessary for my family; but about this time one of my old neighbors, who had settled down on the lake about twenty-five miles from me, came to my house and told me he wanted me to go down and kill some bears about in his parts. He said they were extremely fat, and very plenty. I know'd that when they were fat, they were easily taken, for a fat bear can't run fast or long. But I asked a bear no favors, no way, further than civility, for I now had *eight* large dogs, and as fierce as painters; so that a bear stood no chance at all to get away from them. So I went home with him, and then went on down towards the Mississippi, and commenced hunting.

The morning came, and we packed our horses with the meat, and had as much as they could possibly carry, and sure enough cut out for home. It was about thirty miles, and we reached home the second day. I had now accommodated my neighbor with meat enough to do him, and had killed in all, up to that time, fifty-eight bears, during the fall and winter.

As soon as the time come for them to quit their houses and come out again in the spring, I took a notion to hunt a little more, and in about one month I killed forty-seven more, which made one hundred and five bears I had killed in less than one year from that time.

Having now closed my hunting for that winter, I returned to my hands, who were engaged about my boats and staves, and made ready for a trip down the river. I had two boats and about thirty thousand staves, and so I loaded with them, and set out for New Orleans. I got out of the Obion River, in which I had loaded my boats, very well; but when I got into the Mississippi, I found all my hands were bad scared, and in fact I believe I was scared a little the worst of any; for I had never been down the river, and I soon discovered that my pilot as ignorant of the business as myself. I hadn't gone far before I determined to lash the two boats together; we did so, but it made them so heavy and obstinate, that it was next akin to impossible to do any thing at all with them, or to guide them right in the river.

That evening we fell in company with some Ohio boats; and about night we tried to land, but we could not. The Ohio men hollered to us to go on and run all night. We took their advice, though we had a good deal rather not; but we couldn't do any other way. In a short distance we got into what is called the Devil's Elbow; and if any place in the wide creation has its own proper name, I thought it was this. Here we had about the hardest work that I ever was engaged in, in my life, to keep out of danger; and even then we were in it all the while. We twice attempted to land at Wood-yards, which we could see, but couldn't reach.

The people would run out with lights, and try to instruct us how to get to shore; but all in vain. Our boats were so heavy that we couldn't take them much any way, except the way they wanted to go, and just the way the current would carry them. At last we quit trying to land, and concluded just to go ahead as well as we could, for we found we couldn't do any better. Sometime in the night I was down in the cabin of one of the boats, sitting by the fire, thinking on what a hobble we had got into; and how much better bear-hunting was on hard land, than floating along on the water, when a fellow had to go ahead whether he was exactly willing or not.

The hatchway into the cabin came slap down, right through the top of the boat; and it was the only, way out except a small hole in the side, which we had used for putting our arms through to dip up water before we lashed the boats together.

We were now floating sideways, and the boat I was in was the hindmost as we went. All at once I heard the hands begin to run over the top of the boat in great confusion, and pull with all their might; and the first thing I know'd after this we went broadside full tilt against the head of an island where a large raft of drift timber had lodged. The nature of such a place would be, as everybody knows, to suck the boats down, and turn them right under this raft; and the uppermost boat would, of course, be suck'd down and go under first. As soon as we struck, I bulged for my hatchway, as the boat was turning under sure enough. But when I got to it, the water was pouring thro' in a current as large as the hole would let it, and as strong as the weight of the river could force it. I found I couldn't get out here, for the boat was now turned down in such a way, that it was steeper than a house-top. I now thought of the hole in the side, and made my way in a hurry for that. With difficulty I got to it, and when I got there, I found it was too small for me to get out by my own dower, and I began to think that I was in a worse box than ever. But I put my arms through and hollered as loud as I could roar, as the boat I was in hadn't yet quite filled with water up to my head, and the hands who

Davy Crockett in 1834, roughly a year and a half before he was killed at the Alamo

were next to the raft, seeing my arms out, and hearing me holler, seized them, and began to pull. I told them I was sinking, and to pull my arms off, or force me through, for now I know'd well enough it was neck or nothing, come out or sink.

By a violent effort they jerked me through; but I was in a pretty pickle when I got through. I had been sitting without any clothing over my shirt: this was torn off, and I was literally skin'd like a rabbit. I was, however, well pleased to get out in anyway, even without shirt or hide; as before I could straighten myself on the boat next to the raft, the one they pull'd me out of went entirely under, and I have never seen it any more to this day. We all escaped on to the raft, where we were compelled to sit all night, about a mile from land on either side. Four of my company were bareheaded, and three barefooted; and of that number I was one. I reckon I looked like a pretty cracklin' ever to get to Congress!!!

We had now lost all our loading; and every particle of our clothing, except what little we had on; but over all this, while I was setting there, in the night, floating about on the drift, I felt happier and better off than I ever had in my life before, for I had just made such a marvelous escape, that I had forgot almost everything else in that; and so I felt prime.

In the morning about sunrise, we saw a boat coming down, and we hailed her. They sent a large skiff, and took us all on board, and carried us down as far as Memphis. Here I met with a friend, that I never can forget as long as I am able to go ahead at anything; it was a Major Winchester, a merchant of that place: he let us all have hats, and shoes, and some little money to go upon, and so we all parted.

A young man and myself concluded to go on down to Natchez, to see if we could hear anything of our boats; for we supposed they would float out from the raft, and keep on down the river. We got on a boat at Memphis, that was going down and so cut out. Our largest boat, we were informed had been seen about fifty miles below where we stove, and an attempt had been made to land her, but without success, as she was as hardheaded as ever.

This was the last of my boats, and of my boating; for it went so badly with me, along at the first, that I hadn't much mind to try it any more. I now returned home again, and as the next August was the Congressional election, I began to turn my attention a little to that matter, as it was beginning to be talked of a good deal among the people.

The Black Hawk War

Black Hawk

Every American child should learn at school the history of the conquest of the West. The names Kit Carson, of General Custer and of Colonel Cody should be as household words to them. . . . Nor should Sitting Bull, the Short Wolf, Crazy Horses [sic], and Rain-in-the-Face be forgotten. They too were Americans, and showed the same heroic qualities as did their conquerors.
—R. B. Cunninghame Graham in a 1917 letter
to Theodore Roosevelt

The seeds of the Black Hawk War were sown in a treaty signed in St. Louis in 1804—the same year Lewis and Clark set out on their expedition. This treaty with the Sauk (Sac) and Fox (Mesquakie) Indians, which they later disputed, took away their land in what is now Wisconsin and Illinois, moving them west of the Mississippi River to area that would become Iowa. Napoleon had just sold France's claim to their territory to the United States as part of the Louisiana Purchase, but the government still had to deal with the Natives.

In 1800 what is now Wisconsin, Michigan, Indiana, and Illinois was then called Indian Territory. According to the 1804 treaty, the Sauk and Foxes' territory was theirs to use until it was surveyed and opened for settlement, but squatters began moving in long before this happened, violating the treaty and setting the stage for conflict. The treaty specified that the government would remove all squatters, but this never happened.

The treaty itself was basically a swindle. The compensation for the about 26.5 million acres was extremely poor. There was a one-time payment of $2,234.50 in goods, the promise to establish a trading post and $1,000 in goods per year. There were about 4,600 Sauk and Foxes in 1804, so the annuity worked out to about 22¢ per person per year, though it's doubtful the average tribe member ever received anything. They also were to receive the friendship and protection of the US government. The Natives who signed the treaty did not have any authority to speak for the tribes, except for one chief—Quashquame, or Jumping Fish—who was an alcoholic. The tribal councils were never consulted. The treaty was organized and signed by William Henry Harrison, who would later become famous as an Indian fighter and for serving as US president for a month.

In 1828 the US government told the tribes it was time to move across the Mississippi, and in 1830 Indian Commissioner William Clark signed another treaty with the Sauk, Foxes, and other tribes, ceding their lands to the government. This time the primary Sauk and Fox chief, Keokuk, was one of those who signed. Keokuk (pronounced kiyo-kaga), or Watchful Fox, was a puppet chief, promoted by the US government when the previous civil chief died. By Sauk tradition, the new chief should have been the previous chief's son, Neapope (pronounced nah-popé), meaning "Broth," but the United States wanted someone they could control. This ended up dividing the tribe. Those who opposed the treaties were led by Neapope and Black Hawk.

Black Hawk, or Makataimeshekiakiak—more accurately "Black Sparrow Hawk"—was a sub-chief who strongly believed in not surrendering their homelands and had no part in the treaties. Up to that time his experiences with the United States had mostly been negative. Explaining why he decided to fight with the British in the War of 1812, he said, "I had not discovered yet one good trait in the character of the Americans who had come to the country. They made fair promises but never fulfilled them, while the British made but few, and we could always rely implicitly on their word."

He and his band of Sauk and Foxes decided to resist the evacuation and continued to return from their winter hunting to their homes—their primary village, or capital, being a well-laid-out town called Saukenuk on the Rock River in northern Illinois. It was one of the largest Native American villages in the West and various tribes would gather there. Its population has been estimated at between 6,000 and 10,000—roughly the size of Savannah, Georgia (7,300), or Buffalo, New York (8,600), at that time. There were about a hundred large, strongly built clan houses that ranged in size from thirty to one hundred feet in length and from sixteen to forty feet in width. A hallway ran down the center of the buildings, with various rooms off each side of the hallway. Here they farmed eight hundred acres of corn, beans, squash, and pumpkins. They were primarily farmers. During the winter, when they couldn't farm, they'd hunt. They believed Saukenuk was the center of their world.

About twenty settler families moved into Saukenuk in 1829, fencing in Sauk fields and destroying homes. The Sauk and Foxes got the US Indian Agent to protest to the government, but nothing was done. The following year most of the village was occupied by settlers, so Black Hawk sought support from the British and other tribes from as far away as Texas. That winter Black Hawk's people nearly starved since they didn't have their corn harvest. In the spring of 1831, some relatively minor clashes caused panic to spread among the settlers and they appealed to the US government for help. The government forced Black Hawk's band to leave Saukenuk, promising to supply them with as much corn as they were currently growing there.

When Black Hawk led the Sauk and Foxes back in 1832, the Illinois volunteer militia and regular army troops set out after Black Hawk and his band of 600 to 800 young men, and about 1,200 old men, women, and children. Thus began the Black Hawk War. Eventually around 9,000 militiamen and 1,500 regulars—about a third of the US Army—would become involved, with the support of more than 300 Winnebago, Menominee, and Potawatomi.

Future president Abraham Lincoln, then age twenty-three, was captain of a company of volunteers, but his role in the war was minor. As with many of the militia and army companies, though his men searched, they were unable to find any hostiles, partly because their Winnebago guides were sympathetic with the Sauk. In general throughout the war, the militia distinguished itself in its ability to flee from mostly imagined enemies, running a number of horses to death in the process. The men were also noted for the quantities of whiskey they drank and for calling themselves "Suckers," after the bottom-feeding fish they often had to eat.

When Black Hawk discovered two brigades—consisting of 275 militiamen—under Major Stillman were nearby, and that he would not be joined by other tribes or the British, he decided to give up his hopes of holding on to their homelands and return to the Iowa Territory, so he sent three men with a white flag to open talks, along with five men to watch what happened.

Some of Stillman's volunteers were drunk, which probably contributed to what happened. These were largely untrained men who had long heard stories of fierce Indians who couldn't be trusted. When the jumpy Suckers noticed the five warriors watching from a ridge, they immediately suspected a trap and shot one of Black Hawk's emissaries. The other two escaped into the bushes, while a group of Suckers set off after the five, killing at least two.

When Black Hawk found out what happened, he was enraged, and his battle chief assembled all the available men—about forty of them—and they set out to battle the troops. When Stillman's men encountered the furious warriors, the undisciplined Suckers quickly turned and fled thirty-five miles back to the fort. They claimed they were running from fifteen hundred Indians, but the truth was clear. This entire encounter was given the ignominious name of the Battle of Stillman's Run—referring to both the river and the retreat. The regular army wanted little to do with the militia after this embarrassing failure. In all, twelve militiamen were killed, along with three to five Native Americans.

Lincoln came upon Stillman's camp after the battle and helped to bury the dead, saying, "I remember just how those men looked as we rode up the little hill where their camp was. The red light of the morning sun was streaming upon them as they lay head towards us on the ground. And every man had a round red spot on top of his head, about as big as a [silver] dollar where the redskins had taken his scalp. It was frightful. . . ."

Black Hawk, perhaps encouraged by his success against the militia, took his people north into Michigan Territory—what is now south-central Wisconsin. There were a number of relatively minor skirmishes and incidents—some related to Black Hawk and some not—and panic once again spread throughout the settlements. More soldiers were shipped from the East, but they came down with cholera and ended up spreading the epidemic across the West. Meanwhile Black Hawk turned northwest and was heading back toward the Mississippi River with his people dying from starvation, eating little but roots and bark, when he finally turned to face the militia chasing him and prepared for the Battle of Wisconsin Heights. Approximately seven hundred militiamen went up against sixty to eighty warriors. The warriors were able to keep the Suckers at bay with musket fire for about half an hour while their people fled across the Wisconsin River. By the time the militia mounted a bayonet charge, Black Hawk and his people were across, and by morning his band was gone. The militia lost one man. It's estimated up to seventy Natives were killed. Colonel Henry Dodge, the commander of the militia, said his men and scouts took at least forty Sauk scalps that day. Black Hawk said they only lost six.

The next morning Neapope, hidden in a tree, called out to Dodge's camp, saying his people wanted to leave the territory in peace and were headed for the Mississippi. Unfortunately there were no translators, so no one in the camp understood him.

By the time Black Hawk and his people reached the Mississippi, a few miles downstream from Bad Axe River, near present-day Victory, Wisconsin, many of the young men had already died in battle and many others—especially children and the elderly—from starvation and exhaustion. At the river they found they were hemmed in. Behind them were the militia with bands of Menominee wanting to kill them and across the Mississippi were their enemy, the Lakota Sioux, who had heard they were coming. As Sauk and Foxes were crossing the Mississippi on August 1, 1832, they were found by the steamboat *Warrior*. This time Black Hawk himself tried to surrender by waving a white flag, and once again the twenty-five Army soldiers on board thought it was a trap and started blasting the Natives with grapeshot from a 6-pounder cannon, while crying "Remember Indian Creek!"

They were referring to the Indian Creek Massacre, which really didn't have anything to do with Black Hawk. Just over two months earlier some squatters built a dam on Indian Creek, which threatened the food supply of a Potawatomi village downstream and violated their water rights. When they refused to remove the dam, beating one of the tribe with a hickory stick, between twenty and forty Potawatomi, with three Sauk warriors, murdered fifteen of the settlers and captured two young women, who were released unharmed a couple weeks later. The militia used this as the justification for the Bad Axe Massacre of Black Hawk's people.

The exhausted Indians were not prepared to fight when they were attacked, and it took a bit before they could fire back. The fight lasted over an hour, and in all twenty-three were killed, including a young woman about nineteen years old. Her baby's arm had to be amputated, but it's thought that he or she survived. The militia didn't lose anyone.

Black Hawk tried to convince everyone to flee north to Chippewa country, but only about three dozen went with him. Perhaps the rest were just too exhausted to flee. Black Hawk was in his sixties, so it had to be rough on him too. The next day the four hundred or so survivors found themselves between the river and about eleven hundred Army troops and militiamen. Then the real massacre began.

It lasted for eight hours and most of those who remained were wiped out. Many died in the Mississippi trying to cross—some were shot and some drowned. Others were killed on land by the soldiers. It was the women and children who were trying to cross to safety, as the men remained behind to face the army. The *Warrior*'s guns killed some who tried crossing the river or who made it to the island. Some were crushed by the *Warrior*'s paddlewheel. As one of the soldiers onboard put it, "We kept steaming back and forth on the river, running down those who attempted to cross, and shooting at the Indians onshore." One mother swam the river clutching her baby by his neck with her teeth. Both somehow survived, but the baby's neck was permanently scarred.

Those who escaped the army were hunted down by the Lakota Sioux and Winnebago, who were supporting the army. Some who made it across the river escaped, but the Lakota Sioux took sixty-eight scalps and twenty-two prisoners. In all, around 120 Natives, mainly women and children, were taken prisoner. Major John Wakefield wrote, "It was a horrid sight to witness little children, wounded and suffering the most excruciating pain, although they were of the savage enemy, and the common enemy of the country."

Only five soldiers died that day. The rest of the soldiers took many scalps, and some cut off long strips of flesh from the backs of the dead Natives to tan as straps for sharpening razors.

Black Hawk survived and later turned himself in. Overall the war turned out badly for both sides. Between 450 and 600 Native Americans died, while about 60 soldiers were killed. Also, thousands of Westerners died from the cholera plague spread by deserting soldiers. At its peak, 500 a day were dying in New Orleans alone. And it cost the government about two million dollars—around half a billion dollars in today's money.

Timothy Flint presented the prevailing US view of the war at that time in his book *Indian Wars of the West* (1833):

It had been confidently hoped and predicted, that the savages, within the limits of the American territories, would never again raise the tomahawk against us. In this hope, the event disappointed us. The Sauk and Foxes, who inhabit the waters of Rock and Fox rivers, claimed a great portion of the country embracing the lead mine district, of which Galena is the center. The greater portion of these tribes were fiercely hostile to us, and took part with the British in the late war [i.e., the War of 1812]; and these Indians seem never to have entirely abandoned the hate generated in that contest. They had, however, made a treaty with us, by which our claims to the lead mines were well defined. The hostile Sauk and Foxes had become parties to the treaty of cession, and had affected to be reconciled to us. But it is now evident, that they still fostered deep and settled purposes of revenge. . . .

The leading war chief of the Sauk and Foxes at this time, was a warrior known among the whites by the name of Black Hawk, which is only the translation of his name in the Sauk dialect. His influence over his fierce people was confirmed by the aid and counsels of his brother [not literally Black Hawk's brother], the Prophet [Wabokieshiek, also known as "The Light" or "White Cloud," who was half Sauk and half Winnebago and had great spiritual influence with both tribes (but it should be noted that Neapope was also a spiritual leader and sometimes called the Prophet)], a chief still more insidious, cruel, and revengeful, than Black Hawk himself. Both these chiefs are supposed always to have been in heart decidedly hostile to the Americans. United to the Sauk and Foxes under these chiefs, were fragments of tribes of the Sioux and Winnebago. They had long practiced horse-stealing, burned some houses, and committed some solitary murders, when their hostility was brought to a head by the following events. A party of the Illinois militia was collected near a body of these Indians. The parties came in collision; some skirmishing ensued, and two or three Indians were killed. In the exercise of their accustomed policy, the party fled, to draw the militia into an ambuscade. As soon as they began to retreat, the militia followed them tumultuously, two or three only together, and at wide intervals; and one collection rushing by the other, as they happened to excel in the fleetness of their horses. In this way they pursued their foe over a wide prairie, until about midnight, they found themselves decoyed into the center of an Indian camp, whence a deadly fire was opened upon them, by which from 12 to 20 of their number were killed. The remainder fled with still more haste and disorder than they had advanced.

Aware that they were now in a position of open war with the whites, they commenced their accustomed assaults, burnings, and massacres, along a frontier of 300 miles, from the borders of Illinois to Green Bay. As in former times, their vengeance was indiscriminate and unsparing. Old and young, mothers and infants, the sick and decrepit, were alike the victims of the merciless tomahawk.

Flint went on to explain the dichotomy of opinions toward Native Americans, saying,

the advocates of removal contend, that the states, within whose limits they reside, have perfect sovereignty in their lands, and an undoubted right either to compel their submission to their laws, or to remove them.

They state that it is impossible that the Indians should exist as an independent people within the populous limits of the whites ... They expatiate on the liberal price paid for their relinquished lands, and the ample appropriation made by the Government for their removal. One party sees nothing in their removal, but oppression, violation of treaties, and of the faith of the United States, cruelty and perfidy on our part, and on their banishment from their homes and the graves of their fathers, poverty, famine, degradation and utter extinction, chargeable to the ingratitude and tyranny of the whites.

On the other hand, the advocates of removal see the race perpetuated in opulence and peace in the fair prairies of the west. Here they are to grow up distinct red nations, with schools and churches, the anvil, the loom, and the plough—a sort of Arcadian race between our borders and the Rocky Mountains, standing memorials of the kindness and good faith of our government.

Today, it's easy to see how things turned out. The advocates for removal dominated, and Native Americans from the East and Midwest were relocated to the Indian Territory set aside for them, but it was only a few years before this land between the Mississippi River and the Rockies was taken back from them and they were relegated to small, often desolate, reservations.

Black Hawk described what the war was like for him in his book, *Autobiography of Ma-ka-tai-me-she-kia-kiak, or Black Hawk* (1833), which was translated by Antoine Le Clair, the US interpreter for the Sauk and Foxes. Le Clair said that Black Hawk came to him, saying he really wanted to tell his story, adding, "In accordance with his request, I acted as interpreter and was particularly cautious to understand distinctly the narrative of Black Hawk throughout—and have examined the work carefully since its completion, and have no hesitation in pronouncing it strictly correct, in all its particulars."

I returned and hunted that winter on the Two Rivers. The whites were now settling the country fast. I was out one day hunting in a bottom, and met three white men. They accused me of killing their hogs. I denied it, but they would not listen to me. One of them took my gun out of my hand and fired it off—then took out the flint, gave it back to me and

Black Hawk

commenced beating me with sticks, ordering me at the same time to be off. I was so much bruised that I could not sleep for several nights.

Some time after this occurrence, one of my camp cut a bee tree and carried the honey to his lodge. A party of white men soon followed him, and told him the bee tree was theirs, and that he had no right to cut it. He pointed to the honey and told them to take it. They were not satisfied with this, but took all the packs of skins that he had collected during the winter, to pay his trader and clothe his family with in the spring, and carried them off.

How could we like a people who treated us so unjustly? We determined to break up our camp for fear they would do worse, and when we joined our people in the spring a great many of them complained of similar treatment.

This summer our agent came to live at Rock Island. He treated us well and gave us good advice. I visited him and the trader very often during the summer, and for the first time heard talk of our having to leave our village. The trader, Colonel George Davenport, who spoke our language, explained to me the terms of the treaty that had been made, and said we would be obliged to leave the Illinois side of the Mississippi, and advised us to select a good place for our village and remove to it in the spring. He pointed out the difficulties we would have to encounter if we remained at our village on Rock River. He had great influence with the principal Fox chief, his adopted brother, Keokuk. He persuaded him to leave his village, go to the west side of the Mississippi and build another, which he did the spring following. Nothing was talked of but leaving our village. Keokuk had been persuaded to consent to go, and was using all his influence, backed by the war chief at Fort Armstrong [in Illinois, five miles from the Sauk and Fox village, Saukenuk] and our agent and trader at Rock Island, to induce others to go with him. He sent the crier through our village, to inform our people that it was the wish of our Great Father that we should remove to the west side of the Mississippi, and recommended the Iowa River as a good place for the new village. He wished his party to make such arrangements, before they started on their winter's hunt, and to preclude the necessity of their returning to the village in the spring.

The party opposed to removing called on me for my opinion. I gave it freely, and after questioning Quashquame [Jumping Fish] about the sale of our lands, he assured me that he "never had consented to the sale of our village." I now promised this party to be the leader, and raised the standard of opposition to Keokuk, with a full determination not to leave our village. I had an interview with Keokuk, to see if this difficulty could not be settled with our Great Father, and told him to propose to give any other land that our Great Father might choose, even our lead mines [The tribes mined and smelted lead here long before the arrival of the Europeans.], to be peaceably permitted to keep the small point of land on which our village was situated. I was of the opinion that the white people had plenty of land and would never take our village from us. Keokuk promised to make an exchange if possible, and applied to our agent, and the great chief at St. Louis [William Clark], who had charge of all the agents, for permission to go to Washington for that purpose.

This satisfied us for a time. We started to our hunting grounds with good hopes that something would be done for us. During the winter I received information that three families of whites had come to our village and destroyed some of our lodges, were making fences and dividing our cornfields for their own use. They were quarreling among themselves about their lines of division. I started immediately for Rock River, a distance of ten days' travel, and on my arrival found the report true. I went to my lodge and saw a family occupying it. I wished to talk to them but they could not understand me. I then went to Rock Island; the agent being absent, I told the interpreter what I wanted to say to these people, viz:

"Not to settle on our lands, nor trouble our fences, that there was plenty of land in the country for them to settle upon, and that they must leave our village, as we were coming back to it in the spring." The interpreter wrote me a paper, I went back to the village and showed it to the intruders, but could not understand their reply. I presumed, however, that they would remove as I expected them to.

I returned to Rock Island, passed the night there and had a long conversation with the trader. He advised me to give up and make my village with Keokuk on the Iowa River. I told him that I would not. The next morning I crossed the Mississippi on very bad ice, but the Great Spirit had made it strong, that I might pass over safe. I traveled three days farther to see the Winnebago sub-agent and converse with him about our difficulties. He gave no better news than the trader had done. I then started by way of Rock River to see the Prophet, believing that he was a man of great knowledge. When we met, I explained to him everything as it was. He at once agreed that I was right, and advised me never to give up our village, for the whites to plow up the bones of our people. He said that if we remained at our village, the whites would not trouble us, and advised me to get Keokuk, and the party that consented to go with him to the Iowa in the spring, to return and remain at our village.

I returned to my hunting ground, after an absence of one moon, and related what I had done. In a short time we came up to our village, and found that the whites had not left it, but that others had come, and that the greater part of our cornfields had been enclosed. When we landed the whites appeared displeased because we came back. We repaired the lodges that had been left standing and built others. Keokuk came to the village, but his object was to persuade others to follow him to the Iowa. He had accomplished nothing towards making arrangements for us to remain, or to exchange other lands for our village. There was no more friend-ship existing between us. I looked upon him as a coward and no brave, to abandon his village to be occupied by strangers. What right had these people to our village, and our fields, which the Great Spirit had given us to live upon?

My reason teaches me that land cannot be sold. The Great Spirit gave it to his children to live upon and cultivate as far as necessary for their subsistence, and so long as they occupy and cultivate it they have the right to the soil, but if they voluntarily leave it, then any other people have a right to settle on it. Nothing can be sold but such things as can be carried away.

In consequence of the improvements of the intruders on our fields, we found considerable difficulty to get ground to plant a little corn. Some of the whites permitted us to plant small patches in the fields they had fenced, keeping all the best ground for themselves. Our women had great difficulty in climbing their fences, being unaccustomed to the kind, and were ill-treated if they left a rail down.

One of my old friends thought he was safe. His cornfield was on a small island in Rock River. He planted his corn, it came up well, but the white man saw it; he wanted it, and took his teams over, ploughed up the crop and replanted it for himself. The old man shed tears, not for himself but on account of the distress his family would be in if they raised no corn. The white people brought whisky to our village, made our people drink, and cheated them out of their homes, guns and traps. This fraudulent system was carried to such an extent that I apprehended serious difficulties might occur, unless a stop was put to it. Consequently I visited all the whites and begged them not to sell my people whisky. One of them continued the practice openly; I took a party of my young men, went to his house, took out his barrel, broke in the head and poured out the whisky. I did this for fear some of the whites might get killed by my people when they were drunk.

Our people were treated very badly by the whites on many occasions. At one time a white man beat one of our women cruelly, for pulling a few suckers of corn out of his field to suck when she was hungry. At another time one of our young men was beat with clubs by two white men for opening a fence which crossed our road to take his horse through. His shoulder blade was broken and his body badly bruised, from the effects of which he soon after died.

Bad and cruel as our people were treated by the whites, not one of them was hurt or molested by our band. I hope this will prove that we are a peaceable people—having permitted ten men to take possession of our corn fields, prevent us from planting corn, burn our lodges, ill-treat our women, and beat to death our men without offering resistance to their barbarous cruelties. This is a lesson worthy for the white man to learn: to use forbearance when injured.

We acquainted our agent daily with our situation, and through him the great chief at St. Louis, and hoped that something would be done for us. The whites were complaining at the same time that we were intruding upon their rights. They made it appear that they were the injured party, and we the intruders. They called loudly to the great war chief to protect their property.

How smooth must be the language of the whites, when they can make right look like wrong, and wrong like right.

During this summer I happened at Rock Island, when a great chief arrived, whom I had known as the great chief of Illinois, (Governor Cole) in company with another chief, who I have been told, is a great writer (Judge James Hall). I called upon them and begged to explain the grievances to them, under which my people and I were laboring, hoping that they could do something for us. The great chief however, did not seem disposed to council with me. He said he was no longer the chief of Illinois; that his children had selected another father in his stead, and that he now only ranked as they did. I was surprised at this talk, as I had always heard that he was a good brave and great chief. But the white people appear to never be satisfied. When they get a good father, they hold councils at the suggestion of some bad, ambitious man, who wants the place himself, and conclude among themselves that this man, or some other equally ambitious, would make a better father than they have, and nine times out of ten they don't get as good a one again. . . .

My object in holding this council was to get the opinion of these two chiefs as to the best course for me to pursue. I had appealed in vain, time after time to our agent, who regularly represented our situation to the chief at St. Louis, whose duty it was to call upon the Great Father to have justice done to us, but instead of this we are told that the white people wanted our county and we must leave it for them!

I did not think it possible that our Great Father wished us to leave our village where we had lived so long, and where the bones of so many of our people had been laid. The great chief said that as he no longer had any authority he could do nothing for us, and felt sorry that it was not in his power to aid us, nor did he know how to advise us. Neither of them could do anything for us, but both evidently were very sorry. It would give me great pleasure at all times to take these two chiefs by the hand.

That fall I paid a visit to the agent before we started to our hunting grounds, to hear if he had any good news for me. He had news. He said that the land on which our village now stood was ordered to be sold to individuals, and that when sold our right to remain by treaty would be at an end, and that if we returned next spring we would be forced to remove.

We learned during the winter that part of the land where our village stood had been sold to individuals, and that the trader at Rock Island, Colonel Davenport, had bought the greater part that had been sold. The reason was now plain to me why he urged us to remove. His object, we thought, was to get our lands. We held several councils that winter to determine what we should do. We resolved in one of them, to return to our village as usual in the spring. We concluded that if we were removed by force, that the trader, agent and others must be the cause, and that if they were found guilty of having driven us from our village they should be killed. The trader stood foremost on this list. He had purchased the land on which my lodge stood, and that of our graveyard also. We therefore proposed to kill him and the agent, the interpreter, the great chief at St. Louis, the war chiefs at Forts Armstrong [and] Rock Island, and [Chief] Keokuk, these being the principal persons to blame for endeavoring to remove us. Our women received bad accounts from the women who had been raising corn at the new village, of the difficulty of breaking the new prairie with hoes, and the small quantity of corn raised. We were nearly in the same condition with regard to the latter, it being the first time I ever knew our people to be in want of provisions.

I prevailed upon some of Keokuk's band to return this spring to the Rock River village, but Keokuk himself would not come. I hoped that he would get permission to go to Washington to settle our affairs with our Great Father. I visited the agent at Rock Island. He was displeased because we had returned to our village, and told me that we must remove to the west of the Mississippi. I told him plainly that we would not. I visited the interpreter at his house, who advised me to do as the agent had directed me. I then went to see the trader and upbraided him for buying our lands. He said that if he had not purchased them some person else would, and that if our Great Father would make an exchange with us, he would willingly give up the land he had purchased to the Government. This I thought was fair, and began to think that he had not acted so badly as I had suspected. We again repaired our lodges and built others, as most of our village had been burnt and destroyed. Our women selected small patches to plant corn, where the whites had not taken them in their fences, and worked hard to raise something for our children to subsist upon. . . .

I returned from [Fort] Malden [at what is now Amherstburg, Ontario, where he hoped to gain the support of the British] late in the fall. My people were gone to their hunting ground, whither I followed. Here I learned that they had been badly treated all summer by the whites, and that a treaty had been held at Prairie du Chien [Michigan Territory, later Wisconsin, in 1825]. Keokuk and some of our people attended it, and found that our Great Father had exchanged a small strip of the land that had been ceded by Quashquame [Jumping Fish] and his party, with the Potawatomi for a portion of their land near Chicago. That the object of this treaty was to get it back again, and that the United States had agreed to give them $16,000 [equal to about $4 million today] a year forever for this small strip of land, it being less than a twentieth part of that taken from our nation for $1,000 a year [in today's dollars it would be $250,000, or about $54 per person]. This bears evidence of something I cannot explain. This land they say belonged to the United States. What reason then, could have induced them to exchange it with the Potawatomi if it was so valuable? Why not keep it? Or if they found they had made a bad bargain with the Potawatomi, why not take back their land at a fair proportion of what they gave our nation for it! If this small portion of the land that they took from us for $1,000 a year, be worth $16,000 a year forever to the Potawatomi, then the whole tract of country taken from us ought to be worth, to our nation, twenty times as much a this small fraction.

Here I was again puzzled to find out how the white people reasoned, and began to doubt whether they had any standard of right and wrong.

When it was ascertained that we would not be permitted to go to Washington, I resolved upon my course, and again tried to recruit some braves from Keokuk's band, to accompany me, but could not.

Conceiving that the peaceable disposition of Keokuk and his people had been in a great measure the cause of our having been driven from our village, I ascribed their present feelings to the same cause, and immediately went to work to recruit all my own band, and making preparations to ascend Rock River, I made my encampment on the Mississippi, where Fort Madison had stood. I requested my people to rendezvous at that place, sending out soldiers to bring in the warriors, and stationed my sentinels in a position to prevent any from moving off until all were ready.

Black Hawk's people peacefully moved up the Rock River trying to gather support so they could make a stand.

On our arrival at Kishwacokee an express was sent to the Potawatomie villages. The next day a deputation arrived. I inquired if they had corn in their villages. They said they had a very little and could not spare any. I asked them different questions and received very unsatisfactory answers. This talk was in the presence of all my people. I afterwards spoke to them privately, and requested them to come to my lodge after my people had gone to sleep. They came and took seats. I asked them if they had received any news from the British on the lake. They said no. I inquired if they had heard that a chief of our British Father was coming to Milwaukee to bring us guns, ammunition, goods and provisions. They said no. I told them what news had been brought to me, and requested them to return to their village and tell the chiefs that I wished to see them and have a talk with them.

After this deputation started, I concluded to tell my people that if White Beaver [General Henry Atkinson] came after us, we would go back, as it was useless to think of stopping or going on without more provisions and ammunition. I discovered that the Winnebago and Potawatomie were not disposed to render us any assistance. The next day the Potawatomie chiefs arrived in my camp. I had a dog killed, and made a feast. When it was ready, I spread my medicine bags, and the chiefs began to eat.

This is the beginning of the Battle of Stillman's Run on May 13, 1882.

When the ceremony was about ending, I received news that three or four hundred white men on horseback had been seen about eight miles off. I immediately started three young men with a white flag to meet them and conduct them to our camp that we might hold a council with them and descend Rock River again. I also directed them, in case the whites had encamped, to return, and I would go and see them. After this party had started I sent five young men to see what might take place. The first party went to the camp of the whites and were taken prisoners. The last party had not proceeded far before they saw about twenty men coming toward them at full gallop. They stopped, and, finding that the whites were coming toward them in such a warlike attitude, they turned and retreated, but were pursued, and two of them overtaken and killed. The others then made their escape. When they came in with the news, I was preparing my flags to meet the war chief. The alarm was given. Nearly all my young men were absent ten miles away. I started with what I had left, about forty, and had proceeded but a short distance, before we saw a part of the army approaching. I raised a yell, saying to my braves, "Some of our people have been killed. Wantonly and cruelly murdered! We must avenge their death!"

In a little while we discovered the whole army coming towards us at a full gallop. We were now confident that our first party had been killed. I immediately placed my men behind a cluster of bushes, that we might have the first fire when they had approached close enough. They made a halt some distance from us. I gave another yell and ordered my brave warriors to charge upon them, expecting that they would all be killed. [It was about 40 Native Americans against 275 militiamen]. They did charge. Every man rushed towards the enemy and fired, and they retreated in the utmost confusion and consternation before my little but brave band of warriors.

After following the enemy for some distance, I found it useless to pursue them further, as they rode so fast, and returned to the encampment with a few braves, as about twenty-five of them continued in pursuit of the flying enemy. I lighted my pipe and sat down to thank the Great

Spirit for what he had done. I had not been meditating long, when two of the three young men I had sent with the flag to meet the American war chief, entered. My astonishment was not greater than my joy to see them living and well. I eagerly listened to their story, which was as follows:

When we arrived near the encampment of the whites, a number of them rushed out to meet us, bringing their guns with them. They took us into their camp, where an American who spoke the Sauk language a little told us that his chief wanted to know how we were, where we were going, where our camp was, and where was Black Hawk? We told him that we had come to see his chief, that our chief had directed us to conduct him to our camp, in case he had not encamped, and in that event to tell him that he, Black Hawk, would come to see him; he wished to hold a council with him, as he had given up all intention of going to war. . . .

At the conclusion of this talk, a party of white men came in on horseback. We saw by their countenances that something had happened. A general tumult arose. They looked at us with indignation, talked among themselves for a moment, when several of them cocked their guns and fired at us in the crowd. Our companion fell dead. We rushed through the crowd and made our escape. We remained in ambush but a short time, before we heard yelling like Indians running an enemy. In a little while we saw some of the whites in full speed. One of them came near us. I threw my tomahawk and struck him on the head which brought him to the ground; I ran to him and with his own knife took off his scalp. I took his gun, mounted his horse, and brought my friend here behind me. We turned to follow our braves, who were chasing the enemy, and had not gone far before we overtook a white man, whose horse had mired in a swamp. My friend alighted and tomahawked the man, who was apparently fast under his horse. He took his scalp, horse and gun. By this time our party was some distance ahead. We followed on and saw several white men lying dead on the way. After riding about six miles we met our party returning. We asked them how many of our men had been killed.

They said none after the Americans had retreated. We inquired how many whites had been killed. They replied that they did not know, but said we will soon ascertain, as we must scalp them as we go back. On our return we found ten men, besides the two we had killed before we joined our friends.

Seeing that they did not yet recognize us, it being dark, we again asked how many of our braves had been killed? They said five. We asked who they were? They replied that the first party of three who went out to meet the American war chief, had all been taken prisoners and killed in the encampment, and that out of a party of five, who followed to see the meeting of the first party with the whites, two had been killed. We were now certain that they did not recognize us, nor did we tell who we were until we arrived at our camp. The news of our death had reached it some time before, and all were surprised to see us again.

The next morning I told the crier of my village to give notice that we must go and bury our dead. . . .

I was never so much surprised in my life as I was in this attack. An army of three or four hundred men, after having learned that we were suing for peace, to attempt to kill the flag bearers that had gone unarmed to ask for a meeting of the war chiefs of the two contending parties to hold a council, that I might return to the west side of the Mississippi, to come forward with a full determination to demolish the few braves I had with me, to retreat when they had ten to one, was unaccountable to me. [Black Hawk obviously thought the militia force against him was twice as large as it actually was.] It proved a different spirit from any I had ever before seen among the pale faces. I expected to see them fight as the Americans did with the British during the last war, but they had no such braves among them. At our feast with the Pottowattomies I was convinced that we had been imposed upon by those who had brought in reports of large re-enforcements to my band and resolved not to strike a blow; and in order to get permission from White Beaver to return and re-cross the Mississippi, I sent a flag of peace to the American war chief, who was reported to be close by with his army, expecting that he would convene a council and listen to what we had to say. But this chief, instead of pursuing that honorable and chivalric course, such as I have always practiced, shot down our flag-bearer and thus forced us into war with less than five hundred warriors to contend against three or four thousand soldiers.

As they prepared to cross the Wisconsin River, the US Army caught up and engaged them in the Battle of Wisconsin Heights.

Neapope, with a party of twenty, remained in our rear, to watch for the enemy, whilst we were proceeding to the Wisconsin, with our women and children. We arrived, and had commenced crossing over to an island, when we discovered a large body of the enemy coming towards us. We were now compelled to fight, or sacrifice our wives and children to the fury of the whites. I met them with fifty warriors, (having left the balance to assist our women and children in crossing) about a mile from the river. When an attack immediately commenced, I was mounted on a fine horse, and was pleased to see my warriors so brave. I addressed them in a load voice, telling them to stand their ground and never yield it to the enemy. At this time I was on the rise of a hill, where I wished to form my warriors, that we might have some advantage over the whites. But the enemy succeeded in gaining this point, which compelled us to fall into a deep ravine, from which we continued firing at them and they at us, until it began to grow dark. My horse having been wounded twice during this engagement, and fearing from his loss of blood that he would soon give out, and finding that the enemy would not come near enough to receive our fire, in the dusk of the evening, and knowing that our women and children had had sufficient time to reach the island in the Wisconsin, I ordered my warriors to return, by different routes, and meet me at the Wisconsin, and was astonished to find that the enemy were not disposed to pursue us.

In this skirmish with fifty braves, I defended and accomplished my passage over the Wisconsin, with a loss of only six men, though opposed by a host of mounted militia. I would not have fought there, but to gain time for our women and children to cross to an island. A warrior will duly appreciate the embarrassments I labored under—and whatever may be the sentiments of the white people in relation to this battle—my nation, though fallen, will award to me the reputation of a great brave in conducting it.

The loss of the enemy could not be ascertained by our party; but I am of the opinion that it was much greater, in proportion, than mine. We returned to the Wisconsin and crossed over to our people.

Here some of my people left me, and descended the Wisconsin, hoping to escape to the west side of the Mississippi, that they might return home. I had no objection to their leaving me, as my people were all in a desperate condition, being worn out with traveling and starving with hunger. Our only hope to save ourselves was to get across the Mississippi. But few of this party escaped. Unfortunately for them, a party of soldiers from Prairie du Chien were stationed on the Wisconsin, a short distance from its mouth, who fired upon our distressed people. Some were killed, others drowned, several taken prisoners, and the balance escaped to the woods and perished with hunger. Among this party were a great many women and children.

I was astonished to find that Neapope and his party of spies had not yet come in, they having been left in my rear to bring the news, if the enemy were discovered. It appeared, however, that the whites had come in a different direction and intercepted our trail but a short distance from the place where we first saw them, leaving our spies considerably in the rear. Neapope and one other retired to the Winnebago village, and there remained during the war. The balance of his party, being brave men, and considering our interests as their own, returned, and joined our ranks.

Myself and band having no means to descend the Wisconsin, I started over a rugged country to go to the Mississippi, intending to cross it and return to my nation. Many of our people were compelled to go on foot, for want of horses, which, in consequence of their having had nothing to eat for a long time, caused our march to be very slow. At length we arrived at the Mississippi, having lost some of our old men and little children, who perished on the way with hunger.

The Massacre of Bad Axe took place on August 1 and 2, 1832.

We had been here but a little while before we saw a steamboat (the *Warrior*) coming. I told my braves not to shoot, as I intended going on board, so that we might save our women and children. I knew the captain (Throckmorton) and was determined to give myself up to him. I then sent for my white flag. While the messenger was gone, I took a small piece of white cotton and put it on a pole, and called to the captain of the boat, and told him to send his little canoe ashore and let me come aboard. The people on board asked whether we were Sauk or Winnebago. I told a Winnebago to tell them that we were Sauk, and wanted to give ourselves up! A Winnebago on the boat called out to us "to run and hide, that the whites were going to shoot!" About this time one of my braves had jumped into the river, bearing a white flag to the boat, when another sprang in after him and brought him to the shore. The firing then commenced from the boat, which was returned by my braves and continued for some time. Very few of my people were hurt after the first fire, having succeeded in getting behind old logs and trees, which shielded them from the enemy's fire.

The Winnebago on the steamboat must either have misunderstood what was told, or did not tell it to the captain correctly; because I am confident he would not have allowed the soldiers to fire upon us if he had known my wishes. I have always considered him a good man, and too great a brave to fire upon an enemy when suing for quarters.

After the boat left us, I told my people to cross if they could, and wished; that I intended going into the Chippewa country. Some commenced crossing, and such as had determined to follow them, remained; only three lodges going with me. Next morning, at daybreak, a young man overtook me, and said that all my party had determined to cross the Mississippi—that a number had already got over safely and that he had heard the white army last night within a few miles of them. I now began to fear that the whites would come up with my people and kill them before they could get across. I had determined to go and join the Chippewa, but reflecting that by this I could only save myself, I concluded to return and die with my people if the Great Spirit would not give us another victory. During our stay in the thicket, a party of whites came close by us, but passed on without discovering us.

Early in the morning [of August 2] a party of whites being in advance of the army [led by General Henry Atkinson, with his subordinate, Zachary Taylor, who would become US president], came upon our people, who were attempting to cross the Mississippi. They tried to give themselves up; the whites paid no attention to their entreaties, but commenced slaughtering them. In a little while the whole army arrived. Our braves, but few in number, finding that the enemy paid no regard to age or sex, and seeing that they were murdering helpless women and little children, determined to fight until they were killed. As many women as could, commenced swimming the Mississippi, with their children on their backs. A number of them were drowned, and some shot before they could reach the opposite shore.

One of my braves, who gave me this information, piled up some saddles before him, (when the fight commenced), to shield himself from the enemy's fire, and killed three white men. But seeing that the whites were coming too close to him, he crawled to the bank of the river without being perceived, and hid himself under the bank until the enemy retired. He then came to me and told me what had been done. After hearing this sorrowful news, I started with my little party to the Winnebago village at Prairie La Cross [now La Cross, Wisconsin]. On my arrival there I entered the lodge of one of the chiefs, and told him that I wished him to go with me to his father, that I intended giving myself up to the American war chief and die, if the Great Spirit saw proper. He said he would go with me. I then took my medicine bag and addressed the chief. I told him that it was "the soul of the Sauk nation—that it never had been dishonored in any battle, take it, it is my life—dearer than life—and give it to the American chief!" He said he would keep it, and take care of it, and if I was suffered to live, he would send it to me.

During my stay at the village, the squaws made me a white dress of deer skin. I then started with several Winnebago, and went to their agent, at Prairie du Chien, and gave myself up.

On my arrival there, I found to my sorrow, that a large body of Sioux had pursued and killed a number of our women and children, who had got safely across the Mississippi. The whites ought not to have permitted such conduct, and none but cowards would ever have been guilty of such cruelty, a habit which had always been practiced on our nation by the Sioux.

The massacre, which terminated the war, lasted about two hours. Our loss in killed was about sixty, besides a number that was drowned. The loss of the enemy could not be ascertained by my braves, exactly; but they think that they killed about sixteen during the action.

I was now given up by the agent to the commanding officer at Fort Crawford [at Prairie du Chien], the White Beaver having gone down the river. We remained here a short time, and then started for Jefferson Barracks [just south of St. Louis], in a steamboat, under the charge of a young war chief, (Lieut. Jefferson Davis [who became president of the Confederacy]) who treated us all with much kindness. . . .

On our way down, I surveyed the country that had cost us so much trouble, anxiety and blood, and that now caused me to be a prisoner of war. I reflected upon the ingratitude of the whites when I saw their fine houses, rich harvests and everything desirable around them; and recollected that all this land had been ours, for which I and my people had never received a dollar, and that the whites were not satisfied until they took our village and our graveyards from us and removed us across the Mississippi.

Shortly after the Black Hawk War ended, President Andrew Jackson told Congress, "Severe as is the lesson to the Indians, it was rendered necessary by their unprovoked aggressions. . . ."

After Black Hawk turned himself in several weeks after the Bad Axe Massacre, he was taken to Jefferson Barracks. Eight months later President Andrew Jackson ordered that Black Hawk, Neapope, the Prophet, and eight other Sauk and Fox leaders be brought to Fort Monroe in Hampton, Virginia. They were transported by carriage, steamer, and train, and all along the route large crowds gathered to see the prisoners. The war was over, and Black Hawk was now a celebrity.

On arriving in Washington, DC, they met with President Andrew Jackson and Secretary of War Lewis Cass. Black Hawk told the president, "We did not expect to conquer the whites. They had too many men. I took up the hatchet to avenge injuries my people could no longer endure. Had I borne them longer without striking, my people would have said, 'Black Hawk is a squaw; he is too old to be our chief; he is no Sauk.' These reflections caused me to raise the war-whoop. The result is known to you. I say no more."

After a few weeks in prison, where they posed for numerous portraits, they were taken on tour through the major Eastern cities, where they drew even larger crowds. At one point Black Hawk and the president crossed paths in Baltimore and Jackson noticed people were more interested in Black Hawk than they were with him. One of his aides wrote that "we concluded we wouldn't have him in our company anymore." That same year Black Hawk's autobiography was published and instantly became a bestseller.

At the end of his autobiography, he concludes,

Before I take leave of the public, I must contradict the story of some of the village criers, who, I have been told, accuse me of having murdered women and children among the whites. This assertion is false! I never did, nor have I any knowledge that any of my nation ever killed a white woman or child. I make this statement of truth to satisfy the white people among whom I have been traveling, and by whom I have been treated with great kindness, that, when they shook me by the hand so cordially, they did not shake the hand that had ever been raised against any but warriors.

It has always been our custom to receive all strangers that come to our village or camps in time of peace on terms of friendship, to share with them the best provisions we have, and give them all the assistance in our power. If on a journey or lost, to put them on the right trail, and if in want of moccasins, to supply them. I feel grateful to the whites for the kind manner they treated me and my party whilst traveling among them, and from my heart I assure them that the white man will always be welcome in our village or camps, as a brother. The tomahawk is buried forever! We will forget what has passed, and may the watchword between the Americans and the Sauk and Foxes ever be—*friendship*.

I am done now. A few more moons and I must follow my fathers to the shades. May the Great Spirit keep our people and the whites always at peace, is the sincere wish of *Black Hawk*.

After the tour, Black Hawk was released back to what would in five years become the Iowa Territory. In 1837 he and Keokuk went with a delegation to Washington, DC, where the government vainly attempted to broker a peace agreement between the Sauk and the Sioux. Black Hawk wasn't there as part of the delegation, but he was taken along because Keokuk was afraid Black Hawk might stir up trouble for him if he left the old warrior behind. They were then taken on a tour of the major cities, with Black Hawk receiving the majority of the attention.

The following year Black Hawk was a special guest at Fort Madison for the Fourth of July celebration. After everyone toasted him, he said,

It has pleased the Great Spirit that I am here today. I have eaten with my white friends. . . . I hope we are all friends here. A few summers ago I was fighting you. I did wrong, perhaps. But that is past. It is buried. Let it be forgotten. Rock River Valley was a beautiful country. I loved my villages, my cornfields and the home of my people. I fought for it. It is now yours. . . . I was once a great warrior. Now I am poor. Keokuk has been the cause of my present situation, but do not attach blame to him. I am now old. I have looked upon the Mississippi since I was a child. I love the great river. I have always dwelt upon its banks from the time I was an infant. I look upon it now. I shake hands with you, and as it is my wish, I hope you are my friends. I may not see you again. Farewell.

He died three months later on October 3, 1838, at about the age of seventy-two. They buried him in the sitting position in a fifteen-inch-deep grave with his torso above the ground. This was covered with a four-foot-high wooden cone that was covered with blue grass. He was dressed in a military uniform that was presented to him by the president's cabinet and wearing three medals presented to him by President Jackson, ex-president John Quincy Adams, and the city of Boston. Also with him were a sword given to him by President Jackson and two canes from Henry Clay and British General Dixon. At the head of his grave was a thirty-foot-tall flagstaff with a silken US flag on it.

The following year on the Fourth of July, his grave was robbed by Dr. Turner of Lexington, Iowa. Black Hawk's skeleton was cleaned and wired together. His sons were horrified and frantically appealed to the governor of Iowa. His skeleton was returned, but it was stolen again and placed in Iowa's Burlington Geographical and Historical Society, where it was destroyed in an 1855 fire.

After being defeated in the Black Hawk War, Black Hawk was frustrated by his inability to do anything about the puppet chief Keokuk, who was half his age. Keokuk was a great speaker, but he was corrupt. He spent the money that the US government had given him for his tribe on himself, on large quantities of alcohol, and on the few favorites and supporters he needed to maintain his power. Meanwhile, he kept selling off more and more of the tribes' land, and the tribes continued to decline. Keokuk died in 1848—some say he was poisoned by a tribesman.

Before the war there were roughly 2,850 Sauk and 1,750 Foxes—about half of which were children. When Sauk and Foxes were moved in 1846 from the newly formed state of Iowa to the unorganized territory that would become Kansas, there were only 1,900 Sauk, 700 Foxes, and a few others who remained behind, hiding in Iowa. When they were moved following the Civil War to unorganized territory that would become Oklahoma, there were 600 Sauk and 100 Foxes, with some still in Iowa and Kansas. Today there are 2,200 Sauk and Foxes in Oklahoma, 1,100 in Kansas, and 400 in Iowa.

Of their original 750,000-acre reservation in Oklahoma, only 1,000 acres remain theirs. The branch of the two tribes that remained in Kansas still has 453 acres. In 1859 one band returned to Iowa, purchasing 80 acres. They fared better than the rest of the tribe and now own 3,200 acres. Before the 1804 treaty, the Sauk and Foxes had 20 million acres.

The Black Hawk War was the final armed conflict with Native Americans east of the Mississippi. The long conflict west of the Mississippi was about to begin, starting in 1836 with the Texas–Indian Wars and ending in 1890 with the Pine Ridge Campaign.

Indians, Buffalo, and Kit Carson

John C. Frémont

One of the great explorers of the Far West, who became a celebrated national hero known as "The Pathfinder," was John Frémont. He was a second lieutenant in the Army Topographical Engineers Corps in 1842 when he set out on a series of expeditions for the US government to survey and map the West. At this time the southern portion of the United States basically extended west to the Rio Grande River, though Mexico still claimed most of what is now Texas and half of what is now New Mexico. Roughly all the area covered by California, Nevada, Utah, Arizona, and the western half of New Mexico were still part of Mexico. The United States also claimed the Oregon Territory—an area that is essentially covered by Washington, Oregon, and Idaho—but this area was also claimed by the British.

Frémont's first expedition mapped the first half of what would become the Oregon Trail and the South Pass in the Rocky Mountains. Immigrants were already heading west and the United States wanted to strengthen its claim on the disputed Oregon Territory. Departing from Missouri, they passed through what is now Kansas, Nebraska, Wyoming, and Colorado.

His second expedition took place in 1843 and 1844 and followed the Oregon Trail to what is now Washington, then turned south through Oregon and into Mexico, illegally passing through what is now Nevada, California, Arizona, and then up through Colorado and Kansas. This expedition made Frémont famous, and in 1845 he was sent back to further explore California. This time his expedition passed through what is now Kansas and illegally into Mexico—what is now Colorado, Utah, Nevada, and into California. Traveling around California, they briefly went up into Oregon, back down to southern California, and then up into Nevada, where they retraced their steps back to the United States.

Kit Carson

Besides surveying and mapping the geography, his reports—like those of Lewis and Clark—contained botanical and geological information, as well as his personal experiences. Congress printed up thousands of copies, and the public quickly bought them up. Of course this contributed to the western expansion of the United States. His reports and maps helped guide thousands of immigrants to Oregon and California, especially once the Gold Rush hit in 1848.

Frémont's fourth and fifth expeditions were failures. In 1848 he led a difficult private expedition to search for mountain passes for an Atlantic to the Pacific railway, but was led astray by a guide, and a third of his men died in a blizzard. Then in 1853 he attempted to complete the intended route of his fourth expedition, but it ended when he and his men almost starved in an unsuccessful attempt to cross the Rockies in the middle of winter. He didn't publish reports of these expeditions.

There were other explorers of the West, but Frémont's narratives were a popular sensation, rivaling those of Lewis and Clark. His first three expeditions made him an international celebrity. His reports also made one of his guides, Kit Carson, famous as something of a frontier superhero.

Christopher "Kit" Carson was from Missouri and had little education. After his father died when he was nine, he had to leave school and work to help support his impoverished family. His mother remarried, but he wasn't able to get along with his stepfather, so at fourteen he was apprenticed to a saddle maker. When he was seventeen he joined a wagon train to Mexico, settling in Taos (now in New Mexico).

Prior to 1821, trappers had reached this portion of what was then New Spain, but Spanish authorities forbade them to trade. This changed when Mexico won its independence. The Santa Fe Trail opened, and traders and trappers began moving into the area. Kit arrived there in 1827.

Although he was unable to read or write, Kit was very good at learning languages. Soon Spanish supplanted English as his primary language. He also learned French and could converse in Apache, Navajo, Comanche, Cheyenne, Arapaho, Piute, Ute, Crow, Blackfeet Sioux, and Shoshone, as well as the sign language used by mountain men and many Native Americans. On one occasion this saved his life, when a group of twenty Cheyenne discussed their plans to murder him, not realizing he could understand what they were saying.

At nineteen Carson was hired for one of mountain man Ewing Young's trapping expeditions to what would become California. From 1829 through 1840 he went on a number of trapping expeditions throughout the Sierra Nevadas and the Rockies. During that time he married twice. The first was to an Arapahoe girl named Waa-nibe, or Singing Grass, who died shortly after giving birth to their second child. The second was a Cheyenne woman named Making-Out-Road, who fourteen months later gave him an Indian-style divorce by throwing his possessions and their surviving daughter out of her tepee. He later, at the age of thirty-four, married a fifteen-year-old Mexican girl named Josefa Jaramillo, who was from a prominent Taos family. They remained together for the rest of their lives and had seven children.

While mountain men tended to be pretty wild, Carson was the opposite. He had a reputation for being brave and honest. Giving up his Presbyterian background, he converted to Catholicism.

Frémont met Carson on a Missouri riverboat in 1842 and hired him as the guide for his first expedition at the rate of $100 per month—around $22,000 in today's dollars. Carson also joined him on the second and third expeditions, and the two became lifelong friends. This chance meeting was very important for Carson, as the days of the trapper were coming to an end because the numbers of animals—especially beavers—were dwindling and because of changes in fashion. The demand for soft pelts was replaced by a demand for buffalo hides. But for expeditions, like Frémont's, buffalo were needed for food.

The following account is from Frémont's *Narrative of the exploring Expedition to the Rocky Mountains in the year 1842, and to Oregon and North California in the years 1843–44* (1846). These events took place during the first expedition on June 28, 1842, in southern Nebraska. On this expedition Frémont and Carson had thirty men with them.

At our evening camp about sunset, three figures were discovered approaching, which our glasses made out to be Indians. They proved to be Cheyenne—two men, and a boy of thirteen. About a month since, they had left their people on the south fork of the river, some three hundred miles to the westward, and a party of only four in number had been to the Pawnee villages on a horse-stealing excursion, from which they were returning unsuccessful. They were miserably mounted on wild horses from the Arkansas plains, and had no other weapons than bows and long spears; and had they been discovered by the Pawnee, could not, by any possibility, have escaped. They were mortified by their ill-success, and said the Pawnee were cowards, who shut up their horses in their lodges at night.

I invited them to supper with me, and Randolph and the young Cheyenne, who had been eyeing each other suspiciously and curiously, soon became intimate friends. After supper we sat down on the grass and I placed a sheet of paper between us on which they traced—rudely, but with a certain degree of relative truth—the water-courses of the country which lay between us and their villages, and of which I desired to have some information. Their companions, they told us, had taken a nearer route over the hills; but they had mounted one of the summits to spy out the country, whence they had caught a glimpse of our party, and, confident of good treatment at the hands of the whites, hastened to join company. Latitude of the camp 40° 39' 51".

We made the next morning sixteen miles. I remarked that the ground was covered in many places with an efflorescence of salt, and the plants were not numerous. In the bottoms were frequently seen *Tradescantia*, and on the dry lenches were *carduus*, *cactus*, and *amorpha*. A high wind during the morning had increased to a violent gale from the northwest, which made our afternoon ride cold and unpleasant. We had the welcome sight of two buffaloes on one of the large islands, and encamped at a clump of timber about seven miles from our noon halt, after a day's march of twenty-two miles.

The air was keen the next morning at sunrise, the thermometer standing at 44°, and it was sufficiently cold to make overcoats very comfortable. A few miles brought us into the midst of the buffalo, swarming in immense numbers over the plains, where they had left scarcely a blade of grass standing. Mr. [Charles] Preuss [the topographer], who was sketching at a little distance in the rear, had at first noted them as large groves of timber. In the sight of such a mass of life, the traveler feels a strange emotion of grandeur. We had heard from a distance a dull and confused murmuring, and, when we came in view of their dark masses, there was not one among us who did not feel his heart beat quicker. It was the early part of the day, when the herds are feeding; and everywhere they were in motion. Here and there a huge old bull was rolling in the grass, and clouds of dust rose in the air from various parts of the bands, each the scene of some obstinate fight.

John C. Frémont

Indians and buffalo make the poetry and life of the prairie, and our camp was full of their exhilaration. In place of the quiet monotony of the march, relieved only by the cracking of the whip, and an *"avance donc! enfant de garce!"* shouts and songs resounded from every part of the line, and our evening camp was always the commencement of a feast, which terminated only with our departure on the following morning. At any time of the night might be seen pieces of the most delicate and choicest meat, roasting *en appolas*, on sticks around the fire, and the guard were never without company.

With pleasant weather and no enemy to fear, an abundance of the most excellent meat, and no scarcity of bread or tobacco, they were enjoying the oasis of a voyageur's life. Three cows were killed today. Kit Carson had shot one, and was continuing the chase in the midst of another herd, when his horse fell headlong, but sprang up and joined the flying band. Though considerably hurt, he had the good fortune to break no bones; and Maxwell, who was mounted on a fleet hunter, captured the runaway after a hard chase. He was on the point of shooting him, to avoid the loss of his bridle—a handsomely mounted Spanish one—when he found that his horse was able to come up with him.

Animals are frequently lost in this way; and it is necessary to keep close watch over them in the vicinity of the buffalo, in the midst of which they scour off to the plains and are rarely retaken. One of our mules took a sudden freak into his head, and joined a neighboring band today. As we were not in a condition to lose horses, I sent several men in pursuit, and remained in camp, in the hope of recovering him; but lost the afternoon to no purpose, as we did not see him again. Astronomical observations placed us in longitude 100° 05' 47", latitude 40° 49' 55" [what is now southern Nebraska].

July. 1st. [1842]—Along our road today the prairie bottom was more elevated and dry, and the river hills which border the right side of the river higher, and more broken and picturesque in the outline. The country, too, was better timbered. As we were riding quietly along the bank, a grand herd of buffalo, some seven or eight hundred in number, came crowding up from the river, where they had been to drink, and commenced crossing the plain slowly, eating as they went. The wind was favorable; the coolness of the morning invited to exercise; the ground was apparently good, and the distance across the prairie—two or three miles—gave us a fine opportunity to charge them before they could get among the river hills. It was too fine a prospect for a chase to be lost; and, halting for a few moments, the hunters were brought up and saddled, and Kit Carson, [hunter Lucien] Maxwell, and I, started together.

They were now somewhat less than half a mile distant, and we rode easily along until within about three hundred yards, when a sudden agitation, a wavering in the band, and a galloping to and fro of some which were scattered along the skirts, gave us the intimation that we were discovered. We started together at a hard gallop, riding steadily abreast of each other; and here the interest of the chase became so engrossingly intense, that we were sensible to nothing else. We were now closing upon them rapidly, and the front of the mass was already in rapid motion for the hills, and in a few seconds the movement had communicated itself to the whole herd.

A crowd of bulls, as usual, brought up the rear, and every now and then some of them faced about, and then dashed on after the band a short distance, and turned and looked again, as if more than half inclined to fight. In a few moments, however, during which we had been quickening our pace, the rout was universal, and we were going over the ground like a hurricane. When at about thirty yards, we gave the usual shout—the hunter's *pas de charge*—and broke into the herd. We entered on the side, the mass giving way in every direction in their heedless course. Many of the bulls, less active and fleet than the cows, paying no attention to the ground, and occupied solely with the hunter, were precipitated to the earth with great force, rolling over and over with the violence of the shock, and hardly distinguishable in the dust. We separated on entering, each singling out his game.

My horse was a trained hunter, famous in the West under the name of Proveau; and, with his eyes flashing and the foam flying from his mouth, sprang on after the cow like a tiger. In a few moments he brought me along-side of her, and rising in the stirrups, I fired at the distance of a yard, the ball entering at the termination of the long hair, and passing near the heart. She fell headlong at the report of the gun; and, checking my horse, I looked around for my companions. At a little distance, Kit was on the ground, engaged in tying his horse to the horns of a cow he was preparing to cut up.

Among the scattered bands, at some distance below, I caught a glimpse of Maxwell; and while I was looking, a light wreath of smoke curled away from his gun, from which I was too far to hear the report. Nearer, and between me and the hills, towards which they were direct-ing their course, was the body of the herd; and, giving my horse the rein, we dashed after them. A thick cloud of dust hung upon their rear, which filled my mouth and eyes, and nearly smothered me. In the midst of this I could see nothing, and the buffalo were not distinguishable until within thirty feet. They crowded together more densely still as I came upon them, and rushed along in such a compact body, that I could not obtain an entrance—the horse almost leaping upon them.

In a few moments the mass divided to the right and left, the horns clattering with a noise heard above everything else, and my horse darted into the opening. Five or six bulls charged on us as we dashed along the line, but were left far behind; and, singling out a cow, I gave her my fire, but struck too high. She gave a tremendous leap, and scoured on swifter than before. I reined up my horse, and the band swept on like a torrent, and left the place quiet and clear.

Our chase had led us into dangerous ground. A prairie-dog village, so thickly settled that there were three or four holes in every twenty yards square, occupied the whole bottom for nearly two miles in length. Looking around, I saw only one of the hunters, nearly out of sight, and the long, dark line of our caravan crawling along, three or four miles distant.

After a march of twenty-four miles, we encamped at nightfall, one mile and a half above the lower end of Brady's Island. The breadth of this arm of the river was eight hundred and eighty yards, and the water nowhere two feet in depth.

The island bears the name of a man killed on this spot some years ago. His party had encamped here, three in company, and one of the number went off to hunt, leaving Brady and his companion together. These two had frequently quarreled, and on the hunter's return he found Brady dead, and was told that he had shot himself accidentally. He was buried here on the bank; but, as usual, the wolves tore him out, and some human bones that were lying on the ground we supposed were his.

Troops of wolves that were hanging on the skirts of the buffalo, kept up an uninterrupted howling during the night, venturing almost into camp. In the morning, they were sitting at a short distance, barking, and impatiently waiting our departure, to fall upon the bones.

———

4th. [July 1842]—The morning was very smoky, the sun shining dimly and red, as in thick fog. The camp was roused by a salute at daybreak, and from our scanty store a portion of what our Indian friends called the "red fire-water" served out to the men. While we were at breakfast, a buffalo-calf broke through the camp, followed by a couple of wolves. In its fright, it had probably mistaken us for a band of buffalo. The wolves were obliged to make a circuit round the camp, so that the calf got a little start, and strained every nerve to reach a large herd at the foot of the hills, about two miles distant; but first one and then another, and another wolf joined in the chase, until his pursuers amounted to twenty or thirty, and they ran him down before he could reach his friends.

There were a few bulls near the place, and one of them attacked the wolves and tried to rescue him, but was driven off immediately and the little animal fell an easy prey, half devoured before he was dead. We watched the chase with the interest always felt for the weak; and had there been a saddled horse at hand, he would have fared better. . . .

As we were riding slowly along this afternoon, clouds of dust in the ravines, among the hills to the right, suddenly attracted our attention, and in a few minutes column after column of buffalo came galloping down, making directly to the river. By the time the leading herds had reached the water, the prairie was darkened with the dense masses. Immediately before us, when the bands first came down into the valley, stretched an unbroken line, the head of which was lost among the river hills on the opposite side; and still they poured down from the ridge on our right. From hill to hill, the prairie bottom was certainly not less than two miles wide; and, allowing the animals to be ten feet apart, and only ten in a line, there were already eleven thousand in view. Some idea may thus be formed of their number when they had occupied the whole plain.

In a short time they surrounded us on every side, extending for several miles in the rear, and forward as far as the eye could reach; leaving around us, as we advanced, an open space of only two or three hundred yards. This movement of the buffalo indicated to us the presence of Indians on the North fork.

⌒⌒

8th. [July 1842]—The morning was very pleasant. The breeze was fresh from S. 50° E., with few clouds; the barometer at six o'clock standing at 25.970, and the thermometer at 70°. Since leaving the forks our route had passed over a country alternately clay and sand, each presenting the same naked waste. On leaving camp this morning, we struck again a sandy region, in which the vegetation appeared somewhat more vigorous than that which we had observed for the last few days; and on the opposite side of the river were some tolerably large groves of timber.

Journeying along, we came suddenly upon a place where the ground was covered with horses' tracks, which had been made since the rain, and indicated the immediate presence of Indians in our neighborhood. The buffalo, too, which the day before had been so numerous were nowhere in sight—another sure indication that there were people near. Riding on, we discovered the carcass of a buffalo recently killed—perhaps the day before.

We scanned the horizon carefully with the glass, but no living object was to be seen. For the next mile or two, the ground was dotted with buffalo carcasses, which showed that the Indians had made a surround here, and were in considerable force. We went on quickly and cautiously, keeping the river bottom, and carefully avoiding the hills; but we met with no interruption and began to grow careless again.

We had already lost one of our horses, and here Basil's mule showed symptoms of giving out, and finally refused to advance, being what the Canadians call *resté*. He therefore dismounted, and drove her along before him; but this was a very slow way of traveling. We had inadvertently got about half a mile in advance, but our Cheyenne, who were generally a mile or two in the rear, remained with him. There were some dark-looking objects among the hills, about two miles to the left, here low and undulating, which we had seen for a little time, and supposed to be buffalo coming in to water; but, happening to look behind, Maxwell saw the Cheyenne whipping up furiously, and another glance at the dark objects showed them at once to be Indians coming up at speed.

Had we been well mounted and disencumbered of instruments, we might have set them at defiance; but as it was, we were fairly caught. It was too late to rejoin our friends, and we endeavored to gain a clump of timber about half a mile ahead; but the instruments and tired state of our horses did not allow us to go faster than a steady canter, and they were gaining on us fast. At first, they did not appear to be more than fifteen or twenty in number, but group after group darted into view at the top of the hills, until all the little eminences seemed in motion; and, in a few minutes from the time they were first discovered, two or three hundred, naked to the breechcloth, were sweeping across the prairie. In a few hundred yards we discovered that the timber we were endeavoring to make was on the opposite side of the river; and before we reached the bank, down came the Indians upon us.

I am inclined to think that in a few seconds more the leading man, and perhaps some of his companions, would have rolled in the dust; for we had jerked the covers from our guns, and our fingers were on the triggers. Men in such cases generally act from instinct, and a charge from three hundred naked savages is a circumstance not well calculated to promote a cool exercise of judgment.

Just as he was about to fire, Maxwell recognized the leading Indian, and shouted to him in the Indian language, "You're a fool, God damn you—don't you know me?"

The sound of his own language seemed to shock the savage; and, swerving his horse a little, he passed us like an arrow. He wheeled, as I rode out towards him, and gave me his hand, striking his breast and exclaiming "Arapaho!"

They proved to be a village of that nation, among whom Maxwell had resided as a trader a year or two previously, and recognized him accordingly. We were soon in the midst of the band, answering as well as we could a multitude of questions; of which the very first was, of what tribe were our Indian companions who were coming in the rear? They seemed disappointed to know that they were Cheyenne, for they had fully anticipated a grand dance around a Pawnee scalp that night.

The chief showed us his village at a grove on the river six miles ahead, and pointed out a band of buffalo on the other side of the Platte, immediately opposite us, which he said they were going to surround. They had seen the band early in the morning from their village, and had been making a large circuit, to avoid giving them the wind, when they discovered us. In a few minutes the women came galloping up, astride on their horses, and naked from their knees down and the hips up. They followed the men, to assist in cutting up and carrying off the meat.

The wind was blowing directly across the river, and the chief requested us to halt where we were for awhile, in order to avoid raising the herd. We therefore unsaddled our horses, and sat down on the bank to view the scene; and our new acquaintances rode a few hundred yards lower down, and began crossing the river.

Scores of wild-looking dogs followed, looking like troops of wolves, and having, in fact, but very little of the dog in their composition. Some of them remained with us, and I checked one of the men, whom I found aiming at one, which he was about to kill for a wolf.

The day had become very hot. The air was clear, with a very slight breeze; and now, at 12 o'clock, while the barometer stood at 25.920, the attached thermometer was at 108°.

Our Cheyenne had learned that with the Arapaho village were about twenty lodges of their own, including their own families; they therefore immediately commenced making their toilette. After bathing in the river, they invested themselves in some handsome calico shirts, which I afterwards learned they had stolen from my own men, and spent some time in arranging their hair and painting themselves with some vermilion I had given them.

While they were engaged in this satisfactory manner, one of their half-wild horses, to which the crowd of prancing animals which had just passed had recalled the freedom of her existence among the wild droves on the prairie, suddenly dashed into the hills at the top of her speed.

She was their pack-horse, and had on her back all the worldly wealth of our poor Cheyenne, all their accoutrements, and all the little articles which they had picked up among us, with some few presents I had given them. The loss which they seemed to regret most were their spears and shields, and some tobacco which they had received from me. However, they bore it all with the philosophy of an Indian, and laughingly continued their toilette. They appeared, however, to be a little mortified at the thought of returning to the village in such a sorry plight.

"Our people will laugh at us," said one of them, "returning to the village on foot, instead of driving back a drove of Pawnee horses." He demanded to know if I loved my sorrel hunter very much; to which I replied, he was the object of my most intense affection. Far from being able to give, I was myself in want of horses; and any suggestion of parting with the few I had available was met with a peremptory refusal.

In the meantime, the slaughter was about to commence on the other side. So soon as they reached it, Indians separated into two bodies. One party proceeded across the prairie, towards the hills, in an extended line, while the other went up the river; and instantly as they had given the wind to the herd, the chase commenced.

The buffalo started for the hills, but were intercepted and driven back towards the river, broken and running in every direction. The clouds of dust soon covered the whole scene, preventing us from having any but an occasional view. It had a very singular appearance to us at a distance, especially when looking with the glass. We were too far to hear the report of the guns, or any sound; and at every instant, through the clouds of dust, which the sun made luminous, we could see for a moment two or three buffalo dashing along, and close behind them an Indian with his long spear, or other weapon, and instantly again they disappeared.

The apparent silence, and the dimly seen figures flitting by with such rapidity, gave it a kind of dreamy effect, and seemed more like a picture than a scene of real life. It had been a large herd when the *cerne* commenced, probably three or four hundred in number; but, though I watched them closely, I did not see one emerge from the fatal cloud where the work of destruction was going on.

After remaining here about an hour, we resumed our journey in the direction of the village. Gradually, as we rode on, Indian after Indian came dropping along, laden with meat; and by the time we had neared the lodges, the backward road was covered with the returning horsemen. It was a pleasant contrast with the desert road we had been traveling. Several had joined company with us, and one of the chiefs invited us to his lodge.

The village consisted of about one hundred and twenty-five lodges, of which twenty were Cheyenne; the latter pitched a little apart from the Arapahoe. They were disposed in a scattering manner on both sides of a broad, irregular street, about one hundred and fifty feet wide, and running along the river.

As we rode along, I remarked near some of the lodges a kind of tripod frame, formed of three slender poles of birch, scraped very clean, to which were affixed the shield and spear, with some other weapons of a chief. All were scrupulously clean, the spear-head was burnished bright; and the shield white and stainless. It reminded me of the days of feudal chivalry; and when, as I rode by, I yielded to the passing impulse, and touched one of the spotless shields with the muzzle of my gun, I almost expected a grim warrior to start from the lodge and resent my challenge.

The master of the lodge spread out a robe for me to sit upon, and the squaws set before us a large wooden dish of buffalo meat. He had lit his pipe in the meanwhile, and when it had been passed around, we commenced our dinner while he continued to smoke. Gradually, however, five or six other chiefs came in, and took their seats in silence.

When we had finished, our host asked a number of questions relative to the object of our journey, of which I made no concealment; telling him simply that I had made a visit to see the country, preparatory to the establishment of military posts on the way to the mountains. Although this was information of the highest interest to them, and by no means calculated to please them, it excited no expression of surprise, and in no way altered the grave courtesy of their demeanor.

The others listened and smoked. I remarked, that in taking the pipe for the first time, each had turned the stem upward, with a rapid glance, as in offering to the Great Spirit, before he put it in his mouth. A storm had been gathering for the past hour, and some pattering drops in the lodge warned us that we had some miles to our camp.

An Indian had given Maxwell a bundle of dried meat, which was very acceptable, as we had nothing; and, springing upon our horses, we rode off at dusk in the face of a cold shower and driving wind. We found our companions under some densely foliaged old trees, about three miles up the river. Under one of them lay the trunk of a large cottonwood, to leeward of which the men had kindled a fire, and we sat here and roasted our meat in tolerable shelter.

Nearly opposite was the mouth of one of the most considerable affluents of the South Fork, *la Fourche aux Castors* (Beaver Fork), heading off in the ridge to the southeast.

According to zoologists, American buffalo are not really buffalo at all—they're actually bison—but the general public disagrees and continues to call them buffalo.

There were close to sixty million buffalo roaming the plains in the early 1800s. Fifty years after Frémont's expedition, they were all but extinct. The construction of the Central Pacific and Union Pacific Transcontinental Railroads in the 1860s and

A pile of buffalo skulls beside railroad tracks in Detroit, Michigan, in the 1880s

the Kansas Pacific Railroad in the 1870s greatly contributed to this. The line not only divided the herds, preventing migrations, it enabled easy transportation of the hides to the East Coast. This peaked during the 1870s, when many young men, such as Wyatt Earp, Bat Masterson, Pat Garrett, Buffalo Bill Cody, and Wild Bill Hickock, became buffalo hunters during the difficult economic times that followed the Civil War. One hunter could kill a hundred buffalo a day. Dodge City soon became the buffalo capital of the world, and it's estimated that 1.5 million buffalo hides were shipped from there between 1872 and 1878.

In the northwestern plains soldiers killed hundreds of thousands of buffalo when they were driving the Native Americans from their hunting grounds. Part of this was for fun and part was General Sherman's policy of wiping out the source of the Indians' means of survival.

During this period another type of hunter arrived on the scene. These were rich sportsmen who hunted for the sport and for trophies. They looked down on the market hunters who had to work at hunting for their livelihood. They felt hunting should be elevated to a recreation, like the fox hunts in England. The market hunters looked down on sports hunters as wasteful dandies, referring to them as "pot hunters" and "game hogs." As the railroads brought tourists to the plains, they brought people who, like many of the soldiers, killed buffalo purely for pleasure. They would blast away from train windows, killing as many as they could, rarely taking trophies. Some trains stopped so the hunters could examine their kills. Some passengers cut locks of hair from the carcasses so they could later claim these were Indian scalps.

The railroads also brought in more market hunters. By the time the Northern Pacific Transcontinental Railroad was completed in 1883, there were at least five thousand hunters scattered along it slaughtering thousands of buffalo and other animals. The following year, the buffalo were gone, except for a few hundred that escaped into the British territory of Manitoba. Then it became a huge business gathering up the millions of bones littering the plains and shipping them off to the East, where they were ground up as fertilizer. In 1897 there were only twenty wild buffalo at Yellowstone National Park, plus a few others that were privately owned.

As the buffalo disappeared from the southern plains, the emphasis shifted to cattle and sheep, and the buffalo hunters gave way to the cowboys.

Kit Carson Pursues Horse Thieves

John C. Frémont

H Fremont

Of Kit Carson, John Frémont wrote, "Mounted on a fine horse, without a saddle, and scouring bare-headed over the prairies, Kit was one of the finest pictures of a horseman I have ever seen."

Buffalo Bill Cody wrote of him, "He was, apparently, at once the polished gentleman and the rough plainsman; shrinking from and courting danger at the same time; an adviser and the reckless mad-cap of his companions; large in his own estimation, yet modest and most unpretentious among his associates; a lover of peace, though still the organizer of discord."

The following excerpt is once again from Frémont's *Narrative of the exploring Expedition to the Rocky Mountains in the year 1842, and to Oregon and North California in the years 1843-44* (1846). This incident took place in 1844 on their second expedition. They had already passed through the Oregon Territory and down into Mexico, illegally entering the territory of Alta California. On April 24, 1844, they were at the edge of the Mohave Desert about fifty miles northeast of Los Angeles, when a Mexican man and a boy came into their camp seeking Frémont's help. This is one of the primary incidents that led to Carson becoming a Western hero in the eyes of his contemporaries.

In the afternoon we were surprised by the sudden appearance in the camp of two Mexicans—a man and a boy. The name of the man was Andreas Fuentes; and that of the boy, (a handsome lad, 11 years old,) Pablo Hernandez. They belonged to a party consisting of six persons, the remaining four being the wife of Fuentes, and the father and mother of Pablo, and

Santiago Giacome, a resident of New Mexico. With a cavalcade of about thirty horses, they had come out from Puebla de los Angeles [now just called Los Angeles], near the coast, under the guidance of Giacome, in advance of the great caravan, in order to travel more at leisure, and obtain better grass.

Having advanced as far into the desert as was considered consistent with their safety, they halted at the Archilette, one of the customary camping-grounds, about 80 miles from our encampment, where there is a spring of good water, with sufficient grass; and concluded to await there the arrival of the great caravan. Several Indians were soon discovered lurking about the camp, who, in a day or two after, came in and, after behaving in a very friendly manner, took their leave without awakening any suspicions. Their deportment begat a security which proved fatal.

In a few days afterwards, suddenly a party of about one hundred Indians appeared in sight, advancing towards the camp. It was too late, or they seemed not to have presence of mind to take proper measures of safety; and the Indians charged down into their camp, shouting as they advanced, and discharging flights of arrows. Pablo and Fuentes were on horse-guard at the time, and mounted according to the custom of the country. One of the principal objects of the Indians was to get possession of the horses, and part of them immediately surrounded the band; but, in obedience to the shouts of Giacome, Fuentes drove the animals over and through the assailants, in spite of their arrows; and, abandoning the rest to their fate, carried them off at speed across the plain. Knowing that they would be pursued by the Indians, without making any halt except to shift their saddles to other horses, they drove them on for about sixty miles and this morning left them at a watering-place on the trail called Agua de Tomaso. Without giving themselves any time for rest, they hurried on, hoping to meet the Spanish caravan, when they discovered my camp. I received them kindly, taking them into my own mess, and promised them such aid as circumstances might put it in my power to give.

25th.—We left the [Mohave] river abruptly, and, turning to the north, regained in a few miles the main trail, (which had left the river sooner than ourselves,) and continued our way across a lower ridge of the mountain, through a miserable tract of sand and gravel. We crossed at intervals the broad beds of dry gullies, where in the seasons of rains and melting snows there would be brooks or rivulets: and at one of these, where there was no indication of water, were several freshly-dug holes, in which there was water at the depth of two feet. These holes had been dug by the wolves, whose keen sense of smell had scented the water under the dry sand. They were nice little wells, narrow, and dug straight down; and we got pleasant water out of them.

The country had now assumed the character of an elevated and mountainous desert; its general features being black, rocky ridges, bald, and destitute of timber, with sandy basins

John C. Frémont

between. Where the sides of these ridges are washed by gullies, the plains below are strewed with beds of large pebbles or rolled stones, destructive to our soft-footed animals, accustomed to the soft plains of the Sacramento Valley. Through these sandy basins sometimes struggled a scanty stream, or occurred a hole of water, which furnished camping-grounds for travelers. Frequently in our journey across, snow was visible on the surrounding mountains; but their waters rarely reached the sandy plain below, where we toiled along, oppressed with thirst and a burning sun. But, throughout this nakedness of sand and gravel, were many beautiful plants and flowering shrubs, which occurred in many new species, and with greater variety than we had been accustomed to see in the most luxuriant prairie countries; this was a peculiarity of this desert. Even where no grass would take root, the naked sand would bloom with some rich and rare flower, which found its appropriate home in the arid and barren spot.

Beyond the first ridge, our road bore a little to the east of north, towards a gap in a higher line of mountains; and, after traveling about 25 miles, we

During the Civil War Kit Carson was a Union colonel of the New Mexico volunteers.

arrived at the Agua de Tomaso—the spring where the horses had been left; but, as we expected, they were gone. A brief examination of the ground convinced us that they had been driven off by the Indians. Carson and [Alexis] Godey volunteered, with the Mexican, to pursue them; and, well mounted, the three set off on the trail. At this stopping-place there are a few bushes, and a very little grass. Its water was a pool; but nearby was a spring, which had been dug out by Indians or travelers. Its water was cool—a great refreshment to us under a burning sun.

In the evening Fuentes returned, his horse having failed; but Carson and Godey had continued the pursuit. . . .

In the afternoon of the next day, a war-whoop was heard, such as Indians make when returning from a victorious enterprise; and soon Carson and Godey appeared, driving before them a band of horses, recognized by Fuentes to be part of those they had lost. Two bloody scalps, dangling from the end of Godey's gun, announced that they had overtaken the Indians as well as the horses. They informed us, that after Fuentes left them, from the failure of his horse, they continued the pursuit alone, and towards night-fall entered the mountains, into which the trail led. After sunset the moon gave light, and they followed the trail by moonshine until late in the night, when it entered a narrow defile, and was difficult to follow. Afraid of losing it in the darkness of the defile, they tied up their horses, struck no fire, and lay down to sleep, in silence and in darkness. Here they lay from midnight until morning. At daylight they resumed the pursuit, and about sunrise discovered the horses; and, immediately dismounting and tying up their own, they crept cautiously to a rising ground which intervened, from the crest of which they perceived the encampment of *four* lodges close by. They proceeded quietly, and had got within 30 or 40 yards of their object, when a movement among the horses discovered them to the Indians.

Giving the war-shout, they instantly charged into the camp, regardless of the number which the *four* lodges would imply. The Indians received them with a flight of arrows shot from their long-bows, one of which passed through Godey's shirt-collar, barely missing the neck: our men fired their rifles upon a steady aim, and rushed in. Two Indians were stretched upon the ground, fatally pierced with bullets. The rest fled, except a little lad that was captured. The scalps of the fallen were instantly stripped off; but in the process, one of them, who had two balls through his body, sprang to his feet, the blood streaming from his skinned head, and uttering a hideous howl. An old squaw, possibly his mother, stopped and looked back from the mountainsides she was climbing, threatening and lamenting. The frightful spectacle appalled the stout hearts of our men; but they did what humanity required, and quickly terminated the agonies of the gory savage.

They were now masters of the camp, which was a pretty little recess in the mountain, with a fine spring, and apparently safe from all invasion. Great preparations had been made to feast a large party, for it was a very proper place to rendezvous, and for the celebration of such orgies as robbers of the desert would delight in. Several of the best horses had been killed, skinned, and cut up; for the Indians living in mountains, and only coming into the plains to rob and murder, make no other use of horses than to eat them. Large earthen vessels were on the fire, boiling and stewing the horse-beef; and several baskets, containing 50 or 60 pairs of moccasins, indicated the presence, or expectation, of a considerable party.

They released the boy, who had given strong evidence of the stoicism, or something else, of the savage character, in commencing his breakfast upon a horse's head, as soon as he found he was not to be killed, but only tied as a prisoner.

Their object accomplished, our men gathered up all the surviving horses, fifteen in number, returned upon their trail, and rejoined us, at our camp, in the afternoon of the same day. They had rode about 100 miles, in the pursuit and return, and all in 30 hours.

The time, place, object, and numbers considered, this expedition of Carson and Godey may be considered among the boldest and most disinterested which the annals of western adventure, so full of daring deeds, can present. Two men, in a savage desert, pursue day and night an unknown body of Indians, into the defiles of an unknown mountain—attack them on sight, without counting numbers—and defeat them in an instant—and for what? To punish the robbers of the desert, and to avenge the wrongs of Mexicans whom they did not know. I repeat: it was Carson and Godey who did this—the former an American, born in the Boon's Lick County of Missouri; the latter a Frenchman, born in St. Louis—and both trained to western enterprise from early life.

Chasing Horse Thieves

Kit Carson

C Carson —

This is Kit Carson's version of the same event, taken from his autobiography.

There are a couple published versions of his autobiography. Since Carson was illiterate, he dictated his life story in 1856 to John Mostin, who was Carson's interpreter and secretary from 1854 to 1859. They then handed the manuscript over to Dr. De Witt C. Peters to prepare it for publication. When Peters rewrote it, he greatly embellished and expanded it, making it much more dramatic. The Peters version was then published as *The Life and Adventures of Kit Carson, the Nestor of the Rocky Mountains, from Facts Narrated by Himself* (1858). Fortunately Carson's original manuscript was preserved and eventually appeared as *Kit Carson's Own Story of His Life as Dictated to Col. and Mrs. D. C. Peters About 1856-57 And Never Before Published* (1926). Despite the title, it was actually dictated to John Mostin. Both books have since been reprinted under various titles.

This selection is from Carson's manuscript.

When we arrived at the Fort [Sutter's Fort, at what is now Sacramento, California, but was then in Mexico's Alta California Territory] we were naked and in as poor a condition as men possibly could be. We were well received by Mr. [John] Sutter and were furnished in a princely manner everything we required by him. We remained about a month at the Fort [and] made all the necessary arrangements for our return, having found no difficulty in getting all we required.

About the first of April, 1844, we were ready to depart. During our stay at the Fort, two of our party became deranged, I presume from the effects of starvation, and through receiving an abundance. One morning one of them jumped up [and] was perfectly wild. [He] inquired for his mule. It was tied close to him, but he started to the mountains to look for it. After some time, when his absence was known, men were sent in search of him. [They] looked through all the neighborhood, made inquiries of the Indians, but could hear nothing of him. [We] remained a few days awaiting his return, but as he did not come in, we departed. [We] left word with Sutter to make search, and if possible, find him. He done so, and, sometime after our departure, he was found. [He] was kept at the Fort and properly cared for until he got well, and then Mr. Sutter sent him to the States.

We took up the valley of the San Joaquin on our way home, we crossed the Sierra Nevada and Coast Range, where they join a beautiful, low pass; [we] continued under the Coast Range till we struck the Spanish trail, then to the Mohave River, a small stream that rises in the Coast Range and is lost in the Great Basin. [We then went] down it to where the trail leaves the Mohave River. [Illegible sentence.] We arrived only on the Mohave where we intended leaving it.

In the evening of the same day a Mexican man and boy came to our camp. They informed us that they were of a party of Mexicans from New Mexico. They and two men and women were encamped a distance from the main party herding horses, that they were mounted, the two men and women were in their camp, that a party of Indians charged on them for the purpose of running off their stock. They told the men and women to make their escape, that they would guard the horses. They ran the animals off from the Indians, left them at a spring in the desert about thirty miles from our camp.

We started for the place where they said they left their animals, found that they had been taken away by the Indians that had followed them.

The Mexican requested Frémont to aid him to retake his animals. He [Frémont] stated to the party that if they wished to volunteer for such purpose, they might do so, that he would furnish animals for them to ride. Godey and myself volunteered with the expectation that some men of our party would join us. They did not. We two and the Mexican took the trail of [the] animals and commenced the pursuit. In twenty miles the Mexican's horse gave out. We sent him back and continued on. Traveled during the night. It was very dark. Had to dismount to feel for the trail. By sign we became aware that the Indians had passed after sunset.

We were much fatigued—required rest, unsaddled, wrapped ourselves in the wet saddle blankets and laid down. Could not make any fire for fear of it being seen. Passed a miserably cold night. In the morning we arose very early, went down in a deep ravine, made a small fire to warm ourselves and, as soon as it was light, we again took the trail.

As the sun was rising [we] saw the Indians two miles ahead of us, encamped having a feast. They had killed five animals. We were compelled to leave our horses; they could not travel. We hid them among the rocks, continued on the trail, crawled in among the horses. A young one got frightened; that frightened the rest. The Indians noticed the commotion among the animals [and] sprung for their arms. We now considered it time to charge on the Indians. They were about thirty in number. We charged. I fired, killing one. Godey fired, missed, but reloaded and fired, killing another. There was only three shots fired and two were killed. The remainder run. I took the two rifles and ascended a hill to keep guard while Godey scalped the dead Indians. He scalped the one he had shot and was proceeded towards the one I had shot. He was not yet dead [and] was behind some rocks. As Godey approached, he raised, let fly an arrow. It passed through Godey's shirt collar. He again fell and Godey finished him.

We gathered the animals, drove them to where we had concealed our own, changed our horses and drove to camp, and safely arrived. [We] had all the animals, with the exception of those killed [by the Indians] for their feast.

We then marched on to where the Mexicans had left the two men and women. [The] men we discovered dead—their bodies horribly mutilated. The women, we supposed, were carried into captivity. But such was not the case, for a party traveling in our rear found their bodies very much mutilated and staked to the ground.

Charles Preuss, the expedition's cartographer, wrote in his diary,

Kit shot an Indian in the back; the bullet went through under the chest, and the Indian was able to run two hundred feet and get behind a rock. In the meantime, Godey had missed the other Indian, but loaded again and ran after him. Without knowing it, he passed within a few paces of the rock, from which the wounded Indian shot an arrow close past Godey's ears. Turning, he first dispatched this one, and then he shot the running Indian. Thus he was entitled to both scalps, for according to Indian custom the scalp belongs to the one who makes the kill. Godey rode into camp with a yelling war cry, both scalps on a rod before him.

An 1874 dime novel featuring Kit Carson. Colonel Henry Inman claimed that shortly before Carson's death in 1868, he was shown a dime novel with a cover depicting him "slaying seven Indians with one hand, while he clasped a fainting maiden with the other," to which he responded, after a long pause, "Gentlemen, that thar may be true, but I hain't got no recollection of it."

This incident and others led to Kit Carson becoming a legendary Western hero, and he was featured in dozens of dime novels, but he hardly fit the image. He was about five feet five inches tall, around 140 pounds, and bowlegged from spending so much time in the saddle. On meeting him in California, William Tecumseh Sherman—who would later become a famous Civil War general, but was at that time a lieutenant—said, "I can't express my surprise at beholding a small, stoop-shouldered man with reddish hair, freckled face, and soft blue eyes, and nothing to indicate extraordinary courage or daring. He spoke a little and answered questions in monosyllables."

Kit Carson knew and understood the Native Americans well from his many years with them. In 1854 he was appointed as the Indian agent for the Ute tribe. In this capacity he brought about many treaties between the Natives and US government. He wanted to live with them on their reservation, but this wasn't allowed. He was a better agent and sided with the Natives more than most agents. As General Sherman explained, "These Red Skins think Kit twice as big a man as me. Why his integrity is simply perfect. They know it, and they would believe him and trust him any day before me." Major General John Pope wrote, "Carson is the best man in the country to control these Indians and prevent war. . . . He is personally known and liked by every Indian."

Carson held this position until 1861, when he returned to the military and served in the Civil War primarily in the New Mexico Territory. As a colonel of the New Mexico volunteers, he fought alongside regular Union soldiers in 1862 in the Battle of Valverde, where they were defeated by Confederates from Texas and New Mexico.

With fewer troops on the frontier, the Natives began staging more raids, so Carson was assigned to deal with them. His campaign against the Mescalero Apache was quick, but dealing with the larger and more scattered Navajo tribe was much more difficult. He was ordered to kill any Navajo men who refused unconditional surrender and to capture all women and children. Though he had some sympathies for the tribe, he followed his orders.

With seven hundred men, Carson had to round up about nine thousand Navajo. Perhaps to minimize bloodshed, his primary tactic was to remove their means of survival by destroying their sheep and cattle; their corn, bean, squash, and melon crops; and their irrigated apple, apricot, and peach orchards. This eventually forced them to come in to save their families from starvation. They were then sent on "the Long Walk"—a succession difficult marches through the desert and across the mountains to a reservation at Fort Sumner in Eastern New Mexico, similar to the Cherokee's Trail of Tears. Many died along the way.

Once there, they and about four hundred Apache suffered for four years in disease-ridden confinement, and although they worked hard at farming in new soils and unfamiliar weather, their crops were wiped out by cutworms and then drought.

Near the end of the Civil War, Carson was promoted to brevet-brigadier general of the volunteers. He then returned to his position as Indian Agent. While he was illiterate before the war, he did learn to read and write by the end of it.

(*Note:* Military rank was a bit confusing during this period. One man could actually hold four ranks at the same time. He had his regular rank, but he could also be given a brevet rank—which was a temporarily higher rank, though without an increase in pay and with only limited authority. Thus an officer could be a colonel and also a brevet-general. In addition, he could hold a regular and brevet rank in the regular army, while also holding a regular and brevet rank in the volunteers. Also, it was common for an officer's men to refer to him by a brevet rank that he no longer held—such as Lieutenant Colonel Custer being referred to as "General Custer" long after his brevet commission was rescinded. Unfortunately, historically, brevet ranks do not usually have the word brevet in front of them, so it's often difficult to distinguish brevet ranks from regular ranks. And if that weren't enough, full ranks—such as brigadier general, lieutenant general, major general, and general—are often combined under the generic rank; in this case, "general.")

Although Carson is hated today by the Navajo and is occasionally blamed for atrocities for which he wasn't responsible, in his day he was popular with many of the chiefs who dealt with him. Throughout his life, he lived within three cultures—white, Mexican, and Native American—and easily passed among them.

"In January 1868," Buffalo Bill Cody wrote of Carson, "he was called to Washington [DC] to give evidence and advice in a matter of dispute between the Government and Apaches, and was accompanied on the trip by a deputation from that tribe. . . . His journey was more like a triumphal tour of some proclaimed hero fresh from the field of decisive battle, for everywhere along his route flags were flung to the breeze and cities put on a holiday attire as a token of the admiration generally felt for his character as a man and heroism as an Indian fighter."

Carson died a few months later. By the end of his life he'd traveled throughout the entire West while it was still wilderness, and he had toured much of the eastern United States as well. He's now considered one of America's greatest frontiersmen.

Indian Conflicts and the War in California

Kit Carson

C Carson

"Manifest Destiny" was basically the belief that God intended the United States to be in control of North America. It originated during the Revolutionary War with the desire to seize Canada, but evolved into the annexation of the West. The idea was used as both a justification and rationalization for a number of actions—from the Louisiana Purchase to the Mexican-American War.

The Mexicans had just won the War of Mexican Independence against Spain in 1821 and the new independent government found itself trying to control a vast expanse of sparsely populated land. It particularly had trouble ruling the distant territory of Alta California, which covered the area that is now California, Nevada, Utah, northern Arizona, western Colorado, and southwestern Wyoming.

After the Republic of Texas seceded from Mexico in 1836, it remained, in its eyes, independent until 1845, when it was annexed by the United States. Throughout its existence Mexico refused to recognize the Republic's independence, regarding it as a rebel province. Mexico had long warned the United States that if it annexed Texas, it would be war. And that's what happened. The Mexican-American War began in 1846.

When Frémont returned from their second expedition in 1844, his report greatly increased the US government's interest in Alta California. The United States was concerned about the possibility of war with Mexico and wanted to make sure Britain didn't use the opportunity to seize California, so they sent Frémont on his third expedition. Ostensibly his mission was to further explore the Great Basin and the Pacific Coast, and to discover pathways from one to the other, but in reality his mission was, in case the war started, to help get California for the United States.

In 1846 the Native American population of Alta California was about 100,000. This was down from the more than 300,000 that were there eighty years earlier.

Kit Carson in the 1860s

Two thirds had died, primarily from disease. There were also around 11,500 Hispanics, plus about 500 immigrants who considered themselves Mexican citizens. In addition to this, there were a couple thousand US citizens who had settled there since 1840. El Pueblo de los Angeles—now Los Angeles—was California's largest town, with 770 residents in 1830.

Kit Carson had a previous confrontation with Mexican authorities while on an illegal trapping expedition headed by Ewing Young in 1830. He wrote about it in the manuscript of his autobiography.

On the first September we struck camp, and returning by the same route which we had come, passing through San Fernando, we traveled to the Pueblo of Los Angeles, where the Mexican authorities demanded our passports. We had none. They wished to arrest us, but fear deterred them. They then commenced selling liquor to the men, no doubt for the purpose of getting the men drunk so that they would have but little difficulty in making the arrest. Mr. Young discovered their intentions, directed me to take three men, all the loose animals, packs, etc., and go in advance. He would remain with the balance of the party and endeavor to get them along. If he did not arrive at my camp by next morning, I was directed to move on as best I could and on my return to report the party killed; for Young would not leave them. They were followed by the Mexicans, furnishing them all the liquor they could pay for. All got drunk except Young.

The Mexicans would have continued with them till they arrived at the Mission of San Gabriel, then, being reinforced, arrest the party, only for a man by the name of James Higgins dismounting from his horse and deliberately shooting James Lawrence. Such conduct frightened the Mexicans, and they departed in all haste, fearing that, if men without provocation would shoot one another, it would require but little to cause them to murder them.

Unfortunately Carson didn't say anything about the reasons behind the shooting.

In the spring of 1845, Frémont, Carson, and sixty-one others set out on the third expedition and arrived in Alta California in December 1845. By the following spring they arrived at Sutter's Fort. This wasn't a military fort. It was actually a settlement built by German-born Swiss business-man Johann "John" Augustus Sutter Sr., who is now best known for his involvement in the discov-ery of gold that launched the California Gold Rush.

John Charles Frémont

He arrived in Yerba Buena, which is now called San Francisco, in 1839. At that time there were no permanent non-Native American settlements in Northern California's interior. He established the first, becoming a Mexican citizen and receiving a land grant of eleven square leagues—48,712 acres. His fort was in the California Central Valley near the junction of the Sacramento and American Rivers, where downtown Sacramento is now. Sutter's Fort became an important stopping point of settlers traveling overland on the California Trail from the United States.

Soon after their arrival in the spring of 1846, they began having trouble with Native Americans and the Mexican authorities.

We went up Carson River to Sutter's Fort; having crossed the Sierra Nevada, arrived safely at the Fort. The old Captain Sutter was there and was happy to see us and furnished everything we wanted.

We remained a few days, purchased about forty head of cattle and a few horses, then started to meet our camp. Went up the San Joaquin Valley, crossed, where it came out of the mountain and then on to King's River, up it to the head waters. During our march, from snow and travel-ing over rocks, our cattle had become very tender-footed. From the head of King's River we started back for the prairie and when we arrived we had no cattle, they having all given out. Had to leave behind all except those we killed for meat. As we were getting from the mountains during the night, some Indians crawled into our camp and killed two of our mules.

Next morning we started back for the fort. Through some mistake we had not found our camp, and, as we had lost nearly all our animals, it became necessary to return. The same evening we came on a party of Indians, killed five, and continued on to the fort. Arrived at the fort safely. All were afoot—lived principally on the meat of wild horses that we killed on the march.

We now started for San José, only remained a few days to recruit. Got a few animals and crossed the coast range to see if we could hear anything of our party under [Lieutenant James Theodore] Talbot. At San José we heard that they were on the San Joaquin. Frémont sent me and two men to meet them. We met them on the San Joaquin. Guided them to San José.

After we had all got together again, we set out for Monterey [the capital of Alta California] to get an outfit. When we arrived within about thirty miles of Monterey, Frémont received a very impertinent order from [Commandante] General [José] Castro [the acting governor of Alta California and its military commander], ordering him to immediately leave the country and, if he did not, that he would drive him out.

We packed up at dark, moved back about ten miles to a little mountain, found a good place and made camp. General Castro came with several hundred men and established his headquarters near us. He would frequently fire his big guns to frighten us, thinking by such demonstrations he could make us leave.

We had in the party about forty men armed with rifles. Castro had several hundred soldiers of cavalry and infantry. José received expresses from Monterey from Americans advising him to leave, that the Mexicans were strong and would surely attack us. He sent them word that he had done nothing to raise the wrath of the Mexican commander, that he was in performance of a duty, that he would let the consequences be what they may, execute, and retreat he would not. [*Note:* Frémont may have been trying to provoke a war.]

We remained in our position on the mountain for three days, had become tired of waiting for the attack of the valiant Mexican general. We then started for the Sacramento River, up it to Peter Lassen's [ranch].

There Frémont intended getting his outfit for the homeward trip. [We] remained some ten days.

During our stay at Lassen's, some Americans that were settled in the neighborhood came in stating that there were about 1,000 Indians in the vicinity making preparations to attack the settlements. [They] requested assistance of Frémont to drive them back. He and party and some few Americans that lived near, started for the Indian encampment. Found them to be in great force, as was stated. They were attacked. The number killed I cannot say. It was a perfect butchery. Those not killed fled in all directions, and we returned to Lassen's. Had accomplished what we went for and given the Indians such a chastisement that [it] would be long before they ever again would feel like attacking the settlements.

Of these supposedly hostile Indians, expedition worker and hunter Thomas Martin later recorded that they killed 24 with their initial rifle attack. Then they fought with sabers for three hours. In the end more than 175 Indians were dead. Expedition member Thomas Breckenridge estimated the dead at between 120 and 150.

We remained some time at Lassen's, received the best of treatment and finished [getting together] our outfit. Started for the Columbia River going up the Sacramento and passing near Shasta Butte [i.e., Mount Shasta]. Traveled on without any molestation, till we reached Klamath Lake at upper end of it.

Attempts by President James Polk to purchase the territories of Alta California and Santa Fé de Nuevo México from Mexico failed, so he annexed Texas and sent a militia under General Zachary Taylor into the new state, some of which was still claimed by Mexico. The Mexican military tried to make the Americans leave the disputed area, prompting Polk to claim the Mexicans had invaded the United States, giving him the justification to declare war, which he did on May 13, 1846.

A few days after we left, information was received in California that war was declared between the United States and Mexico. Lieutenant [Archibald] Gillespie, U.S. Marines, and six men were sent after us to have us come back. He had traveled about three hundred miles. His animals were giving out and, the rate he was traveling, he had but poor hopes of overtaking us. He then concluded to mount two men on his best animals and send them in advance. They come up to us on the lake, gave the communications to Frémont, and he, having but poor faith in the Klamath Indians, feared the situation of Gillespie and party; concluded to go and meet him. Took ten picked men, traveled about sixty miles, and met him encamped for the night.

He [Frémont] sat up till 12 or 1 o'clock reading the letters which he had received from the States. [Richard] Owens [a guide] and myself were rolled in our saddle blankets laying near the fire, the night being cold. Shortly after Frémont had laid down I heard a noise as of an axe striking, jumped up, saw there were Indians in camp, gave the alarm. The Indians had then tomahawked two men, [guide Basil] Lajeunesse and a Delaware, and were proceeding to the fire, where four Delaware were lying. They heard the alarm. Crane, a Delaware, got up, took a gun, but not his own. The one he had was not loaded. He was not aware of it and kept trying to fire; stood erect, received five arrows in the breast—four mortal—then fell.

The evening before I fired off my gun for the purpose of cleaning it, accidentally broke the tube, [so] had nothing but my pistol. Rushed on him, fired, cut the string that held his tomahawk. Had to retire, having no other [weapon]. [Lucien] Maxwell [the expedition's chief hunter] fired on him, hit him in the leg. As he was turning, Step [Joseph Stepperfeldt, hunter and gunsmith] fired, struck him in the back, ball passing near the heart, and he fell. The balance of his party then run. He was the bravest Indian I ever saw. If his men had been as brave as himself, we surely would all have been killed.

We lost three men and one slightly wounded. If we had not gone to meet Gillespie, he and party would have been murdered. The Indians evidently were on his trail for that purpose.

We apprehended no danger that night, and the men being much fatigued, no guard was posted. It was the first and last time that we failed in posting guard. Of the three men killed, Lajeunesse was particularly regretted. He had been with us in every trip that had been made. All of them were brave, good men. The only consolation we had for the loss was that if we had not arrived, Gillespie and his four men would have been killed. We lost three, so two lives had been saved.

After the Indians left, each of us took a tree, expecting that they would return. We remained so posted until daylight. We then packed up, took the bodies of the dead, and started for camp of the main party.

[We] had proceeded about ten miles. Could not possibly carry the bodies any farther. [We] went about half a mile off the trail and interred them, covering the graves with logs and brush, so that there was but little probability of their being discovered. [We] would have taken the bodies to our camp, but on account of the timber being so thick, the bodies knocked against the trees and, becoming much bruised, we concluded to bury them when we did.

We met our camp this evening. They had received orders to follow our trail. Camped for [the] night. Next morning [we planned] only to go a few miles. Left fifteen men in our old camp, concealed for the purpose of discovering the movements of the Indians. We had not left more than half an hour when two Indians came. They were killed and in short time their scalps were in our camp.

Frémont concluded to return to California, but [to] take a different route from that [by] which we had last entered the country, by going on the opposite side of the Lake. We were now encamped on a stream of the lake, nearly opposite to the place where we were encamped when we had the three men killed. In the morning, I was sent ahead with ten chosen men, with orders that if I discovered any large village of Indians to send word, and in case I should be seen by them, for me to act as I thought best.

I had not gone more than ten miles [when] I discovered a large village of about fifty lodges and, at the same time, by the commotion in their camp I knew that they had seen us and, considering it useless to send for reinforcements, I determined to attack them, charged on them, fought for some time, killed a number, and the balance fled.

Their houses were built of flag, beautifully woven. They had been fishing [and] had in their houses some ten wagon loads of fish they had caught. All their fishing tackle, camp equipage, etc. was there. I wished to do them as much damage as I could, so I directed their houses to be set on fire. The flag being dry it was a beautiful sight. The Indians had commenced the war with us without cause, and I thought they should be chastised in a summary manner. And they were severely punished.

Frémont saw at a distance the fire, [and] knowing that we were engaged, hurried to join us, but arrived too late for the sport. We moved on about two miles from where the Indian village had been, and camped for the night. After encamping, Owens and twenty men were sent back to watch for Indians. In an hour he sent us word that fifty Indians had returned to camp, I suppose to hunt their lost and bury their dead.

As soon as the information was received Frémont, with six men, started to him, taking a route different from that which Owens had taken, so as to keep concealed. As we got near the camp [we] only saw one Indian. As soon as he was seen, we charged him. I was in advance [and] got within ten feet of him. My gun snapped. He drew his bow to fire on me. I threw myself on one side of my horse to save myself. Frémont saw the danger in which I was, run horse over the Indian, throwing him on the ground, and before he could recover, he was shot. I considered that Frémont saved my life for, in all probability, if he had not run over the Indian as he did, I would have been shot. We could find no more Indians and, fearing that the party seen by Owens had returned to attack our camp, we returned. Arrived, but the Indians did not make an attack.

Next morning we struck out for the Valley of the Sacramento, about four days march. Maxwell and [hunter Auguste] Archambeau were traveling parallel with the party about three miles distant, hunting. They saw an Indian coming towards them. As soon as the Indian saw them, he took from his quiver some young crows that were tied thereon, concealed them in the grass, and continued approaching. As soon as he was within forty yards, he commenced firing. They did not intend to hurt him, wishing to talk, but the Indian keeping up a continuous fire and having shot rather close, they were compelled through self-defense to fire on him. They done so and [at] the first shot he fell, was immediately scalped.

We kept on till we struck the Sacramento and, in passing down the river, there was ahead of us a deep and narrow canyon. The Indians, supposing that we would go through it, placed themselves on each side for the purpose of attacking us as we passed. But we crossed the river and did not go into the canyon.

When we saw the Indians, Godey, myself, and another man—I have forgotten his name—took after them. We were mounted on mules. They could not be caught. One man, braver than the rest, hid himself behind a large rock and awaited our approach. We rode up near him. He came from his hiding place and commenced firing arrows very rapidly. We had to run back, being kept so busy dodging from his arrows, that it was impossible to fire. Retreating from the reach of his arrows, I dismounted and fired. My shot had the desired effect. He was scalped. [He] had a fine bow and beautiful quiver of arrows, which I presented to Lt. Gillespie. He was a brave Indian [and] deserved a better fate, but he had placed himself on the wrong path.

Continued our march and the next day, in the evening, Step and another man had gone out to hunt. We had nothing to eat in our camp; [were] nearly starving. They saw an Indian watching the camp. I presume he was waiting so that he might steal a mule. They gradually approached him—he was unaware of their presence—and, when near enough, fired. He received his death wound and then was scalped. The hunters then returned, having found no other game. We kept on our march to Peter Lassen's, and had no difficulty on the route. Then down the Sacramento to the Buttes. Here camp was made to await positive orders in regard to the war and [also] to hunt.

A party was sent from here to surprise Sonoma, a military post. They captured it, took one general and two captains prisoners, several cannon, and a number of small arms. After the fort had been taken, Frémont had heard positively of the war being declared. [He] then marched forward to Sonoma and found it in the possession of the men he had sent in advance.

This was the beginning of the Bear Flag Revolt, in which about thirty settlers calling themselves Osos, which is Spanish for "Bears," surrounded Mexican general Mariano Vallejo's house early on the morning of June 14, 1846. Outnumbered and unprepared, General Vallejo surrendered and was taken prisoner. The Osos declared what is now Northern California to be an independent republic, much like the Texans had done a decade earlier, and raised a flag designed by Abraham Lincoln's nephew that was similar to California's state flag, with a star, red stripe, a bear, and the words "California Republic." General Vallejo thought the bear looked more like a pig.

While Frémont supported the revolt and may have planned it, he tried to remain in the background so as not to officially commit US troops to the rebellion. There were soon around 90 Osos, though with a constant stream of immigrants arriving, Frémont was able to form the California Battalion with about 160 men by the time he reached Monterey. He was then promoted to the rank of major.

During our stay here, General Castro ordered one of his captains and a large force from San Francisco to attack us and drive us from the country. He [the captain] came over, found two of our men that were carrying news to the settlers that Sonoma was taken and war declared, whom he brutally murdered. He found that we were anxious to meet him and commenced his retreat. We followed him some six days and nights. He could not be found. He made his escape, leaving his animals, and he reached San Francisco and from there went to [the] Pueblo of Los Angeles, General Castro joining him, their object being to reorganize their forces.

This is the flag raised at Sonoma on June 14, 1846, during the Bear Flag Rebellion. It flew for almost a month before it was replaced with the US flag. It was designed by William Todd, a nephew of Abraham Lincoln's wife. He painted the words "California Republic" using blackberry juice. The flag was destroyed in the shake and bake of San Francisco's devastating 1906 earthquake and fire. A later version became California's state flag in 1911.

Frémont left a strong force at Sonoma. All the American settlers by this time had joined him. He then departed for Sutter's Fort and arrived safe. He placed the fort under military command. Left General Vallejo, the two captains, and an American named [Jacob] Leese—brother-in-law of the General—as prisoners there, in charge of the gentleman to whom he gave the command.

[He] then departed to Monterey. It had been taken before our arrival [on July 19, 1846], by the Navy, under command of Commodore [John] Sloat. A few days after our arrival, Sloat left and [Commodore Robert] Stockton [commander of US Naval Forces in the Pacific] assumed the command. Here we learned that General Castro had made his escape, [and] had gone to Los Angeles to organize. We found that we could not catch the Mexicans by following them on land, so Frémont proposed, if furnished a frigate, to take his men to San Diego. He then [would] get animals and go drive the Mexican troops from Los Angeles. The frigate *Cyane* was furnished him, com'd by Captain [Samuel] Dupont, a noble-souled fellow. In four days [we] arrived at our destination. Our forces were landed, 150 strong. Sufficiency of horses could not be procured at San Diego. Men were sent to scour the country [and to] press into service horses. We finally were mounted [and] started for Los Angeles. The Mexicans hearing of our approach, though they were 700 strong, fled—the Gen., Gov., and other officers for Sonora, the balance to all parts—so they did not come in contact with Americans.

We arrived within a league of the town, awaited a short time and Stockton, agreeable to the plan arranged before our departure from Monterey, arrived with a party of sailors and marines. The sailors and marines were as brave men as I ever saw and for the Commodore, it is useless for me to say anything, as he is known to be the bravest of the brave. We took possession of the town, remained some time, and, on the 5 Sept. '46, I was ordered to Washington [DC] as bearer of dispatches, having with me fifteen men.

I was ordered to go to Washington in sixty days, which I would have done if not directed by [Brigadier] General [Stephen] Kearny to join him. When I got within ten miles of Copper Mines I discovered an Apache village. It was about 10 a.m. They were at war. I knew that by staying where we were we would be seen, and, if we endeavored to pass them, they would also see us. So I had a consultation with Maxwell and we came to the conclusion to take for the timber and approach them cautiously, and if we were seen, to be as close as possible to them at the time of discovery. We kept on, had arrived about 100 yards of their village when they saw us. They were somewhat frightened to see us. We said we were friends, were en route to New Mexico [and] wished to trade animals. They appeared friendly. We chose a good place for our camp. They visited us and we commenced trading and procured of them a remount which was much required, our animals all having nearly given out.

We then started and in four days arrived at the first of the settlements. At our departure from California we had only 25 lbs. of dried meat, having a quantity of pinola. At the River village we got some corn. We would dry the corn by the fire, parch the corn, then eat it. Not having other food during our trip we suffered considerably for food.

On the 6th of October, [18]46 [near Socorro, New Mexico], I met General Kearny on his march to California. He ordered me to join him as his guide. I done so and [guide Thomas "Tom"] Fitzpatrick continued on with the dispatches.

General Kearny was the commander of the ground forces sent to seize the Alta California and New Mexico territories. He had already taken the New Mexico Territory and was appointed its military governor on August 18, 1846. After a difficult 850-mile march across the Sonora Desert, they were approaching San Diego.

On the 18th of October we left the Rio Del Norte, December 3rd arrived at Warner's Ranch [about fifty miles northeast of San Diego], and marched on for San Diego. On the 6th we heard of a party of Californians encamped on our route, probably one hundred in number. When we arrived within ten or fifteen miles of their camp, General Kearny sent Lieutenant [Thomas] Hammond with three or four Dragoons ahead to examine their position. He went, was accidentally discovered, [and] saw the encampment as reported. They were in an Indian village. He then returned to us and gave the information found. The General then determined to attack them. We packed up about one o'clock in the morning and moved on. When within a mile of their camp we discovered their spies that were out watching the road, and our movements. The trot and then the gallop was ordered to pursue the spies. They retreated to their camp.

This was the beginning of the Battle of San Pasqual, just southeast of what is now the city of Escondido—about thirty miles north of San Diego.

I was ordered to join Captain [Abraham] Johnston. He had fifteen men under his command. We were to proceed in advance. Our chief object was to get the animals belonging to the Californians. Captain [Benjamin] Moore, having a part of two companies of Dragoons and a party of twenty-five volunteers that had come from San Diego, was ordered to attack the main body. They were attacked, only fought about ten or fifteen minutes, then they retreated. When we were within 100 yards of their camp, my horse fell, threw me and my rifle was broken into two pieces. I came very near being trodden to death. Being in advance, the whole command had to pass over me. I finally saved myself by crawling from under them. I then ran on about 100 yards to where the fight had commenced. A Dragoon had been killed, I took his gun and cartridge box and joined the melee. Johnston and two or three of the dragoons were then killed. The Californians retreated, pursued by Moore for about three quarters of a mile. Moore had about 40 men mounted on horses, the balance on mules.

Two or three days before, we heard of a party of Californians that were en route to Sonora. Lieutenant [John "Black Jack"] Davidson and twenty-five dragoons and I were sent to surprise them. Done so and captured 70 or 80 head of animals, from which Moore got some 40 horses that were gentle and on which he mounted his men. The command in the pursuit had got very much scattered. The enemy saw the advantage, wheeled and cut off the forty that were in advance, and out of the forty [they] killed and wounded thirty-six. Captain Moore [was] among the slain, also Lieutenant Hammond. General Kearny [was] severely wounded and nearly every officer of the command was wounded.

Lieutenant Davidson, in charge of two Howitzers, came up. Before he could do anything every one of his party were killed or wounded, and one piece taken by the enemy. They captured it by lassoing the horse, fastening the lasso to the saddle and then running off. They got about 300 yards and endeavored to fire it at us, but could not. It was impossible for Lieutenant Davidson to do anything, having lost all his men, and one piece, and was himself lanced several times through the clothing, and one [ball] passing through [the] cantle of his saddle, which if the Californian had not missed his aim he also would be numbered among the slain.

We rallied in a point of rocks near where the advance had been defeated, remained there that night, the reason [being we did] not dare move on, and having a number of dead to bury. The dead were buried at the hours of 12 or 1 o'clock that night.

Next day we moved on. I had command of about fifteen men and was ordered in advance. Marched about seven miles. During the night the Californians had received reinforcements. They were now about 150 strong. During the day they would show themselves on every hill ahead of us.

Late in the evening we [were] still on the march, being within about 400 yards from the water where we intended to camp. They then charged on us, coming in two bodies. We were compelled to retreat about 200 yards to a hill of rocks that was to our left. After we had gained our position on the hill, the Californians took another hill, about 100 yards still to our left, and then commenced firing. Captains [William] Emory and [Henry] Turner took the command of what dragoons we had, charged the enemy on the hill, routed them, giving us full possession of their position. There [we] remained for the night.

The day on which we had the first fight, Kearny had sent three men as [an] express to San Diego to Commodore Stockton. This morning they had returned within five hundred yards of our camp. Were taken prisoners by the enemy in our sight. The day previous the horse of a Mexican Lieutenant was shot and he [was] taken prisoner. The parley was sounded and then [they] exchanged the Lieutenant for one of our men that was prisoner.

The place on which we were stationed had barely water enough for the men to drink. We had nothing to eat but mule meat. The animals were turned loose. As soon as any would get from the reach of our guns, they would be driven off by the enemy. The Mexicans had command of the water—probably about 500 yards in advance. Kearny concluded to march on, let the consequences be what they would. About 12 o'clock we were ready for the march, the wounded in ambulances [i.e., in litters on mule back]. The enemy, seeing our movements, saddled up, formed in our rear about 500 yards, the men being placed about 10 feet apart so that our artillery could do them but little damage.

Kearny had a council with his officers, they all knew that, as soon as we would leave the hill, we would again have to fight and, in our present condition it was not advisable. They came to the conclusion to send for reinforcements to San Diego. Lieutenant [Edward] Beale, of the Navy, and myself, volunteered to undertake to carry the intelligence to Stockton.

As soon as dark we started on our mission. In crawling over the rocks and brush our shoes making noise we took them off; fastened them under our belts. We had to crawl about two miles. We could see three rows of sentinels, all ahorseback. We would often have to pass within 20 yards of one. We got through, but had the misfortune to have lost our shoes, had to travel over a country, covered with prickly pear [cactus] and rocks, barefoot.

Got to San Diego the next night. Stockton immediately ordered 160 or 170 men to march to Kearny's relief. They were under the command of a Lieutenant, [and had] one cannon, which was drawn by the men by attaching to it ropes.

I remained at San Diego, Lieutenant Beale was sent aboard of frigate *Congress*; had become deranged from fatigue of the service performed, did not entirely recover for two years.

The next night the reinforcements reached Kearny. They lay by during the day, traveled by night. The enemy, however, discovered their approach, then fled. Kearny and [the] party then joined and moved on to San Diego having no further molestation.

Remained in San Diego about a month or so, till the wounded recovered. Then a force of 600 men were organized and started for Los Angeles under Stockton and Kearny. There were at Los Angeles about 700 Mexicans.

On the 8th January [18]47, we arrived within fifteen miles of Los Angeles. The Mexicans had a good position, being in command of a hill where we had to pass the river. We had two pieces of cannon. Stockton directed them. The Mexicans only stood a few rounds of fire, retreated, and we crossed the river, took possession of the hill, and encamped for the night.

On the 9th we approached within three miles of the Pueblo, having to fight during the day. Nothing however was necessary to be employed but the artillery. They could not make their appearance near us but Stockton, from his unerring aim of his guns, would make them leave.

On the 10th we took possession of the Pueblo. The place was evacuated by the Mexicans. They went to attack Frémont. He was thirty [miles] distant from the Pueblo, on the march thither with about 400 men that he had raised in the vicinity of Monterey. They met him, would not fight him, [and] surrendered to him in preference to any other of the commanders.

On the 12th, I think, Frémont found us at Los Angeles. We remained there during the winter without any further molestation.

General Kearny lost twenty-two men in the battle and had to be rescued by Stockton's marines. While his men recovered, Stockton and Frémont completed the conquest. For California the war ended on January 12, 1847, when Lieutenant-Colonel John Frémont and Mexican General Andres Pico signed the Treaty of Cahuenga. A year later gold was discovered in the hills above Sutter's Fort, prompting thousands of people to flood into California.

The war continued down in Mexico with various battles until Mexico City was invaded on September 13, 1847. The war was essentially over, though it wasn't official until a treaty was signed the following year, when Mexico signed over to the United States approximately half a million square miles—about 40 percent of Mexico's territory. The United States had lost only about seventeen hundred soldiers in battle, though another thirty-six thousand died from disease and other causes, but the real cost of the war came later. The acquisition of the new territory created heated debates over slavery and whether any of the new states should be slave states, which ultimately sparked the Civil War.

The Mexican–American War was not popular at the time. Then-Senator Abraham Lincoln was one of those who strongly criticized President Polk's reasons for starting the war, and the US House of Representatives passed an amendment to a bill stating it was "a war unnecessarily and unconstitutionally begun by the President of the United States."

Almost forty years later, President Ulysses S. Grant, who served in Mexico under General Zachary Taylor, wrote that the war was "one of the most unjust ever waged by a stronger against a weaker nation. It was an instance of a republic following the bad example of European monarchies, in not considering justice in their desire to acquire additional territory." Grant also said, "Texas had no claim beyond the Nueces River, and yet we pushed on to the Rio Grande and crossed it. I am always ashamed of my country when I think of that invasion." He believed the Civil War was God's punishment of the United States for what it did to Mexico, saying, "We got our punishment in the most sanguinary and expensive war of modern times."

John Frémont initially did not fare well after the war and found himself at the center of a dispute between General Kearny and Commodore Stockton. On taking control of California, Stockton appointed Frémont as its military commandant and civil governor, but Kearny had been sent out to establish the occupation government. Frémont remained loyal to Stockton, but the government sided with Kearny, so Kearny arrested Frémont in August 1847, shipping him back to Washington to be court-martialed. In January 1848 he was found guilty of mutiny, disobeying orders and conduct prejudicial to military discipline. He was sentenced to be dismissed from the service, but President Polk reversed the sentence, even though he approved of the verdict, except for the part about mutiny.

Frémont resigned and moved to his land in California's Mariposa County— the heart of what would be California's Gold Country. He had bought the forty-four thousand–acre land grant in 1846 from Mexico's last governor of Alta California. Once California was annexed to the United States, he spent six years in court establishing his ownership. He finally prevailed and became a multimillionaire during the Gold Rush. In 1850 he was elected as one of California's first two US senators.

In 1856 he was nominated as the Republican Party's first presidental candidate and campaigned on an anti-slavery platform, but lost to Democrat James Buchanan, who argued that slavery was a state issue and that outlawing it would lead to a civil war.

When the Civil War started and a secessionist movement in Missouri threatened its neutrality, Lincoln appointed Frémont a major general in the Union Army and made him the commander of the Army's Department of the West, headquartered in St. Louis. Frémont declared martial law and freed the slaves of all those who fought against the Union, but Lincoln felt this was premature and would drive neutrals and slave owners in the border states to join the Confederates. Frémont refused to change his proclamation, so Lincoln allowed Missouri's governor to rescind it and he replaced Frémont.

Frémont returned to the West and became involved in financing and building the railroads, but ended up losing his Gold Rush fortune and was convicted in 1873 for being part of a swindle. In 1878 President Hayes appointed him governor of the Arizona Territory, an office he held until 1883. After this he became destitute, relying on earnings from his wife's writing. In 1890 at the age of seventy-seven, he died in New York City from a burst appendix.

Discovering Gold

John Sutter

For a few years in the nineteenth century, John Sutter was the head of his own little empire. He was the first non-Native American to build a permanent settlement in Northern California's interior, and his fort played a vital role in Frémont's expeditions and the Mexican–American War.

Sutter was born in Germany to Swiss parents. In Switzerland, after becoming bankrupt at the age of thirty-one, he fled from his creditors to America, leaving behind his wife and four kids. Passing through New York, he headed to the backwoods of Indiana and then on to Missouri, where he was a merchant and innkeeper on the Santa Fe Trail for several years. Eventually he joined a party of fur traders and traveled across the Rocky Mountains to Fort Vancouver, at what is now Vancouver, Washington. Here he decided to create a colony in Alta California, but he had to figure out how to get there. Catching a ship, he ended up in the Sandwich Islands—now called Hawaii—for five months and then in Alaska, which at that time still belonged to Russia. Eventually he made it to Yerba Buena—now San Francisco—and then to Monterey, the capital of Alta California, where he applied for a land grant.

When Sutter arrived in 1839, Mexico was trying to maintain its foothold in Alta California by building its population there, and one of the ways it was doing this was by giving land grants to foreigners. When the Spanish first colonized the area in the 1700s, they did so through the mission system. The missions were religious outposts that were to spread Catholicism among the Native Americans, while also confirming Spanish claims on a region. Since the missionaries were almost self-supporting, they were an inexpensive way to colonize an area. Most had two priests and six to eight soldiers. They were built by what amounted to the slave labor of the Natives.

In 1853 John Sutter was appointed as an honorary major
general in the California militia.

Missions were constructed throughout New Spain, including a string of them
along the California Coast. During the 1600s, the Jesuits built fifteen missions running up Baja California, until they were forcibly expelled by King Charles III in 1767.
He replaced them with Dominicans and directed the Franciscans to begin building
missions, starting in San Diego. They ended up building twenty-one missions running
up the coast to Sonoma, thirty miles north of San Francisco. Each was separated by
a day's ride—about thirty miles. The division between the Jesuit and Franciscan missions became roughly the dividing line between Baja and Alta California.

Shortly after gaining independence from Spain, the Mexican government
ordered that all Spaniards under the age of sixty be deported from Mexican territories. Then in 1833 the Mexican congress passed an act selling the missions to raise
money for the further colonization of Baja and Alta California. Many of the missions
were sold for small amounts.

In addition to the missions, the Spanish established four presidios and three
pueblos. The presidios were military bases that were each responsible for a military
district. They were located at San Diego, Santa Barbara, Monterey, and Yerba Buena

(San Francisco). The Mexican military established a fifth one in Sonoma. The pueblos, or towns, were San José, El Pueblo de Nuestra Señora la Reina de los Angeles del Río de Porciúncula (Los Angeles), and Villa de Branciforte (Santa Cruz). Most of these were sparsely populated. For instance, the day Yerba Buena was taken by the United States in 1846, one historian's census listed that the town had a population of 149, the mission had 102, and there were 30 people in the presidio.

Another method for populating the territory was through land grants. These were given to reward someone, to encourage the creation or importation of food and supplies, and to encourage settlers by providing them with land. Some were single lots in towns, some were huge rancho grants. While the government of New Spain had only granted about thirty large ranchos, primarily to wealthy families, the Mexican government handed out more than eight hundred rancho grants, mainly to spur population growth.

Probably the primary reason Mexico wasn't able to hold on to Alta California was because its population wasn't growing fast enough. From 1800 to 1846, Mexico's population went from about 6 million to 8 million. The United States, on the other hand, was growing by leaps and bounds, largely because of immigration. The Irish potato famine and slow economies in Europe prompted many to flock to the States, plus about half a million Africans were brought into the country as slaves, causing the US population to balloon from about 5.3 million to 20.3 million during that same period of time. The population of Mexicans in California was only slowly increasing when American settlers suddenly began flooding in. Around 1,500 arrived in covered wagons in the single year of 1846. And this was before the Gold Rush.

Sutter was one of the earliest non-Spanish Europeans to settle on the West Coast. On arriving in Monterey in 1838, he went to the territory's governor and applied for a land grant in the California Central Valley. The governor probably thought Sutter was a touch insane to try to build a farm way out in the middle of Indian country, about sixty miles from any assistance, but this was what he needed to start populating that area.

The requirements to get the land were that Sutter had to become a Mexican citizen, convert to Catholicism, serve as an official of the Mexican government, and get the Native Americans under control. He also had to get twelve non-Native settlers to join him, build a permanent settlement, and then survive out there for a year. On completing these requirements, he would then receive a land grant of 11 square leagues—48,712 acres. That is what he did.

From what is now San Francisco Bay, he sailed up the largest river he could find, into the California Central Valley. Here he built his fort—what he hoped would become a new colony. He named it New Helvetia, or "New Switzerland," but everyone called it Sutter's Fort. With the help of the Native Americans, he soon had wheat fields, orchards, vineyards, and thirteen thousand cattle. Then in 1844 he was made a captain in the Alta California militia and was given another land grant of 22 square leagues, giving him a total of 146,136 acres.

In *The Exploring Expedition to the Rocky Mountains, Oregon and California* (1852), John Frémont described Sutter's Fort as it was when his second expedition arrived there in March 1844.

He had, at first, some trouble with the Indians; but, by the occasional exercise of well-timed authority, he has succeeded in converting them into a peaceable and industrious people. The ditches around his extensive wheat-fields; the making of the sun-dried bricks, of which his fort is constructed; the plowing, harrowing, and other agricultural operations, are entirely the work of these Indians, for which they receive a very moderate compensation—principally in shirts, blankets, and other articles of clothing. In the same manner, on application to the chief of a village, he readily obtains as many boys and girls as he has any use for. There were at this time a number of girls at the fort, in training for a future woolen factory; but they were now all busily engaged in constantly watering the gardens, which the unfavorable dryness of the season rendered necessary. . . .

A few years since, the neighboring Russian establishment of [Fort] Ross [on the coast about 120 miles west of Sutter's Fort], being about to withdraw from the country, sold to him a large number of stock, with agricultural and other stores, with a number of pieces of artillery and other munitions of war; for these, a regular yearly payment is made in grain.

The fort is a quadrangular adobe structure, mounting twelve pieces of artillery (two of them brass), and capable of admitting a garrison of a thousand men; this, at present, consists of forty Indians in uniform—one of whom was always found on duty at the gate. As might naturally be expected, the pieces are not in very good order. The whites in the employment of Capt. Sutter, American, French, and German, amount, perhaps, to thirty men. The inner wall is formed into buildings, comprising the common quarters, with blacksmith and other workshops; the dwelling-house, with a large distillery-house, and other buildings, occupying more the center of the area.

It is built upon a pond-like stream, at times a running creek communicating with the Rio de los Americanos [the American River], which enters the Sacramento [River] about two miles below. The latter is here a noble river, about three hundred yards broad, deep and tranquil, with several fathoms of water in the channel, and its banks continuously timbered. There were two vessels belonging to Capt. Sutter at anchor near the landing—one a large two-masted lighter, and the other a schooner, which was shortly to proceed on a voyage to Fort Vancouver for a cargo of goods.

In the seven years before the Gold Rush, twenty-seven hundred settlers reached California overland in covered wagons, and the California Trail was one of the three main overland trails that they took. Once in California, Sutter's Fort was the first major stopover on the primary branch of this trail, which then went on to San Francisco. In 1846, when the Donner Party became trapped by snow in the Sierra Nevadas, thirty-nine of the eighty-seven pioneers died, and some were forced to resort to cannibalism to survive. Sutter sent five relief parties that rescued the survivors and brought them back to his fort.

Things were looking good for Sutter. He had assisted Frémont leading up to and during the Mexican–American War, and suddenly when the western border of the United States jumped from Texas to the Pacific Ocean, he was in the perfect position to profit from it.

Then in 1848 gold was discovered at Sutter's Mill in the foothills of the Sierra Nevada. When word leaked out, everything went crazy. Practically the entire population of San Francisco headed for the hills. Schools closed. California's military governor requested the help of the general public in finding and arresting army and navy deserters. At the same time down in Los Angeles, Kit Carson left with dispatches for Washington, DC, along with news that gold had been found.

Suddenly people began flooding in from as far away as Australia, and the prices of everything shot through the roof. Early in 1848, lots in San Francisco were selling between sixteen dollars and fifty dollars each. By the end of the year, they were ten thousand dollars. In the next five years more than 300,000 people, mostly men, arrived. The population of San Francisco went from about 1,000 to around 25,000 in just two years—by 1870 it was 150,000. Meanwhile, the Native American population dropped during the same period from about 100,000 to 30,000 from disease, starvation, and attacks from settlers.

John Sutter's account of the first discovery of gold originally appeared in the November 1857 issue of *Hutchings' California Magazine*. Although there is general agreement that the discovery took place on January 24, 1848, James Marshall—the man who actually found the first nugget—claimed the date was actually between the 18th and the 20th.

It was in the first part of January 1848, when the gold was discovered at Coloma, where I was then building a sawmill. The contractor and builder of this mill was James W. Marshall, from New Jersey. In the fall of 1847, after the mill seat had been located, I sent up to this place Mr. P. [Peter] L. Wimmer with his family, and a number of laborers, from the disbanded Mormon Battalion; and a little later I engaged Mr. [Charles] Bennet from Oregon to assist Mr. Marshall in the mechanical labors of the mill. Mr. Wimmer had the team in charge, assisted by his young sons, to do the necessary teaming, and Mrs. Wimmer did the cooking for all hands.

I was very much in need of a new sawmill to get lumber to finish my large flouring mill of four run of stones at Brighton, which was commenced at the same time, and was rapidly progressing; likewise for other buildings, fences, etc., for the small village of Yerba Buena (now San Francisco). [Yerba Buena was renamed San Francisco in 1847. In 1848, before the Gold Rush, it had 200 buildings and a population of 812.] In the City Hotel, (the only one) at the dinner table this enterprise was unkindly called "another folly of Sutter's," as my first settlement at the old fort near Sacramento City was called by a good many, "a folly of his," and they were about right in that, because I had the best chances to get some of the finest locations near the settlements; and even well-stocked rancho's had been offered to me on the most reasonable conditions; but I refused all these good offers, and preferred to explore the wilderness, and select a territory on the banks of the Sacramento.

It was a rainy afternoon when Mr. Marshall arrived at my office in the Fort, very wet. I was somewhat surprised to see him, as he was down a few days previous; and then, I sent up to Coloma a number of teams with provisions, mill irons, etc., etc. He told me then that he had some important and interesting news which he wished to communicate secretly to me, and wished me to go with him to a place where we should not be disturbed, and where no listeners could come and hear what we had to say.

I went with him to my private rooms; he requested me to lock the door; I complied, but I told him at the same time that nobody was in the house except the clerk, who was in his office in a different part of the house; after requesting of me something which he wanted, which my servants brought and then left the room, I forgot to lock the doors, and it happened that the door was opened by the clerk just at the moment when Marshall took a rag from his pocket, showing me the yellow metal: he had about two ounces of it; but how quick Mr. M. put the yellow metal in his pocket again can hardly be described. The clerk came to see me on business, and excused himself for interrupting me, and as soon as he had left I was told, "now lock the doors; didn't I tell you that we might have listeners?" I told him that he need fear nothing about that, as it was not the habit of this gentleman; but I could hardly convince him that he need not to be suspicious. Then Mr. M. began to show me this metal, which consisted of small pieces and specimens, some of them worth a few dollars; he told me that he had expressed his opinion to the laborers at the mill, that this might be gold; but some of them were laughing at him and called him a crazy man, and could not believe such a thing.

James Marshall described his discovery this way:

While we were in the habit at night of turning the water through the tailrace we had dug for the purpose of widening and deepening the race, I used to go down in the morning to see what had been done by the water through the night; and about half past seven o'clock on or about the 19th of January—I am not quite certain to the day, but it was between the 18th and the 20th of that month—1848, I went down as usual, and after shutting off the water from the race I stepped into it, near the lower end, and there, upon the rock, about six inches beneath the surface of the water, I discovered the gold. I was entirely alone at the time.

I picked up one or two pieces and examined them attentively; and having some general knowledge of minerals, I could not call to mind more than two which in any way resembled this—sulphuret of iron, very bright and brittle; and gold, bright, yet malleable; I then tried it between two rocks, and found that it could be beaten into a different shape, but not broken. I then collected four or five pieces and went up to Mr. Scott (who was working at the carpenter's bench making the mill wheel) with the pieces in my hand and said, "I have found it."

After having proved the metal with *aqua fortis* [i.e., a solution of nitric acid], which I found in my apothecary shop, likewise with other experiments, and read the long article "gold" in the *Encyclopedia Americana*, I declared this to be gold of the finest quality, of at least 23 carats. After this Mr. M. had no more rest nor patience, and wanted me to start with him immediately for Coloma; but I told him I could not leave as it was late in the evening and nearly supper time, and that it would be better for him to remain with me till the next morning, and I would travel with him, but this would not do. He asked me only, "Will you come to-morrow morning?" I told him yes, and off he started for Coloma in the heaviest rain, although already very wet, taking nothing to eat.

I took this news very easy, like all other occurrences good or bad, but thought a great deal during the night about the consequences which might follow such a discovery. I gave all my necessary orders to my numerous laborers, and left the next morning at 7 o'clock, accompanied by an Indian soldier, and *vaquero* [i.e., cowboy], in a heavy rain, for Coloma.

About half way on the road I saw at a distance a human being crawling out from the brushwood. I asked the Indian who it was: he told me "the same man who was with you last evening." When I came nearer I found it was Marshall, very wet; I told him that he would have done better to remain with me at the fort than to pass such an ugly night here but he told me that he went up to Coloma, (54 miles) took his other horse and came half way to meet me; then we rode up to the new El Dorado. In the afternoon the weather was clearing up, and we made a prospecting promenade.

The next morning we went to the tailrace [water from the mill's waterwheel flows out of the mill through the tailrace] of the mill, through which the water was running during the night, to clean out the gravel which had been made loose, for the purpose of widening the race; and after the water was out of the race we went in to search for gold. This was done every morning: small pieces of gold could be seen remaining on the bottom of the clean washed bed rock. I went in the race and picked up several pieces of this gold, several of the laborers gave me some which they had picked up, and from Marshall I received a part. I told them that I would get a ring made of this gold as soon as it could be done in California; and I have had a heavy ring made, with my family's coat of arms engraved on the outside, and on the inside of the ring is engraved, "The first gold, discovered in January, 1848." Now if Mrs. Wimmer possesses a piece which has been found earlier than mine Mr. Marshall can tell, as it was probably received from him. I think Mr. Marshall could have hardly known himself which was exactly the first little piece, among the whole.

The Wimmer Nugget is now on display in the Bancroft Library at the University of California, Berkeley. It is most likely the first one found by Marshall.

The next day I went with Mr. M. on a prospecting tour in the vicinity of Coloma, and the following morning I left for Sacramento. Before my departure I had a conversation with all hands. I told them that I would consider it as a great favor if they would keep this discovery secret only for six weeks, so that I could finish my large flour mill at Brighton—with four run of stones—which had cost me already about from 24 to 25,000 dollars [roughly $660,000 today]—the people up there promised to keep it secret so long. On my way home, instead of feeling happy and contented, I was very unhappy, and could not see that it would benefit me much, and I was perfectly right in thinking so; as it came just precisely as I expected. I thought at the same time that it could hardly be kept secret for six weeks, and in this I was not mistaken, for about two weeks later, after my return, I sent up several teams in charge of a white man, as the teamsters were Indian boys. This man was acquainted with all hands up there, and Mrs. Wimmer told him the whole secret; likewise the young sons of Mr. Wimmer told him that they had gold, and that they would let him have some too; and so he obtained a few dollars' worth of it as a present.

As soon as this man arrived at the fort he went to a small store in one of my outside buildings, kept by Mr. [Charles] Smith, a partner of Samuel Brannan, and asked for a bottle of brandy, for which he would pay the cash; after having the bottle he paid with these small pieces of gold. Smith was astonished and asked him if he intended to insult him; the teamster told him to go and ask me about it; Smith came in, in great haste, to see me, and I told him at once the truth—what could I do? I had to tell him all about it. He reported it to Mr. S. Brannan, who came up immediately to get all possible information, when he returned and sent up large supplies of goods, leased a larger house from me, and commenced a very large and profitable business; soon he opened a branch house of business at Mormon Island.

Brannan was the Mormon Church's first president of its California mission. He had arrived in 1846 at the head of a group of 230 Mormon settlers.

Mr. Brannan made a kind of claim on Mormon Island, and put a tolerably heavy tax on "The Latter Day Saints." I believe it was 30 per cent, which they paid for some time, until they got tired of it, (some of them told me that it was for the purpose of building a temple for the honor and glory of the Lord.)

So soon as the secret was out my laborers began to leave me, in small parties first, but then all left, from the clerk to the cook, and I was in great distress; only a few mechanics remained to finish some very necessary work which they had commenced, and about eight invalids, who continued slowly to work a few teams, to scrape out the mill race at Brighton. The Mormons did not like to leave my mill unfinished, but they got the gold fever like everybody else. After they had made their piles they left for the Great Salt Lake. So long as these people have been employed by me they have behaved very well, and were industrious and faithful laborers, and when settling their accounts there was not one of them who was not contented and satisfied.

Then the people commenced rushing up from San Francisco and other parts of California, in May, 1848. In the former village, only five men were left to take care of the women and children. The single men locked their doors and left for "Sutter's Fort," and from there to the El Dorado. For some time the people in Monterey and farther south would not believe the news of the gold discovery, and said that it was only a "Ruse de Guerre" of Sutter's, because he wanted to have neighbors in his wilderness. From this time on I got only too many neighbors, and some very bad ones among them.

What a great misfortune was this sudden gold discovery for me! It has just broken up and ruined my hard, restless, and industrious labors, connected with many dangers of life, as I had many narrow escapes before I became properly established.

From my mill buildings I reaped no benefit whatever, the mill stones even have been stolen and sold.

My tannery, which was then in a flourishing condition, and was carried on very profitably, was deserted, a large quantity of leather was left unfinished in the vats; and a great quantity of raw hides became valueless as they could not be sold; nobody wanted to be bothered with such trash, as it was called. So it was in all the other mechanical trades which I had carried on; all was abandoned, and work commenced or nearly finished was all left, to an immense loss for me. Even the Indians had no more patience to work alone, in harvesting and threshing my large wheat crop out; as the whites had all left, and other Indians had been engaged by some white men to work for them, and they commenced to have some gold for which they were buying all kinds of articles at enormous prices in the stores; which, when my Indians saw this, they wished very much to go to the mountains and dig gold. At last I consented, got a number of wagons ready, loaded them with provisions and goods of all kinds, employed a clerk, and left with about one hundred Indians, and about fifty Sandwich Islanders (Kanakas) [now known as Hawaiians] which had joined those which I brought with me from the Islands. The first camp was about ten miles above Mormon Island, on the south fork of the American River.

In a few weeks we became crowded, and it would no more pay, as my people made too many acquaintances. I broke up the camp and started on the march further south, and located my next camp on Sutter Creek (now in Amador County), and thought that I should there be alone. The work was going on well for a while, until three or four traveling grog-shops surrounded me at from one and half to two miles distance from the camp; then, of course, the gold was taken to these places for drinking, gambling, etc., and then the following day they were sick and unable to work, and became deeper and more indebted to me, and particularly the Kanakas. I found that it was high time to quit this kind of business, and lose no more time and money. I therefore broke up the camp and returned to the Fort, where I disbanded nearly all the people who had worked for me in the mountains digging gold. This whole expedition proved to be a heavy loss to me.

At the same time I was engaged in a mercantile firm in Coloma, which I left in January, 1849—likewise with many sacrifices. After this I would have nothing more to do with the gold affairs. At this time, the Fort was the great trading place where nearly all the business was trans-acted. I had no pleasure to remain there, and moved up to Hock Farm, with all my Indians, and who had been with me from the time they were children. The place was then in charge of a Major Domo.

It is very singular that the Indians never found a piece of gold and brought it to me, as they very often did other specimens found in the ravines. I requested them continually to bring me some curiosities from the mountains, for which I always recompensed them. I have received ani-mals, birds, plants, young trees, wild fruits, pipe clay, stones, red ochre, etc., etc., but never a piece of gold. Mr. [James] Dana of the scientific corps of the expedition under Com. [Charles] Wilkes' Exploring Squadron, told me that he had the strongest proof and signs of gold in the vicinity of Shasta Mountain, and further south. A short time afterwards, [Swedish naturalist] Doctor [G. M. Waseurtz af] Sandels, a very scientific traveler, visited me, and explored a part of the country in a great hurry, as time would not permit him to make a longer stay.

He told me likewise that he found sure signs of gold, and was very sorry that he could not explore the Sierra Nevada. He did not encour-age me to attempt to work and open mines, as it was uncertain how it would pay and would probably be only for a government. So I thought it more prudent to stick to the plow, notwithstanding I did know that the country was rich in gold, and other minerals. An old attached Mexican servant who followed me here from the United States, as soon as he knew that I was here, and who understood a great deal about working in placers, told me he found sure signs of gold in the mountains on Bear Creek, and that we would go right to work after returning from our campaign in 1845, but he became a victim to his patriotism and fell into the hands of the enemy near my encampment, with dispatches for me from Gen. [Manuel] Micheltorena [the governor of Alta California from 1842 to 1845], and he was hung as a spy, for which I was very sorry.

By this sudden discovery of the gold, all my great plans were destroyed. Had I succeeded for a few years before the gold was discovered, I would have been the richest citizen on the Pacific shore; but it had to be different. Instead of being rich, I am ruined, and the cause of it is the long delay of the United States Land Commission of the United States Courts, through the great influence of the squatter lawyers. Before my case will be decided in Washington, another year may elapse, but I hope that justice will be done me by the last tribunal—the Supreme Court of the United States. By the Land Commission and the District Court it has been decided in my favor. The Common Council of the city of Sacramento, composed partly of squatters, paid Adelpheus Felch, (one of the late Land Commissioners, who was engaged by the squatters during his office), $5,000, from the fund of the city, against the will of the taxpayers, for which amount he has to try to defeat my just and old claim from the Mexican Government, before the Supreme Court of the United States in Washington.

When the Gold Rush hit, Sutter's employees abandoned him to search for gold. Squatters took chunks of his land. New arrivals and bandits stole everything, even his millstone. His cattle were slaughtered and his crops destroyed. Sutter instantly became famous, but he was left bankrupt once again and had to sell his fort. His family came over from Switzerland to join him, and he retired to a ranch in Marysville for a few years until squatters once again took his land, rustlers his cattle, and some men set his house on fire.

After California became part of the United States, he spent thirty-two years in court fighting to get some of his land back, or at least compensation, but failed. Shortly before he died in 1880, he was awarded a pension from the State of California.

During the Gold Rush, an average of seventy-six tons of gold were mined each year. In ten years, $550 million worth came out of California. That's something like $177 billion in today's dollars.

Riding for the Pony Express

Buffalo Bill Cody

[signature: W. F. Cody / Buffalo Bill]

With the Gold Rush raging and the population west of the Rockies booming, there was a great need for communication with the East. At that time, St. Joseph, on the western border of Missouri, was the farthest west that the railroads and telegraphs reached. Sending letters by sea took twenty-six to thirty days, while sending them by stagecoach from St. Louis to San Francisco took twenty-two to twenty-five days. With the Civil War looming, getting information back and forth became very important. In order to provide speedier mail, a freight company began a horse-relay service called the Pony Express.

They had messengers who transported the letters by train from both New York and Washington, DC, to St. Joseph. Then with about 500 top-rate horses and between 90 and 200 lightweight riders, they carried the letters through between 119 and 190 relay stations along the 2,000-mile trail from St. Joseph to Sacramento, where the letters were taken by steamer to San Francisco.

Service began on April 3, 1860. Riding around the clock, day and night, it usually took seven to ten days to complete the journey one way in summer and twelve to sixteen days during winter. Once a week riders began the journey from each end of the route at 5 p.m. on Tuesday, though departures from St. Joseph were soon moved to 9 a.m. on Friday. After three months they expanded the service to twice a week.

The route passed through the territories of Kansas, Nebraska, Utah, and Nevada—what are now the states of Kansas, Nebraska, Colorado, Wyoming, Utah, and Nevada. Parts of the route—both riders and stations—illegally trespassed on Native American land, which inevitably resulted in violent conflicts that often disrupted the service. This was especially true during the Pyramid Lake Indian War near the silver mines of western Nevada Territory, which was sparked at the Williams Station in Carson Valley.

According to the *San Francisco Daily Evening Bulletin* of May 24, 1860, "an old Indian man went to [James O.] Williams's house with a squaw, when four white men tied the buck Indian, and then each committed an atrocious outrage upon the Indian woman. They then let the buck go. He afterwards came back with other Indians, and put a white woman, who was in the house, out of doors, and also three white men who had nothing to do with the outrage. They then bound the four white men who abused the squaw, and burned them in the house."

The miners and settlers, fearing an Indian uprising, raised a volunteer militia with the intention of "ridding the area" of all the Natives. This provoked further raids by the Native Americans, usually on easy targets like the Pony Express riders and stations. The conflict stopped the Pony Express service for a while and slowed it down considerably when the riders needed military escorts. Some stations had to be converted into fortresses. By January 1861 practically the entire Pony Express route was covered by snow, creating more delays.

Initially it cost $5 in gold to send an ounce of mail, or a fraction thereof—approximately $120 in today's dollars. Special lightweight paper made it possible to send an eight- to ten-page letter for about half that amount. The price eventually dropped to $2 per ounce. Each run transported up to twenty pounds of mail.

In order to keep weight to a minimum, the riders had to be small and thin. One ad in a California newspaper stated, "Wanted. Young, skinny, wiry fellows. Not over 18. Must be expert riders. Willing to risk death daily. Orphans preferred." Actually, the riders ranged in age from eleven to mid-forties, though most of them were around twenty. Their average weight was about 120 pounds, and very few, if any, were orphans.

Buffalo Bill claimed he was one of these riders, and most historians include him as the most famous of the Pony Express riders.

William "Buffalo Bill" Cody is now primarily known as a showman, similar to P. T. Barnum, but he was actually very different. While he did stage Wild West shows throughout the United States and Europe, Cody was an authentic Western celebrity. He was a drover, a trapper, prospector, stagecoach driver, wagon master, and buffalo hunter—which was where he received his nickname. Off and on for many years, he served as a scout and guide for the army. At the age of eighteen he became a Union soldier, serving for nineteen months until the end the Civil War. He then became a civilian scout for the Army, tracking and fighting Native Americans, and took part in the campaign that followed Custer's defeat in 1876. In 1872 he received the Medal of Honor—America's highest military award. Shortly after that he joined the theater as an actor. Eventually he began staging his huge Wild West shows.

Though Buffalo Bill had little schooling, he did teach himself to write, since writing books and articles became a good source of income for him. Many of his books were published pretty much as he wrote them, except that he didn't use capital letters or punctuation, so his editors had to fix that. He even wrote a few of the early dime novels that

Buffalo Bill at age eighteen or nineteen in about 1864 or 1865 as a private in the 7th Kansas Cavalry

bear his name, but he seems to have quickly tired of this and soon had ghostwriters—such as Colonel Prentiss Ingraham—penning them for him. He did continue writing nonfiction Western and frontier history. He particularly enjoyed writing about scouts, pioneers, and frontiersmen, such as Daniel Boone, Davy Crockett, and Kit Carson. As was common at the time, he did tend to exaggerate, much like Mark Twain. Later in his life he was more prone to exaggeration and, unfortunately for historians, he did tell some tall tales, but that was because he knew it was what the public wanted. His primary goal was to entertain.

Buffalo Bill's autobiography was originally published as *The Life of Hon. William F. Cody, Known as Buffalo Bill the Famous Hunter, Scout and Guide* (1879). It was reprinted in various editions under various titles. While a few people have suggested it may have been ghostwritten, most scholars have concluded that he wrote it himself.

I have blended together the best of four editions of the book to produce this selection and the one about Custer that appears later in this book. These editions were *The Life of Hon. William F. Cody, Known as Buffalo Bill the Famous Hunter, Scout and Guide* (1879), *Story of the Wild West and Camp-fire Chats* (1888), *The Life and Adventures of "Buffalo Bill"* (1917), and the posthumous *An Autobiography of Buffalo*

Bill (Colonel W. F. Cody) (1920). Some editions contain details not found in the others, though for the most part they are just worded a bit differently, making them easier to read. I also compared these to *The Adventures of Buffalo Bill* (1904). I did not use *True Tales of the Plains* (1908), which appears to be a compilation by several ghostwriters and contains some outlandish tales, such as how at age fourteen he saved the life of a three-year-old girl by shooting a charging buffalo with the buffalo crashing to the ground, dying at her feet.

Unfortunately, Buffalo Bill's autobiographies are unreliable. For the most part he wrote the truth, with some exaggerations and errors of memory. But he also mixed fact with fiction, drawing elements from the plays he performed and from the dime novels written about him. He probably saw this as an extension of the frontier tradition of telling tall tales around the campfire. It helped further his career and people loved it. They were looking for a Wild West hero, and he gave it to them.

Buffalo Bill was only fourteen years old in the winter of 1860–1861—the date at which this selection begins. This is one of the most hotly debated sections of his autobiography. Some cite it as the prime example of his tall tales, saying he was exaggerating his job as a messenger boy for the Russell, Majors, & Waddell Company—the company that owned the Overland Stage Company and the Pony Express—and that he was actually in school that year. Others point out that there were people who knew him at that time who later confirmed that Buffalo Bill worked for the Pony Express, but these sources are unreliable. Records from this time are sketchy.

He did work for the company as a messenger for two months in the summer of 1857 when he was eleven, riding three miles between the company's office and the telegraph office at Fort Leavenworth. The following year he worked for the company on a freight wagon train, herding and tending the train's horses. He did attend school in 1860 and 1861, but it's possible he was in school part of the time, while also riding in the Pony Express. He did have a history of working for the company. On the other hand, his account does contain a number of things that are known to be untrue. For example, Hickok was not a rider and Cody did not go with Hickok to retrieve horses stolen by Native Americans. He also combined a couple of incidents that happened in 1859 and 1862, and placed them in 1861. Those parts of his account are not included here.

So far the evidence is inconclusive, though his story is looking more like fiction. We just won't know for sure one way or the other until new evidence comes to light.

Here is what he wrote about it.

The great Pony Express, about which so much has been said and written, was at that time just being started. The line was being stocked with horses and put into good running condition. At Julesburg I met Mr. George Chrisman, the leading wagonmaster of Russell, Majors & Waddell, who had always been a good friend to me. He had bought out "Old Jules," and was then the owner of Julesburg ranch, and the agent of the Pony Express line. He hired me at once as a Pony Express rider, but as I was so young he thought I would not be able to stand the fierce riding which was required of the messengers. He knew, however, that I had been raised in the saddle—that I felt more at home there than in any other place.

The route was from St. Joseph, Missouri, to Sacramento, California, a distance of two thousand miles, across the Plains, over a dreary stretch of sagebrush and alkali desert, and through two great mountain ranges.

The system was really a relay race against time. Stations were built at intervals averaging fifteen miles apart. A rider's route covered three stations, with an exchange of horses at each, so that he was expected at the beginning to cover close to forty-five miles—a good ride when one must average fifteen miles an hour.

The firm undertaking the enterprise had been busy for some time picking the best ponies to be had for money, and the lightest, most wiry and most experienced riders. This was a life that appealed to me, and I struck for a job. I was pretty young in years, but I had already earned a reputation for coming safe out of perilous adventures, and I was hired.

Naturally our equipment was the very lightest. The messages which we carried were written on the thinnest paper to be found. These we carried in a waterproof pouch, slung under our arms. We wore only such clothing as was absolutely necessary.

The first trip of the Pony Express was made in ten days—an average of two hundred miles a day. But we soon began stretching our riders and making better time. Soon we shortened the time to eight days. President Buchanan's last Presidential message in December, 1860, was carried in eight days. President Lincoln's inaugural, the following March, took only seven days and seventeen hours for the journey between St. Joseph and Sacramento.

We soon got used to the work. When it became apparent to the men in charge that the boys could do better than forty-five miles a day, the stretches were lengthened. The pay of the rider was from $100 to $125 a month [$16,000 to $20,000 today]. It was announced that the further a man rode the better would be his pay. That put speed and endurance into all of us.

Stern necessity often compelled us to lengthen our day's work even beyond our desires. In the hostile Indian country, riders were frequently shot. In such an event the man whose relief had been killed had to ride on to the next station, doing two men's ride. Road-agents were another menace, and often they proved as deadly as the Indians.

In stretching my own route I found myself getting further and further west. Finally I was riding well into the foothills of the Rockies. Still further west my route was pushed. Soon I rode from Red Buttes to Sweetwater, a distance of seventy-six miles [in what was then part of the Nebraska Territory that would later become Wyoming]. Road-agents and Indians infested this country. I never was quite sure when I started out when I should reach my destination, or whether I should never reach it at all.

I wrote to mother and told her how well I liked the exciting life of a Pony Express rider. She replied, and begged of me to give it up, as it would surely kill me. She was right about this, as fifteen miles an hour on horseback would, in a short time, shake any man "all to pieces"; and there were but very few, if any, riders who could stand it for any great length of time. Nevertheless, I stuck to it for two months, and then, upon receiving a letter informing me that my mother was very sick, I gave it up and went back to the old home in Salt Creek Valley.

Adventures on the Overland Road

As the warm days of summer [1861] approached I longed for the cool air of the mountains; and to the mountains I determined to go. After engaging a man to take care of the farm, I proceeded to Leavenworth and there met my old wagonmaster and friend, Lewis Simpson, who was fitting out a train at Atchison and loading it with supplies for the Overland Stage Company, of which Mr. Russell, my old employer, was one of the proprietors. Simpson was going with this train to Fort Laramie and points further west.

"Come along with me, Billy," said he, "I'll give you a good lay-out. I want you with me."

"I don't know that I would like to go as far west as that again," replied I, "but I do want to ride the Pony Express once more; there's some life in that."

"Yes, that's so; but it will soon shake the life out of you," said he. "However, if that's what you've got your mind set on, you had better come to Atchison with me and see Mr. Russell, who I'm pretty certain will give you a situation."

I replied that I would do that. I then went home and informed mother of my intention, and as her health was very poor I had great difficulty in obtaining her consent. I finally convinced her that as I was of no use on the farm, it would be better and more profitable for me to return to the plains. So after giving her all the money I had earned by trapping, I bade her good-bye and set out for Atchison.

I met Mr. Russell there and asked him for employment as a Pony Express rider; he gave me a letter to Mr. [Joseph Alfred "Alf" or "Jack"] Slade, who was then the stage agent for the division extending from Julesburg to Rocky Ridge. Slade had his headquarters at Horseshoe Station, thirty-six miles west of Fort Laramie and I made the trip thither in company with Simpson and his train.

Almost the very first person I saw after dismounting from my horse was Slade. I walked up to him and presented Mr. Russell's letter, which he hastily opened and read. With a sweeping glance of his eye he took my measure from head to foot, and then said:

"My boy, you are too young for a Pony Express rider. It takes men for that business."

"I rode two months last year on Bill Trotter's division, sir, and filled the bill then; and I think I am better able to ride now," said I.

"What! are you the boy that was riding there, and was called the youngest rider on the road?"

"I am the same boy," I replied, confident that everything was now all right for me.

"I have heard of you before. You are a year or so older now, and I think you can stand it. I'll give you a trial anyhow and if you weaken you can come back to Horseshoe Station and tend stock."

That ended our first interview. The next day he assigned me to duty on the road from Red Buttes on the North Platte, to the Three Crossings of the Sweetwater—a distance of seventy-six miles—and I began riding at once. It was a long piece of road, but I was equal to the undertaking; and soon afterwards had an opportunity to exhibit my power of endurance as a Pony Express rider.

One day when I galloped into Three Crossings, my home station, I found that the rider who was expected to take the trip out on my arrival, had gotten into a drunken row the night before and been killed. This left that division without a rider and as it was very difficult to engage men for the service in that uninhabited region, the superintendent requested me to make the trip until another rider could be secured. The distance to the next station, Rocky Ridge, was eighty-five miles and through a very bad and dangerous country, but the emergency was great and I concluded to try it. I therefore started promptly from Three Crossings without more than a moment's rest and pushed on with usual rapidity, entering every relay station on time and accomplishing the round trip of 322 miles back to Red Buttes without a single mishap and on time. This stands on the records as being the longest Pony Express journey ever made.

Slade heard of this feat of mine, and one day as he was passing on a coach he sang out to me, "My boy, you're a brick, and no mistake. That was a good run you made when you rode your own and Miller's routes, and I'll see that you get extra pay for it."

Slade, although rough at times and always a dangerous character—having killed many a man—was always kind to me. Sober, he was cool and self-possessed, but never a man to be trifled with. Drunk, he was a living fury. His services to the company for which he worked were of high value. He was easily the best superintendent on the line. But his habit of man-killing at last resulted in his execution. During the two years that I worked for him as Pony Express rider and stage-driver, he never spoke an angry word to me.

Legends paint Jack Slade as a mad killer, but that's an exaggeration, though it is known that he killed at least two people. Slade's father had been a congressman and US Marshal for Illinois. Those who knew Slade describe him as generous and considerate, and he was a competent manager for the Overland Stage Line, but he was very aggressive and dangerous when drunk. Mark Twain described meeting Slade, saying, "He was so friendly and so gentle-spoken that I warmed to him in spite of his awful history. It was hardly possible to realize that this pleasant person was the pitiless scourge of the outlaws, the raw-head-and-bloody-bones the nursing mothers of the mountains terrified their children with."

Eventually Slade was fired from the stage line after a drunken spree at Fort Halleck. Moving on to Virginia City, Montana, he was soon arrested for shooting up a saloon and tearing up his arrest warrant. Even though Slade was a member of the Committee on Vigilance, the vigilantes made him dance the "Strangulation Jig," hanging him on March 10, 1864.

Like many Wild West figures, Slade may have been a deadly desperado to some people, but to others he was a hero.

A Black Speck Against the Sky

Mark Twain

In spite of having virtually no formal education, Mark Twain—whose real name was Samuel Clemens—went on to become one of America's greatest authors. William Faulkner labeled him "the father of American literature." Twain's classic works include "The Celebrated Jumping Frog of Calaveras County" (1865), *The Adventures of Tom Sawyer* (1876), *The Adventures of Huckleberry Finn* (1884), *A Connecticut Yankee in King Arthur's Court* (1889), and *Pudd'n'head Wilson* (1894). He came to prominence during a period when America was still strongly divided into North and South, but oddly he was a blend of the two, with a heavy dose of the West thrown in.

After the Civil War broke out, he formed a Confederate militia with some friends, but after two weeks half of them left—or "resigned," as he put it—and he went to the Nevada Territory with his brother, who had just been appointed secretary to the territory's governor. Here he tried his hand as a prospector and miner. Unsuccessful, he turned to writing and created his pen name. It was his jumping frog story that really launched his career as a humorist. Unfortunately his form of humor soon almost landed him in several duels. He described his experiences in the West in his book *Roughing It* (1872), from which this selection is taken.

Twain was probably running away from the war when he headed west in July 1861. He and his brother traveled by stagecoach for twenty days from St. Joseph, Missouri, to Carson City, which is now the capital of Nevada. The fare was $150 per person, or about $3,700 today, and this was for a very unpleasant ride, but it did include meals.

One traveler, Demas Barnes, described it as "fifteen inches of seat, with a fat man on one side, a poor widow on the other, a baby in your lap, a bandbox over your head, and three or more persons immediately in front, leaning against your knees, making the picture, as well as your sleeping place for the trip."

In the winter, metal foot warmers containing hot coals were provided for heat. During the summer, while crossing deserts, the passengers had leather shades to block out the sun and dust. Meals of salted meat, boiled beans, and coffee were provided at "home stations," which were about six to eight hours apart, if there weren't any delays from storms, flooded roads, breakdowns, or Indian attacks. These meals had to be eaten rapidly so they could quickly get moving again.

They were passing through the Nebraska Territory when Mark Twain saw a Pony Express rider streak by the stage.

Mark Twain in 1851 or 1852 at age sixteen or seventeen

In a little while all interest was taken up in stretching our necks and watching for the "pony-rider"—the fleet messenger who sped across the continent from St. Joe to Sacramento, carrying letters nineteen hundred miles in eight days! Think of that for perishable horse and human flesh and blood to do!

The pony-rider was usually a little bit of a man, brimful of spirit and endurance. No matter what time of the day or night his watch came on, and no matter whether it was winter or summer, raining, snowing, hailing, or sleeting, or whether his "beat" was a level straight road or a crazy trail over mountain crags and precipices, or whether it led through peaceful regions or regions that swarmed with hostile Indians, he must be always ready to leap into the saddle and be off like the wind!

There was no idling-time for a pony-rider on duty. He rode fifty miles without stopping, by daylight, moonlight, starlight, or through the blackness of darkness—just as it happened. He rode a splendid horse that was born for a racer and fed and lodged like a gentleman; kept him at his utmost speed for ten miles, and then, as he came crashing up to the station where stood two men holding fast a fresh, impatient steed, the transfer of rider and mail-bag was made in the twinkling of an eye, and away flew the eager pair and were out of sight before the spectator could get hardly the ghost of a look.

Both rider and horse went "flying light." The rider's dress was thin, and fitted close; he wore a "round-about," and a skull-cap, and tucked his pantaloons into his boot-tops like a race-rider. He carried no arms—he carried nothing that was not absolutely necessary, for even the postage on his literary freight was worth *five dollars a letter*.

He got but little frivolous correspondence to carry—his bag had business letters in it, mostly. His horse was stripped of all unnecessary weight, too. He wore a little wafer of a racing-saddle, and no visible blanket. He wore light shoes, or none at all. The little flat mail-pockets strapped under the rider's thighs would each hold about the bulk of a child's primer. They held many and many an important business chapter and newspaper letter, but these were written on paper as airy and thin as gold-leaf, nearly, and thus bulk and weight were economized.

The stagecoach traveled about a hundred to a hundred and twenty-five miles a day (twenty-four hours), the pony-rider about two hundred and fifty. There were about eighty pony-riders in the saddle all the time, night and day, stretching in a long, scattering procession from Missouri to California, forty flying eastward, and forty toward the west, and among them making four hundred gallant horses earn a stirring livelihood and see a deal of scenery every single day in the year.

We had had a consuming desire, from the beginning, to see a pony-rider, but somehow or other all that passed us and all that met us managed to streak by in the night, and so we heard only a whiz and a hail, and the swift phantom of the desert was gone before we could get our heads out of the windows. But now we were expecting one along every moment, and would see him in broad daylight. Presently the driver exclaims, "Here he comes!"

Every neck is stretched further, and every eye strained wider. Away across the endless dead level of the prairie a black speck appears against the sky, and it is plain that it moves. Well, I should think so! In a second or two it becomes a horse and rider, rising and falling, rising and falling—sweeping toward us nearer and nearer—growing more and more distinct, more and more sharply defined—nearer and still nearer, and the flutter of the hoofs comes faintly to the ear—another instant a whoop and a hurrah from our upper deck, a wave of the rider's hand, but no reply, and man and horse burst past our excited faces, and go winging away like a belated fragment of a storm!

So sudden is it all, and so like a flash of unreal fancy, that but for the flake of white foam left quivering and perishing on a mail-sack after the vision had flashed by and disappeared, we might have doubted whether we had seen any actual horse and man at all, maybe. . . .

We breakfasted at Horseshoe Station [in what is now Wyoming], six hundred and seventy-six miles out from St. Joseph. We had now reached a hostile Indian country, and during the afternoon we passed Lapierelle [or La Prele] Station, and enjoyed great discomfort all the time we were in the neighborhood, being aware that many of the trees we dashed by at arm's length concealed a lurking Indian or two.

During the preceding night an ambushed savage had sent a bullet through the pony-rider's jacket, but he had ridden on just the same because pony-riders were not allowed to stop and inquire into such things except when killed. As long as they had life enough left in them they had to stick to the horse and ride, even if the Indians had been waiting for them a week and were entirely out of patience.

About two hours and a half before we arrived at Lapierelle Station, the keeper in charge of it had fired four times at an Indian, but he said with an injured air that the Indian had "skipped around so's to spile everything—and ammunition's blamed skurse, too."

The most natural inference conveyed by his manner of speaking was, that in "skipping around," the Indian had taken an unfair advantage.

The Pony Express service lasted only a year and a half. In the spring of 1861, financial and other difficulties led to other companies—such as Wells, Fargo & Co.—taking over parts of the Pony Express routes, but it all became obsolete with the completion of the transcontinental telegraph and ceased service on October 26, 1861. Basically it was replaced by the new technology.

Some credit the Pony Express with keeping California and its gold in the Union during the early days of the war. It was through the Pony Express that President

Lincoln found out that General Albert Johnston—who commanded the Department of the Pacific—intended to turn California's arsenal over to the Confederacy. Lincoln sent a replacement, but before he arrived, Johnston resigned and joined the South.

By the summer of 1861, the Pony Express was carrying thirty-two pounds of government mail per month, some of it going directly to President Lincoln.

Ultimately the Pony Express reduced communication times between the two coasts and helped maintain ties between California and the Union during the war. Also, many newspapers relied heavily on it for bringing them the latest news, with some of them bringing out special "pony extra" editions. Others featured "by Pony Express" columns. Sometimes thousands of people gathered in San Francisco to await the messenger's arrival with the news. The service also demonstrated that travel across the continent was possible in all seasons.

Altogether, 308 runs were made each way, carrying 34,753 pieces of mail—two thirds of it heading east. That's equal to riding a horse 24 times around the earth. Financially, it was a failure—costing $700,000 and making only $500,000. The owners had hoped to pick up the government's overland mail contract, but this was awarded to the Butterfield Overland Stage Company. Losing the contract, along with the high costs of operating the service, ultimately drove the owners to bankruptcy. One of their creditors took over their stagecoach and freight business and was able to make it profitable again, but he didn't attempt to resurrect the Pony Express.

While Buffalo Bill included his tribute to the Pony Express in his Wild West shows, with the rider changing horses mid-gallop, it didn't really become a patriotic symbol of Western strength and heroism until the turn of the twentieth century.

Smitten with the Silver Fever

Mark Twain

Mark Twain

In 1859, America's second great mining boom began when silver was discovered in Nevada. The Comstock Lode soon turned Virginia City into the West's most famous boomtown and for twenty years it was the world's most important mining camp. During the Civil War the Comstock Lode produced more than $45 million—roughly $7.5 billion today—in silver and gold, enabling the US government to maintain its credit, which greatly contributed to the Union's victory. The Lode went on to produce $400 million, or around $66.6 billion today.

Nevada's silver mines were not like California's gold mines, where forty-niners with a pick, shovel, gold pan and sluice could separate gold from dirt and sand in streambeds. It was generally not the prospectors who struck it rich, but the speculators, developers, and middlemen. George Hearst, father of the media mogul William Randolph Hearst, was an exception to this. He got established in the beginning when the silver was near the surface. Initially gold was discovered, but then it was found that the blue-gray mud that stuck to their equipment was actually silver ore. Some of the heavy crusts were worth up to $27,000 a ton. Later the mines had to go extremely deep, while huge rock crushing mills and smelting furnaces were required to extract the ore from stone. This required large teams of men and lots of expensive equipment. Of the thousands who joined the boom, hundreds became moderately wealthy, and only a few dozen made huge fortunes.

Before coming to Virginia City, George Hearst was an unsuccessful forty-niner turned storekeeper. On hearing of the Comstock discovery, he rushed to the site, acquired an interest in a nearby mine for three thousand dollars, and then returned to California to raise the money. He and his friends spent the next two

Mark Twain in 1870

months digging out thirty-eight tons of silver ore and used a mule train to haul it over the Sierra Nevadas to San Francisco, where it was smelted into more than ninety thousand dollars of silver bullion and he was on his way to becoming one of the world's great tycoons. He eventually owned major interests in the Comstock Mine; the Homestake Gold Mine near Deadwood, South Dakota; and the Anaconda Copper Mine of Butte, Montana.

As the Comstock miners drilled deeper and deeper, soon a three-mile stretch of the mountains that Virginia City is nestled in were riddled with tunnels. "The 'city' of Virginia claimed a population of 18,000," wrote Mark Twain, "and all day long half of this little army swarmed the streets like bees, and the other half swarmed among the drifts and tunnels of the Comstock, hundreds of feet down in the earth directly under those same streets. Often we felt our chairs jar, and heard the faint boom of a blast down in the bowels of the earth under the office."

It's estimated that there are up to seven hundred miles of tunnels that make up the forty-six mines in the Comstock Lode. They run to a depth of more than thirty-two hundred feet. Working in the tunnels was extremely dangerous, and men were often killed or seriously injured by fires, cave-ins, or falling into shafts. At the deepest depths the temperature was more than 120°F, and the air was filled with clouds of steam. Some shafts filled with water hot enough to scald a man to death. The miners had to wear gloves because their wooden pick handles would become too hot to hold. They could only work fifteen minutes out of an hour, and each man was given a daily allotment of ninety-five pounds of ice. They suffered from heat exhaustion, rheumatism, and pneumonia, among other things. The mountains for hundreds of miles around were stripped of their forests to provide the timber needed to shore up the tunnels. And yet the average yield of the ore was only around fifty dollars per ton. Still, that was enough to turn a profit.

When Mark Twain and his brother arrived in Nevada, they began investing in mining claims and eventually owned feet in at least thirty different ledges in the Esmeralda Mining District around Aurora, which is three miles from the California border and about halfway between Carson City and Las Vegas. The claims were nominally worth around five thousand dollars, though the brothers probably only made down payments on them and would have paid off the rest if the claims became profitable. Apparently none of these earned a dime.

After failing as a miner, Twain moved on to Virginia City and in 1863 began writing for the town's newspaper, the *Territorial Enterprise*, taking on his now famous pen name—Mark Twain. With this he was much more successful. In *Roughing It* (1872), he wrote of the difficulties and sudden rewards of prospecting.

In 1858 silver lodes were discovered in "Carson County," and then the aspect of things changed. Californians began to flock in, and the American element was soon in the majority. Allegiance to Brigham Young and Utah was renounced, and a temporary territorial government for "Washoe" was instituted by the citizens. Governor [Isaac] Roop was the first and only chief magistrate of it [e.g., the Utah Territory]. In due course of time [1861] Congress passed a bill to organize "Nevada Territory," and President Lincoln sent out Governor [James] Nye to supplant Roop.

At this time the population of the Territory was about twelve or fifteen thousand, and rapidly increasing. Silver mines were being vigorously developed and silver mills erected. Business of all kinds was active and prosperous and growing more so day by day.

———

By and by I was smitten with the silver fever. "Prospecting parties" were leaving for the mountains every day, and discovering and taking possession of rich silver-bearing lodes and ledges of quartz. Plainly this was the road to fortune. The great "Gould and Curry" mine [the richest of the Comstock Lode mines] was held at three or *four hundred dollars a foot* when we arrived; but in two months it had sprung up to eight hundred. The "Ophir" had been worth only a mere trifle, a year gone by, and now it was selling at nearly *four thousand dollars a foot* [about $100,000 a foot in today's dollars]! Not a mine could be named that had not experienced an astonishing advance in value within a short time. Everybody was talking about these marvels. Go where you would, you heard nothing else, from morning till far into the night. Tom So-and-So had sold out of the "Amanda Smith" for $40,000—hadn't a cent when he "took up" the ledge six months ago. John Jones had sold half his interest in the "Bald Eagle and Mary Ann" for $65,000, gold coin, and gone to the States for his family. The widow Brewster had "struck it rich" in the "Golden Fleece" and sold ten feet for $18,000—hadn't money enough to buy a crape bonnet when Sing-Sing Tommy killed her husband at Baldy Johnson's wake last spring. The "Last Chance" had found a "clay casing" and knew they were "right on the ledge"—consequence, "feet" that went begging yesterday were worth a brick house apiece today, and seedy owners who could not get trusted for a drink at any bar in the country yesterday were roaring drunk on champagne today and had hosts of warm personal friends in a town where they had forgotten how to bow or shake hands from long-continued want of practice. Johnny Morgan, a common loafer, had gone to sleep in the gutter and waked up worth a hundred thousand dollars, in consequence of the decision in the "Lady Franklin and Rough and Ready" lawsuit. And so on—day in and day out the talk pelted our ears and the excitement waxed hotter and hotter around us.

I would have been more or less than human if I had not gone mad like the rest. Cart-loads of solid silver bricks, as large as pigs of lead, were arriving from the mills every day, and such sights as that gave substance to the wild talk about me. I succumbed and grew as frenzied as the craziest.

Every few days news would come of the discovery of a brand-new mining region; immediately the papers would teem with accounts of its richness, and away the surplus population would scamper to take possession. By the time I was fairly inoculated with the disease, "Esmeralda" had just had a run and "Humboldt" was beginning to shriek for attention. "Humboldt! Humboldt!" was the new cry, and straightway Humboldt, the newest of the new, the richest of the rich, the most marvelous of the marvelous discoveries in silver-land was occupying two columns of the public prints to "Esmeralda's" one. I was just on the point of starting to Esmeralda, but turned with the tide and got ready for Humboldt. That the reader may see what moved me, and what would as surely have moved him had he been there, I insert here one of the newspaper letters of the day. It and several other letters from the same calm hand were the main means of converting me. I shall not garble the extract, but put it in just as it appeared in the *Daily Territorial Enterprise*:

But what about our mines? I shall be candid with you. I shall express an honest opinion, based upon a thorough examination. Humboldt County is the richest mineral region upon God's footstool. Each mountain range is gorged with the precious ores. Humboldt is the true Golconda.

The other day an assay of mere *croppings* yielded exceeding *four thousand dollars to the ton*. A week or two ago an assay of just such surface developments made returns of *seven thousand* dollars to the ton. Our mountains are full of rambling prospectors. Each day and almost every hour reveals new and more startling evidences of the profuse and intensified wealth of our favored county. The metal is not silver alone. There are distinct ledges of auriferous ore. A late discovery plainly evinces cinnabar. The coarser metals are in gross abundance. Lately evidences of bituminous coal have been detected. My theory has ever been that coal is a ligneous formation. I told Col. Whitman, in times past, that the neighborhood of Dayton (Nevada) betrayed no present or previous manifestations of a ligneous foundation, and that hence I had no confidence in his lauded coal mines. I repeated the same doctrine to the exultant coal discoverers of Humboldt. I talked with my friend Captain Burch on the subject. My pyrhanism vanished upon his statement that in the very region referred to he had seen petrified trees of the length of two hundred feet. Then is the fact established that huge forests once cast their grim shadows over this remote section. I am firm in the coal faith. Have no fears of the mineral resources of Humboldt County. They are immense—incalculable.

Let me state one or two things which will help the reader to better comprehend certain items in the above. At this time, our near neighbor, Gold Hill, was the most successful silver mining locality in Nevada. It was from there that more than half the daily shipments of silver bricks came. "Very rich" (and scarce) Gold Hill ore yielded from $100 to $400 to the ton; but the usual yield was only $20 to $40 per ton—that is to say, each hundred pounds of ore yielded from one dollar to two dollars. But the reader will perceive by the above extract, that in Humboldt from one fourth to nearly half the mass was silver! That is to say, every one hundred pounds of the ore had from *two hundred* dollars up to about *three hundred and fifty* in it. Some days later this same correspondent wrote:

I have spoken of the vast and almost fabulous wealth of this region—it is incredible. The intestines of our mountains are gorged with precious ore to plethora. I have said that nature has so shaped our mountains as to furnish most excellent facilities for the working of our mines. I have also told you that the country about here is pregnant with the finest mill sites in the world. But what is the mining history of Humboldt? The Sheba mine is in the hands of energetic San Francisco capitalists. It would seem that the ore is combined with metals that render it difficult of reduction with our imperfect mountain machinery. The proprietors have combined the capital and labor hinted at in my exordium. They are toiling and probing. Their tunnel has reached the length of one hundred feet. From primal assays alone, coupled with the development of the mine and public confidence in the continuance of effort, the stock had reared itself to eight hundred dollars market value. I do not know that one ton of the ore has been converted into current metal. I do know that there are many lodes in this section that surpass the Sheba in primal assay value. Listen a moment to the calculations of the Sheba operators. They purpose transporting the ore concentrated to Europe. The conveyance from Star City (its locality) to Virginia City will cost seventy dollars per ton; from Virginia to San Francisco, forty dollars per ton; from thence to Liverpool, its destination, ten dollars per ton. Their idea is that its conglomerate metals will reimburse them their cost of original extraction, the price of transportation, and the expense of reduction, and that then a ton of the raw ore will net them twelve hundred dollars. The estimate may be extravagant. Cut it in twain, and the product is enormous, far transcending any previous developments of our racy Territory.

A very common calculation is that many of our mines will yield five hundred dollars to the ton. Such fecundity throws the Gould & Curry, the Ophir and the Mexican, of your neighborhood, in the darkest shadow. I have given you the estimate of the value of a single developed mine. Its richness is indexed by its market valuation. The people of Humboldt County are *feet* crazy. As I write, our towns are near deserted. They look as languid as a consumptive girl. What has become of our sinewy and athletic fellow-citizens? They are coursing through ravines and over mountain tops. Their tracks are visible in every direction. Occasionally a horseman will dash among us. His steed betrays hard usage. He alights before his adobe dwelling, hastily exchanges courtesies with his townsmen, hurries to an assay office and from thence to the District Recorder's. In the morning, having renewed his provisional supplies, he is off again on his wild and unbeaten route. Why, the fellow numbers already his feet by the thousands. He is the horse-leech. He has the craving stomach of the shark or anaconda. He would conquer metallic worlds.

This was enough. The instant we had finished reading the above article, four of us decided to go to Humboldt. We commenced getting ready at once. And we also commenced upbraiding ourselves for not deciding sooner—for we were in terror lest all the rich mines would be found and secured before we got there, and we might have to put up with ledges that would not yield more than two or three hundred dollars a ton, maybe. An hour before, I would have felt opulent if I had owned ten feet in a Gold Hill mine whose ore produced twenty-five dollars to the ton; now I was already annoyed at the prospect of having to put up with mines the poorest of which would be a marvel in Gold Hill.

Hurry, was the word! We wasted no time. Our party consisted of four persons—a blacksmith sixty years of age, two young lawyers, and myself.

We bought a wagon and two miserable old horses. We put eighteen hundred pounds of provisions and mining tools in the wagon and drove out of Carson on a chilly December afternoon. The horses were so weak and old that we soon found that it would be better if one or two of us got out and walked. It was an improvement. Next, we found that it would be better if a third man got out. That was an improvement also. It was at this time that I volunteered to drive, although I had never driven a harnessed horse before and many a man in such a position would have felt fairly excused from such a responsibility. But in a little while it was found that it would be a fine thing if the driver got out and walked also. It was at this time that I resigned the position of driver, and never resumed it again. Within the hour, we found that it would not only be better, but was absolutely necessary, that we four, taking turns, two at a time, should put our hands against the end of the wagon and push it through the sand, leaving the feeble horses little to do but keep out of the way and hold up the tongue. Perhaps it is well for one to know his fate at first, and get reconciled to it. We had learned ours in one afternoon. It was plain that we had to walk through the sand and shove that wagon and those horses two hundred miles. So we accepted the situation, and from that time forth we never rode. More than that, we stood regular and nearly constant watches pushing up behind.

We made seven miles, and camped in the desert. Young Clagett (now member of Congress from Montana) unharnessed and fed and watered the horses; Oliphant and I cut sagebrush, built the fire and brought water to cook with; and old Mr. Ballou the blacksmith did the cooking. This division of labor, and this appointment, was adhered to throughout the journey. We had no tent, and so we slept under our blankets in the open plain. We were so tired that we slept soundly.

We were fifteen days making the trip—two hundred miles; thirteen, rather, for we lay by a couple of days, in one place, to let the horses rest.

We could really have accomplished the journey in ten days if we had towed the horses behind the wagon, but we did not think of that until it was too late, and so went on shoving the horses and the wagon too when we might have saved half the labor. Parties who met us, occasionally, advised us to put the horses *in* the wagon, but Mr. Ballou, through whose iron-clad earnestness no sarcasm could pierce, said that that would not do, because the provisions were exposed and would suffer, the horses being "bituminous from long deprivation." The reader will excuse me from translating. What Mr. Ballou customarily meant, when he used a long word, was a secret between himself and his Maker. He was one of the best and kindest hearted men that ever graced a humble sphere of life. He was gentleness and simplicity itself—and unselfishness, too. Although he was more than twice as old as the eldest of us, he never gave himself any airs, privileges, or exemptions on that account. He did a *young* man's share of the work; and did his share of conversing and entertaining from the general stand-point of *any* age—not from the arrogant, over-awing summit-height of sixty years. His one striking peculiarity was his Partingtonian fashion of loving and using big words *for their own sakes*, and independent of any bearing they might have upon the thought he was purposing to convey. He always let his ponderous syllables fall with an easy unconsciousness that left them wholly without offensiveness. In truth his air was so natural and so simple that one was always catching himself accepting his stately sentences as meaning something, when they really meant nothing in the world. If a word was long and grand and resonant, that was sufficient to win the old man's love, and he would drop that word into the most out-of-the-way place in a sentence or a subject, and be as pleased with it as if it were perfectly luminous with meaning.

We four always spread our common stock of blankets together on the frozen ground, and slept side by side; and finding that our foolish, long-legged hound pup had a deal of animal heat in him, Oliphant got to admitting him to the bed, between himself and Mr. Ballou, hugging the dog's warm back to his breast and finding great comfort in it. But in the night the pup would get stretchy and brace his feet against the old man's back and shove, grunting complacently the while; and now and then, being warm and snug, grateful and happy, he would paw the old man's back simply in excess of comfort; and at yet other times he would dream of the chase and in his sleep tug at the old man's back hair and bark in his ear. The old gentleman complained mildly about these familiarities, at last, and when he got through with his statement he said that such a dog as that was not a proper animal to admit to bed with tired men, because he was "so meretricious in his movements and so organic in his emotions." We turned the dog out.

It was a hard, wearing, toilsome journey, but it had its bright side; for after each day was done and our wolfish hunger appeased with a hot supper of fried bacon, bread, molasses and black coffee, the pipe-smoking, song-singing and yarn-spinning around the evening camp-fire in the still solitudes of the desert was a happy, care-free sort of recreation that seemed the very summit and culmination of earthly luxury.

It is a kind of life that has a potent charm for all men, whether city or country-bred. We are descended from desert-lounging Arabs, and countless ages of growth toward perfect civilization have failed to root out of us the nomadic instinct. We all confess to a gratified thrill at the thought of "camping out."

Once we made twenty-five miles in a day, and once we made forty miles (through the Great American Desert), and ten miles beyond—fifty in all—in twenty-three hours, without halting to eat, drink or rest. To stretch out and go to sleep, even on stony and frozen ground, after pushing a wagon and two horses fifty miles, is a delight so supreme that for the moment it almost seems cheap at the price.

We camped two days in the neighborhood of the "Sink of the Humboldt." We tried to use the strong alkaline water of the Sink, but it would not answer. It was like drinking lye, and not weak lye, either. It left a taste in the mouth, bitter and every way execrable, and a burning in the stomach that was very uncomfortable. We put molasses in it, but that helped it very little; we added a pickle, yet the alkali was the prominent taste and so it was unfit for drinking.

The coffee we made of this water was the meanest compound man has yet invented. It was really viler to the taste than the unameliorated water itself. Mr. Ballou, being the architect and builder of the beverage felt constrained to endorse and uphold it, and so drank half a cup, by little sips, making shift to praise it faintly the while, but finally threw out the remainder, and said frankly it was "too technical for *him*."

But presently we found a spring of fresh water, convenient, and then, with nothing to mar our enjoyment, and no stragglers to interrupt it, we entered into our rest.

After leaving the Sink, we traveled along the Humboldt River a little way. People accustomed to the monster mile-wide Mississippi, grow accustomed to associating the term "river" with a high degree of watery grandeur. Consequently, such people feel rather disappointed when they stand on the shores of the Humboldt or the Carson and find that a "river" in Nevada is a sickly rivulet which is just the counterpart of the Erie Canal in all respects save that the canal is twice as long and four times as deep. One of the pleasantest and most invigorating exercises one can contrive is to run and jump across the Humboldt River till he is overheated, and then drink it dry.

On the fifteenth day we completed our march of two hundred miles and entered Unionville, Humboldt County [Nevada Territory], in the midst of a driving snowstorm. Unionville consisted of eleven cabins and a liberty-pole. Six of the cabins were strung along one side of a deep canyon, and the other five faced them. The rest of the landscape was made up of bleak mountain walls that rose so high into the sky from both sides of the canyon that the village was left, as it were, far down in the bottom of a crevice. It was always daylight on the mountain tops a long time before the darkness lifted and revealed Unionville.

We built a small, rude cabin in the side of the crevice and roofed it with canvas, leaving a corner open to serve as a chimney, through which the cattle used to tumble occasionally, at night, and mash our furniture and interrupt our sleep. It was very cold weather and fuel was scarce. Indians brought brush and bushes several miles on their backs; and when we could catch a laden Indian it was well—and when we could not (which was the rule, not the exception), we shivered and bore it.

I confess, without shame, that I expected to find masses of silver lying all about the ground. I expected to see it glittering in the sun on the mountain summits. I said nothing about this, for some instinct told me that I might possibly have an exaggerated idea about it, and so if I betrayed my thought I might bring derision upon myself. Yet I was as perfectly satisfied in my own mind as I could be of anything, that I was going to gather up, in a day or two, or at furthest a week or two, silver enough to make me satisfactorily wealthy—and so my fancy was already busy with plans for spending this money. The first opportunity that offered, I sauntered carelessly away from the cabin, keeping an eye on the other boys, and stopping and contemplating the sky when they seemed to be observing me; but as soon as the coast was manifestly clear, I fled away as guiltily as a thief might have done and never halted till I was far beyond sight and call. Then I began my search with a feverish excitement that was brimful of expectation—almost of certainty. I crawled about the ground, seizing and examining bits of stone, blowing the dust from them or rubbing them on my clothes, and then peering at them with anxious hope. Presently I found a bright fragment and my heart bounded! I hid behind a boulder and polished it and scrutinized it with a nervous eagerness and a delight that was more pronounced than absolute certainty itself could have afforded. The more I examined the fragment the more I was convinced that I had found the door to fortune. I marked the spot and carried away my specimen. Up and down the rugged mountain side I searched, with always increasing interest and always augmenting gratitude that I had come to Humboldt and come in time. Of all the experiences of my life, this secret search among the hidden treasures of silver-land was the nearest to unmarred ecstasy. It was a delirious revel.

By and by, in the bed of a shallow rivulet, I found a deposit of shining yellow scales, and my breath almost forsook me! A gold mine, and in my simplicity I had been content with vulgar silver! I was so excited that I half believed my overwrought imagination was deceiving me. Then a fear came upon me that people might be observing me and would guess my secret. Moved by this thought, I made a circuit of the place, and ascended a knoll to reconnoiter. Solitude. No creature was near. Then I returned to my mine, fortifying myself against possible disappointment, but my fears were groundless—the shining scales were still there. I set about scooping them out, and for an hour I toiled down the windings of the stream and robbed its bed. But at last the descending sun warned me to give up the quest, and I turned homeward laden with wealth. As I walked along I could not help smiling at the thought of my being so excited over my fragment of silver when a nobler metal was almost under my nose. In this little time the former had so fallen in my estimation that once or twice I was on the point of throwing it away.

The boys were as hungry as usual, but I could eat nothing. Neither could I talk. I was full of dreams and far away. Their conversation interrupted the flow of my fancy somewhat, and annoyed me a little, too. I despised the sordid and commonplace things they talked about. But as they proceeded, it began to amuse me. It grew to be rare fun to hear them planning their poor little economies and sighing over possible privations and distresses when a gold mine, all our own, lay within sight of the cabin and I could point it out at any moment. Smothered hilarity began to oppress me, presently. It was hard to resist the impulse to burst out with exultation and reveal everything; but I did resist. I said within myself that I would filter the great news through my lips calmly and be serene as a summer morning while I watched its effect in their faces. I said, "Where have you all been?"

"Prospecting."

"What did you find?"

"Nothing."

"Nothing? What do you think of the country?"

"Can't tell, yet," said Mr. Ballou, who was an old gold miner, and had likewise had considerable experience among the silver mines.

"Well, haven't you formed any sort of opinion?"

"Yes, a sort of a one. It's fair enough here, may be, but overrated. Seven thousand dollar ledges are scarce, though."

"That Sheba may be rich enough, but we don't own it; and besides, the rock is so full of base metals that all the science in the world can't work it. We'll not starve, here, but we'll not get rich, I'm afraid."

"So you think the prospect is pretty poor?"

"No name for it!"

"Well, we'd better go back, hadn't we?"

"Oh, not yet—of course not. We'll try it a riffle, first."

"Suppose, now—this is merely a supposition, you know—suppose you could find a ledge that would yield, say, a hundred and fifty dollars a ton—would *that* satisfy you?"

"Try us once!" from the whole party.

"Or suppose—merely a supposition, of course—suppose you were to find a ledge that would yield two thousand dollars a ton—would *that* satisfy you?"

"Here—what do you mean? What are you coming at? Is there some mystery behind all this?"

"Never mind. I am not saying anything. You know perfectly well there are no rich mines here—of course you do. Because you have been around and examined for yourselves. Anybody would know that, that had been around. But just for the sake of argument, suppose—in a kind of general way—suppose some person were to tell you that two-thousand-dollar ledges were simply contemptible—contemptible, understand—and that right yonder in sight of this very cabin there were piles of pure gold and pure silver—oceans of it—enough to make you all rich in twenty-four hours! Come!"

"I should say he was as crazy as a loon!" said old Ballou, but wild with excitement, nevertheless.

"Gentlemen," said I, "I don't say anything—*I* haven't been around, you know, and of course don't know anything—but all I ask of you is to cast your eye on *that*, for instance, and tell me what you think of it!" and I tossed my treasure before them.

There was an eager scramble for it, and a closing of heads together over it under the candlelight. Then old Ballou said, "Think of it? I think it is nothing but a lot of granite rubbish and nasty glittering mica that isn't worth ten cents an acre!"

So vanished my dream. So melted my wealth away. So toppled my airy castle to the earth and left me stricken and forlorn.

Moralizing, I observed, then, that "all that glitters is not gold."

Mr. Ballou said I could go further than that, and lay it up among my treasures of knowledge, that *nothing* that glitters is gold. So I learned then, once for all, that gold in its native state is but dull, unornamental stuff, and that only low-born metals excite the admiration of the ignorant with an ostentatious glitter. However, like the rest of the world, I still go on underrating men of gold and glorifying men of mica. Commonplace human nature cannot rise above that.

True knowledge of the nature of silver mining came fast enough. We went out "prospecting" with Mr. Ballou. We climbed the mountain sides, and clambered among sage-brush, rocks and snow till we were ready to drop with exhaustion, but found no silver—nor yet any gold. Day after day we did this. Now and then we came upon holes burrowed a few feet into the declivities and apparently abandoned; and now and then we found one or two listless men still burrowing. But there was no appearance of silver. These holes were the beginnings of tunnels, and the purpose was to drive them hundreds of feet into the mountain, and someday tap the hidden ledge where the silver was. Someday! It seemed far enough away, and very hopeless and dreary. Day after day we toiled, and climbed and searched, and we younger partners grew sicker and still sicker of the promiseless toil. At last we halted under a beetling rampart of rock which projected from the earth high upon the mountain. Mr. Ballou broke off some fragments with a hammer, and examined them long and attentively with a small eyeglass; threw them away and broke off more; said this rock was quartz, and quartz was the sort of rock that contained silver. *Contained* it! I had thought that at least it would be caked on the outside of it like a kind of veneering. He still broke off pieces and critically examined them, now and then wetting the piece with his tongue and applying the glass. At last he exclaimed, "We've got it!"

We were full of anxiety in a moment. The rock was clean and white, where it was broken, and across it ran a ragged thread of blue. He said that that little thread had silver in it, mixed with base metal, such as lead and antimony, and other rubbish, and that there was a speck or two of gold visible. After a great deal of effort we managed to discern some little fine yellow specks, and judged that a couple of tons of them massed together might make a gold dollar, possibly. We were not jubilant, but Mr. Ballou said there were worse ledges in the world than that. He saved what he called the "richest" piece of the rock, in order to determine its value by the process called the "fire-assay." Then we named the mine "Monarch of the Mountains" (modesty of nomenclature is not a prominent feature in the mines), and Mr. Ballou wrote out and stuck up the following "notice," preserving a copy to be entered upon the books in the mining recorder's office in the town.

NOTICE.

We the undersigned claim three claims, of three hundred feet each (and one for discovery), on this silver-bearing quartz lead or lode, extending north and south from this notice, with all its dips, spurs, and angles, variations and sinuosities, together with fifty feet of ground on either side for working the same.

We put our names to it and tried to feel that our fortunes were made. But when we talked the matter all over with Mr. Ballou, we felt depressed and dubious. He said that this surface quartz was not all there was of our mine; but that the wall or ledge of rock called the "Monarch of the Mountains," extended down hundreds and hundreds of feet into the earth—he illustrated by saying it was like a curb-stone, and maintained a nearly uniform thickness—say twenty feet—away down into the bowels of the earth, and was perfectly distinct from the casing rock on each side of it; and that it kept to itself, and maintained its distinctive character always, no matter how deep it extended into the earth or how far it stretched itself through and across the hills and valleys. He said it might be a mile deep and ten miles long, for all we knew; and that wherever we bored into it above ground or below, we would find gold and silver in it, but no gold or silver in the meaner rock it was cased between. And he said that down in the great depths of the ledge was its richness, and the deeper it went the richer it grew. Therefore, instead of working here on the surface, we must either bore down into the rock with a shaft till we came to where it was rich—say a hundred feet or so—or else we must go down into the valley and bore a long tunnel into the mountain side and tap the ledge far under the earth. To do either was plainly the labor of months; for we could blast and bore only a few feet a day—some five or six. But this was not all. He said that after we got the ore out it must be hauled in wagons to a distant silver-mill, ground up, and the silver extracted by a tedious and costly process. Our fortune seemed a century away!

But we went to work. We decided to sink a shaft. So, for a week we climbed the mountain, laden with picks, drills, gads, crowbars, shovels, cans of blasting powder and coils of fuse and strove with might and main. At first the rock was broken and loose and we dug it up with picks and threw it out with shovels, and the hole progressed very well. But the rock became more compact, presently, and gads and crowbars came into play. But shortly nothing could make an impression but blasting powder.

That was the weariest work! One of us held the iron drill in its place and another would strike with an eight-pound sledge—it was like driving nails on a large scale. In the course of an hour or two the drill would reach a depth of two or three feet, making a hole a couple of inches in diameter. We would put in a charge of powder, insert half a yard of fuse, pour in sand and gravel and ram it down, then light the fuse and run. When the explosion came and the rocks and smoke shot into the air, we would go back and find about a bushel of that hard, rebellious quartz jolted out. Nothing more. One week of this satisfied me. I resigned. Clagget and Oliphant followed. Our shaft was only twelve feet deep. We decided that a tunnel was the thing we wanted.

So we went down the mountain side and worked a week; at the end of which time we had blasted a tunnel about deep enough to hide a hogshead in, and judged that about nine hundred feet more of it would reach the ledge. I resigned again, and the other boys only held out one day longer. We decided that a tunnel was not what we wanted. We wanted a ledge that was already "developed." There were none in the camp.

We dropped the "Monarch" for the time being.

Meantime the camp was filling up with people, and there was a constantly growing excitement about our Humboldt mines. We fell victims to the epidemic and strained every nerve to acquire more "feet." We prospected and took up new claims, put "notices" on them and gave them grandiloquent names. We traded some of our "feet" for "feet" in other people's claims. In a little while we owned largely in the "Gray Eagle," the "Columbiana," the "Branch Mint," the "Maria Jane," the "Universe," the "Root-Hog-or-Die," the "Samson and Delilah," the "Treasure Trove," the "Golconda," the "Sultana," the "Boomerang," the "Great Republic," the "Grand Mogul," and fifty other "mines" that had never been molested by a shovel or scratched with a pick. We had not less than thirty thousand "feet" apiece in the "richest mines on earth" as the frenzied cant phrased it—and were in debt to the butcher. We were stark mad with excitement—drunk with happiness—smothered under mountains of prospective wealth—arrogantly compassionate toward the plodding millions who knew not our marvelous canyon—but our credit was not good at the grocer's.

It was the strangest phase of life one can imagine. It was a beggars' revel. There was nothing doing in the district—no mining—no milling— no productive effort—no income—and not enough money in the entire camp to buy a corner lot in an eastern village, hardly; and yet a stranger would have supposed he was walking among bloated millionaires. Prospecting parties swarmed out of town with the first flush of dawn, and swarmed in again at nightfall laden with spoil—rocks. Nothing but rocks. Every man's pockets were full of them; the floor of his cabin was littered with them; they were disposed in labeled rows on his shelves.

It was in this Sacramento Valley . . . that a deal of the most lucrative of the early gold mining was done, and you may still see, in places, its grassy slopes and levels torn and guttered and disfigured by the avaricious spoilers of fifteen and twenty years ago. You may see such disfigurements far and wide over California—and in some such places, where only meadows and forests are visible—not a living creature, not a house, no stick or stone or remnant of a ruin, and not a sound, not even a whisper to disturb the Sabbath stillness—you will find it hard to believe that there stood at one time a fiercely-flourishing little city, of two thousand or three thousand souls, with its newspaper, fire company, brass band, volunteer militia, bank, hotels, noisy Fourth of July processions and speeches, gambling hells crammed with tobacco smoke, profanity, and rough-bearded men of all nations and colors, with tables heaped with gold dust sufficient for the revenues of a German principality—streets crowded and rife with business—town lots worth four hundred dollars a front foot—labor, laughter, music, dancing, swearing, fighting, shooting, stabbing—a bloody inquest and a man for breakfast every morning—*everything* that delights and adorns existence—all the appointments and appurtenances of a thriving and prosperous and promising young city,—and *now* nothing is left of it all but a lifeless, homeless solitude. The men are gone, the houses have vanished, even the *name* of the place is forgotten. In no other land, in modern times, have towns so absolutely died and disappeared, as in the old mining regions of California.

The comment about the town having "a man for breakfast every morning" was a common phrase people in the West used to convey deadly violence. It meant that at every sunrise a dead body would be found in the streets. This was, of course, a great exaggeration.

It was a driving, vigorous, restless population in those days. It was a *curious* population. It was the *only* population of the kind that the world has ever seen gathered together, and it is not likely that the world will ever see its like again. For observe, it was an assemblage of two hundred thousand *young* men—not simpering, dainty, kid-gloved weaklings, but stalwart, muscular, dauntless young braves, brimful of push and energy, and royally endowed with every attribute that goes to make up a peerless and magnificent manhood—the very pick and choice of the world's glorious ones. No women, no children, no gray and stooping veterans,—none but erect, bright-eyed, quick-moving, strong-handed young giants—the strangest population, the finest population, the most gallant host that ever trooped down the startled solitudes of an unpeopled land. And where are they now? Scattered to the ends of the earth—or prematurely aged and decrepit—or shot or stabbed in street affrays—or dead of disappointed hopes and broken hearts—all gone, or nearly all—victims devoted upon the altar of the golden calf—the noblest holocaust that ever wafted its sacrificial incense heavenward. It is pitiful to think upon.

It was a splendid population—for all the slow, sleepy, sluggish-brained sloths staid at home—you never find that sort of people among pioneers—you cannot build pioneers out of that sort of material. It was that population that gave to California a name for getting up astounding enterprises and rushing them through with a magnificent dash and daring and a recklessness of cost or consequences, which she bears unto this day—and when she projects a new surprise, the grave world smiles as usual and says, "Well, that is California all over."

But they were rough in those times! They fairly reveled in gold, whisky, fights, and fandangoes, and were unspeakably happy. The honest miner raked from a hundred to a thousand dollars out of his claim a day, and what with the gambling dens and the other entertainments, he hadn't a cent the next morning, if he had any sort of luck. They cooked their own bacon and beans, sewed on their own buttons, washed their own shirts—blue woolen ones; and if a man wanted a fight on his hands without any annoying delay, all he had to do was to appear in public in a white shirt or a stove-pipe hat, and he would be accommodated. For those people hated aristocrats. They had a particular and malignant animosity toward what they called a "biled shirt."

It was a wild, free, disorderly, grotesque society! *Men*—only swarming hosts of stalwart *men*—nothing juvenile, nothing feminine, visible anywhere!

In those days miners would flock in crowds to catch a glimpse of that rare and blessed spectacle, a woman! Old inhabitants tell how, in a certain camp, the news went abroad early in the morning that a woman was come! They had seen a calico dress hanging out of a wagon down at the camping-ground—sign of emigrants from over the great plains. Everybody went down there, and a shout went up when an actual, bona fide dress was discovered fluttering in the wind! The male emigrant was visible. The miners said, "Fetch her out!"

He said, "It is my wife, gentlemen—she is sick—we have been robbed of money, provisions, everything, by the Indians—we want to rest."

"Fetch her out! We've got to see her!"

"But, gentlemen, the poor thing, she—"

"Fetch her out!"

He "fetched her out," and they swung their hats and sent up three rousing cheers and a tiger; and they crowded around and gazed at her, and touched her dress, and listened to her voice with the look of men who listened to a *memory* rather than a present reality—and then they collected twenty-five hundred dollars in gold and gave it to the man, and swung their hats again and gave three more cheers, and went home satisfied.

Once I dined in San Francisco with the family of a pioneer, and talked with his daughter, a young lady whose first experience in San Francisco was an adventure, though she herself did not remember it, as she was only two or three years old at the time. Her father said that, after landing from the ship, they were walking up the street, a servant leading the party with the little girl in her arms. And presently a huge miner, bearded, belted, spurred, and bristling with deadly weapons—just down from a long campaign in the mountains, evidently-barred the way, stopped the servant, and stood gazing, with a face all alive with gratification and astonishment. Then he said, reverently, "Well, if it ain't a child!" And then he snatched a little leather sack out of his pocket and said to the servant, "There's a hundred and fifty dollars in dust, there, and I'll give it to you to let me kiss the child!"

That anecdote is *true*.

But see how things change. Sitting at that dinner-table, listening to that anecdote, if I had offered double the money for the privilege of kissing the same child, I would have been refused. Seventeen added years have far more than doubled the price.

And while upon this subject I will remark that once in Star City, in the Humboldt Mountains [Nevada Territory], I took my place in a sort of long, post-office single file of miners, to patiently await my chance to peep through a crack in the cabin and get a sight of the splendid new sensation—a genuine, live Woman! And at the end of half of an hour my turn came, and I put my eye to the crack, and there she was, with one arm akimbo, and tossing flap-jacks in a frying-pan with the other.

And she was one hundred and sixty-five years old (Being in calmer mood, now, I voluntarily knock off a hundred from that.—M.T.), and hadn't a tooth in her head.

Interestingly, Mark Twain's life was bracketed by Halley's comet. This comet swings by Earth and reaches its closest point to the sun once every seventy-five years. He was born fifteen days after the comet reached this point, and he died the day after it once again reached perihelion. Writing in his autobiography a year before his death, he said, "I came in with Halley's Comet in 1835. It is coming again next year (1910), and I expect to go out with it. It will be the greatest disappointment of my life if I don't go out with Halley's Comet. The Almighty has said, no doubt, 'Now here are these two unaccountable freaks; they came in together, they must go out together.'"

Rebel Guerrillas and Bank Robbers

Jesse James

Jesse W James

Jesse James is one of America's most famous antiestablishment rebels. The myths surrounding his exploits began well before his death. Dime novels painted him as a hero of the working class. Even President Teddy Roosevelt said, "Jesse W. James is America's Robin Hood."

Jesse was a rebel. He was one of the last of the South's Rebels, fighting against the Northerners long after the Civil War was over. He did this by robbing Northerners and Northern companies. Between February 13, 1866, and September 7, 1881, it's claimed the James–Younger Gang and the subsequent James Gang robbed twelve banks, seven trains, six stagecoaches, three stores, a paymaster, and the gate cash box of the ticket booth at the Kansas City Exposition. The exact number of his robberies is unknown, but it's estimated his gang stole between $82,000 and $450,000—roughly between $11 million and $69 million in today's money. Jesse eluded the authorities for fifteen years, some of it under intense publicity—that alone makes him one of America's most successful robbers.

Jesse and his gang were outlaws, but they were political outlaws with an agenda—and that agenda stemmed from the Civil War.

During the war most states north of the Mason–Dixon Line were Unionist, while most to the south were Confederate, but things were more complex in Missouri—the northernmost of the border slave states. Missouri was part of the Confederacy, but it was more internally divided than most. There the war was fought on a smaller scale and was more personal. Families attacked and killed their next-door neighbors because of their differing politics. Missouri's Unionists formed themselves into militia groups in order to protect themselves from the more violent secessionist guerrillas.

These guerrillas saw the Unionists as traitors of the first order who should be executed, even if they weren't armed or had surrendered.

There were guerilla bands on both sides of the war. The Southern variety were known as bushwhackers, while the Northern gangs were called Jayhawkers. These were self-established groups of irregulars that answered to no one but themselves, and rarely received orders from their respective governments or militaries. They had no specific objectives, other than to kill, punish, destroy, and loot. Most of the guerrillas were between seventeen and twenty-five years old and were brave, reckless, and ruthless.

Seventeen-year-old Jesse James in 1864 at Platte City, Missouri

Two of the most notorious secessionist bushwhackers were William "Bloody Bill" Anderson and William Quantrill. Jesse James served with Anderson and probably with Quantrill. While Quantrill is usually described as a vicious killer, Anderson was said to be "a blood-lusting lunatic."

The guerrillas rarely fought battles with the Union army and were more likely to have skirmishes with Union militias, but usually they were miles away from the front lines, attacking fellow Missourians—robbing and killing civilian Unionists. There were atrocities on both sides, but Anderson's and Quantrill's bands committed some of the worst.

Jesse's brother, Alexander Franklin "Frank" James, was the first to join the bushwhackers. In May 1863, their family farm was raided by Union militia searching for Frank's band. Frank escaped, but sixteen-year-old Jesse was beaten, and they tried to get his stepfather to reveal Frank's location by putting a noose around his neck, throwing it over a branch, and lifting him off the ground. He immediately led them to the guerillas' camp.

Frank joined Quantrill's Raiders and took part in the early morning August 21, 1863, massacre at Lawrence, Kansas. Lawrence was the abolitionist capital of

Kansas and the primary recruiting center for buffalo soldiers, though daily life there was pretty much like anywhere else in the county.

In one of the worst atrocities of the war, about 200 men—some estimate up to 450 men—raided the town. Quantrill had told his men, "Lawrence should be thoroughly cleansed, and the only way to cleanse it is to kill! Kill!" All men and boys of gun-bearing age were summarily executed. Estimates of the dead range from one hundred to more than two hundred, with the higher number probably being more accurate. Many were dragged from their beds and shot in cold blood in front of their families. Some were bludgeoned or knifed. Other unknown victims were burned alive when their homes were torched. By the time Quantrill's men rode out of town at about 9 a.m., they had looted the town and most of it was on fire. They had also robbed two of the town's banks.

Frank then went with Quantrill to Texas during the winter of 1863–1864 and on his return, he and Jesse joined Bloody Bill Anderson's band and took part in the Centralia Massacre.

On September 27, 1864, Anderson and eighty men descended on the town of Centralia and proceeded to loot the place. Some of Anderson's men were waiting for the train and had blocked off the track. As the train approached, some of Anderson's men rode alongside, firing their guns. When the train stopped, Anderson's men swarmed aboard. Anderson, Frank James, and a few others raided the baggage car, where they found thousands of dollars in cash.

Of the 125 passengers, the bushwhackers found 23 who were Union soldiers on leave. Some were wounded. One was on crutches. All were unarmed. The passengers were taken from the train and separated from the soldiers, who were ordered to strip. Anderson then called for an officer. A sergeant stepped forward, expecting to be killed. Instead Anderson had his men open fire, killing the other 22. They saved the sergeant for a prisoner exchange. While robbing the other passengers, they killed a few who tried to hide their valuables. Anderson's men then scalped the dead—they were known for tying Unionist scalps to their saddles and bridles—and they torched the depot. After sending the train on down the tracks toward its next stop in flames, they rode out of town.

Later that day Major Andrew V. E. "Ave" Johnston and the newly formed battalion of the 39th Missouri Infantry, US Volunteers, arrived. Leaving 35 men in town, he set off in pursuit of Anderson's men with 120 of his new recruits. On encountering guerrillas, Johnston ordered his men to dismount and form a battle line. Anderson's men made a mounted charge and their revolvers easily overwhelmed the Unionists' muzzle-loading Minié rifles. Anderson's men killed 123 of Johnston's volunteers. Anderson lost only about three men. Most were shot as they fled or tried to surrender. Frank James later said it was Jesse who killed Major Johnston. Finally they mutilated the bodies.

Because of the James brothers' guerilla activities, their family was exiled from Missouri. Anderson was killed in an ambush the following month. Frank went with Quantrill to Kentucky, and Jesse went with Archie "Little Arch" Clement, one of Anderson's lieutenants, to Texas. Jesse was shot in the chest by a Union cavalry patrol—not while trying to surrender, as was later claimed—and he returned to Missouri to recuperate.

After the war was over, the remnants of Anderson's band returned home, and in 1866, under Arch Clement, they began robbing banks. It's not known when Jesse recovered enough to join them, but Frank was with them. Eventually Clement and some of his men were captured or killed, so essentially the James brothers were all that remained. They were soon joined by Coleman "Cole" Younger, along with his two teenage brothers, and the gang became known as the James–Younger Gang.

During the war Cole was a captain among the bushwhackers, having served with Quantrill, Bloody Bill Anderson, and the James brothers and taken part in the Lawrence massacre. His hatred of the Unionists was inflamed when his father was murdered by Kansas Jayhawkers—Unionist guerrillas who launched many brutal raids into Missouri. Then in 1863—in an attempt to subdue the guerrillas or perhaps to draw them into the open—the Unionists imprisoned many of their female relatives in a three-story building in Kansas City. The building collapsed, killing five—including two of Cole's cousins. One of his sisters was very badly injured and later died from her injuries. Both legs of another of his sisters were broken, crippling her for the rest of her life. It was rumored among the Confederates that the Unionists sabotaged the building, causing it to collapse.

While the James–Younger Gang mainly robbed Republican-owned trains, banks, and businesses, it's said they also helped terrorize black voters. On at least one occasion they robbed a train while wearing full Ku Klux Klan garb.

Jesse became famous in December 1869 when he murdered the unarmed cashier John Sheets during the robbery of the Daviess County Savings Association in Gallatin, Missouri. He mistakenly thought Sheets was Major Samuel Cox, who lived in Gallatin and was credited with killing Bloody Bill Anderson years earlier. As Jesse rode away, he called out that he had shot Cox in revenge for Anderson's death, not knowing he had killed the wrong man. He later claimed that Captain Sheets was one of the company responsible for killing Anderson.

As the newspapers began following the exploits of the James–Younger Gang, Jesse began leaving press releases at the crime scenes. He also started writing letters to newspapers, proclaiming his innocence and establishing alibis. He was using the media to rally support from former Confederates and to portray himself as a victim.

The Jameses had many highs and lows in their lives, but for the most part they were fairly well-off. Most of the years growing up, their family owned slaves—considered a sign of wealth in the South. After their father died of disease as a forty-niner searching for gold in California, they went through a couple of years of poverty, but this changed when their mother remarried. Their stepfather owned a tobacco farm with seven slaves.

The James brothers saw themselves as Southern aristocratic gentleman and used their loot to live the high life. They dressed like cattlemen—wearing new suits, long dusters, and shiny black boots—and they were often dressed this way during their robberies. They bought and sold the finest quality stock, and they rode the best horses. They spent a lot of time at the racetracks racing their thoroughbreds, and they loved to gamble on them. The Youngers shared the James brothers' interest in horseracing and raced thoroughbreds in Missouri, Louisiana, Texas, and Indian Territory (present-day Oklahoma). They were all expert riders and they took special care of their horses, especially since they were essential for quick escapes and eluding posses. They also enjoyed staying at health resorts, which were popular among the wealthy.

When they were committing holdups, they could be fierce and brutal, but they also liked to act charming and joke around with their victims. They were gracious, bowing to the ladies and showing kindness to children. Frank recited Shakespeare and quoted from the Bible, while Jesse occasionally gave some people back a few dollars or their watches. Usually they would ask their victims if they had fought for the Confederacy. If someone said he had, the gang would either not rob him or would return what they had taken from him. But if someone displeased them or showed signs of resistance, Jesse and his men didn't hesitate to shoot him.

The gang loved making dramatic exits, and if the citizens or lawmen weren't already shooting at them, they would fire their guns into the air and dare posses to chase them. Jesse would rear his horse and bow to the crowd or his victims.

Jesse was more impulsive and outgoing than his brother. Frank was quiet and introspective. While Jesse didn't have much of an education, Frank loved to read and would snatch up any book he could find, especially when they were out in the wilderness.

The brothers spent fifteen years on the run, not counting their time as bushwhackers. When not involved in a robbery, they kept a very low profile. This took a toll. As time went on, Jesse became more and more afraid of everybody. He'd accuse people of being Pinkerton agents and is thought to have shot at least one of his gang members who he believed might turn him over to the law.

Since no photographs of him or Frank had yet been published, few people knew what they looked like. For a while Jesse hid his identity by using such aliases as John Davis "Dave" Howard, Thomas "Tom" Howard, and J. T. Jackson, while Frank was Benjamin "Ben" J. Woodson.

Among gang members Frank was known as "Buck," while Jesse was affectionately known as "Dingus." One evening during his time with Quantrill, while sitting around the campfire either loading or cleaning his gun, Jesse accidentally blew off the tip of the middle finger of his left hand. Calmly looking down at the damage, he said, "Now ain't that the most dingus-dangest thing you ever seen?" This got the others to laughing and resulted in them dubbing him "Dingus."

Many in the defeated South considered the guerrillas to be heroes and their crimes to be just a continuation of their guerrilla activities. One of Jesse's staunchest defenders and admirers was Confederate Major John Newman Edwards, a co-founder of the pro-Democrat *Kansas City Times*. Writing in editorials, such as "The Chivalry of Crime," he was largely responsible for the Jesse-James-as-underdog myth and used Jesse to rally against the excesses of the Reconstruction, portraying him as a heroic Southern knight who continued to fight the Lost Cause against Northern oppression by robbing from the rich and giving to the poor. The outlaws latched onto this.

In an anonymous letter to the *Times*—probably written by Jesse—the robbers claimed, "We are not thieves—we are bold robbers . . . [we] rob the rich and give to the poor." But it's doubtful they gave any money to the poor. Their idea of "giving to the poor" was usually giving large tips and overpaying for supplies to ensure their supplier's silence. They did like to throw money around. Sometimes they allowed former bushwhackers or ex-Confederate soldiers to join them on a robbery so they could support their family or pay off their mortgage, but, ultimately, the James–Youngers kept most of the spoils for themselves.

The gang was very popular in Missouri, where many saw them as freedom fight-ers who were striking a blow against the occupation forces. Having this kind of sup-port was extremely important to the James brothers. Before there were forensics and crime-scene investigators, it was very difficult to convict someone of a crime. Trials were essentially based on the testimony of witnesses. Usually the outlaw had friends testify that he was nowhere near the scene of his crime. Since it boiled down to their word against that of the eyewitnesses, the defense attorney could often cre-ate enough doubt that the criminal would be released. Outlaws needed a network of friends to hide, protect, and assist them, and to provide them with alibis.

The myths and disinformation generated by Jesse, Edwards, and other defend-ers generated a network of sympathetic supporters. This was very important and enabled them to escape capture for more than a decade while often hiding in plain sight using their aliases.

What follows is an interview with Jesse James that originally appeared in a spe-cial section of the *St. Louis Dispatch* of November 22, 1873. It was conducted by Major John Edwards and titled "A Terrible Quintette"; the quintet being Jesse and Frank James, Cole and John Younger, and Arthur McCoy—the core of the gang. It is probably Jesse's longest interview. In it Jesse provides alibis for just about every crime he'd been accused of up to that point. In addition to building sympathy, this would be important to his defense if he were captured and put on trial. Later on he came to enjoy his notoriety and often introduced himself to his victims during robberies.

In framing the interview, John Edwards wrote,

In going south from Kearney to the home of the brothers, one has of necessity to ride through heavy timber, and across creeks having bottoms and banks good for ambushment. Big trees grow by the roadside. Paths and blind ways lead off through the undergrowth, excellent avenues for the sudden dash of horsemen, and for the exercise of that sudden marks-manship which is always so fatal because always so near. Your correspon-dent rode unarmed and alone. When one hunts for information one does not hunt with either revolver or shotgun. Others who are paid for it do this, but not those who seek to satisfy that great hungry devil-fish—pub-lic curiosity. On the left, two miles and a half out from Kearney, a large gate opens into a large woods pasture. The gate opens and shuts easily, as if men who had been used to soldiering had been in the habit of riding through. Beyond the gate the timber thickens, and at noonday it is dark there. In the turn of the nights specters may abound there, for in riding into it one feels like riding into the unknown.

Suddenly a remarkably clear and penetrating voice called out "Halt," and before its echoes died away, two men, superbly mounted and splendidly armed, rode out from a clump of bushes into the middle of the road and drew up their horses as picquets [i.e., pickets] on an outpost. Neither gun nor pistol was presented. Between the man having a mission of peace and a man having a mission of war, it was not difficult to distinguish. They rode forward after a few brief seconds of observation and extended their hands. The man on the right was Jesse and the man on the left was Frank James—two horsemen unsurpassed for skill and endurance in the West, and

Two Pistol Shots

without a peer in all Missouri. Each one had a Spencer rifle, with sixty rounds of ammunition to the gun, and each had also three breech-loading dragoon-size Smith and Wesson English pistols, the deadliest and most accurate patent in the known world. A long talk was demanded, and all dismounted and took a seat in the shade of the trees. Not once, however, was a hand released from its hold upon the bridle-rein, and not once did the look of quiet caution and determination die out from the eyes of the men who had over their heads the shadow of an official outlawry.

Jesse James, the youngest [of the two brothers], has a face as smooth and as innocent as the face of a school girl. The blue eyes, very clear and penetrating, are never at rest. His form is tall, graceful and capable of great endurance and great effort. There is always a smile on his lips, and a graceful word or a compliment for all with whom he comes in contact. Looking at his small white hands, with their long, tapering fingers, one would not imagine that with a revolver they were among the quickest and deadliest hands in all the West. Frank is older and taller. Jesse's face is a perfect oval—Frank's is long, wide about the mouth and chin, and set always in a look of fixed repose. Jesse laughs at everything—Frank at nothing at all. Jesse is light-hearted, reckless, devil-may-care—Frank sober, sedate, a dangerous man always in ambush in the midst of society.

Jesse knows there is a price upon his head and discusses the whys and wherefores of it—Frank knows it, too, but it chafes him sorely and arouses all the tiger that is in his heart. Neither will be taken alive. Killed—that may be. Having long ago shaken hands with life, when death does come it will come to those who, neither surprised nor disappointed, will greet him with the exclamation: "How now, old fellow."

"You are accused of a multitude of bank robberies," the correspondent said, "and I have come to you for a full history of your lives, embracing of course your connection with the guerrilla service, and a recital of some of the most important actions connected therewith. If the newspaper reports can be relied on, you are certainly two of the most wonderful men in Missouri."

Jesse complied with alacrity, breaking in often upon his narrative to sweep all of the horizon possible from beneath the undergrowth, and listening ever and anon as an Indian might to catch the sound of approaching hoofs or the tramp of

Armed and Marching Men.

"During the war," he commenced, "Frank and myself served under [William] Quantrill, [George] Todd, [William "Bloody Bill"] Anderson and [Fletcher] Taylor.

"Many of your readers will recognize these names—all of them certainly, the names of Quantrill and Anderson. George Todd was a Jackson County man, living in Kansas City when the war broke out. At first he was a lieutenant under Quantrill, and afterwards organized a company of his own and did border service that was remarkable for its desperation even in a land of desperadoes. Taylor in turn was a lieutenant under Todd, and afterwards he, too, organized a company and exhibited all the enterprise and daring of his famous leaders. Of this terrible quartette, Taylor alone survives. One of his arms was shot away in a desperate combat. The sight of one eye was for a long time endangered by another wound; for months he lay at the point of death with a bullet through his right lung, he was wounded in the left thigh and through his remaining arm, but he still survives a maimed, reticent, quiet citizen, making no moan over the past and well content that he got back from the strife with even as much of his frame as was left to him. Quantrill was killed in Kentucky,

Anderson in Ray County, and Todd, while leading a forlorn charge in the Price Raid of 1864, upon the rear of the Second Colorado Cavalry. The heavy ball from a Spencer rifle struck him fair in the throat, severed the jugular vein, and the man was dead almost before he touched the ground."

Jesse continued:

"Under some one of these four men we served during the war. On the 15th of May, 1865, I was wounded near Lexington, Mo., in a fight with some Wisconsin cavalry men—soldiers, I believe, of the Second Wisconsin. On the 21st of the same month I surrendered at Lexington. I was in a dreadful fix. A Minie ball had gone through my right lung and everybody thought the wound would be mortal. The militia were clamoring for the death of all guerrillas, and people were afraid to come near me or about me. A Mr. Boosman, however, generously and fearlessly came to my relief, borrowed a carriage from Mrs. Early and hauled me into Lexington. On the 13th of June, 1865, I went to Kansas City, where, at my uncle's in Harlem, just across the river. Dr. Johnson Lykins—a Christian if there ever was one in this world—visited me daily and did everything for my wound possible. So also did Dr. Jo. Wood, one of the noblest and best men God ever created. You see I am very particular about these things, for I want first to get at the

Bank Robberies and Murders

with which Frank and myself are charged. On the 15th of July, 1865, I went up the river to Rulo in Nebraska, were my family were. On the 26th of August I returned towards home again, but such was the condition of my wound that I was unable to be hauled to my mother's house in Clay County. Again I stopped in Harlem, at the house of my uncle, and it was here that I received the visits of Dr. Wood.

"Just able barely to mount a horse and ride about a little in the spring of 1866, my life was threatened daily, and I was forced to go heavily armed. The whole country was then full of militia, robbing, plundering and killing. As for Frank, he was never permitted to come home at all. True, he did come, but it was in defiance of the orders of the authorities and at his own peril. After remaining at home awhile he went to Nelson County, Kentucky, and while at Brandenburgh, got into a fight with four Federal soldiers. Two of these he killed, the third he wounded badly, and the fourth

shot Frank in the point of the left hip, inflicting a terrible wound. This was in June, 1866. Frank wrote for me to come to him at once, and although my own wound was still very bad, I started immediately and stayed with him at the house of Mr. Alexander Severe, in Nelson County, until he recovered, which was in September. From Nelson County we went to Logan County to see some relatives we had there, and after staying until the middle of October, I returned alone to my home in Missouri. During the winter of 1866 and '67 I came almost to death's door. My wound would not heal, and I had had several hemorrhages.

"On the night of February 18th, 1867, an effort

Was Made to Kill Me.

Five militia men, well-armed and mounted, came to my mother's house and demanded admittance. The weather was dreadfully cold and I was in bed, scarcely able to get up. My pistols, however, I always kept by me. My stepfather heard them as they walked upon the front porch and asked them what they wanted. They told him to open the door. He came to my room upstairs and asked me what he should do. I requested him to help me to the window that I might look out. He did so. There was snow on the ground and the moon was shining. I saw that the horses hitched to the fence all had on cavalry saddles, and then I knew that the men were soldiers. I had but one thing to do—to drive them away or die. Surrender had played out for good with me. Incensed at my stepfather's absence, they were hammering at the door with the butts of their muskets, and calling out for me to come down, swearing that they knew I was in the house and would have me out dead or alive. I went downstairs softly, got close up to the front door and listened until from the talk of the men I thought I might be able to get a pretty good range. Then putting my pistol up to within about three inches of the upper panel, I fired. One hallowed and fell. Before the surprise was off, I threw the door wide open and with a pistol in each hand began a rapid fusillade. One I killed as he ran, two more were wounded besides the one on the porch, and the fifth man got clear without a scratch. So complete was the surprise that not a man among the whole five fired a shot."

This night attack, just as it is here recorded, actually took place, the circumstances being vouched for by a large number of people in Clay County, who were quite familiar with them.

"The four wounded men were brought into my mother's house, my stepfather went for a doctor, and they all recovered in a short time. Three of them are living in Clay County today, and are as good friends as Frank and myself have anywhere.

"I knew, however, that the next morning after the fight I would have to get away, and I did just in time, for a full company came early to look for me and were furious because I had escaped them.

"Being recommended to consult the celebrated Confederate surgeon, Dr. Paul Eve, of Nashville, Tennessee, I went there in June, 1867, and remained under his care for three weeks. He told me that my lung was so badly decayed that

I was Bound to Die,

and that the best thing I could do was to go home and die among my people. I had hope, however. I had been wounded seven times during the war, and once before in this same lung; and I did not believe I was going to die. I went from Nashville, Tennessee, to Logan County, Kentucky, and remained with my relatives until the first of November, 1867, when I again returned to Missouri. In December I went back to Kentucky and remained in Logan County until the latter part of January, 1868, and then went to Claplin, Nelson County."

The gate leading down from the road was heard to open and latch at this point in Jesse's narrative, and the two men were on horseback and on guard before a bird, startled from its perch among the leaves overhead, had gained another tree not fifty feet away. Horses and riders seemed carved from the same block. Instinctively, the steeds knew the wishes of their masters, and not an ear moved or an eyelid quivered. They had been well trained—trained indeed as only guerrillas know how to train horses when a neigh might bring down ruin or catastrophe. This newcomer was only an old neighbor farmer, however, who gave good day pleasantly and rode down under the hill to the house. Jesse and Frank again dismounted, and again reclined lazily in the shade, an arm through the rein of each bridle, and ever and anon an eye well to the front that watched not only the woods, but listened as well.

"About the bank robberies, Jesse," your correspondent asked, "tell me about them. According to the newspapers you and Frank have now about money enough to start a newspaper yourself, or take a goodly pile of stock in the Northern Pacific Railroad."

"It was to get at the question of these robberies," Jesse replied, "that has caused me to be so minute in introducing my career since the close of the war. The first robbery with which our names have been connected was the robbery of the bank at

Russellville, Kentucky,

which took place on March 20th, 1868. Russellville is in Logan County, and when the bank was robbed on the 20th of March, Frank and myself were at the Marshall Hotel in Claplin, Nelson County. Should occasion ever require proof on this point, we could bring two hundred respectable people to swear that on the day of the robbery we were fifty miles from the town of Russellville. About the first of April, after suffering dreadfully from my wound, I came back to Missouri, leaving Frank behind. It was not safe for him to come to Clay County, and he did not always want to be killing.

"In May, 1868, being recommended by Dr. Joe Wood, of Kansas City, to take a sea voyage, I went to New York City to find a ship going to San Francisco. The *Santiago de Cuba* sailed on the 8th of June and I took passage in her. On board was a regular officer of the U.S. Army with whom I became well acquainted. Major Gregg was a noble specimen of the old-time American army officer—of that time when they had gentlemen in the army, and not shysters, Negroes, and Yankee dead-beats whom the sutlers [i.e., authorized civilian vendors who followed Army camps and sold supplies to the soldiers] did not trust and who did not pay their gambling debts. I went with Major Gregg to Gen. Halleck's headquarters, met the General there, and had a long conversation with him concerning the nature of guerrilla warfare as practiced along the border between Missouri and Kansas. Halleck appearing to be much interested in the reminiscences I gave him of

Quantrill, Todd, Anderson, Blunt, Pool,

and the rest. He proffered me assistance in any manner and advised me to leave the seacoast with my wound. I did so at once, going to the house of my uncle, D. W. James, who owned the Paso Robles Hot Sulphur Springs, San Luis Obispo County, California. These waters cured me in three weeks, as if by a miracle. My wound healed, my lung got sound and strong, and from that day to this I have never felt any inconvenience from it in any manner.

"I was back again at home in Missouri, on the 28th of October, and went to work in good faith and with bright hopes for the future. Threats were made against me, however. The militia still swore that Frank should not come home, and that I should not remain there. What was I to do? Would you believe it, I plowed day in and day out with three pistols strapped about me. Around some of our fields there were thick woods and at any time I might have been shot from the bush, helpless and unable to defend myself.

"While working quietly at home, in December, 1869, Frank and myself were accused of robbing the bank in Gallatin, Daviess County, Missouri, and of killing at the same time its cashier, Capt. John W. Sheets. Knowing our innocence, and feeling justly indignant at a charge so infamous and untrue, Frank and myself saddled our horses, took what arms we needed to protect ourselves from our enemies and rode boldly into Kearney. Our purpose was to get affidavits from men whom the whole county knew to be truthful, and who would testify as to our whereabouts on the day of the robbery. We did get these affidavits. They were published in the columns of the

Kansas City Times,

a paper that has never been afraid to speak its mind on any subject, and to say a kind word even for a dog if he deserves it. These affidavits, sworn to by men of unimpeachable veracity, declared that both Frank and myself were in the town of Kearney, at 8 o'clock on the night preceding the morning of the robbery, and that we were in several stores and bought goods from several merchants. From Kearney to Gallatin is eighty miles. The robbery was committed on the 16th of December, 1869, and on the 15th of December, at 8 o'clock in the evening, both Frank and myself were buying goods in Kearney, eighty miles from Gallatin. These facts were proved by half a dozen of the best men of Clay County. Fifty more affidavits could have been procured on the same point if they had been deemed necessary. But this is not all. The night of the 16th we were again in Kearney, and again talked to a dozen or more of its citizens. To have killed Sheets and robbed the bank, and to have been in Kearney both on the nights of the 15th and 16th, it was necessary that we should have ridden one hundred and sixty miles in thirty hours on horseback.

At the time we published these affidavits, I wrote a letter to Col. McClurg, then the Governor of Missouri, pledging ourselves to surrender immediately to the officers of the law if he would protect us from a Daviess County mob—a county full of the militia the commands to which we had belonged had invariably routed. Governor McClurg did not answer my letter, but he did say, after carefully reading the evidence, that both Frank and myself were innocent of the

Gallatin Bank Robbery.

"If the Governor had given us protection we would have gone to Gallatin cheerfully and proved to the State that we had been lied upon and slandered; but he made no motion towards it, and we were too young and too brave to be first caught and then killed as rats are killed in a trap.

"Soon after the robbery, however, the deputy sheriff of Clay County, Mr. Thomason, came to arrest me with four men. It was snowing hard at the time, and I did not recognize any of them at first. I dreaded a mob, and I had long ago made up my mind never to be taken alive. Frank and myself were soon mounted and coming to close quarters with the posse. They did not stand worth a cent. I killed Thomason's horse, and it was not until then that I knew who composed the attacking party. We rode away after the posse fled, not caring even to pursue them, much less to make a circuit, as we might have done, ambushing and killing them every one. Without one single particle of evidence to connect us with the robbery— with an abundance of undisputable testimony in our favor—the attack upon the bank was laid at our door and we were held responsible for it. Governor McClurg, however, refused to offer any reward, so convinced was he of our entire innocence in the matter."

This interview was had before the reward of $2,000 had been offered for the arrest of each by Gov. Woodson, although they knew at the time that Daviess County had offered two hundred dollars for their arrest, and the widow of Capt. Sheets four hundred more.

"But, Jesse," your correspondent proceeded, "have neither you nor Frank an idea of this Gallatin matter? Why should Sheets have been killed, who made no objection to giving up his money?"

"Yes, we have an idea of the whole thing, and a pretty clear one at that. I will tell you why

Sheets was Killed.

"In Bill Anderson's command there were probably fifty men who had formed what was known as the Brotherhood of Death. To become a member of it, one had to swear that he would avenge the killing of a brother no matter how killed, or when, or where. Each member had a companion-in-arms, upon whom the pact became especially binding, and who could make it much more easy of observance. When Bill Anderson was killed a captain by the name of Cox, a militia captain, boasted openly and persistently of having shot him. He showed the revolver that fired the fatal ball. He came upon the body after life was extinct and carried it into Richmond, Ray County, where a photographer could be found. Many pictures were taken of the dead lion, with his great mane of a beard, and that indescribable pallor of death on his bronzed face. One of these pictures can be seen yet, I am told, in the State Arsenal, at Jefferson City. Cox, however, did not kill Bill Anderson, although he says he did. A line of infantry, a brigade strong, was drawn up across a road Anderson was traveling to reach the Missouri River. He was a man who rode over things in preference to riding round them. He ordered a charge as soon as he struck the skirmishers and dashed ahead as he always did—the foremost rider in a band that had devils for riders. The ball that killed him was a Minie ball—Cox had only his revolver—but it was something for a militiaman to have killed the savage tiger of all the bushwhackers, and so he boasted of it, and paraded his pictures everywhere as an Indian might his scalps. Some of the Brotherhood survived the war—not many, it is true, but enough to make good the oath they had sworn. Two or three declared to me that they meant to kill Cox, if he could be got at high or low, and as Cox is said to have been a bold man they thought they would have no difficulty in finding him. I am satisfied Sheets was killed through a mistake. I am almost convinced that one of the Brotherhood did it, and that he thought he was killing Cox. At any rate Cox himself thought so, for in a very short time he sold out his property in Gallatin and removed immediately to California. This is all I can tell you of Sheets and the robbery business.

"In August, 1870, Frank and myself went to Texas, and well down upon the frontier, where we remained until the winter of 1871. With a man by the name of D. C. Wells, we visited the Indian Nation, spending some time among the Choctaws and Chickasaws. One day, I think it was on the 22nd of February, and about seven miles south of Perryville, in the Creek Nation, Wells, Frank and myself met

Deputy Sheriff Thomason and Five Men,

face to face—our old antagonist of the Clay County battle. They were all well armed and so were we. A fight was expected on our side, but as they made no hostile movement, we certainly did not, and so after a little parley it was proposed that we should all dine together. Two hours were spent in this way quite pleasantly. Each party was ever on guard, but while each kept strict watch and ward, not a word was spoken that indicated in the least either vigilance or suspicion. Indeed, the deputy sheriff was greatly in need of money, and it gave me great pleasure to loan him fifty dollars, which I did then and there.

"In April, 1871, I came home again, well knowing, however, the hazard of the proceeding. On the 3rd of June, 1871, a bank was robbed in Corydon, Iowa, and straightway the crime was charged upon Frank and myself. Again it was the James Boys who had done it—and again was a great hue and cry raised over our daring recklessness."

"But where were you on the third, you and Frank?"

"Frank was home in bed with a severe attack of intermittent fever, and I was in West Kansas City, at the house of Mr. Lee B. McMurtry. Mr. McMurtry was living then in the same house with Policeman McKnight, of the patrol force. I conversed freely with these two gentlemen, and with many others about the depots in the bottom. Also with a reporter from the *Times* by the name of Timlin. On the 5th of June a pursuing party from Corydon overtook the robbers in Daviess County and had a fight with them. The robbers whipped the Iowa men and drove them back. The day of this fight I was at home, as I can prove by three of our neighbors who were over to see us, leaving at sundown for the house of Mr. Allen Moberly, in Greenville, Clay County, where I remained until about 12 o'clock.

"On the 28th of April, 1872, the bank at Columbia, Kentucky, was
Robbed and the Cashier Killed.
Again it was declared that Frank and myself had a hand in this robbery, and that we were not only bullet proof, but ubiquitous as well. I understand, however, where most of these charges against us came from. Detective Bligh, of Louisville, had an especial hatred against us, and for very good reasons. Whenever he could hear of a robbery that was somewhat remarkable for its boldness and its bravado, he would telegraph all over the country that the James Boys had a hand in it. He has written long letters to Major C. C. Rainwater, of the St. Louis Board of Police Commissioners, filled with his bare-faced and unscrupulous lies. Once in a fight with him our command whipped his to death, and he has never forgiven Frank and myself for the part we took in it. We know Major Rainwater well, although he does not know us. He was a gallant Confederate officer, and one who will do his duty under all circumstances. He is respected by all brave men, and I do not believe he was ever imposed on by Bligh's sensational letters and dispatches. At the time the bank was robbed in Columbia, I was in Lafayette County, Missouri. It was just after the mob in Cass County had stopped the train at Gun Town, and had killed Cline; Stevenson and Detro. Gen. Jo. O. Shelby was on the train at the time, and Frank and myself rode over to his place to learn from him the particulars of the massacre. We found him at his barn and had a long talk with him in the presence of several of his workmen. These will testify to out whereabouts.

"Again in November of the same year, I was in Lafayette County. A Negro boy at work for Gen. Shelby had been over in Aullville, had got into a fight with a white boy and had shot at him. A mob arose and pursued the Negro with the purpose of hanging him. They had a rope along ready for his neck. I galloped down to them and bade them halt, getting between the boy and his pursuers. Covering the leader with a double-barreled shotgun, I made the first and the last speech of my life. I told the mob that I was

An Outlaw Myself,

and that I had been driven away from home with a price upon my head. I knew nothing of the case, I said, but I was determined to resist the execution of mob-law in every shape, and that the first man who made a step further in pursuit would be certainly killed. Nobody moved, and I saved the Negro. Afterwards he was tried fairly and acquitted.

"It takes me some time to tell you all about these bank robberies, but if you want a full confession, I propose to give it to you. The attack on the bank at Ste. Genevieve, Missouri, took place, I believe, about the 26th of May, 1873. Frank and myself were accused of being there, of course. No matter where a bank is robbed, there we are in the midst of those who suffer. Now, if Governor Woodson, today would pledge his official honor to protect me from the savages of a cowardly mob, I would go at once to Jefferson City and stand trial for every crime I have been charged with. So, also would Frank. When the Ste. Genevieve bank was robbed, we were in Lafayette County. I could bring as witnesses to prove my whereabouts on the 25th of May, the day preceding the robbery, twenty citizens of that county whose oaths would be taken in the court of Heaven. They saw me, talked to me, and would remember perfectly the circumstances of my meeting with each of them.

"I now come down to the

Iowa Train Robbery,

which occurred on the 21st of July, 1873, and which filled all Western Missouri with spies, detectives, and armed men in search of us. The newspapers made me out the leader of the band. With me, according to reports, were Frank James, Arthur McCoy, and the two Youngers [John and Cole]. You remember the outlines of the robbery. A rail was removed from the track, a train thrown off, an engineer killed, and a general rifling had of an express car, thought to contain money belonging to the United States. An Iowa Sheriff named Brinkhoff came down to Kansas City with a pocket full of requisitions. He made some magnificent promises—not a few threats—hunted everywhere except in the right place, and, as far as I am informed, is still in Kansas City waiting for something to turn up.

"If we were ravenous animals, we could not have been more bitterly, more unreasonably, and more savagely abused and denounced. The lying reports of the cowardly and baffled Detective Bligh had been taken as gospel truth, and public sentiment, without stopping a moment to reason or to analyze, clamored viciously for our summary arrest and punishment. The Radical [Republican] papers of the State declared with emphasis that there was an organized band of robbers in Western Missouri, and that especially in Jackson County, had various members of the band been harbored and protected. Since the Iowa train robbery, however, I have not been in Jackson County, and of the day of the robbery, I had a long interview with a prominent county official, whose name I do not propose to give, even to a correspondent of the *Dispatch*—a paper for which I have so much regard. I remained with him about five hours, and during that time I saw and talked with seven men who will swear that I was not in Iowa the day the

Attack was Made Upon the Train.

"When it is safe for Frank and myself to surrender to the authorities of Missouri, we will do so openly and cheerfully. But it is not safe now, and so we do not mean to surrender. We may be killed, very well. It is a long lane that never has a turn. I have been shot seven times, and Frank five. Perhaps we have done a little shooting ourselves in all these years, but of that it does not become me to speak. Ask of my comrades in Jackson County, should you go back through Kansas City, what kind of soldiers we made. The best judge of a soldier on earth, is another soldier. Some of them are very hard to please, it may be, and have besides a very high standard, but when one soldier says that another soldier will fight, put it down always as gospel, that he will fight. I propose to be judged by the verdict of those with whom I served. I do not boast. In all I have said to you, I have confined myself to the God's truth, and I have tried to be brief. Should you print it, please print it as near my own way of saying it as possible."

The career of the James–Younger Gang lasted for another eight years after this interview—fifteen years altogether. Here is a list of the robberies attributed to them:

Date	Location	Target	Suspects (Reports vary in their list of suspects, so there may be more suspects than gunmen.)	Take	Victims	Comment
February 13, 1866	Liberty, Missouri	Clay County Savings Association (bank)	10 to 14 gunmen: Frank James, Cole and Jim Younger, John Jarrette, George and Oliver "Ol" or "Oll" Sheppard, Archie "Little Arch" Clements, Bill Anderson, Bud and Donny Pence, Jim and Bill Wilkerson, Frank Gregg, Joab Perry, Ben Cooper, Allen Parmer, Redman Munkers (or Red Monkus)	$58,072.64	19-year-old George "Jolly" Wymore killed	Said to be the first day-time bank robbery during peacetime. Jesse helps plan the raid, but can't participate because of his chest wound.
October 30, 1866	Lexington, Missouri	The Alexander Mitchell and Co. Bank	4 gunmen and 5 backup men: Jesse and Frank James, Cole Younger, John Jarrette, George and Ol Shepard, John and Dave Pool, Jesse Hamlett, Little Arch Clements, Hedge Reynolds	$2,011.50		Possibly Jesse's first robbery
March 2, 1867	Savannah, Missouri	Judge John McClain Banking House	5 or 6 gunmen: R. McDaniels, Robert Pope, Fitzgerald, John Jarrette	$0	John McClain wounded	Robbers are forced to flee under fire. Some believe this wasn't a James–Younger robbery, but a copycat.
May 22, 1867	Richmond, Missouri	The Hughes and Wasson Bank	12 gunmen: Frank and Jesse James, Cole and Bob Younger, Dick Burns, Payne Jones, Andy McGuire, John and James White, Allen Parmer, Bill Hulse, Felix Bradley, Tom Little, Bud Pence, Fred Meyers, James Devers, Issac Flannery	$3,500 to $4,000	Lieutenant Frank Griffin, B. G. Griffin (Frank's father), and the town's mayor John Shaw killed	
November 27, 1867	Independence, Missouri	Stone, McCoy & Co. Bank		$20,000 to $50,000		Not committed by the James–Younger Gang. Frank James is charged for this robbery, but the charges are dropped for lack of evidence.

Date	Location	Target	Suspects (Reports vary in their list of suspects, so there may be more suspects than gunmen.)	Take	Victims	Comment
March 20, 1868	Russellville, Kentucky	Nimrod Long Banking Co.	4 to 8 gunmen: Jesse and Frank James, Cole and Jim Younger, John Jarrette, George and Ol Shepard, Arthur McCoy, Jim White	$9,000 in paper currency, $3,000 in gold coins	One local wounded, one bandit killed and another captured.	George Shepard goes to prison for this robbery.
December 7, 1869	Gallatin, Arkansas	Daviess County Savings Bank	2 or 3 gunmen: Jesse and Frank James, Arthur McCoy, Jim Anderson	$700 to $1,000	Cashier John Sheets killed and clerk William McDowell wounded	Jesse kills Sheets thinking he is Cox. This is the first time Jesse's name is in newspapers. A $3,000 reward is offered for their capture.
June 3, 1871	Corydon, Iowa	Ocobock Brothers' Bank	4 to 7 gunmen: Jesse and Frank James, Cole and Jim Younger, Cleland or McClelland "Clell" Miller, Jim Cummins, Charley Pitts (real name Samuel "Sam" Wells)	$6,000 to $10,000		The Pinkerton Detective Agency is hired to catch the gang.
April 29, 1872	Columbia, Kentucky	Bank of Columbia	5 gunmen: Jesse and Frank James, Cole and John Younger, Clell Miller	$600 to $1,000	Cashier R. A. C. Martin killed and citizen James Garrett wounded	The cashier refuses to open the safe.
September 26, 1872	Kansas City	Kansas City Industrial Exposition Ticket Office	3 gunmen: Jesse James; Cole, Bob, and John Younger	$978	A little girl shot in the calf	30 minutes earlier the ticket office had $12,000. John Edwards describes the robbery as a "feat of stupendous nerve and fearlessness."
May 27, 1873	Ste. Genevieve, Arkansas	Ste. Genevieve Savings Association (bank)	4 gunmen: Jesse and Frank James, Cole and John Younger, Clell Miller, Bill Chadwell (real name William "Bill" Stiles)	$4,100		

Date	Location	Target	Suspects (Reports vary in their list of suspects, so there may be more suspects than gunmen.)	Take	Victims	Comment
July 21, 1873	4 miles from Adair, Iowa	Chicago, Rock Island, and Pacific Railroad	9 to 11 gunmen: Jesse and Frank James, Cole, Jim, John, and Bob Younger, Clell Miller, Charley Pitts, Bill Chadwell, George Sheperd, Arthur McCoy	$2,337	Engineer John Rafferty is killed when his neck snaps in the crash and several passengers are seriously injured.	The gang robs the express car and passengers. They expect a large cash shipment of up to $100,000, but it is on an earlier train. A $5,000 reward is offered, plus $1,000 each for Jesse and Frank.
January 8, 1874	Bienville Parish, Louisiana	Monroe-Shreveport Stagecoach	? gunmen	Unknown		Possibly not the James–Younger Gang
January 15, 1874	At Gulpha Creek between Malvern and Hot Springs, Arkansas	El Paso Stagecoach	5 or 6 gunmen: Jesse and Frank James, Cole, Bob, and John Younger, Clell Miller, Arthur McCoy	$1,000 to $8,000 in cash and jewels		Jesse had a watch from this robbery when he died.
January 31, 1874	Near Gad's Hill, Missouri	Iron Mountain Railroad	5 gunmen: Jesse and Frank James; Cole, John, and Bob Younger; Clell Miller; Arthur McCoy; Jim Reed	$2,000 to $5,000		Afterward the robbers telegraphed a press release.
February 1874	Bentonville, Arkansas	Craig and Son General Store	5 to 7 gunmen: Jesse and Frank James; Cole, John, and Bob Younger; Clell Miller; Arthur McCoy; Jim Reed	About $200		
March 11, 1874	Near Blue Hills, Missouri		Probably Jesse James and others		Pinkerton agent Joseph Whicher found murdered after being tortured	
April 7, 1874	Near Austin, Texas	San Antonio Stagecoach	5 gunmen: Jesse and Frank James, Bob Younger, Clell Miller, Arthur McCoy, Bill Chadwell, Charley Pitts	Around $3,000		

Date	Location	Target	Suspects (Reports vary in their list of suspects, so there may be more suspects than gunmen.)	Take	Victims	Comment
August 30, 1874	Lexington, Missouri	Waverly-Lexington Omnibus Stagecoach	3 gunmen: Jesse and Frank James, one of the Youngers, Arthur McCoy	Probably $100 to $200		The man with $5,000 they expected to rob was on the previous day's stagecoach.
August 30, 1874	Between Waverly and Carrollton, Missouri	Waverly-Lexington Omnibus Stagecoach	3 gunmen: Jesse and Frank James, one of the Youngers, Arthur McCoy			Some say the same 3 gunmen robbed this second stage 25 miles from the first.
December 7, 1874	Corinth, Mississippi	Tishomingo Savings Bank	4 gunmen: Jesse and Frank James, Cole Younger. Robbers gave their names as J. C. White, Ed Mason, Lewis, Castle—probably aliases	$5,000 in cash and $5,000 in jewelry		It's doubtful the James-Younger gang committed this one because of the next day's robbery, but they may have split the gang.
December 8, 1874	Muncie, Kansas	Kansas Pacific Railroad	5 gunmen: Jesse and Frank James, Cole and Bob Younger, Clell Miller, Jack Keen (aka Tom Webb), Sol Reed, Bill Ryan, Ed Miller, Jim Cummins, Billy Judson, Thompson "Tom" and Bill "Bud" McDaniel	Almost $30,000 or $50,000	Bud McDaniel was arrested, then killed, after escaping.	Rewards rise to $7,500 per robber.
May 13, 1875	Henry County, 12 miles north of Clinton, Missouri	Store/Post Office	4 gunmen: Jesse and Frank James, Cole and Bob Younger, Clell Miller, Jack Keen, Sol Reed, Tom McDaniel	Unknown. Mrs. D. A. Lambert and Bessie Sharp said the robbers stole "every cent we had in the world."		Jessie claimed it was Clell Miller, Jack Keen, Sol Reed, and Tom McDaniel.

Date	Location	Target	Suspects (Reports vary in their list of suspects, so there may be more suspects than gunmen.)	Take	Victims	Comment
September 6, 1875	Huntington, West Virginia	Bank of Huntington	4 gunmen: Jesse and Frank James, Cole Younger, Tom McDaniel, Jack Keen	$10,000 to $20,000	Tom McDaniel was killed. Jack Keen was sent to prison.	This was Jesse's 28th birthday.
April 13 or 19, 1876	Baxter Springs, Kansas	Crowell Bank	2 gunmen: Bill Chadwell, Charley Pitts	Almost $3,000		Probably masterminded by Cole and the Jameses
July 7, 1876	Rocky Cut, near Otterville, Missouri	Missouri Pacific Railroad	7 or 8 gunmen: Jesse and Frank James, Cole and Bob Younger, Clell Miller, Bill Chadwell, Charley Pitts, Hobbs Kerry, Jim Younger	$18,300	Hobbs Kerry sent to prison.	This robbery finances the gang's trip to Minnesota. Kerry identified the others and provided descriptions.
September 7, 1876	Northfield, Minnesota	First National Bank	8 gunmen: Jesse and Frank James, Cole, Jim and Bob Younger, Charley Pitts, Bill Chadwell, Clell Miller	$26.70	Cashier Joseph Heywood and citizen Nicholas Gustavson killed, with citizen Alonzo Bunker wounded. Gang members Charley Pitts, Bill Chadwell, and Clell Miller killed. Cole, Jim, and Bob Younger wounded and captured.	The James–Younger gang were informed a deposit of $75,000 had been made into the bank, though on that day the vault held only $15,455. Heywood was shot by Jesse or Frank. Only the James brothers escaped.

Date	Location	Target	Suspects (Reports vary in their list of suspects, so there may be more suspects than gunmen.)	Take	Victims	Comment
October 8, 1879	Glendale, Missouri	Chicago, Alton & St. Louis Railroad	6 gunmen: Jesse James, Bill Ryan (aka Tom Hill), Dick Liddil, Tucker Bassham, Ed Miller, Wood Hite	Between $6,000 and $50,000	One injured	The gunmen leave behind a press release, but it has no political content. Reconstruction was over, and even John Edwards stopped answering Jesse's letters.
September 3, 1880	Near Mammoth Cave, Kentucky	The Florida sightseeing stagecoach	2 gunmen: Jesse James, Bill Ryan	Around $1,800 or $2,000 in cash and jewelry		Jesse gets a diamond ring he gives to his wife.
October 15, 1880	Mercer, Kentucky	Doveys' store	3 gunmen: Jesse James, Bill Ryan, Dick Liddil	$13 and one watch		The robbers expected to get the Dovey Coal Mines' payroll.
March 11, 1881	Near Muscle Shoals, Alabama	Government paymaster	3 gunmen: Jesse James, Bill Ryan, either Clarence or Wood Hite	$5,240.18		
July 15, 1881	Near Winston, Missouri	Chicago, Rock Island & Pacific Railroad	5 gunmen: Jesse and Frank James, Wood and Clarence Hite, Dick Liddil	Around $600 or $2,000 in cash and jewelry	Conductor William Westfall and passenger Frank McMillan killed	According to Liddil, Jesse killed Westfall and Frank killed McMillan.
September 7, 1881	Blue Cut, near Glendale, Missouri	Chicago & Alton Railroad	6 gunmen: Jesse and Frank James, Wood and Clarence Hite, Dick Liddil, Charlie Ford	Between $950 and $3000 in cash and jewelry		The 5th anniversary of the Northfield robbery

Such a high-profile life of crime was particularly dangerous. The following gang members were killed:

- Archie "Little Arch" Clements (lynched, 1866)
- Oliver "Ol" Shepard (1868)
- Bill "Bud" McDaniel (1874)
- John Younger (1874)
- Thomas "Tom" McDaniel (1875)
- Cleland "Clell" Miller (1876)
- Charley Pitts (1876)
- Bill Chadwell (1876)
- Wood Hite (killed by two gang members, 1881)
- Ed Miller (shot by Jesse, 1881)
- Jesse James (killed by gang member, 1882)

Also, Archie Samuel—Jesse's eight-year-old half-brother—was killed by Pinkertons in 1875. And the following landed in prison:

- Clarence Hite (9 months)
- Hobbs Kerry (served 2 years)
- George Shepard (3 years)
- Bill Ryan, aka Tom Hill (7.5 years)
- Jack Keen, aka Tom Webb (8 years)
- Cole Younger (25 years)
- Jim Younger (25 years)
- Bob Younger (died in prison)

The Northfield Robbery in 1876 almost put an end to the gang. Pitts and Chadwell were killed and the Younger brothers were wounded, captured and sent to prison with life terms, though they were eventually paroled after twenty-five years. The James brothers barely escaped and were all that was left of the gang. Frank and Jesse laid low for three years before Jesse reformed the gang, but the new gang was plagued by paranoia, infighting, defections, mistrust and betrayal. In 1881, Jesse killed Ed Miller, the brother of dead gang member Clell Miller. It's uncertain why, but it's thought Jesse was afraid Ed might turn him in for the reward money. Then, later that same year, Wood Hite and Dick Liddil got into a gunfight over money and over Hite's stepmother, with whom Liddil was said to be having an affair. Hite was shot in the arm and Liddil in the thigh. Then Bob Ford entered the fray and shot Hite in the head, killing him. Hite was Jesse's cousin and he probably would've killed both Liddil and Ford, if he had found out.

Eventually Jesse had only two members he felt he could trust—Charlie and Robert "Bob" Ford. His trust was

Jesse James in about 1876 at the age of twenty-eight

misplaced, as the twenty-two-year-old Bob was in negotiations with the governor to betray Jesse. Perhaps it was out of fear for their lives; perhaps it was for the reward; perhaps it was because Jesse roughed up Bob's fifteen-year-old cousin; perhaps it was a bit of all of these, but whatever the reason, Bob shot Jesse in the head while Jesse's back was turned. The Ford brothers were living at Jesse's house in St. Joseph, Missouri, at the time. They were planning to leave the next day to rob a bank in Platte City, Missouri.

Bob later described what happened to the governor:

On the morning of April 3, [1882] Jess and I went downtown, as usual, before breakfast, for the papers. We got to the house about eight o'clock and sat down in the front room. Jess was sitting with his back to me, reading the *St. Louis Republican*. I picked up the *Times*, and the first thing I saw in big headlines was the story about Dick Liddil's surrender. Just then Mrs. James came in and said breakfast was ready. Beside me was a chair with a shawl on it, and as quick as a flash I lifted it and shoved the paper under. Jess couldn't have seen me, but he got up, walked over to the chair, picked up the shawl and threw it on the bed, and taking the paper, went out to the kitchen. I felt that the jig was up, but I followed and sat down at the table opposite Jess.

Mrs. James poured out the coffee and then sat down at one end of the table. Jesse spread the paper on the table in front of him and began to look over the headlines. All at once Jess said: "Hello, here. The surrender of Dick Liddil." And he looked across at me with a glare in his eyes.

"Young man, I thought you told me you didn't know that Dick Liddil had surrendered," he said.

I told him I didn't know it.

"'Well," he said, "it's very strange. He surrendered three weeks ago and you was right there in the neighborhood. It looks fishy."

He continued to glare at me, and I got up and went into the front room. In a minute I heard Jess push his chair back and walk to the door. He came in smiling, and said pleasantly, "Well, Bob, it's all right, anyway."

Instantly his real purpose flashed upon my mind. I knew I had not fooled him. He was too sharp for that. He knew at that moment as well as I did that I was there to betray him. But he was not going to kill me in the presence of his wife and children. He walked over to the bed, and deliberately unbuckled his belt, with four revolvers in it, and threw it on the bed. It was the first time in my life I had seen him without that belt on, and I knew that he threw it off to further quiet any suspicions I might have.

He seemed to want to busy himself with something to make an impression on my mind that he had forgotten the incident at the breakfast table, and said, "That picture is awful dusty." There wasn't a speck of dust that I could see on the picture, but he stood a chair beneath it and then got upon it and began to dust the picture on the wall.

As he stood there, unarmed, with his back to me, it came to me suddenly, "Now or never is your chance. If you don't get him now, he'll get you tonight." Without further thought or a moment's delay I pulled my revolver and leveled it as I sat. He heard the hammer click as I cocked it with my thumb and started to turn as I pulled the trigger. The ball struck him just behind the ear and he fell like a log, dead.

The body of Jesse James. The exit wound is visible above his left eye.

Jesse was killed at the age of thirty-four.

The Fords were tried and convicted of murder, and were sentenced to hang, but they were immediately pardoned by the governor. Some say the rewards were for Jesse's capture, so were not awarded. Others say a small reward was eventually given, but it was divided among the Fords and detectives. In 1884, Charlie Ford— suffering from tuberculosis and morphine addiction—committed suicide. Bob Ford eventually made his way to Las Vegas, New Mexico Territory, where he ran a saloon with Dick Liddil and served as a police officer. Bob was killed in Creede, Colorado, in 1892 by a shotgun blast to the throat.

The Disastrous Northfield Bank Robbery

Cole Younger

Cole Younger

Jesse may have captured the public's imagination, but he wasn't really the leader of the gang until he reformed it three years after the failed Northfield Raid. The gang was democratic in its decisions, though during robberies Jesse was usually the first to go in and the last to come out. The planning and coordination appears to have been done by Jesse, Frank, and Cole Younger. Cole definitely played a major role in the gang up until Northfield. And, as the oldest and most experienced of the four Younger brothers in the gang, it was only natural for them to look up to him.

The boldness and notoriety of the James–Younger Gang made things much more difficult for bandits, including themselves. By the mid-1870s, banks had better protection and robbing them became more dangerous, so the gang turned to holding up stagecoaches, but they didn't seize enough cash, so they began attacking trains. Soon the railroad companies increased their security, placing armed guards with valuable shipments and keeping the schedules secret. So the gang began hitting banks again.

They selected Northfield's First National Bank for monetary and political reasons. Besides being a major Northern bank, two of its largest depositors played significant roles in the Union's occupation of the South. These were former Union Generals Benjamin Butler and Adelbert Ames.

Butler was a Massachusetts senator who became a major general during the war and was the controversial commander of the Union's occupation forces in New Orleans in 1862, where he was referred to by Southerners as "Brute" and "Beast." While he didn't really commit any atrocities, other than having a man hanged for tearing down a Union flag from the US Mint in New Orleans, he was arrogant,

Cole [left] and Jim Younger around the time of the Civil War. Daguerreotypes, tin-types, and other similar early photographs usually depict a mirror image of their subject. One way to spot whether an image is correct is by the buttons. Men's buttons are normally on the person's right, buttoning to the left, while women's are usually on the left and button to the right. Also, coat pockets are generally on the left. This and some of the other images in this book have been corrected to show the subjects as they really were.

insensitive, and harsh. His time there is best known for his order stating that any woman who insulted a Union soldier would be treated as a prostitute. President Lincoln quickly replaced him. After the war he served in the US House of Representatives. After the Northfield raid he again served in the House of Representatives and became governor of Massachusetts. He had been the author of the Civil Rights Act of 1871—also known as the Ku Klux Klan Act of 1871—which provided federal protection of individual civil rights. It was largely designed to put an end to Ku Klux Klan violence, lynching, and voting violations by allowing federal troops to arrest and federal courts to try Klansmen, accomplishing what the states were unable to do.

Adelbert Ames was also a major general for the Union. He fought at Fredericksburg and Gettysburg and had served under General Butler in the Bermuda Hundred Campaign and the Siege of Petersburg, eventually marrying Butler's daughter. After the war he was a carpetbagger politician, first being appointed as provisional governor of Mississippi in 1868 and then elected governor in 1874. He was also a US senator from Mississippi from 1870 to 1874. He moved to Northfield a month before the raid to help run the family flour mill there. Cole later said he'd heard Ames and Butler had just deposited seventy-five thousand dollars in the bank.

In ten years of crime, the gang had never had any serious setbacks. All this changed with this raid. Previously they maintained the elements of surprise and intimidation, but this time they quickly lost both of these. They seriously underestimated the people of Northfield, Minnesota.

The townspeople were primarily God-fearing, hard-working, patriotic farmers, cattlemen, and tradesmen, who put a high value on obeying the law and working hard to earn money. They were largely of Swedish descent and were quick to welcome strangers, but were highly suspicious of anyone acting strangely. Many of them had fought for the Union.

When the gang rode into town, they immediately stood out with their rich clothes, rifles, and horses. One witness commented, "They were all first-class horses and would attract attention anywhere." Their Southern accents didn't help. They immediately caught the attention of merchants as they rode by the shop windows. Curiosity held the merchants' attention until the first sign of trouble, which caused the residents to quickly snap up their guns. Surprise and intimidation were gone and the shooting began. They were caught in a crossfire with nowhere to hide.

The town's marshal rapidly appeared on the scene, but he was unarmed, so he began throwing rocks at the outlaws. Adelbert Ames, the man whose deposit inspired the robbery, was at the flour mill nearby and came running at the sound of gunfire. He, too, was unarmed and could only watch the fight, but several times came very close to getting shot, which would have greatly pleased the robbers. The gang rode right past the mill on their way into town without knowing he was there.

What follows is Cole Younger's description of the Northfield raid from his book, *The Story of Cole Younger* (1903). His book is similar to Jesse James's interview in that he portrays himself as a loyal Confederate soldier and an avenger of the South, while covering up his crimes—except for his involvement in the Northfield raid, which he obviously couldn't deny. For the most part his account of the raid is pretty accurate, though he did try to conceal the role of Jesse and Frank, probably because Frank was still alive when he wrote this and probably because this was the way he'd been telling the story since it happened. Jesse and Frank were the only two robbers to escape. Since Cole and the others were wounded, they were not able to travel very fast, so Jesse and Frank took off on their own, hoping to draw their pursuers away from those they left behind. After being captured, Cole would have changed certain facts in his account to protect Jesse and Frank. In his account here, he starts off saying they were both dead, even though it's very likely he knew Frank was still alive. He did, in fact, get together with Frank for the first time in twenty-seven years right after his book was published. Then he tries to make it seem that he and Jesse didn't get along and wanted nothing to do with each other.

In order to remove the Jameses from the story, he replaces them in spots with other gang members. I have corrected this by adding the names of the most likely culprits, based on other testimony and evidence, in brackets.

Cole also blames alcohol for their downfall in this account, but this appears to be a later addition to his story and is probably not true.

SOME PRIVATE HISTORY

Every blood-and-thunder history of the Younger brothers declares that Frank and Jesse James were the two members of the band that entered Northfield who escaped arrest or death. They were not, however. One of those two men was killed afterward in Arizona [*sic*, Missouri] and the other died from fever some years afterward.

There were reasons why the James and the Younger brothers could not take part in any such project as that at Northfield.

Frank James and I came together as soldiers [sic, bushwhackers] some little time before the Lawrence Raid. He was a good soldier, and while he never was higher than a private, the distinctions between the officers and the men were not as finely drawn in Quantrill's command as they are nowadays in military life. As far back as 1862, Frank James and I formed a friendship, which has existed to this day.

Jesse James I never met, as I have already related, until the early summer of 1866. The fact that all of us were liable to the visits of posses when least expected gave us one interest in common, the only one we ever did have, although we were thrown together more or less through my friendship with Frank James.

The beginning of my trouble with Jesse came in 1872, when George W. Shepherd returned to Lee's Summit after serving a term in prison in Kentucky for the bank robbery at Russellville in 1868.

Jesse had told me that Shepherd was gunning for me, and accordingly one night, when Shepherd came late to the home of Silas Hudspeth, where I was, I was prepared for trouble, as in fact, I always was anyway.

When Shepherd called, Hudspeth shut the door again, and told me who was outside. I said, "Let him in." And stepping to the door with my pistol in my hand, I said, "Shepherd, I am in here. You're not afraid, are you?"

"That's all right," he answered. "Of course I'm not afraid."

The three of us talked till bedtime, when Hudspeth told us to occupy the same bed. [It was common practice up until the twentieth century for people to share beds. Part of the reason was lack of space, but it was primarily done for warmth. Entire families would share a bed. Even strangers slept together in boarding houses. Dogs were often included. The term "a three-dog night" refers to a night that is so cold one has to sleep with three dogs to keep warm.] I climbed in behind, and as was my custom, took my pistol to bed with me. Shepherd says he did not sleep a wink that night, but I did. At breakfast next morning, I said, "I heard yesterday that you intended to kill me on sight. Have you lost your nerve?"

"Who told you that, Cole?" he answered.

"I met Jess yesterday and he told me that you sent that message to me by him."

Soon after I met Jesse James, and but for the interference of friends we would have shot it out then and there.

My feeling toward Jesse became more bitter in the latter part of that year, when after the gate robbery at the Kansas City Fair, he wrote a letter to the *Times* of that city declaring that he and I had been accused of the robbery, but that he could prove an alibi. So far as I know that is the first time my name was ever mentioned in connection with the Kansas City robbery.

In 1874, when Detective [Joseph] Whicher [a Pinkerton agent] was killed on a trip to arrest Frank and Jesse James, I was angered to think that Jesse and his friends had brought Whicher from Kearney to the south side of the river, which I then believed was done to throw suspicion on the boys in Jackson County, of whom, perhaps, I would be most likely to get the credit. I have since learned, however, from the men who did kill Whicher, that Jesse did not kill him, but had believed his story and had been inclined to welcome him as a fellow wanderer.

Whicher was killed by Jesse, Frank, and one other gang member.

Whicher declared that he had murdered his wife and children in the East and he was seeking a refuge from the officers of the law. But Jesse's comrades were skeptical, and when they found on Whicher a pistol bearing Pinkerton's mark, they started with him for Kansas City intending to leave him dead in the street there. Shortly after they crossed to the Independence side of the river, the sound of a wagon on the frozen ground impelled them to finish the job where they were, as it was almost daybreak and they did not want to be seen with their captive.

But Jesse and I were not on friendly terms at any time after the Shepherd affair, and never were associated in any enterprises.

❦

We took a trip into town that forenoon [September 7, 1876], and I looked over the bank. We had dinner at various places and then returned to the camp. While we were planning the raid it was intended that I should be one of the party to go into the bank. I urged on the boys that whatever happened we should not shoot anyone.

Cole Younger

"What if they begin shooting at us?" someone suggested.

"Well," said Bob, "if Cap is so particular about the shooting, suppose we let him stay outside and take his chances."

So at the last minute our plans were changed, and when we started for town Bob [Younger], [Charley] Pitts and [Bill] Howard [actually Jesse, Frank and Charley] went in front, the plan being for them to await us in the square and enter the bank when the second detachment came up with them. [Clell] Miller and I went second to stand guard at the bank, while the rest of the party [Bob and Jim Younger and Bill Chadwell] were to wait at the bridge for the signal—a pistol shot—in the event they were needed. There were no saddle horses in evidence, and we calculated that we would have a considerable advantage. Wrecking the telegraph office as we left, we would get a good start, and by night would be safe beyond Shieldsville, and the next day could ride south across the Iowa line and be in comparative safety.

But between the time we broke camp and the time they reached the bridge the three who went ahead drank a quart of whisky, and there was the initial blunder at Northfield. I never knew Bob to drink before, and I did not know he was drinking that day till after it was all over.

When Miller and I crossed the bridge the three [Jesse, Frank, and Charley Pitts] were on some dry goods boxes at the corner near the bank, and as soon as they saw us went right into the bank, instead of waiting for us to get there.

When we came up I told Miller to shut the bank door, which they had left open in their hurry. I dismounted in the street, pretending to tighten my saddle girth. J. S. Allen, whose hardware store was near, tried to go into the bank, but Miller ordered him away, and he ran around the corner, shouting, "Get your guns, boys. They're robbing the bank."

Dr. H. M. Wheeler, who had been standing on the east side of Division Street, near the Dampier house, shouted "Robbery! Robbery!" and I called to him to get inside, at the same time firing a pistol shot in the air as a signal to the three boys at the bridge that we had been discovered. Almost at this instant I heard a pistol shot in the bank. Chadwell, Woods [Bob Younger] and Jim rode up and joined us, shouting to people in the street to get inside, and firing their pistols to emphasize their commands. I do not believe they killed anyone, however. I have always believed that the man Nicholas Gustavson, who was shot in the street, and who, it was said, did not go inside because he did not understand English, was hit by a glancing shot from Manning's or Wheeler's rifle. If any of our party shot him it must have been Woods.

Witnesses said Cole shot Gustavson in the head.

A man named Elias Stacy, armed with a shotgun, fired at Miller just as he was mounting his horse, filling Clell's face full of bird shot. Manning took a shot at Pitts' horse, killing it, which crippled us badly. Meantime the street was getting uncomfortably hot. Every time I saw anyone with a bead on me I would drop off my horse and try to drive the shooter inside, but I could not see in every direction. I called to the boys in the bank to come out, for I could not imagine what was keeping them so long. With his second shot Manning wounded me in the thigh, and with his third he shot Chadwell through the heart. Bill fell from the saddle dead. Dr. Wheeler, who had gone upstairs in the hotel, shot Miller, and he lay dying in the street.

At last the boys who had been in the bank came out. Bob ran down the street toward Manning, who hurried into Lee & Hitchcock's Store, hoping in that way to get a shot at Bob from behind. Bob, however, did not see Wheeler, who was upstairs in the hotel behind him, and Wheeler's third shot shattered Bob's right elbow as he stood beneath the stairs. Changing his pistol to his left hand, Bob ran out and mounted Miller's mare. Howard [actually this was Jesse *and* Frank] and Pitts had at last come out of the bank. Miller was lying in the street, but we thought him still alive. I told Pitts to put him up with me, and I would pack him out, but when we lifted him I saw he was dead, and I told Pitts to lay him down again. Pitts' horse had been killed, and I told him I would hold the crowd back while he got out on foot. I stayed there pointing my pistol at anyone who showed his head until Pitts had gone perhaps thirty or forty yards, and then, putting spurs to my horse, I galloped to where he was and took him up behind me.

"What kept you so long?" I asked Pitts.

Then he told me they had been drinking and had made a botch of it inside the bank. Instead of carrying out the plan originally formed, seizing the cashier at his window and getting to the safe without interruption, they leaped right over the counter and scared Heywood at the very start. As to the rest of the affair inside the bank I take the account of a Northfield narrator:

"With a flourish of his revolver one of the robbers pointed to Joseph L. Heywood, head bookkeeper, who was acting as cashier in the absence of that official, and asked, 'Are you the cashier?'

"'No,' replied Heywood, and the same question was put to A. E. Bunker, teller, and Frank J. Wilcox, assistant bookkeeper, each of whom made the same reply.

"'You are the cashier,' said the robber, turning upon Heywood, who was sitting at the cashier's desk. 'Open that safe quick or I'll blow your head off.'

"Pitts then ran to the vault and stepped inside, whereupon Heywood followed him and tried to shut him in.

"One of the robbers seized him and said, 'Open that safe now or you haven't but a minute to live.'

"'There's a time lock on,' Heywood answered, 'and it can't be opened now.'"

The safe was actually unlocked.

Howard [Jesse or Frank] drew a knife from his pocket and made a feint to cut Heywood's throat, as he lay on the floor where he had been thrown in the scuffle, and Pitts told me afterward that Howard fired a pistol near Heywood's head to scare him.

Top three photographs: citizen August Suborn (whose real name was Asle Oscar Sorbel), who discovered the fleeing outlaws; murdered cashier Joseph Heywood; and Sheriff James Glispin. Center photograph: The captions of Clell Miller and Bill Chadwell (whose real name was Bill Stiles) are reversed. Miller's body is on the left. Bottom four pictures: a battered Cole Younger, Jim Younger, the body of Charley Pitts (whose real name was Samuel "Sam" Wells), and Bob Younger. Jim Younger looks like he has a bloody nose, but that's the bullet hole that shattered his upper jaw.

Bunker tried to get a pistol that lay near him, but Pitts saw his movement and beat him to it. It was found on Charley when he was killed, so much more evidence to identify us as the men who were in Northfield.

"Where's the money outside the safe?" Bob asked.

Bunker showed him a box of small change on the counter, and while Bob [Jesse or Frank] was putting the money in a grain sack Bunker took advantage of the opportunity to dash out of the rear window. The shutters were closed, and this caused Bunker an instant's delay that was almost fatal. Pitts chased him with a bullet. The first one missed him, but the second went through his right shoulder.

As the men left the bank Heywood clambered to his feet and Pitts [probably Jesse], in his liquor, shot him through the head, inflicting the wound that killed him.

We had no time to wreck the telegraph office, and the alarm was soon sent throughout the country.

Gov. John S. Pillsbury first offered $1,000 reward for the arrest of the six who had escaped, and this he changed afterward to $1,000 for each of them, dead or alive. The Northfield bank offered $700 and the Winona & St. Peter Railroad $500.

A Chase to the Death

A little way out of Northfield we met a farmer and borrowed one of his horses for Pitts to ride. We passed Dundas on the run, before the news of the robbery had reached there, and at Millersburg, too, we were in advance of the news, but at Shieldsville, we were behind it. Here a squad of men, who, we afterwards learned, were from Faribault, had left their guns outside a house. We did not permit them to get their weapons until we had watered our horses and got a fresh start. They overtook us about four miles west of Shieldsville, and shots were exchanged without effect on either side. A spent bullet did hit me on the "crazy bone," and as I was leading Bob's horse it caused a little excitement for a minute, but that was all.

We were in a strange country. On the prairie our maps were all right, but when we got into the big woods and among the lakes we were practically lost.

There were a thousand men on our trail, and watching for us at fords and bridges where it was thought we would be apt to go.

That night it started to rain, and we wore out our horses. Friday we moved toward Waterville, and Friday night we camped between Elysian and German Lake. Saturday morning we left our horses and started through on foot, hiding that day on an isle in a swamp. That night we tramped all night and we spent Sunday about four miles south of Marysburg. Meantime our pursuers were watching for horsemen, not finding our abandoned horses, it seems, until Monday or Tuesday.

Bob's shattered elbow was requiring frequent attention, and that night we made only nine miles, and Monday, Monday night and Tuesday we spent in a deserted farm-house close to Mankato. That day a man named Dunning discovered us and we took him prisoner. Some of the boys wanted to kill him, on the theory that "dead men tell no tales," while others urged binding him and leaving him in the woods. Finally we administered to him an oath not to betray our whereabouts until we had time to make our escape, and he agreed not to. No sooner, however, was he released than he made posthaste into Mankato to announce our presence, and in a few minutes another posse was looking for us.

Suspecting, however, that he would do so, we were soon on the move, and that night we evaded the guard at the Blue Earth River bridge, and about midnight made our way through Mankato. The whistle on the oil mill blew, and we feared that it was a signal that had been agreed upon to alarm the town in case we were observed, but we were not molested.

Howard and Woods, who had favored killing Dunning, and who felt we were losing valuable time because of Bob's wound, left us that night and went west. As we afterward learned, this was an advantage to us as well as to them, for they stole two horses soon after leaving us, and the posse followed the trail of these horses, not knowing that our party had been divided.

Accordingly, we were not pursued, having kept on a course toward Madelia to a farm where I knew there were some good horses, once in possession of which we could get along faster.

We had been living on scant rations, corn, watermelon and other vegetables principally, but in spite of this Bob's arm was mending somewhat.

The Youngers, clockwise from their sister Henrietta—Cole, James, and Robert

He had to sleep with it pillowed on my breast, Jim being also crippled with a wound in his shoulder, and we could not get much sleep. The wound in my thigh was troubling me and I had to walk with a cane I cut in the brush. One place we got a chicken and cooked it, only to be interrupted before we could have our feast, having to make a quick dash for cover.

At every stopping place we left marks of blood from our wounds, and could have been easily trailed had not the pursuers been led in the track of our recent companions.

It seems from what I have read since, however, that I had myself left with my landlord at Madelia, Col. [Thomas] Vought, of the Flanders house, a damaging suggestion which proved the ultimate undoing of our party. I had talked with him about a bridge between two lakes near there, and accordingly when it became known that the robbers had passed Mankato, Vought thought of this bridge and it was guarded by him and others for two nights. When they abandoned the guard, however, he admonished a Norwegian boy named Oscar Suborn to keep close watch there for us, and Thursday morning, Sept. 21, just two weeks after the robbery, Oscar saw us, and fled into town with the alarm. [This seventeen-year-old Norwegian boy's real name was Asle Oscar Sorbel. He said his name was August Suborn or Oscar Oleson Suborn out of fear of reprisals by other members of the James–Younger Gang and their friends.] A party of forty was soon out in search for us, headed by Capt. W.[illiam] W. Murphy, Col. Vought and Sheriff [James] Glispin. They came up with us as we were fording a small slough, and unable to ford it with their horses, they were delayed somewhat by having to go around it. But they soon after got close enough so that one of them broke my walking stick with a shot. We were in sight of our long-sought horses when they cut us off from the animals, and our last hope was gone. We were at bay on the open prairie, surrounded by a picket line of forty men, some of whom would fight. Not prepared to stand for our last fight against such odds on the open field, we fell back into the Watonwan River bottoms and took refuge in some bushes.

We were prepared to wait as long as they would, but they were not of the waiting kind. At least some of them were not, and soon we heard the captain, who, we afterward learned, was W. W. Murphy, calling for volunteers to go in with him and rout us out. Six stepped to the front, Sheriff Glispin, Col. T. L. Vought, B. M. Rice, G. A. Bradford, C. A. Pomeroy and S. J. Severson.

Forming in line four paces apart, he ordered them to advance rapidly and concentrate the fire of the whole line the instant the robbers were discovered.

Meanwhile we were planning, too.

"Pitts," I said, "if you want to go out and surrender, go on."

"I'll not go," he replied, game to the last. "I can die as well as you can."

"Make for the horses," I said. "Every man for himself. There is no use stopping to pick up a comrade here, for we can't get him through the line. Just charge them and make it if we can."

I got up as the signal for the charge and we fired one volley.

I tried to get my man, and started through, but the next I knew I was lying on the ground, bleeding from my nose and mouth, and Bob was standing up, shouting, "Coward!"

One of the fellows in the outer line, not brave enough himself to join the volunteers who had come in to beat us out, was not disposed to believe in the surrender, and had his gun leveled on Bob in spite of the handkerchief which was waving as a flag of truce.

Sheriff Glispin, of Watonwan County, who was taking Bob's pistol from him, was also shouting to the fellow, "Don't shoot him or I'll shoot you."

All of us but Bob had gone down at the first fire. Pitts, shot through the heart, lay dead. Jim, including the wound in the shoulder he received at Northfield, had been shot five times, the most serious being the shot which shattered his upper jaw and lay imbedded beneath the brain, and a shot that buried itself underneath his spine, and which gave him trouble to the day of his death. Including those received in and on the way from Northfield I had eleven wounds.

A bullet had pierced Bob's right lung, but he was the only one left on his feet. His right arm useless, and his pistol empty, he had no choice.

"I surrender," he had shouted. "They're all down but me. Come on. I'll not shoot."

And Sheriff Glispin's order not to shoot was the beginning of the protectorate that Minnesota people established over us.

We were taken into Madelia that day and our wounds dressed and I greeted my old landlord, Col. Vought, who had been one of the seven to go in to get us. We were taken to his hotel and a guard posted.

"I don't want any man to risk his life for us," I said to him, "but if they do come for us give us our pistols so we can make a fight for it."

"If they do come, and I weaken," he said, "you can have your pistols."

But the only mob that came was the mob of sightseers, reporters and detectives.

After fleeing Northfield, Jesse, Frank, Pitts, and the wounded Youngers slowly headed southwest for a week in the rain dodging posses. They had abandoned their horses along the way. By this time there were a thousand men searching for them. Extremely hungry and suffering from exposure, they decided it was time to split up. The Jameses headed off on their own, while Pitts remained behind to assist the wounded. Frank and Jesse stole a horse from a nearby farm, which they both rode, and continued toward the Dakota Territory. At one point they were hit by shotgun fire from a guard post. Stealthily dropping off their galloping horse, they allowed it to lead the posse away. Frank was wounded in the right foot, Jesse in the right knee, and one of them in the side. They soon stole two more horses and headed off again.

They reached Sioux Falls in the Dakota Territory on September 18, 1876—after eleven days on the run with little food or sleep and no change of clothes. With posses still in hot pursuit, they rode their horses across the Sioux River into Iowa. On the 20th they encountered a doctor, who Jesse forced to swap clothes with him. Riding off to the south, they disappeared, and the posses lost their trail. The next day, back in Minnesota, the Youngers were captured and Pitts killed.

It's uncertain where the Jameses went. Some say they headed down through Indian Territory (now Oklahoma) and into southern Missouri, where they hid at friends' houses, before eventually moving on to settle near Nashville with their families. Others say they traveled east through Iowa and Wisconsin, turning south through Illinois and Kentucky to Tennessee. After many months they reached Nashville, where they lived quietly for three years before resuming their criminal careers.

In order to avoid the death penalty, the Youngers pled guilty to being accessories to murder and each was sentenced to life imprisonment. They were sent to Stillwater Prison at Stillwater, Minnesota. Eight years later Bob died of tuberculosis. Cole and Jim were considered model prisoners and in 1901 were paroled after serving twenty-five years. A year later, Jim committed suicide. Cole received a complete pardon in 1903. In 1912 he repented his past and became a Christian. He died in 1916 at seventy-two years of age.

"I am not exactly a lead man," Cole Younger wrote, "but it may surprise you to know that I have been shot between twenty and thirty times and am now carrying over a dozen bullets which have never been extracted. How proud I should have been had I been scarred battling for the honor and glory of my country."

Breaking Off from My Bohemian Life

Frank James

[signature: Frank James]

After the Northfield raid, Jesse and Frank laid low for three years. Then Jesse began to scout around for a new gang. Frank, short on cash, decided to rejoin him. They carefully chose criminals they felt they could trust. But one of them, Bob Ford, shot Jesse in the back of the head in 1882. Jesse was only thirty-four years old. Jesse's death really took a lot out of Frank. Six months later he had decided to turn himself in. He explained,

I was tired of an outlaw's life. I have been hunted for twenty-one years. I have literally lived in the saddle. I have never known a day of perfect peace. It was one long, anxious, inexorable, eternal vigil. When I slept it was literally in the midst of an arsenal. If I heard dogs bark more fiercely than usual, or the feet of horses in a greater volume of sound than usual, I stood to arms. Have you any idea of what a man must endure who leads such a life? No, you cannot. No one can unless he lives it for himself.

Journalist Frank O'Neill interviewed Frank James both before and after his October 5, 1882, surrender to Missouri governor Thomas Crittenden. In the interview, Frank discussed his life on the run, Bob Ford, and Jesse's death, but he refused to talk about his involvement in any crimes—probably out of fear that anything he said would be used against him in court. He maintained this silence in public throughout most of his life.

The governor refused to promise Frank either an amnesty or a pardon, offering only "a fair and impartial trial." Frank was accompanied by journalists Frank O'Neill,

John Newman Edwards, and Finis Farr—the governor's secretary. On meeting the governor, Frank said—offering him his cartridge belt and pistols—"Governor Crittenden, I want to hand over to you that which no living man except myself has been permitted to touch since 1861, and to say I am your prisoner."

O'Neill's interview with Frank James appeared in the *St. Louis Republican* the following day.

I have returned to Missouri to try and regain a home and a standing among her people. I have been hunted like a wild animal from state to state. I have known no home, I have slept in all sorts of places—here today—there tomorrow. I have been charged with every great crime committed in Missouri or in her neighboring states. I have been taught to suspect my nearest and dearest friends of treachery and where is the end to be?

I am tired of this life of taut nerves of night-riding and day-hiding, of constant listening, for footfalls, cracking twigs and rustling leaves and creaking doors; tired of seeing Judas on the face of every friend I know— and God knows I have none to spare—tired of the saddle, the revolver and the cartridge belt; tired of the hoofs and horns with which popular belief has equipped me. I want to see if there is not some way out of it.

I intend to work—oh, so hard—to make amends for the past. If I am not allowed to do this, I don't know what I shall do. Of course the world is wide and I can go where my safety is absolute but I have had enough of exile. I don't want any more.

I think I can give the state substantial proof for what I ask and I think the dignity of the law will not suffer if I prove myself worthy of mercy. I have proved my ability at good citizenship and I think I can demonstrate it in Missouri. . . .

In August 1877 I arrived in Nashville accompanied by my wife. I was then in very poor health and had been for some time. A great many emigrants from Ohio were arriving that time and it was easy for us to assume that character. I went by the name of B. J. Woodson. We first applied to a farmer named Ben Drake who received us kindly and strangers though we were, made us comfortable for a week.

We then moved over to a house of Mrs. Ledbetter, a widowed sister of Mr. Drake and we stayed there until I effected the rental of a piece of land from a man named Josiah Walton, on White Creek, a few miles from Nashville.

My health rapidly improved and I worked on the farm, seldom failing to put ten hours a day in the fields. At the end of the year I engaged to team for one year on for Jeff Hyde's place for the Indiana Lumber Company and I carried out this agreement to the letter, driving a four-mule team.

I took my meals in the woods with the darkies, never missing a full day's work. At the expiration of teaming I rented a farm from Felix Smith on White Creek and I remained there until the time of my departure in April of 1881.

During those four years I was never absent from my work and I maintained a reputation for good citizenship equal to any man in the county.

Among my many friends was J. B. Shute, a member of the legislature and he will undoubtedly be surprised that he was in the company of the notorious Frank James. I went with Shute to many political meetings but I never took any prominent part. In my whole experience down there I never had but one approach to trouble.

One day I was sitting in the blacksmith shop of Dood Young, brother of the constable, when Dood who had been drinking freely, came in. He had suddenly conceived I was one of those damn Yankees who had come down to run things. Being in a belligerent mood he cursed me out and said he intended to slap my face. He was a great big double-fisted fellow and I was no match for him. For a moment I was in a great dread. I knew if he started to beat me I could not restrain myself from killing him. And then it would be goodbye to this long endeavor to settle down.

I took all he said good naturedly and tried to reason with him and by this pacific course I finally quieted him down and was able to slip away. Subsequently we became good friends and I have no doubt he will read your newspaper with a great deal of interest.

That reminds me of a couple of Nashville citizens who will also take a particular interest in your newspapers if this comes out.

Among the detectives in Nashville was a man named Fletch Horn and a man named Watson. Horn is a Falstaffian sort of fellow, full of good nature and I always liked him. Watson, on the other hand, was morose, saying little and staring at everything and everybody.

One day Jim Cummins came down to visit me and we were in War-ner's Restaurant and Watson was standing nearby.

You know Jim Cummins is an apprehensive, nervous sort of a chap, who always feared the worst. I jerked him by the sleeve and asked him to come over and be introduced to a detective.

He paled and grew very fidgety. As he backed away he said, "Not by a —— sight. Do you think I'm a —— fool?" He got as far back in the restaurant as he could and all I could get out of him was, "You know you don't have a bit of —— sense. Someday you'll get pulled in by your brashness."

I explained to Jim the safest course for us was "cheeking it out" and the man most liable to get pulled in was the man who sneaked. But I never converted him to that view as the results will show.

Was Cummins there with you?

No, he was there with Jess.

What! Did Jesse live there too?

I forgot to tell you about that. It was something curious. I had not seen Jesse for two years and I had no idea where he was. One day in the Spring after my arrival, I stopped in the grain store of Ray & Sons to buy some red oats. Whom should I see in the office talking to Ike Ray but Jess! Ike knew him as Joe Howard. Jess was as surprised as I was and we stepped out and had a chat. He told me he was living near Waverly, Humphreys County, West Tennessee, and had come up to sell some corn. After some talk we separated. A year and a half later he moved to North Nashville.

What was Jesse's occupation?

He was a great patron and lover of the race tracks and spent much of his time there. He had several fine horses, among them the great Jim Malone, which won a big race not long ago in St. Louis, a four-mile race in Louisville and a big cup at Atlanta, Georgia. Jesse moved with perfect freedom down there.

When did Cummins go there?

He and Dick Liddil came down in the fall of 1880. Dick came on horseback and Jim came through by the cars [i.e., train]. Jim was a happy-go-lucky, trampish sort of a fellow, not fond of work and I'll bet that wherever he is, he doesn't have ten dollars to his name.

He is not at all dangerous and the state does not have to worry about him. I have no doubt if he reads that I am telling you, he will say (with a most comical drawl), " 'Yass, there's that damn fool go in 'n turned state's evidence. I'll kill the —— scoundrel as soon as I lay eyes on him. By —— I will!"

But Jim won't you know, that's one of his plays of fancy. He frequently has them and he never kills anybody. It's just too much trouble. Jim stopped with Jesse and so did Jack Ryan. Dick Liddil stayed with me and was a right good industrious young chap. I never thought there was anything vicious about Dick but he was easily influenced.

Well, our residence in Nashville was cut short due to a curious circumstance and it was a strong illustration, try as we may, to break off from my bohemian life, something would always occur to drive us back. Jim Cummins had always been the fearful frightened wretch that I have described and he somehow got the idea that he wasn't safe at Jesse's place. His fidgeting and restlessness attracted Jesse's attention and he become suspicious that Jim was nerving himself up to betray us.

We both kept a close watch on Jim and made it our business to know where he was going and what he was doing. One night in April, 1881, he was at my house and was more nervous than usual. He started up and I asked him where he was going. He said he was going to Jesse's. I asked him if he was coming back that night and he said he might but then he might not.

He did go to Jesse's but after staying a short time he said he was coming back to my place. But he never showed up. When Jesse found that Jim had not taken his overcoat and overshoes he became suspicious and came to see me. Considering his abandonment of his clothing, we agreed that Jim had gone to betray us. We decided to take proper caution, we kept our accoutrements in readiness, saddled our horses, and staying away from the house, waited all night for the officers to make their appearance.

They never appeared and this satisfied us that Jim had not said anything to the Nashville police.

We then thought it possible that Jim had gone to some distant point to meet officers from Missouri whom he had sent for, so during the next week, we were constantly in the saddle and in the balance had our horses ready in the barn.

Our fears proved groundless and we became convinced, and I still am, that Jim ran away because he feared capture and not to raise any mischief. Jesse wrote to several places making inquiries about him but we never saw Jim again.

Then just as we were settling down to security again, and less than two weeks after Jim Cummins' departure, Jack Ryan, known here as Bill Ryan, got drunk one day and was arrested in White Creek for disorderly conduct by Squire Erthman, who I knew well and who lived three miles from my place.

When they arrested him they found him heavily armed and with evidence as to his real identity and character. He was removed, as you know to Missouri to answer a charge there. As soon as we heard of his arrest, we mounted our horses, rode away and have never been back since.

Jess went one way with Dick Liddil and I went another. I never saw Jess again. I need hardly tell you that since that time I have done very little business. Those four years of an upright life were the happiest I have ever spent since my boyhood, notwithstanding the hard labor attending them. My old life grew the more detestable the more I got away from it and it was with a sense of despair that I rode away from our little house on the Smith place to again become a wanderer.

Did you attend public gatherings at Nashville freely and without fear of identification?

I did. For example I took the prize for exhibiting the Poland-China hogs at the Nashville and Jackson fairs, and I entered my horse, Jewel Maxey for the gents stakes at Nashville two years in succession, winning the first prize the first time and second money, the second time.

I rode myself the second time and would have taken first money, I believe if the starter, Ben Cockrell, had not ruled me down unfairly at the start. A year ago last Christmas, I took dinner with Clint Cantwell in the home of County Clerk Eastman who is Mr. Cantwell's son-in-law.

And no one in that region knew your identity?

Nobody but those of my own household and of Jesse's. Before I leave that subject I would like to mention that my little boy was born on the Walton place near Nashville.

When did you hear of Jesse's death?

The morning after it occurred. I went out early that morning to take a walk with my son and by the way I would like to say that he is the brightest four-year-old that ever blessed a family. When I returned my wife had the *New York Herald* in her hand. She told me that Jesse had been killed.

I asked by whom. She said by Bob Ford. When she said that I knew it was true, Jesse never trusted Bob. He loved Charlie but he suspected Bob of treachery. I believe that if the whole truth were known, Charlie took no part in that assassination, no matter what he may have been drawn into saying since it occurred.

Charlie Ford was always a warm-hearted boy and Jesse always treated him as if he was a brother. You may have noticed from the statements of the police that they did not consider Charlie in their employ. Charlie never fired a shot that day and anybody knows Charlie is a quicker man with a pistol than Bob. No, I can't believe Charlie was in it.

I don't blame Governor Crittenden for the part he had in the affair. I am satisfied there was no contract for assassination. If I were governor charged with upholding the laws of a great state cursed by such a band of outlaws who terrorized the state, I would take desperate measures to meet such desperate men. They would have to go as in this case they have gone. Such is the fate of all such bands. But what must be the suffering of such a pitiful creature as Bob Ford. For a few paltry dollars he has, while on the verge of manhood, brought upon himself a blighting curse that will never leave him in all the years to come.

Did you notice how remorse seized him soon after he got his blood money? He was rushing away from his victim with all the horror of Macbeth when the poor, desolate wife called to him to come back. What did he say? "I swear to God I did not do it."

Again like Macbeth, "I'll go no more. I'm afraid to think of what I have done. Look upon it again I dare not." Watch him again in New York. He is certain he saw the face of my wife there while as a fact she was at her father's home in Missouri. His imagination has already started to begin its deadly work and he sees blood and horror wherever he looks.

They said, as they have said many idle things, that I have sworn vengeance against the assassin and that I would have a life for a life. Would that be vengeance? Would it be vengeance to shorten a life which is now an agonizing torture to him? Would it be vengeance to send a corpse to break the heart of a mother who loves him as mine does me? Would it be vengeance to come home to my wife and my mother and show the red brand of a murderer?

No. When I took the paper and read the account of Jesse's death that morning, my wife and I sat down and talked about it. I said then the air would be full of rumors of what I would do and I proposed to do nothing. I have never made a threat against the life of any man in my lifetime and I was not going to now.

It was rumored that you came to Missouri that time. Did you?

I did not. What sort of generalship would it have been to come when everyone was expecting me?

After his surrender, Frank James was something of a celebrity. Crowds swarmed around him, eager to get a glimpse of the famous outlaw and to shake his hand.

There were indictments against him for an 1867 bank robbery in Independence, Missouri, and for the 1874 murder of Pinkerton detective Joseph Whicher, but at the recommendation of the prosecutor, the charges were dismissed. Indictments for the 1869 Gallatin bank robbery and for killing passenger Frank McMillan during the 1881 train robbery of the Chicago, Rock Island & Pacific Railroad remained.

In 1883 Frank went on trial in Gallatin, Missouri, for McMillan's murder, and the staunchly Democrat jury found him innocent. He then went on trial in Huntsville, Alabama, for the 1881 holdup of the government paymaster in Muscle Shoals. Once again he was found not guilty. Then he was sent back to Missouri to be tried for the 1876 Rocky Cut train robbery of the Missouri Pacific Railroad, but the case was dropped right before the trial because a court ruling stated a felon could not testify in a trial unless he had been pardoned, and prosecutors were unable to obtain a pardon for Dick Liddil, their primary witness.

There were no other charges against him in Missouri, and the newly elected governor—a former Confederate general—was not about to hand him over to Minnesota authorities for the Northfield raid.

Cole Younger was released from prison in 1901, and his book was published two years later. On its publication in March 1903, Cole phoned Frank. The two friends decided to give lecture tours together. They bought an interest in the Buckskin Bill Wild West Show, and renamed it the Great Cole Younger and Frank James Historical

Wild West Show. As a condition of his parole, Cole was not allowed "to exhibit himself," so he sat in a reserved box signing autographs, shaking hands, and lecturing on the evils of gambling and alcohol. The show was a disaster, but when Frank and Cole demanded to be released from their contract, they were refused. Eventually Cole threatened one of the owners with his pistol to get out of the show, and it closed.

Frank James in 1898

The following year, Cole became president of the Hydro-Carbon Old Burner Company, but he soon quit. About a year later the former train robber became president of the production company of the Kansas City, Lee's Summit, & Eastern Railroad. Frank died in 1915 at the age of seventy-two. Cole died the following year.

For years Jesse's mother made money by selling pebbles from Jesse's grave in her front yard for a quarter apiece. Jesse's son, Jesse Edward James, was arrested in 1898 for robbing the Missouri Pacific Express train just outside Kansas City. Jesse insisted he was innocent, and his attorneys said he was framed by the police. He was acquitted. With the help of former governor Crittenden—the governor who was elected on the promise that he would break up the James–Younger Gang—he went to law school and became a lawyer.

The Massacre of Some of Custer's Men

George Armstrong Custer

In 1874 one of Lieutenant Colonel George Custer's men proved there was gold in the Black Hills of what is now South Dakota, sparking a gold rush into an Indian reservation that led on June 25, 1876, to the Battle of the Little Bighorn, where Custer and between 207 and 225 of his men died. Custer was famous during his lifetime, but his final battle made him a legend, and it became the most famous battle in frontier history.

Custer's military career was a checkered one. He came close to being expelled each of his four years at the US Military Academy, often because of his penchant for practical jokes. He graduated last in his class and was court-martialed a few days later for failure of duty because, as officer of the guard, he didn't break up a fight between two cadets. He was saved because the outbreak of the Civil War created a shortage of officers.

During the war, in spite of the unusually high casualty rates of his units, his fearless aggression in battle resulted in rapid promotions—a characteristic that later contributed to his death. Custer's first battle was at Bull Run in 1861. At that time he was a second lieutenant. Two years later, at the age of twenty-three, he was a brevet-brigadier general. His brigade fought at Gettysburg and in Shenandoah Valley. He was the one who received the Confederate flag of truce and was present when General Robert E. Lee surrendered at Appomattox. He was promoted to brevet-major general before the end of the Civil War. Like many others, he reverted to his regular rank of captain when the war was over.

In 1866 he was appointed lieutenant colonel and commander of the newly formed 7th Cavalry. He was then sent to fight in the Indian Wars.

Life in the cavalry was difficult and involved lots of marching, riding, and moving about. George Custer outlined a typical day in the 7th Cavalry in his book, *My Life on the Plains* (1874), which was originally published serially in *The Galaxy* from 1872 to 1874. The day he described was June 2, 1867, in Kansas, shortly after setting off on a thousand mile march with 350 men and 20 wagons.

A cavalry camp immediately after reveille always presents an animated and most interesting scene. As soon as the rolls are called and the reports of absentees made to

Cadet George Custer at West Point in about 1859

headquarters, the men of the companies, with the exception of the cooks, are employed in the care of the horses. The latter are fed, and while eating are thoroughly groomed by the men, under the superintendence of their officers. Nearly an hour is devoted to this important duty. In the meanwhile the company cooks, ten to each company, and the officers' servants are busily engaged preparing breakfast, so that within a few minutes after the horses have received proper attention breakfast is ready, and being very simple it requires but little time to dispose of it. Immediately after breakfast the first bugle call indicative of the march is the "General," and is the signal for tents to be taken down and everything packed in readiness for moving. A few minutes later this is followed by the bugler at headquarters sounding "Boots and saddles," when horses are saddled up and the wagon train put in readiness for pulling out. Five minutes later "To horse" is sounded, and the men of each company lead their horses into line, each trooper standing at the head of his horse. At the words "Prepare to mount," from the commanding officer, each trooper places his left foot in the stirrup; and at the command "Mount," every man rises on his stirrup and places himself in his saddle, the whole command presenting the appearance to the eye of a huge machine propelled by one power. Woe betide the unfortunate trooper who through carelessness or inattention fails to place himself in his saddle simultaneously with his companions. If he is not for this offense against military rule deprived of the services of his horse during the succeeding half day's march, he escapes luckily.

As soon as the command is mounted the "Advance" is sounded, and the troops, usually in column of fours, move out. The company leading the advance one day march in rear the following day. This successive changing gives each company an opportunity to march by regular turn in advance. Our average daily march, when not in immediate pursuit of the enemy, was about twenty-five miles. Upon reaching camp in the evening the horses were cared for as in the morning, opportunities being given them to graze before dark. Pickets were posted and every precaution adopted to guard against surprise.

Four years earlier, in 1862, gold was discovered in what was then the Nebraska Territory—but would the following year become the Montana Territory—prompting the creation of the Bozeman Trail, which was actually a series of trails. This five-hundred-mile trail provided a shortcut from the Oregon–California Trail to the gold fields, reducing travel by four hundred miles. Unfortunately it ran across Sioux, Arapaho, and Cheyenne territory and right through their last remaining hunting grounds—the Powder River Country—where the travelers not only disrupted the herds, but killed many buffalo. In order to protect the travelers, the Army built a series of forts along the trail. Travel on the trail dropped off in 1866 because of hostilities, though it was still used as a military supply route for the forts until it was closed in 1868.

Between 1863 to 1866 only thirty-five thousand emigrants used the trail, but it was enough to spark the Sioux War of 1866–1868—also known as Red Cloud's War. The Natives resented these incursions, and some committed thefts, rapes, and murders of travelers, settlers, and soldiers—often brutally. (While Native Americans are usually portrayed as a major threat to the emigrants on the overland trails, statistics show that between 1840 and 1860, Native Americans killed 362 out of a total of 296,259 pioneers on the trails, while the pioneers killed 426 Native Americans during that time.) In 1866 tensions were high and things were getting more violent.

(*Note:* The Great Sioux Nation is a confederation of seven tribes made up of three divisions—the Dakota, Nakota, and Lakota—all of which mean "allies" or "friends" in their different dialects. The eastern division, called the Dakota or Santee, is made up of the Mdewakanton, Sisseton, Wahpekute, and Wahpeton tribes. The middle division, the Nakota, is composed of the Yankton and Yanktonai tribes. The western division consists of the Lakota [or Teton] tribe. The Sioux Wars were primarily fought by this tribe. After 1720, the Lakota divided into seven bands—the Blackfeet Sioux [also known as the Sihasapa and not to be confused with the Algonquian Blackfeet tribe of Montana and Canada], Brulé [Sićangu], Hunkpapa, Miniconjou, Oglala, Sans Arcs [Izipaco or Itazipacola], and Two Kettle [Ooinunpa].)

The purpose of Custer's excursion in 1867 was to intimidate the tribes into stopping the violence and to prevent a large-scale outbreak along the Bozeman Trail and other travel routes. Custer tried to locate the tribes, but all he found were small war parties that constantly harassed his men. Marching from Fort Hays in central Kansas, he and his men headed south in a semicircle and up through southern Nebraska to Fort Sedgwick into the northeastern corner of the Colorado Territory, then south to Fort Wallace in Western Kansas and back to Fort Hays.

A month into their march, Lieutenant Lyman Kidder—with a Sioux guide and ten soldiers—was sent from Fort Sedgwick carrying dispatches for Custer. Kidder was supposed to head for Custer's command post at the forks of the Republican River in southern Nebraska. If Custer wasn't there, he was to trail Custer and catch up with him. When Custer reached Riverside Station—a telegraph station about fifty miles west of Fort Sedgwick—he telegraphed the Fort and was told Kidder had been sent after him. Since Lieutenant Kidder's detachment was long overdue, Custer became very concerned about their safety and set out to find them. His account is a spooky foreshadowing of his own end.

The third night after leaving the Platte [River], my command encamped in the vicinity of our former camp near the forks of the Republican. So far nothing had been learned which would enable us to form any conclusion regarding the route taken by Kidder. [Will] Comstock, the guide, was frequently appealed to for an opinion which, from his great experience on the Plains, might give us some encouragement regarding Kidder's safety. But he was too cautious and careful a man, both in word and deed, to excite hopes which his reasoning could not justify. When thus appealed to he would usually give an ominous shake of the head and avoid a direct answer.

On the evening just referred to, the officers and Comstock were grouped near headquarters discussing the subject which was then uppermost in the mind of every one in camp. Comstock had been quietly listening to the various theories and surmises advanced by different members of the group, but was finally pressed to state his ideas as to Kidder's chances of escaping harm.

"Well, gentle*men*," emphasizing the last syllable as was his manner, "before a man kin form any ijee as to how this thing is likely to end, thar are several things he ort to be acquainted with. For instance, now, no man need tell me any p'ints about Injuns. Ef I know anything, it's Injuns. I know jest how they'll do anything and when they'll take to do it; but that don't settle the question, and I'll tell you why. Ef I knowed this young lootenint—I mean Lootenint Kidder—ef I knowed what for sort of a man he is, I could tell you mighty near to a sartainty all you want to know; for you see Injun huntin' and Injun fightin' is a trade all by itself, and like any other bizness a man has to know what he's about, or ef he don't he can't make a livin' at it. I have lots uv confi*dence* in the fightin' sense of Red Bead, the Sioux chief who is guidin' the lootenint and his men, and ef that Injun kin have his own way thar is a fair show for his guidin' 'em through all right; but as I sed before, there lays the difficulty. Is this lootenint the kind of a man who is willin' to take advice, even ef it does cum from an Injun? My experience with you army folks has allus bin that the youngsters among ye think they know the most, and this is particularly true ef they hev just cum from West P'int. Ef some of them young fellars knowed half as much as they b'lieve they do, you couldn't tell them nothin'. As to rale book-larnin', why I 'spose they've got it all; but the fact uv the matter is, they couldn't tell the difference twixt the trail of a war party and one made by a huntin' party to save their necks. Half uv 'em when they first cum here can't tell a squaw from a buck, just because both ride straddle; but they soon larn. But that's neither here nor thar. I'm told that the lootenint we're talkin' about is a newcomer and that this is his first scout. Ef that be the case it puts a mighty onsartain look on the whole thing, and twixt you and me, gentle*men*, he'll be mighty lucky ef he gits through all right. Tomorrow we'll strike the Wallace Trail and I kin mighty soon tell ef he has gone that way."

But little encouragement was to be derived from these expressions. The morrow would undoubtedly enable us, as Comstock had predicted, to determine whether or not the lieutenant and his party had missed our trail and taken that leading to Fort Wallace [down near the central western border of Kansas].

At daylight our column could have been seen stretching out in the direction of the Wallace Trail. A march of a few miles brought us to the point of intersection. Comstock and the Delaware had galloped in advance, and were about concluding a thorough examination of the various tracks to be seen in the trail, when the head of the column overtook them. "Well, what do you find, Comstock?" was my first inquiry. "They've gone toward Fort Wallace, sure," was the reply; and in support of this opinion he added, "The trail shows that twelve American horses, shod all round, have passed at a walk, goin' in the direction of the fort; and when they went by this p'int they were all right, because their horses were movin' along easy and there are no pony tracks behind 'em, as wouldn't be the case ef the Injuns had got an eye on 'em." He then remarked, as if in parenthesis, "It would be astonishn' ef that lootenint and his layout gits into the fort without a scrimmage. He may; if he does, it will be a scratch ef ever there was one, and I'll lose my confidence in Injuns."

The opinion expressed by Comstock as to the chances of Lieutenant Kidder and party making their way to the fort across eighty miles of danger unmolested was the concurrent opinion of all the officers. And now that we had discovered their trail, our interest and anxiety became immeasurably increased as to their fate. The latter could not remain in doubt much longer, as two days' marching would take us to the fort. Alas! we were to solve the mystery without waiting so long.

Pursuing our way along the plain, heavy trail made by [Lieutenant Samuel] Robbins and [Colonel William] Cooke [of the 7th Cavalry], and directing Comstock and the Delawares to watch closely that we did not lose that of Kidder and his party, we patiently but hopefully awaited further developments. How many miles we had thus passed over without incident worthy of mention, I do not now recall. The sun was high in the heavens, showing that our day's march was about half completed, when those of us who were riding at the head of the column discovered a strange-looking object lying directly in our path, and more than a mile distant. It was too large for a human being, yet in color and appearance, at that distance, resembled no animal frequenting the Plains with which any of us were familiar. Eager to determine its character, a dozen or more of our party, including Comstock and some of the Delawares, galloped in front.

Before riding the full distance the question was determined. The object seen was the body of a white horse. A closer examination showed that it had been shot within the past few days, while the brand, U.S., proved that it was a government animal. Major [Joel] Elliot then remembered that while at Fort Sedgwick he had seen one company of cavalry mounted upon white horses. These and other circumstances went far to convince us that this was one of the horses belonging to Lieutenant Kidder's party. In fact there was no room to doubt that this was the case.

Almost the unanimous opinion of the command was that there had been a contest with Indians, and this only the first evidence we should have proving it. When the column reached the point where the slain horse lay, a halt was ordered to enable Comstock and the Indian Scouts to thoroughly examine the surrounding ground to discover, if possible, any additional evidence, such as empty cartridge shells, arrows, or articles of Indian equipment, showing that a fight had taken place. All the horse's equipments, saddle, bridle, etc. had been carried away, but whether by friend or foe could not then be determined.

While the preponderance of circumstances favored the belief that the horse had been killed by Indians there was still room to hope that he had been killed by Kidder's party and the equipments taken away by them; for it frequently happens on a march that a horse will be suddenly taken ill and be unable for the time being to proceed farther. In such a case, rather than abandon him alive, with a prospect of his recovering and falling into the hands of the Indians to be employed against us, orders are given to kill him, and this might be the true way of accounting for the one referred to.

The scouts being unable to throw any additional light upon the question, we continued our march, closely observing the ground as we passed along. Comstock noticed that instead of the trail showing that Kidder's party was moving in regular order, as when at first discovered, there were but two or three tracks to be seen in the beaten trail, the rest being found on the grass on either side.

We had marched two miles perhaps from the point where the body of the slain horse had been discovered, when we came upon a second, this one, like the first, having been killed by a bullet, and all of his equipments taken away. Comstock's quick eyes were not long in detecting pony tracks in the vicinity, and we had no longer any but the one frightful solution to offer: Kidder and his party had been discovered by the Indians, probably the same powerful and blood-thirsty band which had been resisted so gallantly by the men under Robbins and Cooke; and against such overwhelming odds, the issue could not be doubtful.

George Armstrong Custer in his brigadier general's uniform in September 1863

We were then moving over a high and level plateau unbroken either by ravines or divides, and just such a locality as would be usually chosen by the Indians for attacking a party of the strength of Kidder's. The Indians could here ride unobstructed and encircle their victims with a continuous line of armed and painted warriors, while the beleaguered party, from the even character of the surface of the plain, would be unable to find any break or depression from behind which they might make a successful defense. It was probably this relative condition of affairs which had induced Kidder and his doomed comrades to endeavor to push on in the hope of finding ground favorable to their making a stand against their barbarous foes.

The main trail no longer showed the footprints of Kidder's party, but instead Comstock discovered the tracks of shod horses on the grass, with here and there numerous tracks of ponies, all by their appearance proving that both horses and ponies had been moving at full speed. Kidder's party must have trusted their lives temporarily to the speed of their horses—a dangerous venture when contending with Indians. However, this fearful race for life must have been most gallantly contested, because we continued our march several miles farther without discovering any evidence of the savages having gained any advantage. How painfully, almost despairingly exciting must have been this ride for life! A mere handful of brave men struggling to escape the bloody clutches of the hundreds of red-visaged demons, who, mounted on their well-trained war ponies, were straining every nerve and muscle to reek their hands in the life-blood of their victims. It was not death alone that threatened this little band. They were not riding simply to preserve life. They rode, and doubtless prayed as they rode, that they might escape the savage tortures, the worse than death which threatened them. Would that their prayer had been granted!

We began leaving the high plateau and to descend into a valley through which, at the distance of nearly two miles, meandered a small prairie stream known as Beaver Creek [in Northwest Kansas]. The valley near the banks of this stream was covered with a dense growth of tall wild grass intermingled with clumps of osiers [*Salix longifolia*, a shrub willow]. At the point where the trail crossed the stream we hoped to obtain more definite information regarding Kidder's party and their pursuers, but we were not required to wait so long. When within a mile of the stream I observed several large buzzards floating lazily in circles through the air, and but a short distance to the left of our trail. This, of itself, might not have attracted my attention seriously but for the rank stench which pervaded the atmosphere, reminding one of the horrible sensations experienced upon a battlefield when passing among the decaying bodies of the dead.

As if impelled by one thought Comstock, the Delaware, and half-a-dozen officers detached themselves from the column and separating into squads of one or two instituted a search for the cause of our horrible suspicions. After riding in all directions through the rushes and willows, and when about to relinquish the search as fruitless, one of the Delaware uttered a shout which attracted the attention of the entire command; at the same time he was seen to leap from his horse and assume a stooping posture, as if critically examining some object of interest. Hastening, in common with many others of the party, to his side, a sight met our gaze which even at this remote day makes my very blood curdle. Lying in irregular order, and within a very limited circle, were the mangled bodies of poor Kidder and his party, yet so brutally hacked and disfigured as to be beyond recognition save as human beings.

Every individual of the party had been scalped and his skull broken—the latter done by some weapon, probably a tomahawk—except the Sioux chief Red Bead, whose scalp had simply been removed from his head and then thrown down by his side. This, Comstock informed us, was in accordance with a custom which prohibits an Indian from bearing off the scalp of one of his own tribe. This circumstance, then, told us who the perpetrators of this deed were. They could be none other than the Sioux, led in all probability by Pawnee Killer.

Red Bead, being less disfigured and mutilated than the others, was the only individual capable of being recognized. Even the clothes of all the party had been carried away; some of the bodies were lying in beds of ashes, with partly burned fragments of wood near them, showing that the savages had put some of them to death by the terrible tortures of fire. The sinews of the arms and legs had been cut away, the nose of every man hacked off, and the features otherwise defaced so that it would have been scarcely possible for even a relative to recognize a single one of the unfortunate victims. We could not even distinguish the officer from his men. Each body was pierced by from twenty to fifty arrows, and the arrows were found as the savage demons had left them, bristling in the bodies. While the details of that fearful struggle will probably never be known, telling how long and gallantly this ill-fated little band contended for their lives, yet the surrounding circumstances of ground, empty cartridge shells, and distance from where the attack began, satisfied us that Kidder and his men fought as only brave men fight when the watchword is victory or death.

As the officer, his men, and his no less faithful Indian guide had shared their final dangers together and had met the same dreadful fate at the hands of the same merciless foe, it was but fitting that their remains should be consigned to one common grave. This was accordingly done. A single trench was dug near the spot where they had rendered up their lives upon the altar of duty. Silently, mournfully, their comrades of a brother regiment consigned their mangled remains to mother earth, there to rest undisturbed, as we supposed, until the great day of final review.

Good Bear told George Bent that he was one of twelve Cheyenne Dog Soldiers involved in the fight. (The Dog Soldiers were an elite Cheyenne military organization that played a major role in Cheyenne resistance to incursions into their territory. They were strongly opposed to the peace policies of chiefs like Black Kettle and Lean Bear, insisting on preserving their original way of life, while resisting confinement on reservations and becoming dependent on the US government.) They and some Brulé Sioux under Pawnee Killer were hunting buffalo when they spotted Lieutenant Kidder and his men near their camp. They quickly sprang into action. The Dog Soldiers rode their horses around Kidder's men firing at them, while the Sioux preferred to fight on foot and fire from the cover of the grass. Throughout the fight, Red Bead called out to the Sioux asking that they let him out, but they ignored him. Two Sioux were killed in the battle, while the Dog Soldiers had two horses shot out from under them.

The mutilation of a corpse was a tradition of warfare for many tribes. Scalping and strangulation were done in the belief that it would kill the person's spirit, taking away his eternal life to save the tribes from having to fight the same enemy again in the afterlife. They wanted to make sure the dead stayed dead. Other mutilations, without scalping or strangulation, were to disfigure and make the person suffer in the afterlife. They believed that the spirit of a person whose body was cut and shot full of arrows would also have those wounds and have spirit arrows sticking out of them, tormenting them for eternity. This was the reason for what appeared to be an expensive waste of arrows.

They believed everything—animals, trees, stones—were manifestations of these objects' spirits. Like many cultures, they thought that weapons, blankets, and personal items that are left with the body would be there to use in the afterlife. Items the person could make for him- or herself were not left. Favorite ponies were sometimes tied up or killed near the body. The items themselves were not thought to go to the afterworld, but as long as they remained with the body until his or her spirit reached there, then the essence of those items would be with the person. Though the physical items quickly served their purpose, the living would never consider taking anything from a grave, even if they were starving to death and needed the weapons to survive.

Some Natives believed the afterlife was much like this one, only more intense. And the fewer enemies to harass them, the better. When dealing with enemies, they often scalped and mutilated the bodies. Besides the reasons already given, they also did this to humiliate their enemy, to demonstrate they were warriors, and to put fear into the surviving enemies. But for an enemy they really hated, they would mutilate, but not scalp the corpse, leaving that person to suffer in torment for eternity. Mutilation was a punishment, but the scalping was seen as merciful. They killed Chief Red Bead because he was with the soldiers. Apparently he wasn't mutilated, since his was the only recognizable body, but he was scalped to prevent his spirit from entering the afterlife.

On reaching Fort Wallace, Custer took a few of his men and headed off to Fort Riley in what is now Northeastern Kansas to see his wife. On arriving there he was arrested and charged with abandoning his command during a campaign in which he ordered pursuers to shoot three deserters without a hearing—one of which died—and several other lesser infractions. Custer was once again court-martialed and suspended from his command for a year. After ten months Lieutenant General Philip Sheridan reinstated him, and two months later, on November 27, 1868, Custer led his men in the attack on a Cheyenne village on the Washita River that has become known as the Washita Massacre.

The Sioux Wars were largely guerrilla wars and—much like the Vietnam and Iraq Wars—it was very difficult for the Army to separate the peaceful civilians from the fighters. Often the fighters would hide out in a peaceful camp. Unfortunately, when the soldiers couldn't locate the hostiles, they would attack those they could find—often peaceful Native Americans.

After being attacked by a small party of warriors, Custer's guides followed the tracks to the Washita village, which was on the Cheyenne reservation in what would eventually become Oklahoma. This was Black Kettle's band and Chief Black Kettle (Motavato) was well known throughout the United States as one of the most peaceful chiefs on the plains. In spite of all the terrible things done to him and his people, Black Kettle consistently lobbied for peace.

(It should be noted that the government never understood that Native American chiefs did not have the same authority over their people as a president or general does. Chiefs would get together to make decisions for their bands or their tribe, but it was up to each person to decide whether or not to follow them. Individuals were free to follow their own hearts, and many changed bands when they didn't agree with the decisions of the chiefs. All chiefs—even war chiefs—had difficulty controlling their young warriors. Many well-planned traps were spoiled when anxious young warriors attacked too soon. And even the most peaceful chiefs could not keep the most hostile warriors from visiting or joining their camps.)

Five years earlier Black Kettle and a number of other chiefs were invited to Washington, DC, where they met President Lincoln and were given medallions and papers certifying they were friends of the United States. Black Kettle was also given a huge US flag and told that if he flew that flag, no soldier would ever fire at him. He was very proud of this flag and always flew it above his tepee when at a permanent encampment.

The following year several chiefs, including Black Kettle, met with the governor of the Colorado Territory to ask for peace. They were told to set up camp at Sand Creek and their Indian agent would give them some provisions. Secretly the governor, the Indian agent, and Colonel John Chivington wanted to provoke a war so they could seize the Natives' lands.

Chivington was the commander of 3rd Colorado Cavalry, which was ridiculed as the "Bloodless Third," because they hadn't fought a battle in the nearly one hundred days of its existence. Chivington arrived at the nearby Fort Lyon with six hundred men, saying he "had come to kill Indians, and believed it to be honorable to kill Indians under any and all circumstances." Because he couldn't find any hostiles in those one hundred days, he was determined to attack the camp of peaceful Indians at Sand Creek.

Black Kettle and his band of about six hundred people spent almost the entire night celebrating the peace they thought they'd achieved, when just before dawn on November 29, 1864, seven hundred soldiers of the "Bloodless Third," along with four howitzers, surrounded his sleeping camp. Two-thirds of those in the camp were women and children, since previously one of Chivington's officers had suggested to the Natives that their warriors should go off to hunt buffalo.

Roused from his sleep, Black Kettle ran out in front of his teepee and waved the large US flag that President Lincoln had given him, assuring his people they would be safe. His white flag was also flying, but Chivington's men ignored it and opened fire.

Twenty-eight Native men and 105 women and children were killed in the Sand Creek Massacre. Many more were wounded. Most of those in the camp were able to escape because of the drunkenness, cowardice, and lack of discipline of Chivington's men.

Just about all of the Native American dead were scalped by the troops, and many were mutilated. Chivington's guide, Robert Bent, later testified before Congress, "I saw one squaw cut open with an unborn child, as I thought, lying by her side. Captain Soule afterwards told me that such was the fact. I saw the body of White Antelope [a seventy-five-year-old chief] with the privates cut off, and I heard a soldier say he was going to make a tobacco pouch out of them. I saw one squaw whose privates had been cut out. . . . I saw a little girl about five years of age who had been hid in the sand; two soldiers discovered her, drew their pistols and shot her, and then pulled her out of the sand by the arm. I saw quite a number of infants in arms killed with their mothers." Lieutenant James Connor testified that this was accurate, adding even more gruesome details. Chivington had previously justified murdering Native American babies by saying, "Nits make lice!"

Although there was a huge public outcry and the government launched three investigations, Colonel Chivington was never charged for the atrocity.

At Sand Creek Chivington and the 3rd Colorado Cavalry essentially wiped out the power of every Cheyenne and Arapaho chief who sought peace with the United States and a localized conflict intensified into a more generalized Indian War—one that lasted for twenty-six years. Unfortunately, many more horrible massacres were committed by both sides before it was over.

Black Kettle escaped the Sand Creek Massacre along with his wife, who was shot nine times. He carried her to Fort Lyon, where the doctors saved her. The following summer, when officials wanted him to sign a new treaty because Denver and many new settlements were on Cheyenne and Arapaho land, he said, "Although the troops have struck us, we throw it all behind and are glad to meet you in peace and friendship. . . . We are different nations, but it seems as if we were but one people, whites and all." He and his people agreed to move onto Kiowa land in what is now Oklahoma, where they were guaranteed "perpetual peace." But just over four years later, Black Kettle found history repeating itself on the new reservation with the Washita Massacre, when Custer and the 7th Cavalry charged into his sleeping camp. Once again Black Kettle was flying his white flag and the Stars and Stripes given to him by President Lincoln. This time both he and his wife were killed. Black Kettle died with his hand raised making the sign for peace. Though a count wasn't made, Custer estimated that 103 Cheyenne and Arapaho warriors were killed. Other witnesses said they were again mostly women, children and old men. Custer ordered all their animals—more than eight hundred—to be slaughtered and their possessions burned. It turned out the horse thieves Custer was chasing weren't even from Black Kettle's band.

The previous year and again just a few days earlier, Black Kettle and Arapaho chief Big Mouth petitioned Colonel William Hazen for protection for his people, requesting the military allow him to move his camp near Fort Cobb. Hazen said only Sheridan could approve it, but Sheridan and Custer were busy preparing for their winter campaign.

The 7th Cavalry had twenty-one soldiers killed at Washita, but between seventeen and twenty of these were a small detachment that chased some fleeing Natives downstream when they encountered hundreds of Cheyenne, Kiowa, and Arapaho coming from the villages below to assist Black Kettle's village. Custer then began to move on the other villages of about five thousand people, but they fled, fearing they'd be massacred like Black Kettle's camp.

Custer was later accused of abandoning that detachment of his men who were killed at the Washita, but overall the Army felt he had redeemed himself. General Sheridan was pleased that Custer had "wiped out old Black Kettle" and the massacre was considered the Army's largest victory to date in the plains wars.

Custer and Little Bighorn

Buffalo Bill Cody

[signature: W. F. Cody / Buffalo Bill]

Buffalo Bill Cody knew Custer well. Though Cody was scouting for the 5th Cavalry at the time of the Battle of the Little Bighorn, he had previously served with Custer and the 7th Cavalry back in the Sioux War of 1866–1868.

The following excerpt is from Buffalo Bill's autobiography. Here is what he wrote about working as one of Custer's guides:

During the winter of 1866-67, I scouted between Fort Ellsworth and Fort Fletcher. In the spring of 1867 I was at Fort Fletcher, when General Custer came out to go on an Indian expedition with General Hancock. I remained at this post until it was drowned out by the heavy floods of Big Creek, on which it was located; the water rose about the fortifications and rendered the place unfit for occupancy; so the Government abandoned the fort, and moved the troops and supplies to a new post—which had been named Fort Hays—located further west, on the south fork of Big Creek. It was while scouting in the vicinity of Fort Hays that I had my first ride with the dashing and gallant Custer, who had come up to the post from Fort Ellsworth with an escort of only ten men. He wanted a guide to pilot him to Fort Larned, a distance of sixty-five miles across the country.

ACTING AS GUIDE TO CUSTER

I was ordered by the commanding officer to guide General Custer to his desired destination, and I soon received word from the General that he would start out in the morning with the intention of making the trip

Buffalo Bill in 1872

in one day. Early in the morning, after a good night's rest, I was on hand, mounted on my large mouse-colored mule—an animal of great endurance—and ready for the journey; when the General saw me, he said, "Cody, I want to travel fast and go through as quickly as possible, and I don't think that mule of yours is fast enough to suit me."

"General, never mind the mule," said I, "he'll get there as soon as your horses. That mule is a good one," as I knew that the animal was better than most horses.

"Very well; go ahead, then," said he, though he looked as if he thought I would delay the party on the road.

For the first fifteen miles, until we came to the Smoky Hill River, which we were to cross, I could hardly keep the mule in advance of the General, who rode a frisky, impatient and ambitious thoroughbred steed; in fact, the whole party was finely mounted. The General repeatedly told me that the mule was "no good," and that I ought to have had a good horse. But after crossing the river and striking the sand-hills, I began letting my mule out a little, and putting the "persuaders" to him. He was soon out-traveling the horses, and by the time we had made about half the distance to Fort Larned, I occasionally had to wait for the General or some of his party, as their horses were beginning to show signs of fatigue.

"General, how about this mule, anyhow?" I asked, at last.

"Cody, you have a better vehicle than I thought you had," was his reply.

From that time on to Fort Larned I had no trouble in keeping ahead of the party. We rode into the fort at four o'clock in the afternoon with about half the escort only, the rest having lagged far behind.

General Custer thanked me for having brought him straight across the country without any trail, and said that if I were not engaged as post scout at Fort Hays he would like to have me accompany him as one of his scouts during the summer; and he added that whenever I was out of employment, if I would come to him he would find something for me to do. This was the beginning of my acquaintance with General Custer, whom I always admired as a man and as an officer.

The Sioux War of 1866–1868 ended the struggle for the Southern Plains, but it was just the beginning of the struggle on the Northern Plains that ended in the defeat of last remaining free-roaming tribes soon after the Battle of the Little Bighorn. That battle took place in 1876—one of the most significant years in the history of the West.
Here is how writer Joseph Geringer described it:

The year 1876, while known as the celebration of America's glorious first centennial, was a nightmare for Western folklore. That shining star, that long-haired hero of the Civil War, that fearless Indian fighter named George Armstrong Custer went to his death at the Little Bighorn River; the Indians won. James Butler "Wild Bill" Hickok, that lightning draw and sharp-witted lawman who cleaned many a cow town of its villains, was shot in the head at a Deadwood, South Dakota card table; the villains won. And Jesse James, who had garnered the hearts of many across the frontier with his romantically daring snubs at sanctimonious do-gooders, was ingloriously turned out from Northfield, Minnesota, the seat of his pants smoking; the sanctimonious do-gooders won.

Geringer accurately portrays the popular sentiment at the time, and how many would view it today. The United States had just marked the end of its first century and was just embarking on its second when suddenly news arrived that Custer and between 207 and 225 of his men had been annihilated. It was July 6, 1876, when the world began to discover what happened. The *New York Times* reported, "Gen. [Richard] Drum, of [General Philip] Sheridan's staff, is of the opinion that Sitting Bull began concentrating his forces after the fight with [General George] Crook, and that no doubt, Custer dropped squarely into the midst of no less than ten thousand red devils and was literally torn to pieces."

To the horrified public, this was the 9/11 of that day. Though initially the military blamed Custer for not accepting additional troops offered to him, for not taking his Gatling guns, for dividing his force when facing a larger enemy, and for ignoring his orders by advancing too quickly on the enemy, the public wasn't interested in any of this or the actual events that led up to the battle. Instead the myths surrounding the Custer massacre arose, highlighted by numerous paintings of "Custer's Last Stand," depicting the Western hero in his buckskins standing defiantly amidst his few remaining desperate soldiers futilely trying to fight off hundreds of bloodthirsty savages. Custer became a gallant victim of "red devils" who were impeding the progress of civilization. The fact that it was Custer and his men who attacked the village was justified by saying that because of their hostility, the tribes brought it on themselves.

The actual causes of the conflict dated back many years earlier, but one could say they were pushed to the brink with the search for gold in the Dakota Territory and its discovery by Custer's men in 1874. Years before the discovery there were rumors that there might be gold in the Lakota Sioux's Black Hills, but generally prospectors who went there didn't come back. The Black Hills are sacred to the Sioux and other tribes, who believe it is the home of the gods. Warriors went there to talk to the Great Spirit and to receive visions. In 1868 the Fort Laramie Treaty formally made the area off-limits to nonNatives, specifying, "the United States now solemnly agrees that no persons, except those herein designated . . . shall ever be permitted to pass over, settle upon, or reside in the territory described in this article." The treaty designated the western half of what is now South Dakota west of the Missouri River and the Powder River Country east of the Bighorn Mountains in the Wyoming and Montana Territories as a permanent reservation for the Sioux and any other tribes they permitted to join them. The US government agreed to abandon military posts in the area and promised to remove all trespassers so the Native Americans could live there peacefully forever.

Just four years later the US secretary of the interior was already talking about taking the land away from the Sioux. Secretary Columbus Delano was responsible for protecting Sioux territorial rights, but in 1872 he wrote in a letter, "I am inclined to think that the occupation of this region of the country is not necessary to the happiness and prosperity of the Indians, and as it is supposed to be rich in minerals and lumber it is deemed important to have it freed as early as possible from Indian occupancy. I shall, therefore, not oppose any policy which looks first to a careful examination of the subject . . . If such an examination leads to the conclusion that country is not necessary or useful to Indians, I should then deem it advisable . . . to extinguish the claim of the Indians and open the territory to the occupation of the whites."

But occasionally Natives brought in chunks of gold to their agency saying they were from the Black Hills, so in the spring of 1874, the secretary of war sent Lieutenant Colonel George Custer to explore the Black Hills with his 7th Cavalry Regiment of 79 officers, 1,451 troops, and 275 wagons, along with cannons, Gatling guns, 300 head of cattle, various reporters, scientists—including a geologist—and two miners.

Custer was eager to get back onto the frontier. For about a year and a half, the 7th Cavalry had been spread out over the seven Southern states, enforcing federal tax laws on distilleries and suppressing the Ku Klux Klan. Custer's primary duty had been to inspect and purchase horses for the Army. As he had political aspirations, he was hoping for chances to distinguish himself.

He and his men were assigned to explore the Black Hills and set up a military post, but their primary mission was to search for gold and other mineral wealth in the hills. The fort they set up was Fort Lincoln, just south of Mandan in the Yellowstone Territories. This became his headquarters for the next three years. The two-month expedition did find gold near today's town of Custer. In his report to General Alfred Terry, Custer wrote, "I have on my table forty or fifty small particles of pure gold . . . most of it obtained today from one panful of earth."

The reporters with the expedition spread the news around the world, describing the Black Hills and its gold in glowing terms. The United States, along with the rest of the world, had just entered the Long Depression, which began with the stock market crash and the Panic of 1873 and continued for the next twenty-three years, so prospectors from around the world responded. By the beginning of the following year there were fifteen thousand miners in the Hills. The path cut by Custer's mile-long supply train was soon dubbed "Thieves' Road" by the Natives.

In the spring of 1875, the Army sent General George Crook onto the Black Hills reservation to remove the trespassing miners, as required by the Fort Laramie Treaty, and they did expel one group. But as prospectors and settlers were flooding in from all directions, Crook soon realized his mission was hopeless. His commander, General Philip Sheridan, stated he was willing to "give a cordial support to the settlement of the Black Hills" if Congress decided to "open up the country for settlement, by extinguishing the treaty rights of the Indians." While the government verbally discouraged illegal settlement of the area, it was being urged to quickly establish military posts before all the best land was grabbed up by the settlers. So while the Army originally went in to protect the Indians and remove the settlers, as required by the treaty, they ended up trying to protect the settlers and remove the Indians.

Meanwhile, Red Cloud and Spotted Tail filed strong protests with Washington, DC, knowing if the chiefs did nothing, the young warriors would begin defending their land. In response the government sent emissaries to negotiate the sale of the Black Hills. The commissioners were met by a group of more than twenty thousand angry Lakota Sioux, Cheyenne, and Arapaho. They were quickly convinced that the tribes had no intention of selling the Black Hills, so they offered to buy the mineral rights. The commissioners also asked for the Powder River Country, which was the last of their hunting grounds. This didn't go over well, although some chiefs argued they should sell the Black Hills because they were going to lose it anyway. In the end the Lakota rejected the offers. The commissioners returned to Washington, DC, and recommended that Congress force the Lakota to sell for "a fair equivalent of the value of the hills."

Since the Lakota refused to negotiate, the government was forced to take another tack. On December 6, 1875, President Grant, using the lame excuse that the Lakota were harassing the Crow in the Montana Territory, issued an order to round up the remaining free Indians of the plains by ordering all Lakota Sioux and Northern Cheyenne to report to the reservation agency offices by January 31, 1876. Anyone who refused would be considered a "hostile" and subject to military action.

(*Note:* The government referred to free Natives as "wild Indians," while the free Natives referred to reservation Natives as "loafers" for their reliance on the government for their food, supplies, and annuities.)

The Army initially intended for this to be a winter campaign, since the Natives were more stationary at their winter camps and many of the warriors would be away from camp hunting, thus making the camps easier to attack. It was also easier to track warriors in snow, and they couldn't move as fast. Also, it was easier to destroy their camp's food supplies in winter. But that winter was a particularly bad one, making it almost impossible for the tribes to report to their agencies. The tribes disbursed for the winter because of scarce resources, so many never received the message, while others lived quietly far out on the northern plains in the Montana Territory legally hunting on as-yet-unceded Indian land, just as they always had, having little or no contact with whites.

The deadline passed, but the harsh weather forced the Army to postpone their campaign. When they were able to begin, their first major skirmish was the Battle of Powder River on March 17 in the Montana Territory. Marching through a blizzard with temperatures dropping to 80°F below zero, Colonel Joseph Reynolds and about three hundred soldiers came across two tracks in the snow that lead them to a Cheyenne village of about six hundred, which they attacked at dawn. One Native and four soldiers were killed in the fight. Reynolds's men gained control of the village and burned what they could. They also captured a large portion of the natives' eight hundred to fifteen hundred ponies, but the Cheyenne took them back during a snowstorm the

A rare photo of George Armstrong Custer in civilian clothes

next morning. The natives joined Crazy Horse's camp several miles away, where they were provided shelter and food.

Then in April 1876 the mother lode of the gold in the Black Hills was discovered near the newly formed town of Deadwood. This was the Homestake Mine, which George Hearst and his partners bought for seventy thousand dollars. Over the next 125 years this mine produced 10 percent of the world's gold.

Custer almost didn't make it to the Little Bighorn Battle. In March he testified before Congress about a scandal involving the secretary of war and President Grant's brother that concerned the selling of licenses for post sutlerships and reservation trading posts. This was just one of many Grant Administration corruption scandals. Grant was so angry that he refused to see Custer and then, because Custer had not paid him a courtesy call before leaving Washington, he had Custer arrested and relieved him of his command. Public outcry forced Grant to reinstate Custer, but he placed him under General Alfred Terry, even though Terry was less experienced at fighting Indians and didn't really want the job.

In May the 7th Cavalry set out from Fort Lincoln to assist in rounding up the remaining free Native Americans. They were part of three columns of troops headed by General George Crook, Colonel John Gibbon, and General Terry. Their planned three-prong attack sounded good, but it was almost impossible to carry out considering 1) the unknown location of the Indian camps, 2) each column had to travel hundreds of miles from different directions, and 3) their inability to communicate with the other columns. Crook proceeded from the south, Gibbon from the west, and Terry from the east.

At around the same time, Sitting Bull called together the seven Lakota Sioux tribes and the Northern Cheyenne to discuss what they should do. They began coming together at Rosebud Creek in the Montana Territory. It was an unusually large gathering. Sitting Bull, as a spiritual leader of the Lakota, then led them in the very difficult and painful Sun Dance ritual of sacrifice and endurance, which was designed to produce visions. Forty-five-year-old Sitting Bull had a hundred pieces of skin about the size of a match head sliced off his arms. His chest was then pierced on each side, and through these piercings he was attached to a central pole by a rawhide line. With no food or water and only a few brief breaks, he danced until around noon the next day, when he had a vision of soldiers falling into their camp like grasshoppers because they had no ears to hear the truth, but warned, "Do not touch the spoils. . . . it will prove to be the downfall of this nation."

Inspired by this vision, Crazy Horse and 500 to 750 warriors set off to fight. They encountered Crook's battalion of 1,300 men in the Battle of the Rosebud and forced the soldiers to retreat, driving off one prong of the three-prong attack. After the battle they moved their camp to the Little Bighorn River, where they were joined by additional people from the reservations. Crook returned to his fort, withdrawing from the campaign.

Gibbon and Terry's columns met to the northeast of the Native American encampment and picked up a trail to the camp, allowing Custer and some of his men to proceed ahead. Custer was moving quickly and came upon the tribes' camp well ahead of the main force. Custer underestimated the camp's size and thought he could take it, so instead of waiting for reinforcement, he decided to attack while he still had the element of surprise. He divided his 590 men into three columns and went up against the camp of between 2,500 and 8,000 Native Americans, including about 1,800 warriors led by Battle Chiefs Gall, Lame White Man, and Crazy Horse, among others. (While Sitting Bull is often listed as being in command, he was caught by surprise and played only a minor role in the battle.) It was on June 25, 1876—only eleven days after Sitting Bull had had his vision—that the 7th Cavalry descended upon their camp. Major Reno with one of Custer's three battalions was to attack from the south, while Custer with another would continue on so he could come in from the east. The column under Major Reno was the first to attack, but was forced to retreat. His column joined up with the battalion under Captain Benteen, and the entire group was surrounded.

An hour after Reno's original attack and a couple miles away, Custer reached a position overlooking the village. Seeing mainly women and children, he figured most of the warriors were away hunting, when they were actually off fighting Reno, but they soon learned of Custer's presence and turned their attention on him. Hopelessly outnumbered, within an hour Custer and five companies of the 7th Cavalry were completely wiped out.

(Technically there were a few exceptions. Custer sent two men back to Benteen with messages, and he released four of his scouts, who he thought were being too fatalistic when they began preparing to die shortly before the attack. These were White Man Runs Him, Curley, Goes Ahead, and Hairy Moccasin. Three of them remained with Reno, while Curley continued on, watching the battle through a spyglass from a mile and a half away. A number of other people claimed to be survivors of the battle, but only one is taken seriously by historians. Frank Finkel, who enlisted as Frank Hall, was in the battle, but said blood got in his eyes, blinding him, and his horse charged past the Sioux, through their village and beyond. When he finally reached Fort Benton, no one would believe his story, so he gave up and went on his way.)

The only surviving eyewitnesses to Custer's Last Stand were the Native Americans, and they had trouble recognizing Custer because he had just cut his hair short and several others were dressed like him. Some historians believe he didn't actually make it to the Last Stand, but died early in the battle when his men reached the river. Others believe Custer made it to Custer Hill for his Last Stand. Some say in the end the Natives overwhelmed the fleeing men in a ravine and Custer never made a Last Stand.

Reno and Benteen's men were surrounded on a hill about a mile southeast of the village. They were able to hold off the Natives for a day and a half, until Sitting Bull called the warriors off and the tribes dissipated. Of Reno and Benteen's 425 or so men, between 53 and 59 were dead, bringing the total dead to between 260 and 268. Estimates of Native American losses range from 36 to 136.

Shortly before the battle, Ree scout Bloody Knife told Custer that at the village "we'll find enough Sioux to keep up fighting two or three days." Custer just smiled and replied, "I guess we'll get through with them in one day." Actually the Sioux "got through" with Custer's column in just over half an hour.

Buffalo Bill was a scout for 5th Cavalry when this happened. Previously in 1872 he received the Medal of Honor—the nation's highest military award. That fall he was elected to the Nebraska Legislature, but failed to claim the seat, saying it was a waste of time making laws that nobody obeyed. He was already famous by then, largely because of dime novels of his fictional exploits, published by Edward Judson under the name "Ned Buntline." Judson was also staging plays, and he talked Buffalo Bill into joining him as a partner and an actor, but between seasons, Buffalo Bill returned to the Army as a scout.

SCOUTING WITH THE FIFTH CAVALRY

The Sioux War [of 1876–1877—sometimes called Sitting Bull's War] was just breaking out. We closed our theatrical season earlier than usual in the spring of 1876, because I was anxious to take part in the Sioux war which was then breaking out.

Colonel [Anson] Mills had written me several times to say that General [George] Crook wanted me to accompany his command. When I left Chicago I had expected to catch up with Crook at the Powder River, but I learned en route that my old command, the gallant Fifth Cavalry, was on its way from Arizona to join him, and that General [Eugene] Carr, my former commander, was at its head.

Carr wanted me as his guide and chief of scouts, and had written to army headquarters in Chicago to learn where I could be reached.

As soon as this news came to me I gave up the idea of overtaking Crook. I hastened to Cheyenne, where the Fifth Cavalry had already arrived, and was met at the depot there by Lieutenant Charles King, adjutant of the regiment, who had been sent by General Carr from Fort D. A. Russell. In later years, as General Charles King, this officer became a widely popular author, and wrote some of the best novels and stories of Indian life that I have ever read.

As I accompanied the lieutenant back to the fort, we passed soldiers who recognized me and shouted greetings. When we entered the Post a great shout of "Here's Buffalo Bill!" arose from the men on the parade ground. It was like old times, and I felt a thrill of happiness to be back among my friends and bound for one of the regular old-time campaigns. The following morning the command pulled out for Fort Laramie. We found General Sheridan there ahead of us, and mighty glad was I to see that brave and able commander once more. Sheridan was accompanied by General [James] Fry and General [George "Sandy"] Forsyth, and all were en route for the Red Cloud Agency, near the center of the Sioux trouble, which was then reaching really alarming proportions. The command was to remain at Laramie for a few days; so, at General Sheridan's request, I accompanied him on his journey. We were able to accomplish little in the way of peace overtures.

The Indians had lately committed many serious depredations along the Black Hills trail. Gold had been discovered there in many new places, and the miners, many of them tenderfoots, and unused to the ways of the red man, had come into frequent conflict with their new neighbors. Massacres, some of them very flagrant, had resulted and most of the treaties our Government had made with the Indians had been ruthlessly broken.

On my return from the agency, the Fifth Cavalry was sent out to scout the country between there and the Black Hills. We operated along the south fork of the Cheyenne and about the foot of the Black Hills for two weeks, and had several small engagements with roving bands of Indians during that time.

All these bands were ugly and belligerent, and it was plain from the spirit they showed that there had been a general understanding among all the redskins thereabout that the time had come to drive the white man from the country.

Brevet-General Wesley Merritt, who had lately received his promotion to the colonelcy of the Fifth Cavalry, now took command of the regiment. I regretted that the command had been taken from General Carr. I was fond of him personally, and it was under him that the regiment made its fine reputation as a fighting organization. I soon became well acquainted with General Merritt, however, and found him to be a brave man and an excellent officer.

REPORT OF THE CUSTER MASSACRE AND CAUSES LEADING THERETO

The regiment did continuous and hard scouting. We soon believed we had driven all the hostile Indians out of that part of the country. In fact, we were starting back to Fort Laramie, regarding the business at hand as finished, when a scout arrived at our camp and reported the massacre of General Custer and his whole force on the Little Bighorn.

The extraordinary and sorrowful interest attaching to the destruction of Custer and his brave followers, felt by the whole civilized world, prompts me to give herewith a brief description of the causes leading thereto, and some of the details of that horrible sacrifice which so melts the heart to pity.

When the Black Hills gold fever first broke out in 1874, a rush of miners into that country resulted in much trouble, as the Indians always regarded that region with jealous interest, and resisted all encroachments of white men. Instead of the Government adhering to the Treaty of 1868 and restraining white men from going into the Hills, Gen. Custer was sent out, in 1874, to intimidate the Sioux. The unrighteous spirit of this order the General wisely disregarded, but proceeded to Prospect Valley, and from there he pushed on to the valley of the Little Missouri. Custer expected to find good grazing ground in this valley, suitable for a camp which he intended to pitch there for several days, and reconnoiter, but the country was comparatively barren and the march was therefore continued to the Belle Fourche Valley [north of the Black Hills in what is now South Dakota], where excellent grazing, water, and plenty of wood was found.

Crossing the Fourche the expedition was now among the outlying ranges of the Hills where a camp was made and some reconnoitering done; but finding no Indians, Gen. Custer continued his march, skirting the Black Hills and passing through a country which he described as beautiful beyond description, abounding with a most luxurious vegetation, cool, crystal streams a profusion of gaudy, sweet smelling flowers, and plenty of game.

Proceeding down this lovely valley, which he appropriately named Floral Park, an Indian campfire, recently abandoned, was discovered, and fearing a collision unless pains were taken to prevent it, Custer halted and sent out his chief scout, Bloody Knife, with twenty friendly Indian allies to trail the departed Sioux. They had gone but a short distance when, as Custer himself relates, "Two of Bloody Knife's young men came galloping back and informed me that they had discovered five Indian lodges a few miles down the valley, and that Bloody Knife, as directed, had concealed his party in a wooded ravine, where they awaited further orders. Taking E company with me, which was afterward reinforced by the remainder of the scouts and Col. [Verlin] Hart's company, I proceeded to the ravine where Bloody Knife and his party lay concealed, and from the crest beyond obtained a full view of the five Indian lodges, about which a considerable number of ponies were grazing. I was enabled to place my command still nearer to the lodges undiscovered. I then dispatched [James] Agard, the interpreter, with a flag of truce, accompanied by ten of our Sioux scouts, to acquaint the occupants of the lodges that we were friendly disposed and desired to communicate with them. To prevent either treachery or flight on their part, I galloped the remaining portion of my advance and surrounded the lodges. This was accomplished almost before they were aware of our presence. I then entered the little village and shook hands with its occupants, assuring them through the interpreter, that they had no cause to fear, as we were not there to molest them, etc."

Finding there was no disposition on the part of Gen. Custer to harm them, the Indians dispatched a courier to their principal village, requesting the warriors to be present at a council with the whites. This council was held on the following day, but though Custer dispensed coffee, sugar, bacon and other presents to the Indians, his advice to them regarding the occupation of their country by miners was treated with indifference, for which, he observes in his official report, "I cannot blame the poor savages."

MINERS IN THE BLACK HILLS

During the summer of 1875, Gen. Crook made several trips into the Black Hills to drive out the miners and maintain the Government's faith, but while he made many arrests there was no punishment and the whole proceeding became farcical. In August of the same year Custer City was laid out and two weeks later it contained a population of six hundred souls. These Gen. Crook drove out, but as he marched from the place others swarmed in and the population was immediately renewed.

It was this inability, or real indisposition, of the Government to enforce the terms of the Treaty of 1868 that led to the bitter war with Sitting Bull and which terminated so disastrously on the 25th of June, 1876.

It is a notorious fact that the Sioux Indians, for four years immediately preceding the Custer massacre, were regularly supplied with the most improved firearms and ammunition by the agencies at Brule, Grand River, Standing Rock, Fort Berthold, Cheyenne and Fort Peck. Even during the campaign of 1876, in the months of May, June and July, just before and after Custer and his band of heroes rode down into the valley of death, these fighting Indians received eleven hundred and twenty Winchester and Remington rifles and 413,000 rounds of patent ammunition, besides large quantities of loose powder, lead and primers, while during the summer of 1875 they received several thousand stand of arms and more than a million rounds of ammunition. With this generous provision there is no cause for wonder that the Sioux were able to resist the Government and attract to their aid all the dissatisfied Cheyenne and other Indians in the Northwest.

Besides a perfect fighting equipment, all the Indians recognized in Sitting Bull the elements of a great warrior, one whose superior, perhaps, has never been known among any tribe; he combined all the strategic cunning of Tecumseh with the cruel, uncompromising hatred of Black Kettle, while his leadership was far superior to both. Having decided to precipitate a terrible war, he chose his position with consummate judgment, selecting a central vantage point surrounded by what is known as the "bad lands," and then kept his supply source open by an assumed friendship with the Canadian French. This he was the better able to accomplish, since some years before he had professed conversion to Christianity under the preaching of Father [Pierre] DeSmet and maintained a show of great friendship for the Canadians.

WAR DECLARED AGAINST THE SIOUX

War against the Sioux having been declared, brought about by the combined causes of Black Hill outrages and Sitting Bull's threatening attitude, it was decided to send out three separate expeditions, one of which should move from the north, under Gen. Terry, from Fort Lincoln; another from the east, under Gen. [John] Gibbon, from Fort Ellis, and another from the south, under Gen. Crook, from Fort Fetterman; these movements were to be simultaneous, and a junction was expected to be formed near the headwaters of the Yellowstone River.

For some cause, which I will refrain from discussing, the commands did not start at the same time. Gen. Crook did not leave Fetterman until March 1st, [1876,] with seven hundred men and forty days' supply. The command was entrusted to Col. [Joseph] Reynolds, of the Third Cavalry, accompanied by Gen. Crook, the department commander. Nothing was heard of this expedition until the 22d following, when Gen. Crook forwarded from Ft. Reno a brief account of his battle on Powder River. The result of this fight, which lasted five hours, was the destruction of Crazy Horse's village of one hundred and five lodges; or that is the way the dispatch read, though many assert that the battle resulted in little else than a series of remarkable blunders which suffered the Indians to make good their escape, losing only a small quantity of their property.

One serious trouble arose out of the Powder River fight, which was found in an assertion made by Gen. Crook, or at least attributed to him, that his expedition had proved that instead of there being 15,000 or 20,000 hostile Indians in the Black Hills and Bighorn country, that the total number would not exceed 2,000. It was upon this estimation that the expeditions were prepared.

The Terry column, which was commanded by Gen. Custer, consisted of twelve companies of the Seventh Cavalry, and three companies of the Sixth and Seventeenth Infantry, with four Gatling guns, and a detachment of Indian scouts. This force comprised twenty-eight officers and seven hundred and forty-seven men, of the Seventh Cavalry, eight officers and one hundred and thirty-five men of the Sixth and Seventeenth Infantry, two officers and thirty-two men in charge of the Gatling battery, and forty-five enlisted Indian scouts, a grand total of thirty-eight officers and nine hundred and fifty-nine men, including scouts.

The combined forces of Crook, Gibbon, Terry and Custer, did not exceed twenty-seven hundred men, while opposed to them were fully 17,000 Indians, all of whom were provided with the latest and most improved patterns of repeating rifles.

On the 16th of June [1876] Gen. Crook started for the Rosebud, on which stream it was reported that Sitting Bull and Crazy Horse were stationed; about the same time a party of Crow Indians, who were operating with Gen. Crook, returned from a scout and reported that Gen. Gibbon, who was on Tongue River, had been attacked by Sitting Bull, who had captured several horses. [At that time, the Crow and Arikara tribes were at war with the Sioux and Cheyenne, who they felt had stolen their land, so they were eager to act as scouts for the Army and to fight alongside the bluecoats. The Crow's friendly ties to the whites were based on a century-old prophecy that going against them would be disastrous and on a 1825 treaty they were determined not to break.] Crook pushed on rapidly toward the Rosebud, leaving his train behind and mounting his infantry on mules. What were deemed accurate reports, stated that Sitting Bull was still on the Rosebud, only sixty miles from the point where Gen. Crook camped on the night of the 15th of June. The command traveled forty miles on the sixteenth, and when within twenty miles of the Sioux's principal position, instead of pushing on, Gen. Crook went into camp.

ATTACKED BY SITTING BULL

The next morning he was much surprised at finding himself attacked by Sitting Bull, who swooped down on him with the first streaks of coming dawn, and a heavy battle followed. Gen. Crook, who had camped in a basin surrounded on all sides by high hills, soon found his position so dangerous that it must be changed at all hazards. The advance was therefore sounded with [Captain Henry] Noyes' battalion occupying a position on the right, [Captain Anson] Mills on the right center, [Colonel Alexander] Chambers in the center, and the Indian allies on the left. Mills and Noyes charged the enemy in magnificent style, breaking the line and striking the rear. The fight continued hot and furious until 2 p.m., when a gallant charge of Col. [William] Royall, who was in reserve, supported by the Indian allies, caused the Sioux to draw off to their village, six miles distant, while Gen. Crook went into camp, where he remained inactive for two days.

Gen. Gibbon was found in camp quietly awaiting developments. A consultation was had with Gens. Gibbon and Custer, and then Gen. Terry definitely fixed upon the plan of action. It was believed the Indians were at the head of the Rosebud, or over on the Little Horn, a dividing ridge only fifteen miles wide separating the two streams. It was announced by Gen. Terry that Gen. Custer's column "would strike the blow."

Having now ascertained the position of the enemy, or reasoned out the probable position, Gen. Terry sent a dispatch to Gen. Sheridan, as follows: "No Indians have been met with as yet, but traces of a large and recent camp have been discovered twenty or thirty miles up the Rosebud. Gibbon's column will move this morning on the north side of the Yellowstone, for the mouth of the Bighorn, where it will be ferried across by the supply steamer, and whence it will proceed to the mouth of the Little Horn, and so on. Custer will go up the Rosebud tomorrow with his whole regiment, and thence to the headwaters of the Little Horn, thence down that stream."

Following this report came an order, signed by E. W. Smith, Captain of the Eighteenth Infantry, Acting Assistant Adjutant-General, directing General Custer to follow the Indian trail discovered, pushing the Indians from one side while Gen. Gibbon pursued them from an opposite direction. As no instructions were given as to the rate each division should travel, Custer, noted for his quick, energetic movements, made ninety miles the first three days, and, discovering the Indians in large numbers, divided his command into three divisions, one of which he placed under Major [Marcus] Reno, another under Major [Frederick] Benteen, and led the other himself.

CUSTER STRIKES THE INDIANS

As Custer made a detour to enter the village, Reno struck a large body of Indians, who, after retreating nearly three miles turned on the troops and ran them pell-mell across Grassy Creek into the woods. Reno overestimated the strength of his enemies and thought he was being surrounded. Benteen came up to the support of Reno, but he too took fright and got out of his position without striking the enemy.

While Reno and Benteen were trying to keep open a way for their retreat, Custer charged on the village, first sending a courier, Trumpeter

[John] Martin, to Reno and Benteen with the following dispatch: "Big village; be quick; send on the packs." This order was too plain to be misconstrued. It clearly meant that he had discovered the village, which he intended attacking at once; to hurry forward to his support and bring up the packs; ambulances, etc. But instead of obeying orders, Reno and Benteen stood aloof, fearful lest they should endanger their position, while the brave Custer and his squad of noble heroes rushed down like a terrible avalanche upon the Indian village. . . .

I have avoided attaching blame to anyone, using only the facts that have been furnished me of how Custer came to attack the Sioux village and how and why he died.

When the news of the terrible massacre was learned, soldiers everywhere made a pilgrimage to the sacred place, and friendly hands reared a monument on that distant spot commemorative of the heroism of Custer and his men; collected together all the bones and relics of the battle and piled them up in pyramidal form, where they stand in sunshine and storm, overlooking the Little Bighorn.

Custer with about 590 men went up against an estimated 1,500 braves with disastrous consequences, but many other battles were fought in the West with similar or worse odds. For example, in the Texas panhandle on November 26, 1864, Colonel Kit Carson leading 325 Union soldiers and 72 Ute and Apache scouts attacked a Kiowa village, not realizing there were other large villages nearby with a total of between 3,000 and 7,000 Natives. Using the nearby ruins of Adobe Walls as a fort—it had been blown up by traders when they abandoned it sixteen years earlier—he was able to successfully hold off at least 1,500 Kiowa and Comanche warriors. Shortly before sunset, after six to eight hours of fighting, Carson's men recaptured the village and set about burning it. After dark, not wanting to remain in the area and concerned about the 75 soldiers and supply wagons he'd left behind, Carson and his men made the three-hour return march to their camp.

This was the first Battle of Adobe Walls, not to be confused with Bat Masterson's and the buffalo hunters' Battle of Adobe Walls ten years later. Kit Carson, unlike Custer, did not leave his heavy guns behind, and it's largely because he had two howitzers that he was able to hold off his attackers. In all, while it's said the Indians lost 60 to 150, he lost just six men.

Custer was only thirty-six years old when he was killed, and his death came as a great shock to the country—largely because the public could hardly believe that "wild savages" were able to defeat a modern well-equipped army. Initially Crook and Terry's columns called for reinforcements and ended up waiting a month before returning to search for villages. Meanwhile the Natives celebrated their victory for a few weeks, and when there was little response from the Army, many assumed the government had halted its campaign and the tribes disbursed. When Crook and Terry finally did begin searching for villages, they could only find one. Crook and Terry returned to their forts. In November Crook and more than 2,400 men set out again, but again only found one village. Also in November the 5th Infantry Regiment under Colonel Nelson Miles set off after Sitting Bull's band and eventually chased them to Canada in December. In January 1877 Miles's men had a battle with Crazy Horse's band, and in May they fought Lame Deer's band in the final battle of the war.

In spite of the Army's initial paralysis after the Battle of the Little Bighorn, there were some minor skirmishes. One of them involved Colonel Miles's 5th Infantry, and Buffalo Bill was at the forefront.

AFTER THE MURDERERS OF CUSTER

This massacre occurred June 25, 1876, and its details are known, or ought to be known, by every schoolboy. Custer was a brave, dashing, headlong soldier, whose only fault was recklessness.

He had been warned many times never to expose a small command to a superior force of Indians, and never to underestimate the ability and generalship of the Sioux. He had unbounded confidence, however, in himself and his men, and I believe that not until he was struck down did he ever doubt that he would be able to cut his way out of the wall of warriors about him and turn defeat into a glorious and conspicuous victory.

The news of the massacre, which was the most terrible that ever overtook a command of our soldiers, was a profound shock to all of us. We knew at once that we would all have work to do, and settled grimly into the preparations for it.

Colonel [William] Stanton, who was with the Fifth Cavalry on this scout, had been sent to the Red Cloud Agency two days before. That night a message came from him that eight hundred warriors had left the agency to join Sitting Bull on the Little Bighorn. [*Note:* There were only about

Lieutenant Colonel George Armstrong Custer in March 1876 at age thirty-five. The photographs taken during this sitting are said to be the last pictures taken of Custer. His hair was cut even shorter than this when he charged into the Battle of the Little Bighorn.

two hundred Natives on the reservation at that time and only some of these left.] Notwithstanding instructions to proceed immediately by way of Fort Fetterman to join Crook, General [Wesley] Merritt took the responsibility of endeavoring to intercept the Cheyenne and thereby performed a very important service.

For this job the general selected five hundred men and horses. In two hours we were making a forced march back to War Bonnet Creek. Our intention was to reach the Indian trail running to the north across this watercourse before the Cheyenne could get there. We arrived the next night.

At daylight the next morning, July 17, I proceeded ahead on a scout. I found that the Indians had not yet crossed the creek. On my way back to the command I discovered a large party of Indians. I got close enough to observe them, and they proved to be Cheyenne, coming from the south. With this information, I hurried back to report.

The cavalrymen were ordered to mount their horses quietly and remain out of sight, while General Merritt, accompanied by two or three aides and myself, went on a little tour of observation to a neighboring hill. From the summit of this we saw the Indians approaching almost directly toward us. As we stood watching, fifteen or twenty of them wheeled and dashed off to the west, from which direction we had come the night before.

Searching the country to see what it was which had caused this unexpected maneuver, we observed two mounted soldiers approaching us on the trail. Obviously they were bearing dispatches from the command of General Merritt.

My Duel with Yellow Hand

It was clear that the Indians who had left their main body were intent on intercepting and murdering these two men. General Merritt greatly feared that they would accomplish this purpose. How to aid them was a problem. If soldiers were sent to their assistance, the Indians would observe the rescuers, and come to the right conclusion that a body of troops was lying in wait for them. This of course would turn them back, and the object of our expedition would be defeated.

The commander asked me if I had any suggestions.

"General," I replied, "why not wait until the scouts get a little nearer? When they are about to charge on the two men, I will take fifteen soldiers, dash down and cut them off from their main body. That will prevent them from going back to report, and the others will fall into our trap."

The general at once saw the possibilities of the scheme. "If you can do that, Cody, go ahead," he said.

I at once rushed back to the command and jumped on my horse.

With fifteen of the best men I could pick in a hurry I returned to the point of observation. I placed myself and my men at the order of General Merritt, and asked him to give me the word at the proper time.

He was diligently studying the country before him with his field-glasses. When he thought the Indians were as close to the unsuspecting scouts as was safe, he sang out, "Go on now, Cody, and be quick about it. They are going to charge on the couriers."

The two messengers were not over four hundred yards from us, and the Indians were only about two hundred yards behind them. We instantly dashed over the bluffs, and advanced on a gallop towards the Indians. A running fight lasted several minutes, during which we drove the enemy some little distance and killed three of their number. The rest of them rode off towards the main body, which had come into plain sight, and halted, upon seeing the skirmish that was going on. We were about half a mile from General Merritt, and the Indians whom we were chasing suddenly turned upon us, and another lively skirmish took place.

One of the Indians, who was handsomely decorated with all the ornaments usually worn by a war chief when engaged in a fight, sang out to me, in his own tongue, "I know you, Pa-he-haska [Long Hair, which was also the Sioux's name for Custer]; if you want to fight, come ahead and fight me."

The name he used was one by which I had long been known by the Indians. It meant Long-Yellow-Hair.

The chief was riding his horse back and forth in front of his men, as if to banter me, and I concluded to accept the challenge. I galloped towards him for fifty yards and he advanced towards me about the same distance, both of us riding at full speed, and then, when we were only about thirty yards apart, I raised my rifle and fired; his horse fell to the ground, having been killed by my bullet. Almost at the same instant my own horse went down, he having stepped into a gopher hole. The fall did not hurt me much, and I instantly sprang to my feet. The chief and I were now both on our feet, not twenty paces apart. We fired at each other at the same instant. My usual luck held. His bullet whizzed harmlessly past my head, while mine struck him full in the breast.

He reeled and fell, but I took no chances. He had barely touched the ground, when I was upon him, knife in hand, and to make sure of him drove the steel into his heart.

A MOMENT OF GREAT DANGER

The whole affair from beginning to end occupied but little time, and the Indians, seeing that I was some little distance from my company, now came charging down upon me from a hill, in hopes of cutting me off. General Merritt had witnessed the duel, and realizing the danger I was in, ordered Colonel [Julius] Mason with Company K to hurry to my rescue. The order came none too soon, for had it been given one minute later I would have had not less than two hundred Indians upon me. As the soldiers came up I swung the Indian chieftain's top-knot and bonnet in the air, and shouted, "*The first scalp for Custer.*"

General Merritt, seeing that he could not now ambush the Indians, ordered the whole regiment to charge upon them. They made a stubborn resistance for a little while, but no eight hundred Indians, or twice that number, for that matter, could make a successful stand against such veteran and fearless fighters as the Fifth Cavalry. They soon came to that conclusion themselves and began a running retreat for the Red Cloud Agency.

For thirty-five miles, over the roughest kind of ground, we drove them before us. Soon they were forced to abandon their spare horses and all the equipment they had brought along. Despite the imminent risk of encountering thousands of other Indians at the Agency, we drove our late adversaries directly into it. No one in our command had any assurance that the Indians gathered there had not gone on the warpath, but little difference that made to us. The Fifth Cavalry, on the warpath itself, would stop at nothing. It was dark when we entered the reservation. All about us we could see the huddling forms of Indians—thousands of them—enough, in fact, to have consummated another Custer massacre. But they showed no disposition to fight.

While at the Agency I learned that the Indian I had killed in the morning was none other than Yellow Hand [Hay-o-wei, actually "Yellow Hair"], a son of old Cut Nose, who was a leading chief of the Cheyenne. The old man learned from the members of Yellow Hand's party that I had killed his son, and sent a white interpreter to me offering four mules in exchange for the young chief's war-bonnet. This request I was obliged to refuse, as I wanted it as a trophy of the first expedition to avenge the death of Custer and his men.

There were actually about thirty Natives—not two hundred. Buffalo Bill and Yellow Hair came upon each other suddenly and both fired at the same time. Neither of them spoke a common language, and there was little time to issue a challenge. It's still debated how Buffalo Bill killed Yellow Hair, but there is now little doubt that he did.

Buffalo Bill kept Yellow Hair's blanket, bridle, whip, shield, girdle, and head-dress as trophies, eventually shipping them, along with the scalp, to his home in New York, whereupon being shown the scalp, his wife promptly fainted. For many years Buffalo Bill exhibited the scalp, along with the rifle he used to shoot Yellow Hair and the Bowie knife he used to cut off the scalp, using them to advertise his shows. They are now at the Buffalo Bill Museum in Golden, Colorado, although the scalp is no longer on display.

Three days after the Battle of the Little Bighorn, General Edward Godfrey arrived on the scene and described Custer's burial.

Buffalo Bill's trophies from his fight with Yellow Hair, along with the scalp at the bottom right. The scalp is described as consisting of a three-inch-square piece of skin with a nearly two-feet length of braided hair. There are also some Indian scalps that Yellow Hair had attached to a shield. Also included are Yellow Hair's headdress, girdle, Remington percussion revolver, knife, blanket, bridle, and whip.

All the bodies, except a few, were stripped of their clothing, according to my recollection nearly all were scalped or mutilated, and there was one notable exception, that of General Custer, whose face and expression were natural: he had been shot in the temple and in the left side. Many faces had a pained, almost terrified expression. . . . I had just identified and was supervising the burial of Boston Custer [one of Col. Custer's two brothers who died at Little Bighorn], when Major Reno sent for me to help identify the dead at Custer Hill.

When I arrived there, General Custer's body had been laid out. He had been shot in the left temple and the left breast. There were no powder marks or signs of mutilation. Mr. F. F. Girard, the interpreter, informed me that he preceded the troops there. He found the naked bodies of two soldiers, one across the other and Custer's naked body in a sitting posture between and leaning against them, his upper right forearm and hand supporting his head in an inclining posture like one resting or asleep.

While Custer's resounding battlefield defeat was only a "massacre" in the broader sense of the term, the government used it as the excuse they were looking for to officially rescind the Fort Laramie Treaty of 1868, which President Grant had unofficially abandoned in 1875. The military assumed control of the reservations in Sioux country, and the Native Americans became prisoners of war—even those who had not left the reservation or been involved in the battle. Their horses and guns were confiscated. After the government made the Natives sign a treaty transferring the Black Hills and the Powder River Country to the United States, their reservation was moved to deforested land in Missouri. This prompted one of the signers to comment, "Tell your people that since the Great Father promised that we should never be removed we have been moved five times. I think you had better put the Indians on wheels so you can run them about wherever you wish."

Seeking revenge for Custer's defeat, many soldiers and civilians set out to kill any Native American they could find who was not on a reservation. Custer was dead, but his legend haunted the Native Americans for decades to come.

In his book, *My Life on the Plains*, Custer expressed his view of Native Americans.

It is to be regretted that the character of the Indian as described in [James Fennimore] Cooper's interesting novels [such as *The Last of the Mohicans*] is not the true one. . . . Stripped of the beautiful romance with which we have been so long willing to envelop him, transferred from the inviting pages of the novelist to the localities where we are compelled to meet with him, in his native village, on the war path, and when raiding upon our frontier settlements and lines of travel, the Indian forfeits his claim to the appellation of the *noble* red man. We see him as he is, and, so far as all knowledge goes, as he ever has been, a *savage* in every sense of the word; not worse, perhaps, than his white brother would be, similarly born and bred, but one whose cruel and ferocious nature far exceeds that of any wild beast of the desert.

Buffalo Bill had a very different view.

I am and always have been a friend of the Indian. I have always sympathized with him in his struggle to hold the country that was his by right of birth.

But I have always held that in such a country as America the march of civilization was inevitable, and that sooner or later the men who lived in roving tribes, making no real use of the resources of the country, would be compelled to give way before the men who tilled the soil and used the lands as the Creator intended they should be used.

In my dealings with the Indians we always understood each other. In a fight we did our best to kill each other. In times of peace we were friends. I could always do more with the Indians than most white men, and I think my success in getting so many of them to travel with my organization was because I understood them and they understood me.

Shrewd as were the generals who conducted the fight against the Indians, I believe they could have done little without the services of the men who all over the West served them in the capacity of scouts. . . .

Of all the Indians I encountered in my years on the Plains the most resourceful and intelligent, as well as the most dangerous, were the Sioux. They had the courage of dare-devils combined with real strategy. They mastered the white man's tactics as soon as they had an opportunity to observe them. Incidentally they supplied all thinking and observing white commanders with a great deal that was well worth learning in the art of warfare. The Sioux fought to win, and in a desperate encounter were absolutely reckless of life.

But they also fought wisely, and up to the minute of closing in they conserved their own lives with a vast amount of cleverness. The maxim

Buffalo Bill in about 1900

put into words by the old Confederate fox, [General Nathan Bedford] Forrest: "Get there fastest with the mostest," was always a fighting principle with the Sioux.

They were a strong race of men, the braves tall, with finely shaped heads and handsome features. They had poise and dignity and a great deal of pride, and they seldom forgot either a friend or an enemy.

The greatest of all the Sioux in my time, or in any time for that matter, was that wonderful old fighting man, Sitting Bull, whose life will someday be written by a historian who can really give him his due.

Sitting Bull it was who stirred the Indians to the uprising whose climax was the massacre of the Little Bighorn and the destruction of Custer's command.

For months before this uprising he had been going to and fro among the Sioux and their allies urging a revolt against the encroaching white man. It was easy at that time for the Indians to secure rifles. The Canadian-French traders to the north were only too glad to trade them these weapons for the splendid supplies of furs which the Indians had gathered. Many of these rifles were of excellent construction, and on a number of occasions we discovered to our cost that they outranged the army carbines with which we were equipped.

After the Sioux's success at the Battle of the Little Bighorn, the Lakota were forced into the Red Cloud Agency Treaty of 1876. (This treaty was ratified by Congress in 1877, so it's sometimes referred to as the Treaty of 1877. It's also sometimes called the Custer's Last Stand Treaty.) Food was becoming scarce in the Black Hills and the Powder River Country, winter was coming on, their guns and horses had been confiscated, the Army said it would kill any Native American who didn't stay at their agency, and Congress had just passed a bill stating that the reservation food allotments would be withheld until they signed the treaty. Facing the prospect of watching their families slowly die from starvation, they had no choice but to sign. Only 10 percent of the adult male Lakota population signed—mostly from the reservation—not the two thirds required by the 1868 treaty.

Beginning in 1923, the Sioux Nations filed a number of lawsuits against the government in federal court and, in 1980, the US Supreme Court ruled in the Sioux's favor, awarding them what they said was fair value for the land in 1877—$17.1

million plus interest. At the time that came to about $106 million, or roughly $1,350 per person. This the court considered was fair compensation for 7.3 million acres, and the gold that was removed before 1877. The estimated $4 billion in natural resources that have been removed since didn't count. So far the Sioux have not accepted the money, for to do so would mean giving up their claim to the Black Hills.

Ironically, while in 1876 the nation was celebrating one hundred years of freedom, the government was busy taking away the independence of the northern plains tribes.

Crazy Horse's Deathbed Statement

Crazy Horse

Crazy Horse (Ta'shunka Witko, literally "His Horse Is Crazy") led the attack on Custer's Hill, which many people believe was the location of Custer's Last Stand during the Battle of the Little Bighorn. In a 1930 interview Short Bull recounted what he remembered of the battle.

In this Custer fight I was helping fight Reno and never noticed Custer coming. We had Reno's men on the run across the creek when Crazy Horse rode up with his men.

"Too late! You've missed the fight!" we called out to him. "Sorry to miss the fight!" he laughed, "But there's a good fight coming over the hill."

I looked where he pointed and saw Custer and his bluecoats pouring over the hill. I thought there were a million of them.

"That's where the big fight is going to be," said Crazy Horse. "We'll not miss that one."

He was not a bit excited, he made a joke of it. He wheeled and rode down the river and a little while later I saw him on his pinto pony leading his men across the ford. He was the first man to cross the river. I saw he had the business well in hand.

They rode up the draw and then there was too much dust, I could not see any more.

Crazy Horse charged right through Custer's line of men, dividing them into two groups, which the other Indians were able to keep separated, making it easier to defeat them. As the battle was coming to a close on the Custer battlefield, Crazy Horse killed one of the last soldiers. "One soldier was running away to the east," said Flying Hawk, "but Crazy Horse saw him and jumped on his pony and went after him. He got him about half a mile from the place where the others were lying dead."

Crazy Horse at the Battle of the Little Bighorn, drawn by Amos Bad Heart Bull, who was about seven years old when he witnessed the fight

Long before this, many of the Sioux considered him the bravest man they'd ever seen. He would often lead his men into battles and approach much closer to their enemy than anyone else. Interestingly Custer was the same in this regard, which was one reason for his rapid promotions during the Civil War. Both leaders were thought to be "bullet proof" by their men. Custer's men called him "Lucky Custer," while Crazy Horse's men were convinced that his medicine and talismans protected him.

Short Bull described him, saying:

Crazy Horse was a man not very tall and not very short, neither broad nor thin. His hair was very light about the color of yours (The interviewer could be described as a medium blonde). He was a trifle under six feet tall. Bad Heart Bull was the same general type.

But Crazy Horse had a very light complexion, much lighter than the other Indians. He usually wore an Iroquois shell necklace; this was the only ornament he wore. His features were not like those of the rest of us. His face was not broad, and he had a sharp, high nose. He had black eyes that hardly ever looked straight at a man, but they didn't miss much that was going on, all the same.

Crazy Horse was a very enigmatic figure, even for those of his own tribe. No one really understood him. He was very quiet and reserved, usually keeping to himself. He didn't take part in the usual celebrations and rarely attended councils. When he did, he didn't participate—just watched and listened. He often spent days alone away from his village, even in the winter. But he was always in the forefront during battles. He distinguished himself as a warrior in his early teens, leading his first war party before he was twenty. He soon became a war chief. He also became "shirt-wearer," which was a position of importance and leadership for young men. They were spokesmen for the community and settled disputes between families and with outsiders.

Crazy Horse was a shirt-wearer for about five years, until he was caught having an affair with the wife of No Water. When caught, No Water shot him in the face; fortunately the gun was small and the powder-charge was weak. The bullet entered his cheek, glancing down his upper jaw, fracturing it, and exited his neck. It left a scar near his left nostril. The wife stayed with her husband and soon had a daughter that some thought looked a lot like Crazy Horse.

Although they took his shirt away, he remained an important leader in his portion of the tribe, which had been divided into four quarters. He was fiercely loyal to his people and put their well-being above all else.

Like his father, Crazy Horse was also considered a spiritual leader of the Oglala Sioux. He was very interested in the spirit world and gained knowledge through visions. He was always seeking insight into how he could better help his band and how to be a better warrior. He wore various talismans and charms to protect him in battle. His people believed he was living partly in the physical world and partly in the spiritual world.

Black Elk, who at age thirteen was at the Battle of Little Big Horn, said:

I think I was a little afraid of him. I was not afraid that he would hurt me; I was just afraid. Everybody felt that way about him, for he was a queer man and would go about the village without noticing people or saying anything. In his own tepee he would joke, and when he was on the warpath with a small party, he would joke to make his warriors feel good. But around the village he hardly ever noticed anybody, except little children. All the Lakota like to dance and sing; but he never joined a dance, and they say nobody ever heard him sing. But everybody liked him, and they would do anything he wanted or go anywhere he said. He was a small man among the Lakota and he was slender and had a thin face and his eyes looked through things and he always seemed to be thinking hard about something. He never wanted to have many things for himself, and did not have many ponies like a chief. They say that when game was scarce and the people were hungry, he would not eat at all.

Black Elk also explained how Crazy Horse received his name from a vision.

Crazy Horse's father was my father's cousin, and there were no chiefs in our family before Crazy Horse; but there were holy men; and he became a chief because of the power he got in a vision when he was a boy. When I was a man, my father told me something about that vision. Of course he did not know all of it; but he said that Crazy Horse dreamed and went into the world where there is nothing but the spirits of all things. That is the real world that is behind this one, and everything we see here is something like a shadow from that world. He was on his horse in that world, and the horse and himself on it and the trees and the grass and the stones and everything were made of spirit, and nothing was hard, and everything seemed to float. His horse was standing still there, and yet it danced around like a horse made only of shadow, and that is how he got his name, which does not mean that his horse was crazy or wild, but that in his vision it danced around in that queer way.

It was this vision that gave him his great power, for when he went into a fight, he had only to think of that world to be in it again, so that he could go through anything and not be hurt. Until he was murdered by the Wasichus [i.e., non-Native Americans] at the Soldiers' Town [Camp Robinson, Nebraska, which became Fort Robinson in 1878] on White River, he was wounded only twice, once by accident and both times by some one of his own people when he was not expecting trouble and was not thinking; never by an enemy.

Originally it was Crazy Horse's father who was named Crazy Horse, but he passed the name on to his son and took on the name Worm (Waglula) for himself.

Natives didn't usually talk to anyone about their visions, believing them to be very personal, but Crazy Horse did tell his cousin, Chief Flying Hawk, about another of his visions. Flying Hawk later said:

I have been in nine battles with Crazy Horse; won them all. Crazy Horse was quiet and not inclined to associate with others. He was in the front of every battle. He was the greatest leader of our tribe. He told me this story once:

> I was sitting on a hill or rise, and something touched me on the head. I felt for it and found it was a bit of grass. I took it to look at. There was a trail nearby and I followed it. It led to water. I went into the water. There the trail ended and I sat down in the water. I was nearly out of breath. I started to rise out of the water, and when I came out I was born by my mother. When I was born I could know and see and understand for a time, but afterwards went back to it as a baby. Then I grew up naturally. At the age of seven I began to learn, and when twelve began to fight enemies. That was the reason I always refused to wear any war-dress; only a bit of grass in the hair. That was why I always was successful in battles. The first fight was with the Shoshones. The Shoshones were chasing the Sioux. I, with my younger brother [Little Hawk] riding double; two of the Shoshones came for us. We started to meet them. I killed one of them, took his horse. We jumped on him, my brother and I double, and escaped.

Crazy Horse was much alone when not in a fight or on travel or on a hunt. He was quiet and never told stories, but he was the first in every kind of trouble. He was married but had no children. [He had one daughter, but she died at the age of two or three.] His younger brother was on a campaign in the country about which is Utah, and was killed there by some settlers who were having trouble with some Indians there. When Crazy Horse learned that his brother was killed, he left the camp and took his wife, and nobody could find where he went. For a long time he was gone. He went to the place where his brother was killed, and camped in the woods, where he could see the settlement, but the thick woods protected his tepee from view. Here he stayed for nine days; every morning he got up and would stand and look. When he saw some enemy he shot him, until he had killed enough to satisfy him; then went back home.

While still a teenager, Crazy Horse is said to have witnessed the Grattan Massacre, also known as the Mormon Cow Incident. In 1854 High Forehead killed a cow he saw wandering in a field. Some say the cow was old and crippled. Apparently it had escaped from a wagon train and belonged to a Mormon immigrant passing through the area. Since the loose cow was wandering around Lakota Sioux land and they had nothing else to eat, they ate the cow. When the Mormon complained to the Army, they met with a friendly chief named Brave Bear, who was also known as Conquering Bear. He had been the first chief to sign the Fort Laramie Treaty of 1851. The Brulé chief did not have the authority to hand over High Forehead, because High Forehead was a free Miniconjou Sioux and could do nothing to harm a guest in his village, but he offered one of his own horses as restitution. The Mormon refused. He then offered one of the cows the government would be sending them, but that was turned down. An Indian trader offered ten dollars, but the Mormon insisted on twenty-five dollars.

Reaching an impasse, the Mormon insisted High Forehead be arrested. So the next day Brevet-Second Lieutenant John Grattan and thirty men went to the village to make the arrest. This was actually in violation of the 1851 treaty, which stated the Natives would "make restitution for any wrongs committed" and the Army had no authority to arrest or punish any Indian. At the village Grattan and his men were surrounded by many of the twelve hundred warriors under Chief Spotted Tail. After hours of discussions and arguments through the Army's drunken, belligerent interpreter, Grattan's jittery men eventually began shooting, mortally wounding Brave Bear. Grattan tried to regain control by firing off his two howitzers, but he accidentally fired too high. Infuriated, the Natives—pretty much armed with only bows and arrows—quickly wiped out Grattan and all his men. Chief Brave Bear was the only Native killed. Thus the Sioux Wars, which spanned forty years, began because of misunderstandings, incompetence, and a lame cow. It's said that after witnessing Brave Bear's death, Crazy Horse began having trance visions.

Just over a decade later, Crazy Horse fought under Red Cloud in the Sioux War of 1866–1868. After the Sand Creek Massacre of Black Kettle's Cheyenne, many Sioux joined with the Cheyenne, including Crazy Horse. He fought at the Battle of Red Buttes, the Platte River Bridge Station Battle, and the Wagon Box Fight. He is sometimes credited with planning the Fetterman Massacre. This was an 1866 battle in which a group of seven decoy Natives led by Crazy Horse lured Captain William Fetterman's brigade from Fort Kearny into a trap, where more than one thousand Indians killed Fetterman and all seventy-nine (or eighty-three) of his men, while estimates of the Native dead ranged from seven to more than sixty. Fetterman had reportedly claimed, "With eighty men I could ride through the whole Sioux nation."

Crazy Horse also helped attack one of the surveying parties with Custer's 1874 expedition into the Black Hills. He led the force that turned back General Crook's battalion in the Battle of the Rosebud and was one of the main leaders in the Battle of the Little Bighorn. Then when the war department ordered all the Lakota Sioux and Cheyenne—both free and reservation—to report to the agencies, Crazy Horse became one of the primary resistance leaders. While Sitting Bull and Gall retreated into Canada, Crazy Horse and his band remained behind.

General Crook talked Spotted Tail—who he had recently appointed as the chief of all Lakota, replacing Red Cloud—into talking Crazy Horse into surrendering. He sent Spotted Tail out to find Crazy Horse with 250 Brulé Sioux and a pack train of gifts. Crook asked Spotted Tail to promise Crazy Horse that if he surrendered, he would be given his own reservation—like Spotted Tail and Red Cloud's agencies—along the Powder River. After many negotiations, Crazy Horse and 899 people, including 217 braves, surrendered at Camp Robinson, near the Red Cloud Agency, on May 6, 1877. To reinforce his commitment to end hostilities forever, he smoked the peace pipe.

"After the pipe of peace was accepted by Crazy Horse, it settled the matter," said Red Cormorant Woman (Susan Bordeaux Bettelyoun), the French-Sioux wife of one of Camp Robinson's interpreters. She went on:

He, by smoking with the envoy, was at peace for once and forever. The peace pipe was considered such a sacred pact that no one ever broke its law. If they did, they came to grief, brought on by their own untruthfulness, for breaking the law of truth. All that was unclean was never practiced with the peace pipe. The white people, [having] little understanding [of] the power of the pipe as something sacred and holy, doubted the veracity of the peace made with the peace pipe. It is often laughed and jested about by them. The peace pipe, like the white man's sacrament, was a symbol of truth and inward grace. Its laws were spiritual and not to be desecrated.

Crazy Horse's surrender stirred up a hornet's nest of rivalries, power struggles, intrigue, deceit, betrayals, and mistrust and even spawned plots to assassinate him. General Crook refused to consider killing him, but was concerned he would resume hostilities, so he decided to arrest him and ship him off to a desolate island prison in the Dry Tortugas, seventy miles west of Florida's Key West. On September 5, 1877, they brought him back to Camp Robinson under arrest, which he had no problem with, but when he suddenly realized they were going to lock him up in the stockade, he began to struggle and was bayoneted. Realizing he was mortally wounded, they took him to the adjutant's office, where he insisted they lay him on the floor, instead of the bed, so he could be closer to the earth. It's said that shortly before he died, he made this statement to Lieutenant Jesse Lee, the Indian Agent for the nearby Spotted Tail Agency who had accompanied him to plead his case to Camp Robinson's commander:

My friend, I do not blame you for this. Had I listened to you this trouble would not have happened to me. I was not hostile to the white man. Sometimes my young men would attack the Indians who were their enemies and took their ponies. They did it in return.

We had buffalo for food, and their hides for clothing, and our tepees. We preferred hunting to a life of idleness on the reservations, where we were driven against our will. At times we did not get enough to eat, and we were not allowed to leave the reservation to hunt.

We preferred our own way of living. We were no expense to the Government then. All we wanted was peace and to be left alone. Soldiers were sent out in the winter, who destroyed our villages. Then "Long Hair" [Custer] came in the same way. They say we massacred him but he would have done the same to us had we not defended ourselves and fought to the last. Our first impulse was to escape with our squaws and papooses, but we were so hemmed in we had to fight.

After that I went up on Tongue River with a few of my people and lived in peace. But the Government would not let me alone. Finally, I came back to the Red Cloud agency . . . I came here with the agent to talk to the Big White Chief, but was not given a chance. They tried to confine me, I tried to escape, and a soldier ran his bayonet into me.

I have spoken.

In what may have been his final words to his father, Worm, Crazy Horse said, "Ahh, my father. I am bad hurt. Tell the people it is no use to depend on me anymore now." He was most likely thirty-six when he died.

Little Bighorn and Custer's Death

Sitting Bull

Sitting Bull

In the summer of 1872 the Northern Pacific Railroad, ignoring the 1868 treaty, sent surveyors to plot the course of the tracks across unceded Native land along the Yellowstone River. During the Battle of Arrow Creek on August 14 against five hundred soldiers who were protecting the survey team, Sitting Bull calmly walked out into an open valley in front of the soldiers' defensive position. Laying down his rifle, bow, and quiver, he called out to his men, "Anyone who wishes to smoke with me, come." White Bull and three other warriors went out between the lines and sat with him, calmly sharing a pipe as the soldiers' bullets whizzed past and kicked up the dirt around them. When they were done, Sitting Bull cleaned the pipe. As the others got up and ran for cover, Sitting Bull calmly walked back. One of them fled so quickly, he left his bow and quiver behind and White Bull had to retrieve it for him. Crazy Horse, armed only with a lance, then rode in front of the soldiers, from one end of their line to the other, followed by White Bull. Crazy Horse was almost back to safety when his horse was shot out from under him. White Bull later described the "smoking party" as a terrifying experience. But in it, Sitting Bull not only demonstrated his bravery, he was also insulting the soldiers.

Bravery was highly prized among the Native Americans and acts such as this increased their status in the tribe. Warfare was looked on as a type of competition. Killing an enemy was not nearly as important as counting coup by physically touching the enemy with one's hand or coup stick. It's said that when Sitting Bull was about twenty-eight, his band was in a fight with a band of Crow. Most of the Crow were forced to retreat, but one Crow warrior remained behind in a narrow ravine, from which he killed several Hunkpapa. Eventually Sitting Bull charged him on horseback. The Crow leapt out, and as Sitting Bull struck him with his coup stick, the Crow poked his empty gun in Sitting Bull's face and jumped back to his cover. On discovering the warrior was out of ammo, Sitting Bull threw the man his own rifle and then returned to his own men. Attacking him again, Sitting Bull was seriously wounded—shot by the enemy with his own gun—while his men killed the Crow. Sitting Bull felt the warrior was very brave, and he did not want to kill the man when he was unarmed.

Sitting Bull

Sitting Bull's bravery was well known among his tribe, and he became a highly respected Hunkpapa chief and a religious leader of the Lakota Sioux. Early on he was a leader of the Strong Heart warrior society and was involved in a tribal welfare group called the Silent Eaters. He became the primary chief of the Lakota in 1868.

Sioux physician and author Dr. Charles Eastman (Ohiyesa) explained in *Indian Heroes and Great Chieftains* (1918),

It is a mistake to suppose that Sitting Bull, or any other Indian warrior, was of a murderous disposition. It is true that savage warfare had grown more and more harsh and cruel since the coming of white traders among them, bringing guns, knives, and whiskey. Yet it was still regarded largely as a sort of game, undertaken in order to develop the manly qualities of their youth. It was the degree of risk which brought honor, rather than the number slain, and a brave must mourn thirty days, with blackened face and loosened hair, for the enemy whose life he had taken. While the spoils of war were allowed, this did not extend to territorial aggrandizement, nor was there any wish to overthrow another nation and enslave its people. It was a point of honor in the old days to treat a captive with kindness. The common impression that the Indian is naturally cruel and revengeful is entirely opposed to his philosophy and training. The revengeful tendency of the Indian was aroused by the white man.

Sitting Bull's name, Tatanka Iyotanka, literally means "Buffalo Bull Sitting Down" or "Buffalo He Sits Down." According to Dr. Eastman, this is how Sitting Bull got his name:

It is told that after a buffalo hunt the boys were enjoying a mimic hunt with the calves that had been left behind. A large calf turned viciously on Sitting Bull, whose pony had thrown him, but the alert youth got hold of both ears and struggled until the calf was pushed back into a buffalo wallow in a sitting posture. The boys shouted, 'He has subdued the buffalo calf! He made it sit down!' And from this incident was derived his familiar name of Sitting Bull.

Apparently Sitting Bull has told several versions of his early life. Here is one recorded in Willis Fletcher Johnson's *Life of Sitting Bull and History of the Indian War of 1890- '91* (1891):

I was born near old Fort George, on Willow Creek, below the mouth of the Cheyenne River. Cannot tell exactly how old I am. We count our years from the moons between great events. The event from which I date my birth is the year in which Thunder Hawk was born. I have always been running around. Indians that remain on the same hunting grounds all the time can remember years better. I have nine children and two living wives and one wife that has gone to the Great Spirit. I have two pairs of twins. I think as much of one as the other. If I did not, I would not keep them. I believe if I had a white wife I would think more of her than the other two. My father's name was The Jumping Bull, and he was a chief. At the age of fourteen I killed an enemy and began to make myself great in battle and became a chief.

In 1875 Sitting Bull gave a speech at the Powder River Council, where he presented his view of people who were flooding into the area. It was written down by Dr.

Eastman, who once met Sitting Bull, but gathered most of his information from other Sioux who knew the chief well. Eastman wrote of him:

His bitter and at the same time well-grounded and philosophical dislike of the conquering race is well expressed in a speech made before the purely Indian council before referred to, upon the Powder River. I will give it in brief as it has been several times repeated to me by men who were present.

"Behold, my friends, the spring is come; the earth has gladly received the embraces of the sun, and we shall soon see the results of their love! Every seed is awakened, and all animal life. It is through this mysterious power that we too have our being, and we therefore yield to our neighbors, even to our animal neighbors, the same right as ourselves to inhabit this vast land.

"Yet hear me, friends! we have now to deal with another people, small and feeble when our forefathers first met with them, but now great and overbearing. Strangely enough, they have a mind to till the soil, and the love of possessions is a disease in them. These people have made many rules that the rich may break, but the poor may not! They have a religion in which the poor worship, but the rich will not! They even take tithes of the poor and weak to support the rich and those who rule. They claim this mother of ours, the Earth, for their own use, and fence their neighbors away from her, and deface her with their buildings and their refuse. They compel her to produce out of season, and when sterile she is made to take medicine in order to produce again. All this is sacrilege.

"This nation is like a spring freshet; it overruns its banks and destroys all who are in its path. We cannot dwell side by side. Only seven years ago we made a treaty by which we were assured that the buffalo country should be left to us forever. Now they threaten to take that from us also. My brothers, shall we submit? or shall we say to them: 'First kill me, before you can take possession of my fatherland!'"

As Sitting Bull spoke, so he felt, and he had the courage to stand by his words. Crazy Horse led his forces in the field; as for him, he applied his energies to state affairs, and by his strong and aggressive personality contributed much to holding the hostiles together.

Sitting Bull gave that speech shortly before the Battle of the Little Bighorn. During the battle he gave some orders, but he wasn't able to fight. The day before, his leg was severely injured when a wounded pack animal kicked him. It appears he was seen by Reno's men, though they didn't know it at the time. Years later Sitting Bull mentioned this when he met First Sergeant John Ryan, who fought with Reno's detachment. Ryan served under Custer for ten years and was with him at the Washita Massacre, when Chief Black Kettle and his wife were killed.

This interview is from the August 8, 1885, issue of the *Boston Record*, as it was reprinted in the Dakota Territory's *Bismarck Daily Tribune*.

CUSTER'S DEATH
AN EXCHANGE OF REMINISCENCES
BY SITTING BULL AND A SOLDIER.

Boston Special: The real facts about the death of General Custer came out a day or two ago in an interview here between Sitting Bull and Sergeant John Ryan, of Newton, who fought under General Reno in the last battle between Custer's regiment and the Indians. When Sergeant Ryan was introduced to the chief, Sitting Bull showed no disposition to talk, but presently Ryan drew from his pocket a blood spattered cavalry guidon and asked Sitting Bull whether he had ever seen a flag like that before. The Indian showed sudden awakening of interest:

"Yes," he said.

"When was it?" asked Sergeant Ryan.

"When we had the fight and killed Custer's men," said Sitting Bull through the interpreter, "we got a number of them. "Where did you get it?"

"On the second day of the fight," answered Ryan, "I saw an Indian riding up and down in front of our lines displaying this flag. Another man and myself, who had long range rifles, fired at him repeatedly, and finally dropped him off his horse. When night came I crawled out and brought the flag in."

"When we struck your trail," Sergeant Ryan continued, "and just before the fight, we found four lodges with dead Indians in them. Who were they?"

"They were Sioux Shawnee scouts," replied Sitting Bull, "killed by men of Gen. Crook's command on the Rosebud on June 17th. On the first day's fight, do you recollect an Indian mounted on a black horse who was armed with a 'camp stick' (an Indian lance), and was cheering and urging on his men?"

"That was when you were trying to break our skirmish line," said Ryan. "The chief was 200 or 800 yards away and I fired on him a number of times."

Sitting Bull (with much merriment) said, "That was I. Soon after that I went to the scene of the fight with Custer and was not in the battle after that day. I remember when two of your pack mules charged down to the water from your camp on the bluff. They were loaded with ammunition, and we used that ammunition, as well as that we got from Custer, in the second day's fight when I went to take charge of the battle at the other end of the valley, where Custer made his attack. I left Crazy Horse in command of my young men, who were fighting you and Reno."

"Was the fight going on when you got there?" asked Ryan.

"Oh, yes; we had them surrounded."

"It has been said that Rain-in-the-Face asserted that he killed Custer. Did he?"

"No. There is no truth in it. So many were firing at Custer at the same time that no one could tell whether he hit him or not."

"You are telling the truth there," said Ryan. "I was in command of the detail that buried Custer after General Terry came up. There were a number of bullets in Custer's body, and a newspaper man named Kelly were the only ones whose bodies had not been mutilated. Who was it that crushed the head of Captain Tom Custer, and what became of the prisoners?"

"I don't know about that," answered Sitting Bull. "The young men and the squaws had to do with that. There were 4,000 warriors and there were in the camp from 6,000 to 7,000 women and children, and the camp was four or five miles long, all in the valley of the Little Big Horn. How many men did you have?"

"Six hundred all told, of whom 207 were killed with Custer."

The two men exchanged many campaign reminiscences. Ryan was in Custer's regiment on the plains for ten years and often skirmished with Sitting Bull and his tribe when they were on the war path.

Chief Crow King said it was Sitting Bull who called the warriors away from Reno and Benteen's men, saying,

Then we went back for the first party [Reno's, after Custer's men were dead]. We fired at them until the sun went down. We surrounded them and watched them all night, and at daylight we fought them again. We killed many of them. Then a chief from the Hunkpapa called our men off. He told them those men had been punished enough, that they were fighting under orders, that we had killed the great leader and his men in the fight the day before, and we should let the rest go home. Sitting Bull gave this order. He said, "This is not my doings, nor these men's. They are fighting because they were commanded to fight. We have killed their leader. Let them go. I call on the Great Spirit to witness what I say. We did not want to fight. Long Hair sent us word that he was coming to fight us and we had to defend ourselves and our wives and children." If this command had not been given we could have cut Reno's command to pieces, as we did Custer's.

After Little Bighorn, Sitting Bull hoped the military would leave him and his people alone, but Colonel Nelson Miles was sent after him, and though he couldn't catch him, Miles was able to harass him and keep him on the move.

On October 16, 1876, one of Colonel Miles's officers found a message from Sitting Bull posted on a stake in the ground. For the previous six days, Sitting Bull's snipers had been taking potshots at Miles's supply wagons as they moved up the Yellowstone River. Sitting Bull's translator wrote for him:

I want to know what you are doing, traveling on this road. You scare all the buffalo away. I want to hunt in this place. I want you to turn back from here. If you don't, I will fight you again. I want you to leave what you have got here and turn back from here.

I am your friend

Sitting Bull

I mean all the rations you have got and some powder. Wish you would write me as soon as you can.

Miles responded by requesting that Sitting Bull meet with him on October 20. According to several Natives who attended the meeting, the colonel said to the chief, "They say you are well known to be hostile to the white man."

Sitting Bull replied, "That's all wrong. All I am looking out for is to see how and where I can find more meat for my people, more game animals for my people, and to find what God has given me to eat."

Miles demanded Sitting Bull surrender, and Sitting Bull demanded Miles leave his country. Then the shooting started. No soldiers died, but five Sioux were killed. It became known as the Battle of Cedar Creek.

In May 1877, Sitting Bull crossed the border into Canada to escape harassment by the military, settling in the country south and east of the Cypress Hills—an area that would sit on the southern border between the future provinces of Alberta and Saskatchewan. He brought with him about a thousand people, while Canada had only thirty-four-year-old Major James Walsh and about ninety members of the newly formed North-West Mounted Police—now known as the Royal Canadian Mounted Police—to maintain control. It was a difficult job, and Major Walsh dealt with it in the proper manner. When he first discovered Sitting Bull's camp, he marched right on into it with just a sergeant and three troopers. This was just eleven months after the Custer massacre. They were quickly surrounded. War Chief Spotted Eagle was impressed, telling the men they were the only white men ever to approach Sitting Bull's camp in such a manner.

Walsh explained to Sitting Bull basic Canadian laws, adding that they apply equally to Natives and whites. Sitting Bull assured Walsh their intensions were peaceful. He then asked for ammunition, saying they'd used most of it in their battles south of the border and needed some in order to hunt for food. Walsh gave them enough for this, after receiving assurances none of it would be used for fighting US soldiers. Sitting Bull's prejudices against white people began to turn around in Canada, he was so impressed by his treatment and the bravery of the Mounties, and of Walsh in particular. In dealing with the Natives, Walsh was firm and fair, but not arrogant or demanding. He treated the Sioux chief with respect. According to Mountie historian John Peter Turner, Sitting Bull said, "Yesterday I was fleeing from white men, cursing them as I went. Today they erect their lodges by the side of mine and defy me. The White Forehead Chief [Walsh] walks to my lodge alone and unarmed. He gives me the hand of peace. Have I fallen? Am I at the end?"

Still, the Canadian government was leery of their presence and requested the US government try to get him to go to a US reservation, so they sent General Terry to offer him a pardon, but just a couple of weeks earlier, Colonel Miles had forced the surrender of Chief Joseph and the Nez Percés, after General Oliver Howard's men had chased them seventeen hundred miles from Oregon to the Montana Territory. A few had escaped and had just arrived at Sitting Bull's camp, telling him what had happened to them. Sitting Bull wanted nothing to do with Terry's pardon or US reservations. He intended to remain in Canada.

Terry was accompanied by a newspaper reporter who interviewed Sitting Bull. The resulting article appeared in the November 16, 1877, issue of the *New York Herald*. Of course one of the reporter's primary interests was in asking Sitting Bull about Custer and the Battle of the Little Bighorn.

SITTING BULL TALKS
VALUABLE INTERVIEW WITH A HERALD CORRESPONDENT
"I AM NO CHIEF."
Graphic Description of the
Rosebud Fight
"HELL—A THOUSAND DEVILS."
"Bullets Were Like Humming Bees
Soldiers Shook Like Aspen Leaves."
———

CUSTER NOBLY VINDICATED
———

"A Sheaf of Corn with All the Ears
Fallen About Him."
———

HE DIED LAUGHING
———

An Implied Charge Against Major Reno
———

Fort Walsh, Northwest Territory,
October 17, 1877.

Lakota Sioux Chiefs. Front row (left to right): Hunkpapa Chief Sitting Bull with Brulé Chiefs Swift Bear and Spotted Tail. Back row: translator Julius Meyer and Oglala Chief Red Cloud.

The conference between Sitting Bull and the United States Commissioners was not, as will presently be seen, the most interesting conference of the day. Sitting Bull and his chiefs so hated the "Americans," especially the American officers, that they had nothing for them but the disdain evinced in the speeches I have reported to you. After the talk with Generals Terry and Lawrence the Indians retired to their quarters.

But through the intercession of Major Walsh, Sitting Bull was persuaded at nightfall to hold a special conference with me. It was explained to him that I was not his enemy, but that I was his good friend. He was told by Major Walsh that I was a great paper chief who talked with a million tongues to all the people in the world. Said the Major, "This man is a man of wonderful medicine; he speaks and the people on this side and across the great water open their ears and hear him. He tells the truth; he does not lie. He wishes to make the world know what a great tribe is encamped here on the land owned by the White Mother. He wants it to be understood that her guests are mighty warriors. The Long Haired Chief (alluding to General Custer) was his friend. He wants to hear from you how he fought and whether he met death like a brave." [*Note:* The "White Mother" was the Native name for Queen Victoria. He's referring to Canada and the Canadians.]

"Agh-howgh!" (It is well) said Sitting Bull.

He finally agreed to come, after dark, to the quarters which had been assigned to me, on the condition that nobody should be present except himself, his interlocutor, Major Walsh, two interpreters and the stenographer I had employed for the occasion.

SITTING BULL AS HE APPEARS

At the appointed time, half-past eight, the lamps were lighted, and the most mysterious Indian chieftain who ever flourished in North America was ushered in by Major Walsh, who locked the door behind him. This was the first time that Sitting Bull had condescended, not merely to visit but to address a white man from the United States. During the long years of his domination he had withstood, with his bands, every attempt on the part of the United States Government at a compromise of interests. He had refused all proffers, declined any treaty. He had never been beaten in a battle with United States troops: on the contrary, his warriors had been victorious over the pride of our army. Pressed hard, he had retreated, scorning the factions of his bands who accepted the terms offered them with the same bitterness with which he scorned his white enemies.

Here he stood, his blanket rolled back head upreared, his right moccasin put forward his right hand thrown across his chest.

I arose and approached him, holding out both hands. He grasped them cordially.

"How!" said he.

"How!"

And now let me attempt a better portrait of Sitting Bull than I was able to dispatch to you at headlong haste by the telegraph. He is five feet ten inches high. He was clad in a black and white calico shirt, black cloth leggings, and moccasins, magnificently embroidered with beads and porcupine quills. He held in his left hand a foxskin cap, its brush drooping to his feet.

I turned to the interpreter and said, "Explain again to Sitting Bull that he is with a friend."

The interpreter explained.

"Banee!" said the chief, holding out his hand again and pressing mine.

Major Walsh here said, "Sitting Bull is in the best mood now that you could possibly wish. Proceed with your questions and make them as logical as you can. I will assist you and trip you up occasionally if you are likely to irritate him."

Then the dialogue went on. I give it literally.

"I AM NO CHIEF."

"You are a great chief," said I to Sitting Bull, "but you live behind a cloud. Your face is dark; my people do not see it. Tell me, do you hate the Americans very much?"

A gleam as of fire shot across his face. "I am no chief."

This was precisely what I expected. It will dissipate at once the erroneous idea which has prevailed that Sitting Bull is either a chief or a warrior.

"What are you?"

"I am," said he, crossing both hands upon his chest, slightly nodding and smiling satirically, "a man."

"What does he mean?" I inquired, turning to Major Walsh.

"He means," responded the Major, "to keep you in ignorance of his secret if he can. His position among his bands is anomalous. His own tribes, the Hunkpapa, are not all in fealty to him. Parts of nearly twenty different tribes of Sioux, besides a remnant of the Hunkpapa, abide with him. So far as I have learned he rules over these fragments of tribes, which compose his camp of 2,500, including between 800 and 900 warriors, by sheer compelling force of intellect and will. I believe that he understands nothing particularly of war or military tactics, at least not enough to give him the skill or the right to command warriors in battle. He is supposed to have guided the fortunes of several battles, including the fight in which Custer fell. That supposition, as you will presently find, is partially erroneous. His word was always potent in the camp or in the field, but he has usually left to the war chiefs the duties appertaining to engagements. When the crisis came he gave his opinion, which was accepted as law.

"What was he, then?" I inquired, continuing this momentary dialogue with Major Walsh. "Was he, is he, a mere medicine man?"

"Don't for the world," replied the Major, "intimate to him, in the questions you are about to ask him, that you have derived the idea from me, or from anyone, that he is a mere medicine man. He would deem that to be a profound insult. [Sitting Bull was not a medicine man in the sense of someone who treats sickness with herbs or native remedies. He was a spiritual visionary and religious leader. The English terms medicine and medicine man were used for both when connected with Native Americans.] In point of fact he is a medicine man, but a far greater, more influential medicine man than any savage I have ever known. He speaks. They listen and they obey. Now let us hear what his explanation will be."

A SAVAGE COMPANION

"You say you are no chief?"

"No!" with considerable hauteur.

"Are you a head soldier?"

"I am nothing—neither a chief nor a soldier."

"What? Nothing?"

"Nothing."

"What, then, makes the warriors of your camp, the great chiefs who are here along with you, look up to you so? Why do they think so much of you?"

Sitting Bull's lips curled with a proud smile. "Oh, I used to be a kind of a chief, but the Americans made me go away from my father's hunting ground."

"You do not love the Americans?"

You should have seen this savage's lips.

"I saw today that all the warriors around you clapped their hands and cried out when you spoke. What you said appeared to please them. They liked you. They seemed to think that what you said was right for them to say. If you are not a great chief, why do these men think so much of you?"

At this Sitting Bull, who had in the meantime been leaning back against the wall, assumed a posture of mingled toleration and disdain.

"Your people look up to men because they are rich; because they have much land, many lodges, many squaws?"

"Yes."

"Well, I suppose my people look up to me because I am poor. That is the difference."

In this answer was concentrated all the evasiveness natural to an Indian.

"What is your feeling toward the Americans now?"

He did not even deign an answer. He touched his hip where his knife was.

I asked the interpreter to insist on an answer.

"Listen," said Sitting Bull, not changing his posture but putting his right hand out upon my knee. "I told them today what my notions were— that I did not want to go back there. Every time that I had any difficulty with them they struck me first. I want to live in peace."

"Have you an implacable enmity to the Americans? Would you live with them in peace if they allowed you to do so; or do you think that you can only obtain peace here?"

"I BOUGHT THEM."
"The White Mother is good."

"Better than the Great Father?"

"Howgh!"

And then, after a pause, Sitting Bull continued, "They asked me today to give them my horses. I bought my horses, and they are mine. I bought them from men who came up the Missouri in macinaws [i.e., flat-bottomed boats]. They do not belong to the Government; neither do the rifles. The rifles are also mine. I bought them; I paid for them. Why I should give them up I do not know. I will not give them up."

"Do you really think, do your people believe, that it is wise to reject the proffers that have been made to you by the United States Commissioners? Do not some of you feel as if you were destined to lose your old hunting grounds? Don't you see that you will probably have the same difficulty in Canada that you have had in the United States?"

"The White Mother does not lie."

"Do you expect to live here by hunting? Are there buffaloes enough? Can your people subsist on the game here?"

"I don't know; I hope so."

"If not, are any part of your people disposed to take up agriculture? Would any of them raise steers and go to farming?"

"I don't know."

"What will they do, then?"

"As long as there are buffaloes that is the way we will live."

"But the time will come when there will be no more buffaloes."

"Those are the words of an American."

POISONED WITH BLOOD
"How long do you think the buffaloes will last?"

Sitting Bull arose. "We know," said he, extending his right hand with an impressive gesture, "that on the other side the buffaloes will not last very long. Why? Because the country there is poisoned with blood—a poison that kills all the buffaloes or drives them away. It is strange," he continued, with his peculiar smile, "that the Americans should complain that the Indians kill buffaloes. We kill buffaloes, as we kill other animals, for food and clothing, and to make our lodges warm. They kill buffaloes—for what? Go through your country. See the thousands of carcasses rotting on the Plains. Your young men shoot for pleasure. All they take from dead buffalo is his tail, or his head, or his horns, perhaps, to show they have killed a buffalo. What is this? Is it robbery? You call us savages. What are they? The buffaloes have come North. We have come North to find them, and to get away from a place where people tell lies."

To gain time and not to dwell importunately on a single point, I asked Sitting Bull to tell me something of his early life. In the first place, where he was born?

"I was born on the Missouri River; at least I recollect that somebody told me so—I don't know who told me or where I was told of it."

"Of what tribe are you?"

"I am a Hunkpapa."

"Of the Sioux?"

"Yes; of the great Sioux Nation."

"Who was your father?"

"My father is dead."

"Is your mother living?"

"My mother lives with me in my lodge."

"Great lies are told about you. White men say that you lived among them when you were young; that you went to school; that you learned to write and read from books; that you speak English; that you know how to talk French?"

"It is a lie."

"You are an Indian?"

(Proudly) "I am a Sioux."

Then, suddenly relaxing from his hauteur, Sitting Bull began to laugh. "I have heard," he said, "of some of these stories. They are all strange lies. What I am, I am," and here he leaned back and resumed his attitude and expression of barbaric grandeur.

PREDESTINATION

"I am a man. I see. I know. I began to see when I was not yet born; when I was not in my mother's arms, but inside of my mother's belly. It was there that I began to study about my people."

Here I touched Sitting Bull on the arm.

"Do not interrupt him," said Major Walsh. "He is beginning to talk about his medicine."

"I was," repeated Sitting Bull, "still in my mother's insides when I began to study all about my people. God (waving his hand to express a great protecting Genius) gave me the power to see out of the womb. I studied there, in the womb, about many things. I studied about the small-pox, that was killing my people—the great sickness that was killing the women and children. I was so interested that I turned over on my side. The God Almighty must have told me at that time (and here Sitting Bull unconsciously revealed his secret) that I would be the man to be the judge of all the other Indians—a big man, to decide for them in all their ways."

"And you have since decided for them?"

"I speak. It is enough."

"Could not your people, whom you love so well, get on with the Americans?"

"No!"

"Why?"

Why He Fought

"I never taught my people to trust Americans. I have told them the truth—that the Americans are great liars. I have never dealt with the Americans. Why should I? The land belonged to my people. I say never dealt with them—I mean I never treated with them in a way to surrender my people's rights. I traded with them, but I always gave full value for what I got. I never asked the United States Government to make me presents of blankets or cloth or anything of that kind. The most I did was to ask them to send me an honest trader that I could trade with and I proposed to give him buffalo robes and elk skins and other hides in exchange for what we wanted. I told every trader who came to our camps that I did not want any favors from him—that I wanted to trade with him fairly and equally, giving him full value for what I got—but the traders wanted me to trade with them on no such terms. They wanted to give little and get much. They told me that if I did not accept what they would give me in trade they would get the Government to fight me. I told them I did not want to fight."

"But you fought."

"At last, yes; but not until after I had tried hard to prevent a fight. At first my young men, when they began to talk bad, stole five American horses. I took the horses away from them and gave them back to the Americans. It did no good. By and by we had to fight."

THE GREAT CUSTER BATTLE EXPLAINED

It was at this juncture that I began to question the great savage before me in regard to the most disastrous, most mysterious Indian battle of the century—Custer's encounter with the Sioux on the Bighorn—the Thermopylae of the Plains. Sitting Bull, the chief genius of his bands, has been supposed to have commanded the Sioux forces when Custer fell.

That the reader may understand Sitting Bull's statements, it will be necessary for him to scan the map of the illustrious battleground, which is herewith presented, and to read the following preliminary sketch. It should be understood, moreover, that, inasmuch as every white man with Custer perished, and no other white man, save one or two scouts, had conferred lately with Sitting Bull or any of his chiefs since the awful day, this is the first authentic story of the conflict which can possibly have appeared out of the lips of a survivor. It has the more historical value since it comes from the chief among Custer's and Reno's foes.

The Indian village, consisting of camps of Cheyenne, Oglala, Miniconjou and Hunkpapa, was nearly three miles long. The accompanying map will show its exact situation, also the routes pursued by Reno's and Custer's forces. It is seen from this map that Reno crossed the Little Bighorn, formed his first line just south of the crossing and charged. He says, "I deployed; and, with the Ree scouts on my left, charged down the valley with great ease for about two and a half miles."

Reno, instead of holding the ground thus gained, retreated, being hard pressed. The map shows the timber in which he made a temporary stand, and it shows, too, his line of retreat back over the valley, and across the Little Bighorn and up the bluffs, on the summit of which he entrenched himself late in the afternoon.

The map expresses the fact that Custer's march to the ford where he attempted to cross the Little Bighorn and attack the Indians in their rear

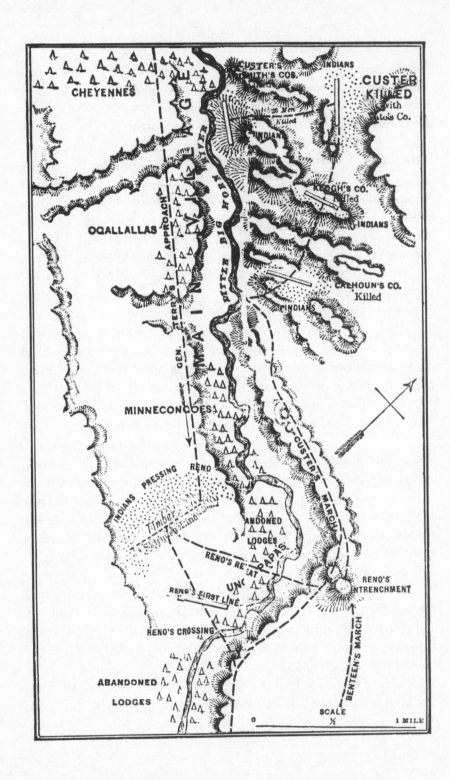

was much longer than Reno's march, consequently Custer's assault was not made until after Reno's.

"WE THOUGHT WE WERE WHIPPED"

The testimony of Sitting Bull, which I am about to give, is the more convincing and important from the very fact of the one erroneous impression he derived as to the identity of the officer in command of the forces which assailed his camp. He confounds Reno with Custer. He supposes that one and the same general crossed the Little Bighorn where Reno crossed, charged as Reno charged, retreated as Reno retreated back over the river and then pursued the line of Custer's march, attacked as Custer attacked and fell as Custer fell.

"Did you know the Long Haired Chief?" I asked Sitting Bull. "No."

"What! Had you never seen him?"

"No. Many of the chiefs knew him."

"What did they think of him?"

"He was a great warrior."

"Was he brave?"

"He was a mighty chief."

"Now, tell me. Here is something that I wish to know. Big lies are told about the fight in which the Long Haired Chief was killed. He was my friend. No one has come back to tell the truth about him, or about that fight. You were there; you know. Your chiefs know. I want to hear something that forked tongues do not tell—the truth."

"It is well."

Here I drew forth the map of the battlefield and spread it out across Sitting Bull's knees and explained to him the names and situations as represented on it, and he smiled.

"We thought we were whipped," he said.

"Ah! Did you think the soldiers were too many for you?"

"Not at first; but by-and-by, yes. Afterwards, no."

"Tell me about the battle. Where was the Indian camp first attacked?"

"Here" (pointing to Reno's crossing on the map).

"About what time in the day was that?"

"It was some two hours past the time when the sun is in the centre of the sky."

CUSTER COMMANDED

"What white chief was it who came over there against your warriors?"

"The Long Hair."

"Are you sure?"

"The Long Hair commanded."

"But you did not see him?"

"I have said that I never saw him."

"Did any of the chiefs see him?"

"Not here, but there," pointing to the place where Custer charged and was repulsed on the north bank of the Little Bighorn.

"Why do you think it was the Long Hair who crossed first and charged you here at the right side of the map?"

"A chief leads his warriors."

"Was there a good fight here, on the right side of the map? Explain it to me."

"It was so," said Sitting Bull, raising his hands. "I was lying in my lodge. Some young men ran in to me and said, 'The Long Hair is in the camp. Get up. They are firing into the camp.' I said, all right. I jumped up and stepped out of my lodge."

"Where was your lodge?"

"Here, with my people," answered Sitting Bull, pointing to the group of Hunkpapa lodges, designated as "abandoned lodges" on the map.

"So the first attack was made then, on the right side of the map, and upon the lodges of the Hunkpapa?"

"Yes."

"Here the lodges are said to have been deserted?"

"The old men, the squaws and the children were hurried away."

"Toward the other end of the camp?"

"Yes. Some of the Miniconjou women and children also left their lodges when the attack began."

"Did you retreat at first?"

"Do you mean the warriors?"

"Yes, the fighting men."

MISTAKING RENO FOR CUSTER

"Oh, we fell back, but it was not what warriors call a retreat; it was to gain time. It was the Long Hair who retreated. My people fought him here in the brush (designating the timber behind which the Indians pressed Reno) and he fell back across here (placing his finger on the line of Reno's retreat to the northern bluffs).

"So you think that was the Long Hair whom your people fought in that timber and who fell back afterward to those heights?"

"Of course."

"What afterward occurred? Was there any heavy fighting after the retreat of the soldiers to the bluffs?"

"Not then; not there."

"Where, then?"

"Why, down here;" and Sitting Bull indicated with his finger the place where Custer approached and touched the river. "That," said he, "was where the big fight was fought, a little later. After the Long Hair was driven back to the bluffs he took this route (tracing with his finger the line of Custer's march on the map), and went down to see if he could not beat us there."

(Here the reader should pause to discern the extent of Sitting Bull's error, and to anticipate what will presently appear to be Reno's misconception or mistake. Sitting Bull, not identifying Reno in the whole of this engagement, makes it seem that it was Custer who attacked, when Reno attacked in the first place and afterward moved down to resume the assault from a new position. He thus involuntarily testified to the fact that Reno's assault was a brief, ineffectual one before his retreat to the bluffs, and that Reno, after his retreat, ceased on the bluffs from aggressive fighting.)

BULL'S DESCRIPTION OF HELL

"When the fight commenced here," I asked, pointing to the spot where Custer advanced beyond the Little Bighorn, "what happened?"

"Hell!"

"You mean, I suppose, a fierce battle?"

"I mean a thousand devils."

"The village was by this time thoroughly aroused?"

"The squaws were like flying birds; the bullets were like humming bees."

"You say that when the first attack was made, up here on the right of the map, the old men and the squaws and children ran down the valley toward the left. What did they do when this second attack came from up here toward the left?"

"They ran back again to the right, here and here," answered Sitting Bull, placing his swarthy finger on the place where the words "Abandoned Lodges" are.

"And where did the warriors run?"

"They ran to the fight—the big fight."

"So that, in the afternoon, after the fight, on the right hand side of the map was over, and after the big fight toward the left hand side began, you say that the squaws and children all returned to the right hand side, and that the warriors, the fighting men of all the Indian camps, ran to the place where the big fight was going on?"

"Yes."

"Why was that? Were not some of the warriors left in front of these entrenchments on the bluffs, near the right side of the map? Did not you think it necessary—did not your war chiefs think it necessary—to keep some of your young men there to fight the troops who had retreated to those entrenchments?"

"No."

"Why?"

"You have forgotten."

"How?"

A CHARGE AGAINST RENO

"You forget that only a few soldiers were left by the Long Hair on those bluffs. He took the main body of his soldiers with him to make the big fight down here on the left."

"So there were no soldiers to make a fight left in the entrenchments on the right hand bluffs?"

"I have spoken. It is enough. The squaws could deal with them. There were none but squaws and papooses in front of them that afternoon."

"Well then," I inquired of Sitting Bull, "Did the cavalry, who came down and made the big fight, fight?"

Again Sitting Bull smiled.

"They fought. Many young men are missing from our lodges. But is there an American squaw who has her husband left? Were there any Americans left to tell the story of that day? No."

"How did they come on to the attack?"

"I have heard that there are trees which tremble."

"Do you mean the trees with trembling leaves?"

"Yes."

"They call them in some parts of the western country Quaking Aspens; in the eastern part of the country they call them Silver Aspens."

"Hah! A great white chief, whom I met once, spoke these words 'Silver Aspens,' trees that shake; these were the Long Hair's soldiers."

"You do not mean that they trembled before your people because they were afraid?"

"They were brave men. They were tired. They were too tired."

"How did they act? How did they behave themselves?"

At this Sitting Bull again arose. I also arose from my seat, as did the other persons in the room, except the stenographer.

As Good Men as Ever Fought

"Your people," said Sitting Bull, extending his right hand, "were killed. I tell no lies about dead men. These men who came with the Long Hair were as good men as ever fought. When they rode up their horses were tired and they were tired. When they got off from their horses they could not stand firmly on their feet. They swayed to and fro—so my young men have told me—like the limbs of cypresses in a great wind. Some of them staggered under the weight of their guns. But they began to fight at once; but by this time, as I have said, our camps were aroused, and there were plenty of warriors to meet them. They fired with needle guns. We replied with magazine guns repeating rifles. It was so (and here Sitting Bull illustrated by patting his palms together with the rapidity of a fusillade). Our young men rained lead across the river and drove the white braves back."

"And then?"

341

"And then, they rushed across themselves."

"And then?"

"And then they found that they had a good deal to do."

"Was there at that time some doubt about the issue of the battle, whether you would whip the Long Hair or not?"

"There was so much doubt about it that I started down there (here again pointing to the map) to tell the squaws to pack up the lodges and get ready to move away."

"You were on that expedition, then, after the big fight had fairly begun?"

"Yes."

"You did not personally witness the rest of the big fight? You were not engaged in it?"

"No. I have heard of it from the warriors."

How Custer was Surrounded

"When the great crowds of your young men crossed the river in front of the Long Hair what did they do? Did they attempt to assault him directly in his front?"

"At first they did, but afterward they found it better to try and get around him. They formed themselves on all sides of him except just at his back."

"How long did it take them to put themselves around his flanks?"

"As long as it takes the sun to travel from here to here" (indicating some marks upon his arm with which apparently he is used to gauge the progress of the shadow of his lodge across his arm, and probably meaning half an hour. An Indian has no more definite way than this to express the lapse of time).

"The trouble was with the soldiers," he continued, "they were so exhausted and their horses bothered them so much that they could not take good aim. Some of their horses broke away from them and left them to stand and drop and die. When the Long Hair, the General, found that he was so outnumbered and threatened on his flanks, he took the best course he could have taken. The bugle blew. It was an order to fall back. All the men fell back fighting and dropping. They could not fire fast enough, though. But from our side it was so," said Sitting Bull, and here he clapped his hands rapidly twice a second to express with what quickness and continuance the balls flew from the Henry and Winchester rifles wielded by the Indians.

"They could not stand up under such a fire," he added.

"Were any military tactics shown? Did the Long Haired Chief make any disposition of his soldiers, or did it seem as though they retreated all together, helter skelter, fighting for their lives?"

No Cowards on Either Side

"They kept in pretty good order. Some great chief must have commanded them all the while. They would fall back across a coulee and make a fresh stand beyond on higher ground. The map is pretty nearly right. It shows where the white men stopped and fought before they were killed. I think that is right—down there to the left, just above the Little Bighorn. There was one part driven out there, away from the rest, and there a great many men were killed. The places marked on the map are where all were killed."

"Did the whole command keep on fighting until the last?"

"Every man, so far as my people could see. There were no cowards on either side."

Duration of the Fight

I inquired of Sitting Bull, "How long did this big fight continue?"

"The sun was there," he answered, pointing to within two hours from the western horizon.

"You cannot certainly depend," here observed Major Walsh, "upon Sitting Bull's or any other Indian's statement in regard to time or numbers. But his answer, indeed all his answers, exactly correspond with the replies to similar questions my own. If you will proceed you will obtain from him in a few moments some important testimony."

I went on to interrogate Sitting Bull:

"This big fight, then, extended through three hours?"

"Through most of the going forward of the sun.

"Where was the Long Hair the most of time?"

"I have talked with my people; I cannot find one who saw the Long Hair until just before he died. He did not wear his long hair as he used to wear it. His hair was like yours," said Sitting Bull, playfully touching my forehead with his taper fingers. "It was short, but it was of the color of the grass when the frost comes."

"Did you hear from your people how he died? Did he die on horseback?"

"No. None of them died on horseback."

"All were dismounted?"

"Yes."

"And Custer, the Long Hair?"

THE LAST TO DIE

"Well, I have understood that there were a great many brave men in that fight, and that from time to time, while it was going on, they were shot down like pigs. They could not help themselves. One by one the officers fell. I believe the Long Hair rode across once from this place down here (meaning the place where Tom Custer's and Smith's companies were killed) to this place up here (indicating the spot on the map where Custer fell), but I am not sure about this. Anyway it was said that up there where the last fight took place, where the last stand was made, the Long Hair stood like a sheaf of corn with all the ears fallen around him."

"Not wounded?"

"No."

"How many stood by him?"

"A few."

"When did he fall?"

"He killed a man when he fell. He laughed."

"You mean he cried out."

"No, he laughed; he had fired his last shot."

"From a carbine?"

"No, a pistol."

"Did he stand up after he first fell?"

"He rose up on his hands and tried another shot, but his pistol would not go off."

344

"Was anyone else standing up when he fell down?"

"One man was kneeling; that was all. But he died before the Long Hair. All this was far up on the bluffs, far away from the Sioux encampments. I did not see it. It is told to me. But it is true."

NOT SCALPED

"The Long Hair was not scalped?"

"No. My people did not want his scalp."

"Why?"

"I have said; he was a great chief."

"Did you at any time," I persisted, "during the progress of the fight believe that your people would get the worst of it?"

"At one time, as I have told you, I started down to tell the squaws to strike the lodges. I was then on my way up to the right end of the camp, where the first attack was made on us. But before I reached that end of the camp where the Miniconjou and Hunkpapa squaws and children were and where some of the other squaws—Cheyenne and Oglala—had gone, I was overtaken by one of the young warriors, who had just come down from the fight. He called out to me. He said, " 'No use to leave camp; every white man is killed.' So I stopped and went no further. I turned back, and by and by I met the warriors returning."

"But in the meantime," I asked, "Were there no warriors occupied up here at the right end of the camp? Was nobody left, except the squaws and the children and the old men, to take care of that end of the camp? Was nobody ready to defend it against the soldiers in those entrenchments up there?"

"Oh," replied Sitting Bull again, "there was no need to waste warriors in that direction. There were only a few soldiers there in those entrenchments, and we knew they wouldn't dare to come out."

A HERO'S DEATH

"While the big fight was going on," I asked Sitting Bull, "could the sound of the firing have been heard as far as those entrenchments on the right?"

"The squaws who were gathered down in the valley of the river heard them. The guns could have been heard three miles and more."

ADIEU KING BULL

As Sitting Bull rose to go I asked him whether he had the stomach for any more battles with the Americans.

He answered, "I do not want any fight."

"You mean not now?"

He laughed quite heartily. "No; not this winter."

"Are your young braves willing to fight?"

"You will see."

"When?"

"I cannot say."

"I have not seen your people. Would I be welcome at your camp?"

After gazing at the ceiling for a few moments, Sitting Bull responded, "I will not be pleased. The young men would not be pleased. You came with this party (alluding to the United States Commissioners) and you can go back with them. I have said enough."

With this Sitting Bull wrapped his blanket around him and, after gracefully shaking hands, strode to the door. Then he placed his fox-skin cap upon his head and I bade him adieu.

After about four years in Canada, with the buffalo rapidly disappearing, both Canada's Natives and Sitting Bull's people were on the verge of starvation. Canada was obligated by treaties to feed only its own Natives, so Sitting Bull's band was forced to return to the States.

Sitting Bull surrendered on July 19, 1881, at Fort Buford in the Montana Territory, saying, "I wish it to be remembered that I was the last man of my tribe to surrender my rifle." He asked for a reservation near the Black Hills and for permission to visit Canada whenever he wished. Instead, he and his people were sent to Fort Randall—in what is now South Dakota—as prisoners of war, where they were held for two years.

While at the prison in Fort Randall in 1882, Sitting Bull summarized his desires, saying, "The life of white men is slavery. They are prisoners in towns and farms. The life my people want is a life of freedom. . . . The white men had many things that we wanted, but we could see that they did not have the one thing we liked best—freedom. I would rather live in a tepee and go without meat when game is scarce than give up my privileges as a free Indian."

One of Sitting Bull's primary concerns was that the Sioux get what was rightfully theirs under the treaties with the US government. He was illiterate, but he knew exactly what was in the treaties. According to Buffalo Bill, "He carried in his head all the treaties that had been made between his people and the white men, and could recite their minutest details, together with the dates of their making and the names of the men who had signed for both sides."

About twelve years earlier Sitting Bull had made one of his more famous speeches, saying:

What treaty that the whites have kept has the red man broken? Not one. What treaty that the white man ever made with us have they kept? Not one. When I was a boy the Sioux owned the world; the sun rose and set on their land; they sent ten thousand men to battle. Where are the warriors today? Who slew them? Where are our lands? Who owns them? What white man can say I ever stole his land or a penny of his money? Yet, they say I am a thief. What white woman, however lonely, was ever captive or insulted by me? Who has ever come to me hungry and unfed? Who has ever seen me beat my wives or abuse my children? What law have I broken? Is it wrong for me to love my own? Is it wicked for me because my skin is red? Because I am Lakota, because I was born where my father dies, because I would die for my people and my country?

Some of this was confirmed by Major James Walsh, who, the day after the Sitting Bull's death, wrote, "Bull had been misrepresented. He was not the bloodthirsty man reports made him out to be. He asked for nothing but justice. . . . He was not a cruel man. He was kind of heart. He was not dishonest. He was truthful. He loved his people and was glad to give his hand in friendship to any man who was honest with him."

After Sitting Bull surrendered, his life as a reservation Indian began. In May 1883 he was released from twenty months imprisonment at Fort Randall, and he and the others who had returned with him from Canada were finally allowed to join the rest of their tribe at the Standing Rock Reservation. Determined that Sitting Bull should not have any special privileges, Agent James McLaughlin even forced Sitting Bull to hoe the fields.

That same year—just seven years after the Battle of the Little Bighorn—Buffalo Bill formed his Wild West show. Even though, as a scout, he tried to track down and kill the Indians involved in Custer's death, he ended up hiring some of them for his show. As he put it, "Nearly one hundred Indians, from several tribes, were engaged, among the number being the world famous Chief Sitting Bull, and several other Sioux that had distinguished themselves in the Custer massacre." Chief Sitting Bull was billed as "the slayer of General Custer."

The show in 1885—performed outdoors on grounds resembling a racetrack—started with a grand processional, beginning with the Pawnee; then the Mexican vaqueros, the Wichita, the cowboys, a sheriff, and the Sioux, led by Chief Sitting Bull; and finally Buffalo Bill Cody, the Army's chief of scouts who had served under ten generals. The exhibitions began with a horserace between a vaquero, a cowboy, and a Native American. Then came the Pony Express demonstration. Next there was a one-hundred-yard race between an Indian on foot and one on horseback. Buffalo Bill then reenacted his fight with Yellow Hair. With the arena full of cowboys and Indians, Cody and the actor playing "Yellow Hand" rode toward each other on horseback while firing their guns. Dismounting, they charged up a mound in the center of the arena for hand-to-hand combat armed with only a spear and knife. After Cody "scalped" his enemy, a general battle broke out, with the cowboys eventually driving off the Indians. Following this, a marksman with a Winchester shot composition balls, and then half-dollars, nickels, and dimes. Then the sixteen-year-old "Cowboy Kid" shot his rifle from several different positions, such as over his head and leaning over backward. Next it was Annie Oakley's turn to dazzle the crowd with her marksmanship.

Cowboys then rode bucking mules and ponies, Tom Clayton tamed the "ferocious" mare Dynamite, and Buck Taylor picked up his hat and handkerchief from the ground as he galloped past. Buffalo Bill did some stunt shooting from horseback. The Deadwood Stage, with members of the audience as passengers, was chased and shot at by yelling Indians, until they are rescued by Buffalo Bill and his men after a blazing battle.

Next, Sioux boys raced bareback and cowboys raced on horses and mules. Then the Pawnee and Wichita performed several of their ceremonies. Mustang Jack jumped over burros and horses. Cowboys and Vaqueros did some rodeo stunts, such as roping steers. An African-American cowboy rode an elk. Buffalo Bill then led the Native Americans in a buffalo hunt. In the finale, the Natives attacked a settler's log cabin and, in the midst of the battle, Buffalo Bill and the cowboys rushed to the rescue with their guns blasting, chasing the Natives in a running battle around grounds.

They had a final farewell with the entire cast in front of the grandstand, where Buffalo Bill invited everyone to visit their camp before going home. The show was a tremendous success and toured for three decades throughout the United States and Europe, often playing to crowds in the tens of thousands for a single show.

Sitting Bull was in Buffalo Bill's show for only four months in 1885. Initially the government didn't want to allow him to leave the reservation, but finally decided he'd be less of a threat away from his people. As a headliner, he made fifty dollars a week—around six thousand dollars in today's dollars—plus whatever he could make selling autographed photos. He only had to make an appearance, calmly riding around the arena at the start of the show. Most American crowds booed, jeered, and ridiculed him as Custer's murderer, but he was viewed differently in Canada, receiving a much warmer reception. He also toured parts of Europe with the show.

While Sitting Bull was touring with the show, Buffalo Bill expressed his admiration for him in an interview, saying,

Sitting Bull is a wonderful general—the greatest of all Indian chiefs and comparatively a greater war general than any white man I know of. His tribe of 6,000 warriors and their families starved almost for three years because he said, 'No. The time has not come when we must ask charity of the white man.' I don't know of any white general who could get from 6,000 to 10,000 people to follow him on the verge of starvation for three years, when all they had to do was to cross the line and agree to the government terms.

After Sitting Bull's time with the show was over, the government turned down requests for him to join the show again, so that was his only season. He returned to the reservation and his duties as chief, but the situation was getting really bad there. Buffalo Bill, in *An Autobiography of Buffalo Bill (Colonel W. F. Cody)* (1920), wrote:

The forfeiture of the Black Hills and unwise reduction of rations kept alive the Indian discontent. When, in 1889, Congress passed a law dividing the Sioux Reservation into many smaller ones so as to isolate the different tribes of the Dakota nation, a treaty was offered them. This provided payment for the ponies captured or destroyed in the war of 1876 and certain other concessions, in return for which the Indians were to cede about half their land, or eleven million acres, which was to be opened up for settlement.

The treaty was submitted to the Indians for a vote. They came in from the woods and the plains to vote on it, and it was carried by a very narrow majority, many of the Indians insisting that they had been coerced by their necessities into casting favorable ballots.

Congress delayed and postponed the fulfillment of the promised conditions, and the Indian unrest increased as the months went by. Even after the land had been taken over and settled up, Congress did not pass the appropriation that was necessary before the Indians could get their money.

Just when things were reaching their lowest point for the Sioux, a new religion appeared known as the Ghost Dance, and it ended up leading to both Sitting Bull's death and the Massacre at Wounded Knee. It was started by a northern Paiute named Wovoka (Wood Cutter) in Nevada. At the age of fourteen, he became close to a Presbyterian rancher's family by the name of Wilson, and he took the name Jack Wilson. By the time he was about thirty, he incorporated many of the Christian beliefs he learned into his Native religion to create the Ghost Dance, which the Natives called the Spirit Dance. Of course messianic religions flourished throughout the United States then, just as they do today, while millennialism among the Native Americans dates back at least to 1618. Still, after what happened to Custer, most US citizens were seriously spooked by the idea of all the remaining Native tribes uniting together in armed rebellion.

On the other hand, for the defeated and humiliated Native Americans trying to scratch out a living on shrinking reservations with little to eat, no hope, and little recourse for wrongs done to them, it's natural that a religion promising a return to their glory days would appeal to them. The idea that their oppressors would be gone, all their dead family and friends would return, and they would have their freedom back in a land of Eden gave them new hope. All they had to do was be morally good people, pray, chant, meditate, perform ceremonial cleansings, and dance the Ghost Dance.

What many didn't understand was that the religion itself was not hostile. Wovoka maintained ties to the Wilson family for about forty years, and he kept the name Jack Wilson throughout his life, even using it to sign his messiah letters. A version of the Ghost Dance dates back to 1869—which may have been led by his father, shortly before he died—but it was transformed by Wovoka after he claimed that he had visions in 1888 and 1889 in which God told him all men are brothers and must live

in peace; that there would be a res-
urrection of the dead—both Native
and white; and that they must not lie,
steal, swear, or drink alcohol. God
said the old world would be remade
through earthquakes, tornados,
floods, and volcanoes, but that Jesus
would come and take the believers up into the clouds above Mount
Grant, Nevada to protect them, while
the floods would drown the foreign
invaders. Nonbelieving Natives would
survive but would shrink to be about
a foot tall. Some would turn to wood
and be burned up. After five days the
believers would return to the new
Eden-like earth. There would be lots
of game and buffalo, and there would
be good times once again.

Later, in one of the messiah letters, Wovoka wrote:

Wovoka (also known as Jack Wilson), the
Paiute religious leader who founded the
Ghost Dance movement

Do not tell the white people about this: Jesus is now on the ground [i.e.,
on Earth]. He [is] just like [a] cloud. Everybody [i.e., the dead] is alive
again. I do not know when he will be here; maybe [it] will be this fall or
in [the] spring. When it happens, it may be this: there will be no sickness
and [everyone will] return to young again.

Do not refuse to work for [the] white man or do not make any trouble with them until you leave them [to gather at Mount Grant]. When
the earth shakes [at the coming of the new world], do not be afraid. It
will not hurt you.

The feature of the religion that attracted the most attention was the dancing. Wovoka
said God told him that every three months they must dance the Ghost Dance for several days and nights without a break. The dance was a circle dance where everyone

stood in a circle facing a fire or a pole in the center. Holding hands, they would dance sideways in a clockwise fashion for a while and then switch to counterclockwise. The tempo would gradually increase. This would go on until they could no longer stand and fell unconscious, hoping to see visions. According to one witness, "When they cannot lose their senses from exhaustion they butt their heads together, beat them on the ground, and do anything to become insensible, so that they may be ushered into the presence of the Messiah. . . . Seven or eight of them died as the result of one dance near Wounded Knee." While the visions were important, the main purpose of the dance was to hasten Christ's return.

For years the reservation Natives had been under the authority of the Bureau of Indian Affairs, but it was so riddled with corruption that instead of helping the Natives, as it was charged with doing, it made their situation drastically worse. In 1890 the buffalo were gone; it was a hot year with little rain, so there were few crops; the government reduced the size of the reservations again; and the government also cut the Sioux's food rations in half. The Sioux were literally starving to death. In speaking of the feelings of desperation that led many people to join the Ghost Dance movement, Chief Red Cloud said:

We felt that we were mocked in our misery. We had no newspapers and no one to speak for us. We had no redress. Our rations were again reduced. You who eat three times each day, and see your children well and happy around you, can't understand what starving Indians feel. We were faint with hunger and maddened by despair. We held our dying children, and felt their little bodies tremble as their souls went out and left only a dead weight in our hands. They were not very heavy, but we ourselves were very faint, and the dead weighed us down. There was no hope on earth, and God seemed to have forgotten us. Someone had again been talking of the Son of God, and said He had come. The people did not know; they did not care. They snatched at the hope. They screamed like crazy men to Him for mercy. They caught at the promises they heard He had made.

While Wovoka's message was one of peace, the government and its citizens thought it was one of war and rebellion. To them, the dancing was riling up the Natives and the idea of them gathering in large crowds made many people very nervous. Perhaps government officials also confused Wovoka's idea of an approaching apocalypse that would wipe out the white invaders, with the idea of an Armageddon where the Indians would wipe out the non-Natives. Maybe even some tribes mixed the ideas.

Added to this was a misunderstanding of the purpose of the ghost shirts that were supposed to protect the Natives from bullets. The army thought their purpose was to protect warriors when they started attacking soldiers. Actually, these were ceremonial shirts that they wore during the dance, which were painted with symbols from the wearers' visions. As the number of soldiers increased at the Standing Rock Reservation, the Sioux became worried they would be attacked, but they came to believe their shirts would protect them if they were. It seems the Sioux were the only ones who believed this, though it was common for Natives to believe their "medicine" or talismans would protect them.

The Bureau of Indian Affairs soon banned the dance, as they did with most Native spiritual rituals, but this didn't stop it. Many people just snuck off into the hills or badlands to perform it secretly. President Benjamin Harrison then ordered the secretary of war to suppress the potential outbreak by force. Sitting Bull reluctantly permitted members of his band to join the dance, though he was skeptical. When the army asked him to use his influence to stop the dance, he refused, thinking it hypocritical. Since the whites had their dances, he didn't see why his people couldn't dance. He was planning on taking a trip to see the dance and find out more of what it was about, but he never made it.

Still, the army blamed Sitting Bull for the dance and wanted to arrest him, but they were afraid to do it in his village. General Miles wanted Buffalo Bill to visit Sitting Bull's camp to see whether he could talk the chief into coming to the agency, where they could arrest him and send him to a military prison. He drew up an order for Buffalo Bill to meet him at Standing Rock, but the agent—who apparently wanted to be the one to have Sitting Bull arrested—was able to get President Henry Harrison to rescind Miles's order, and Buffalo Bill was ordered to leave. Miles went ahead with the arrest, sending forty-three Native policemen, accompanied by a detachment of soldiers, to Sitting Bull's log cabin before dawn on December 15, 1890. Things did not go well, and a Sioux named Catch-the-Bear shot Lieutenant Henry Bull Head, who was one of the arresting officers. Lieutenant Bull Head and another arresting officer fired back. Both shots hit Sitting Bull—one in the head. Seven policemen died in the ensuing fight, along with Sitting Bull and seven of his people. It's said that five years earlier Sitting Bull had a vision where a meadowlark told him, "Your own people, Lakotas, will kill you."

The army hoped to prevent more trouble by disarming the Lakota and arresting their chiefs. As news of Sitting Bull's death spread, hundreds of frightened Hunkpapa Lakota fled from Standing Rock to the Pine Ridge Reservation. Many went to Red Cloud's Brulé Lakota camp. Up to a hundred went to the Miniconjou Lakota camp of Chief Big Foot. Hoping to avoid trouble, Big Foot was moving his camp toward the agency when they were intercepted by some of Colonel James Forsyth's men. Big Foot immediately ran up his white flag, and the soldiers had him set up his village next to their encampment at Wounded Knee Creek. Big Foot had a bad case of pneumonia—he was coughing up blood and could barely stand—so one of the officers set up a heated tent for him and had the camp's surgeon attend to him.

Unlike Colonel Chivington and his men at Sand Creek, it's unlikely the soldiers intended to massacre the Native Americans when they entered Big Foot's village to disarm it on December 29, 1890. It was a peaceful camp of 350 to 400 Native Americans. In fact for the previous decade, the Sioux had not been hostile, nor had they shown any inclination to fight. In spite of having four Hotchkiss guns—which were revolving-barrel cannons—trained on them, the Natives were in good spirits because they expected to reach the agency later that day, where they would see their relatives. Lieutenant W. W. Robinson Jr., commented, "I observed the children of all ages . . . playing among the tepees, and had commented . . . that there was no hostile intent on the part of the Indians."

But Forsyth's 470 soldiers were members of the 7th Cavalry, and some were itching for revenge. Captain George Wallace was quoted by one newspaper as saying, "The Seventh has bloody score to settle with them."

Fourteen years had passed since the Battle of the Little Bighorn and the 7th Cavalry hadn't had the chance to fight Indians again, so some felt they had something to prove. Most were newer inexperienced recruits. In addition Sitting Bull had been killed just two weeks earlier, and with the Ghost Dances going on, the soldiers were already nervous and jumpy. They set about disarming the camp, but the Natives were reluctant to give up their weapons, as they needed them for hunting. They hadn't done anything wrong and couldn't understand why they had to give up their guns, knives, hatchets, and beading awls, but they did, begrudgingly. Soldiers searched the women, wagons, and tepees, confiscating most of their weapons, and began searching the men, who were separated from the village. One man held his rifle over his head, saying he paid a lot of money for it and didn't want to give it up without compensation. Some soldiers tried to take it away from him, and it went off in the struggle.

Sitting Bull and Buffalo Bill in Montreal in August 1885

The soldiers in the village suddenly opened fire on the men and the tepees, while the soldiers on a nearby hill began firing the Hotchkiss guns, each capable of firing a 2.6-pound explosive shell every 1.2 seconds. With four of these guns firing, the explosions and flying shrapnel did considerable damage. Chief Big Foot was one of the first to die. Since the village was surrounded by soldiers, and there were soldiers in the village, some soldiers were killed in the crossfire by their own men, just like at the Sand Creek Massacre. Many of the women and children made it to the ravine behind their tepees. The men had to fight their way through a line of soldiers to get back to their village. After the main fight was over, soldiers chased those in the ravine for several miles and scattered shots were heard for hours after the attack. Witnesses later gave accounts of brutality similar to that at the Sand Creek Massacre. Twenty-nine soldiers died, while from 146 to more than 200 Lakota were killed—most were old men, women, and children. Four babies were found with their skulls crushed. General Miles wanted Colonel Forsyth punished, but nothing was done, and within seven years, Forsyth was promoted to the rank of brigadier general and then major general. Eighteen soldiers were awarded Medals of Honor for the Wounded Knee Massacre—one went to an artilleryman who kept firing his Hotchkiss gun after his commanding officer was wounded and who continually moved it so he could get better shots.

Chief Black Elk later said, "I did not know then how much was ended. When I look back now from this high hill of my old age, I can still see the butchered women and children lying heaped and scattered all along the crooked gulch as plain as when I saw them with eyes still young. And I can see that something else died there in the bloody mud, and was buried in the blizzard. A people's dream died there."

The Ghost Dance continued, off and on, possibly as late as 1926—Wovoka, himself, was involved in some of the revivals—but this massacre ended the Indian wars. With the Native Americans subdued and confined to reservations, the West was opened to tourism and America's frontier era came to an end.

Recommended Reading Bibliography

I used perhaps a thousand or more sources while researching and writing my portions of this book. This is not a list of sources or even a listing of the sources I used the most, though many of those are listed. My purpose here is to provide a brief bibliography of related books that I felt were particularly notable.

✶ Bell, Bob Boze, *Bad Men: Outlaws & Gunfighters of the Wild West*, Phoenix: Tri Star-Boze Productions, 1999.

Coleman, William, *Voices of Wounded Knee*, Lincoln: University of Nebraska Press, 2000.

Dunlay, Tom, *Kit Carson and the Indians*, Lincoln: University of Nebraska Press, 2005.

Horan, James D., *The Gunfighters*, New York: Gramercy Books, 1976.

———*The Lawmen*, New York: Gramercy Books, 1980.

———*The Outlaws*, New York: Gramercy Books, 1977.

McMurtry, Larry, *Crazy Horse*, New York: Viking, 1999.

———*Oh What a Slaughter: Massacres in the American West: 1846–1890*, New York: Simon & Schuster, 2006.

Rosa, Joseph G., and Robin May, *Buffalo Bill and His Wild West*, Lawrence: University of Kansas Press, 1989.

♟ Sandoz, Mari, *Crazy Horse: The Strange Man of the Oglalas*, New York: Alfred A. Knopf, 1942. Though presented as nonfiction, this book is actually a historical novel and should not be used for research.

✶ Stiles, T. J., *Jesse James: Last Rebel of the Civil War*, New York: Alfred A. Knopf, 2002.

Utley, Robert M., *Billy the Kid: A Short and Violent Life*, Lincoln: University of Nebraska Press, 1989.

———*Cavalier in Buckskin: George Armstrong Custer and the Western Military Frontier*, Norman: University of Oklahoma Press, 1988.

———*The Lance and the Shield: The Life and Times of Sitting Bull*, New York: Henry Holt & Co., 1993. Also published as *Sitting Bull: The Life and Times of an American Patriot.*

Viola, Herman J., *Little Bighorn Remembered: The Untold Indian Story of Custer's Last Stand*, Westminster, Maryland: Times Books, 1999.

Welch, James with Paul Stekler, *Killing Custer: The Battle of the Little Bighorn and the Fate of the Plains Indians*, New York: W. W. Norton & Co., 1994.

Wilson, R. L., with Greg Martin, *Buffalo Bill's Wild West: An American Legend*, Edition, New Jersey: Chartwell Books, 1998.

INDEX

Italicized page numbers indicate illustrations.

About the Author/Editor

John Richard Stephens is the author/editor of twenty-one books, which include *Gold, Commanding the Storm, Humor and the Civil War, Wyatt Earp Speaks, The Wild, Wild West,* and *Wildest Lives of the Wild West.*

Before becoming a writer, John gained experience in a wide variety of occupations ranging from work as a psychiatric counselor in two hospitals and three mental health facilities to being an intelligence officer and squadron commander in the US Air Force.

His books have been selections of the Preferred Choice Book Club, the Quality Paperback Book Club, and the Book of the Month Club. His work has been published as far away as India and Singapore and has been translated into Japanese and Finnish.

John also has the distinguished honor of being quoted around the world next to such luminaries as Abraham Lincoln, Mark Twain, Lord Byron, and Franz Kafka.